KEY ISSUES IN POPULATION AND FOOD POLICY

Capon Springs Public Policy Conference #2

Edited by
Eliot Glassheim
Charles Cargille
Population/Food Fund

University Press
of America™

Library of Congress Catalog Card Number: 78-63063

DEDICATION

To Margaret Mead

and

Roger Revelle

for inspiration, encouragement and help in
the task of creating Population/Food Fund.

A WORLD GOAL

. . . to mobile society to solve the population problem by achieving a balance between population size and available resources for life support in a stable and healthful environment.

TABLE OF CONTENTS

Food Policy

SCIENTIFIC PAPERS AND POLICY ANALYSES

I. OVERPOPULATION

Policy Analyses

Family Planning

II. WORLD HUNGER AND MALNUTRITION

Responses at the Personal Level

Increasing Available Food

ix

Institutional Responses

Nutrition

III. POPULATION/FOOD PROPOSALS

PREFACE

The Second Capon Springs Public Policy Conference, on Population and Food Policy, was unique for a number of reasons. First, it brought together scholars who crossed many disciplines. Anthropologists, economists, nutritionists, agricultural scientists, demographers, philosophers and teachers of literature and business administration focused their different backgrounds on the related problems of overpopulation and world hunger. Secondly, lay people with no academic expertise rubbed shoulders in an open forum with Congressmen, representatives from governmental agencies, farmers and academics. Thirdly, there were a significant number of participants from developing countries whose first hand experience of Third World population and food problems was a welcome addition to the conference.

The diversity of the participants in the conference was a hopeful sign. It was also encouraging to find population people concerned about hunger and malnutrition, and food people worried about overpopulation. The number of papers calling for integrated, or ecological approaches to population-food problems was another positive aspect of the conference format.

As is to be expected, this diversity of backgrounds also led to some lively disagreements. Perhaps the most basic split which surfaced time and again throughout the conference was one between those who argue that we must control nature and those who argue that we must control human greed. The neo-Malthusians saw excessive population growth as a natural disaster of great magnitude which must be brought under control. The neo-Marxist camp--which includes elements of Catholic and liberal thought--argued that human economic and social arrangements are at the root of the world's suffering and that social justice and equitable distribution of resources throughout the world would solve the problems connected with population growth.

Another basic disagreement was expressed in the exchange between Charles Cargille of the Population/Food Fund and R. T. Ravenholt, administrator of the Agency for International Development population program. Dr. Cargille argued that AID's plans and budget requests had vastly underestimated the seriousness of global overpopulation, with the result that world population growth was out of control. Dr. Ravenholt cited declines in the world's growth rate and spelled out AID projections for 1985 and 2000 which suggested that things were under control.

A third unresolved issue was what role America should play in helping hungry people and overpopulated lands. Even assuming the purest of motives for American foreign policy, there was little agreement on what action the people or the government of the United States should take.

Should we change our eating habits from grain-fed meat to grass-fed meat, or cut down drastically on meat consumption, in order to make more grains available to hungry people? A number of speakers offered calculations to show how many more people could be fed in this fashion. But others suggested that (a) the amount of grain freed for poor countries would not be sufficient to feed everyone and (b) without money, poor countries could not purchase food even if more were available.

Should the United States put conditions on our foreign aid? Again, even assuming that our conditions would express what we felt was best for countries with population and food problems rather than our own selfish interests, there was little agreement about the propriety or effectiveness of attaching strings to our gifts. Should we tie food and development aid to reductions in population growth rates? Should we tie population and health assistance to targeted decreases in population growth? If we don't, will we not be wasting our money? If we do, what country will want our money?

Should we lower trade barriers to allow underdeveloped countries to earn foreign exchange? How can we help developing countries which are ruled by elites which will not take steps to help their poorest people? Is it acceptable to interfere in foreign countries on behalf of poor people against their leaders? Assuming, as most participants did, that widespread land reform will result in both more food and fewer babies, how is the United States to bring about land reform in countries which are not interested?

A fourth area of indecision was the means by which population growth can best be reduced. There was widespread agreement that family planning alone is not enough. There was also agreement that changes in the roles of women, improved health services, land reform, decreases in infant mortality rates, better education, higher incomes and social security all make a lowered fertility rate more likely. Yet there was little concrete information about the costs of achieving these improvements, the time they would take, or the means by which they could be accomplished.

The institutions which should be charged with responsibility for lowering growth rates were also disputed. During one spirited debate the Department of Defense was nominated, because of the national security implications of overpopulation and hunger, but the weight of opinion rejected this proposal. The ability of the United Nations to take on the task was called into question. An alliance of industrial democracies was proposed, as was a new federal agency within the U.S. The effectiveness of the Agency for International Development's population program was both attacked and defended. Perhaps the most far-fetched, yet interesting proposal, was one calling for an international covenant to be ratified by individual countries agreeing that birth rates must be brought down in both developed countries, where resource use was excessive, and developing countries, where the population was excessive in relation to global resources.

Despite these areas of disagreement and lack of consensus, a number of core ideas commanded general support. Three areas of agreement were:

Carrying Capacity. The importance of the notion of global carrying capacity was widely discussed. There was agreement that we lacked hard data on the absolute numerical limits which the earth could sustain, with estimates widely ranging between five and thirty billion people. There was also some skepticism about the technical possibility of establishing such a number, since the factors which go into such an equation are so complex. But, given Lester Brown's outline of the diminishing ability of major biological systems (grasslands, fisheries, forests and croplands) to sustain human life, there was general agreement that research to more precisely define the natural limits of the earth would be worthwhile.

Appropriate Social Organization. With so much recent interest in Appropriate Technology, it was refreshing to hear speakers from a variety of backgrounds speak of the importance of appropriate social organization. Though less concrete than windmills or small tractors, the idea of retaining appropriate, small-scale, decentralized social organization may be of greater significance. Several anthropologists argued that disturbances to traditional economic, social and agricultural arrangements were contributing to population and food problems throughout the world.

Changes in Lifestyle. An unexpected number of speakers suggested that as a response to world overpopulation and impending food and resource scarcity there would be widespread changes in the way people in the United States and other developed countries lived. Changes in diet and in values were among the two most frequently mentioned. The most extreme, yet believable, alternative was represented by members of The Farm, an intentional community of 1100 people in Tennessee who live a simple life, share their bounty and skills with the poor in other countries, and yet do not repudiate modern technology. Other participants upheld the virtues of community gardening, vegetarianism, natural foods, and rejection of the materialistic values which have dominated Western thinking. There was some disagreement about the timing of these changes. Congressmen, who are attuned to what is socially acceptable today to the majority, generally felt these changes would take place in an indefinite future, while other participants described their current alternative lifestyles as harbingers of more widespread social change.

xv

Although the number of people whose energies are engaged in solving population and food problems, and the budgets devoted to them, are still miniscule compared to the stakes involved, the variety of disciplines and life experiences which the conference brought to bear on these problems leads one to hope that solutions are not far away. Though conferences don't solve problems, they may act as a magnifying glass to focus human energy towards effective action.

As money becomes available, the Population/Food Fund intends to use its continuing Capon Springs Public Policy Conference Series to debate policy proposals for solving population, food, resource and environmental problems with the purpose of funding the best policy proposals to come out of each conference. In this way we hope to lessen the time between thought and effective action and to hasten the realization of a world which is both stable and just.

ELIOT GLASSHEIM
Population/Food Fund

CARRYING CAPACITY--BIOLOGICAL SYSTEMS AND HUMAN NUMBERS

Lester R. Brown
Worldwatch Institute

My comments this morning will be drawn from a book published in April, 1978, entitled The Twenty-Ninth Day, and subtitled Accommodating Human Needs and Numbers to the Earth's Resources. The title of the book derives from a riddle which the French use to teach school children the concept of exponential growth. The riddle begins with a lily pond that has one leaf in it the first day, and each day the number of leaves doubles--two the second day, four the third day, and so forth. Question: If the pond fills on the thirtieth day, when is it half full? Answer: The twenty-ninth day. As I look at our global lily pond, I have the feeling it's very close to half full; hence, the title of the book.

The Twenty-Ninth Day attempts to look at both nonrenewable and renewable resources and relate those to carrying capacity. The years since The Limits to Growth was published have been years in which we have focused on the nonrenewable resources in public discussions. Because renewable resources are renewable, we've overlooked them. In fact, I think that we need to be paying far more attention to the renewable resources.

In the opening chapters of The Twenty-Ninth Day, I focus on four biological systems on which we depend heavily: namely, fisheries, forests, grasslands, and croplands. Those four biological systems provide not only all of our food, but, in addition, all of the raw materials for industry except minerals and petrochemicals. Let me repeat that because it's a fundamental point. These four biological systems provide not only all of our food, but also all the raw materials for industry except minerals and petrochemicals. We cannot separate what happens to these biological systems from what happens to the economic system.

Looking first at fisheries, the world fish catch increased from 22 million tons in 1950 to 70 million tons in 1970 and became one of our major global sources of high quality protein. The fish catch peaked in 1970 and has been fluctuating between 65 and 70 million tons since then. This means that in per capita terms, the fish catch has declined by some 14% since 1970. This helps to explain why, when

1

you go to the supermarket to buy seafood, the price often seems to go up from week to week.

High quality protein is scarce. Probably the best single indicator of this is the price of soybeans, which during the 1960s averaged $2.46 per bushel, and since 1972 has fluctuated between $5 and $12 per bushel.

If you look at oceanic fisheries today, overfishing is now the rule, not the exception. This overfishing has come about in an effort to meet the needs of 4 billion consumers. The question we have not resolved analytically or conceptually is what happens to oceanic fisheries as we move toward 8 and 10 and 11 or 12 or 16 billion people?

The second biological system upon which we depend heavily is forests. We depend on forests for firewood, for lumber, for newsprint. For a third of mankind, firewood is the principal source of fuel. Lumber is still the universal building material.

In 1956 I spent a year living in villages in India, one of them located in central India on the Deccan Plateau. At the time I was there, it was a heavily forested area. I remember traveling for miles and miles through the woods to get to the village where I was staying.

I've been back many times since then. The thing that has impressed me most about that part of India is the rate of deforestation. Today there are almost no trees left. As population has grown, as the demand for firewood and building materials has increased, the claims on the forests have begun to exceed their sustainable yield. And the deforestation that I've seen in a very personal way in central India is now commonplace in much of the Third World. At the turn of the century, Ethiopia was half covered with forests; today, only 5% of Ethiopia is forested.

While we've focused on the 4 or 5-fold increase in the price of oil during the 1970s, almost exactly the same thing has been happening to the price of firewood in many Third World villages. There are some countries in Africa now where the fuel to heat the pot to cook the food may cost more than the food inside the pot itself. Such is the scarcity of fuel for cooking.

A few months ago, here in Washington, Patricia Harris, Secretary of Housing and Urban Development, announced an investigation into why the cost of housing in the United States has gone up so rapidly. In 1960, just over half of all Americans could someday expect to own their own home. Today, that has dropped to 32%, and only in the last few months have economists begun to link what's happening to the cost of housing and what's happening to the world's forests. As the forests shrink, the cost of housing goes up.

We see the impact of deforestation in other areas. We see it in

2

the communications industry, for example. We see it in the closing
of newspapers. Hardly a week goes by but that another important newspaper in some city around the country closes or is absorbed by another
paper. And some newspapers have converted from the standard format to
a tabloid format--recently the <u>Christian Science Monitor</u>, for ex-
ample--in order to conserve on newsprint.

What's happening to forests now will affect us in very real ways
in the years ahead, and the fact is that the world is now being
rapidly deforested as the claims of 4 billion people exceed the regenerative capacity of forests. What we have not reckoned with analytically and where there's an enormous gap between biologists and
ecologists on the one hand, and economists on the other, is establishing the link between carrying capacity and population size.

The third biological system which is under stress are grasslands.
One of the recent Worldwatch papers was entitled "Spreading Deserts--
The Hand of Man," prepared for the UN Conference on Desertification
held in Nairobi. The conclusion of that paper was that in large
areas of the world, particularly in Africa, the Middle East and parts
of West Asia, deserts are expanding rapidly as overgrazing reduces
the area in grassland.

Grass, I should remind you, is the source of much of our high
quality protein--meat, milk, cheese. It's also the source of raw
material--leather for the leather goods industry, wool, and so forth.

The fourth biological system is croplands. Man has substantially altered this system in contrast to the other three biological
systems--fisheries, forests and grasslands--which are still essentially natural. What we find with croplands is that overplowing is
now commonplace in large areas of the world. Marginal croplands are
being brought into use in areas where rainfall is either too low or
undependable, or where the soils are too steeply sloping, as in large
areas of the East African Plateau, the Andean countries of Latin
America and Central America, and the northern part of the Indian
subcontinent. We find that topsoil is being lost and cropland is
being abandoned as more and more pressure is put on the land. Fal-
low systems of agriculture, whether practiced in dry land areas such
as the Western Great Plains or the Soviet Union, are under pressure
as the demands for food go up. The same is true for the slash-and-
burn cultivation in the subtropical regions. In Nigeria, for example,
shifting cultivation is extensively practiced. Formerly the land
used to be cleared and farmed for three years and then abandoned for
20 to 25 years to give it time to regenerate; but that cycle is being
shortened now down to 10 to 15 years, and the land does not have time
to regenerate fully.

A recent article in <u>Science</u> magazine, reporting on a survey of
soils in Wisconsin, indicated that in the area surveyed the loss of
topsoil was averaging about 9 tons per acre per year, whereas the

3

regenerative capacity of soil formation through natural processes totaled only 4 tons per year. The loss of topsoil exceeded the tolerance factor by some 5 tons per acre. It is now believed that this characteristic may apply to a large share of the cropland in the United States, perhaps even a majority of it. It is becoming a subject of research and concern in the Department of Agriculture.

Biological systems have a parallel in economics, though most economists do not recognize it. We have in economics the concept of an endowment; a philanthropic foundation, for example, has an endowment and it makes grants from the interest on that endowment. If a foundation has a $100 million endowment, and its endowment is earning 6% interest per year, that foundation can disburse grants at the rate of up to $6 million a year indefinitely. But if the project officers become overly enthusiastic and begin disbursing funds at $10 million a year, then it's only a matter of time until that foundation will have to close its doors. And that is basically what is happening today with biological systems. We're consuming the capital along with the interest. That's what deforestation is all about. That's what overfishing is all about. And what we are saying is that the productive resource base is beginning to shrink.

Malthus told us that demand would tend to grow exponentially as a result of population growth, and, indeed, demand has grown rapidly and has put pressure on resources. But what we're now beginning to see is that continuing population growth beyond current levels has a double-edged effect. It not only contributes to the growth in demand. But, by putting too much pressure on biological systems, population growth can also lead to a shrinkage of the productive resource base itself--the forests, the fisheries, cropland and grasslands. And that concept is new. We have not integrated that concept into our thinking, and the projections being made in the various global economic models entirely overlook this phenomenon. It's one that we're going to have to reckon with. And I think, in the policy area, we're going to have to begin undertaking the sorts of analyses that permit national political leaders to gain an understanding of what the carrying capacities of their forests and grasslands are. We need analyses that permit the international community to begin to acquire some understanding of what the long term sustainable yield of oceanic fisheries is, assuming that they can be managed ideally and that we can eliminate overfishing.

It seems to me that carrying capacity as a concept has long been understood, appreciated, and used by ecologists, but it has not been used by economists. To most economists, the concept of carrying capacity is an alien one. What I attempt to do in The Twenty-Ninth Day is to establish some links between what's happening to biological systems and what's happening to the economic system.

Every day we read in the newspaper about stresses in the economic system. We read about inflation, unemployment, slowing growth rates,

4

and therefore rising pressures for protectionism, whether it's in steel, textiles or agriculture. These economic stresses are manifestations of the deteriorating relationship between 4 billion people and the biological systems on which we depend. It seems to me that analytically we've got to begin to understand this relationship and to realize that in economic planning and policymaking we can no longer treat population as an exogenous variable, as something independent, as something that's given. We're reaching the point where we have to begin thinking about population growth and consumption levels--both of which influence the overall level of demand on the earth's biological systems--as variables which we do need to directly address in policy. The situation now calls for us to begin formulating incentives and disincentives and allocating resources for slowing population growth.

My summary point is that the sort of accommodation that's required to stabilize the relationship between ourselves and the biological systems on which we depend, and without which we cannot survive, is going to require an enormous social change. The change ahead over the next couple of decades in adjusting lifestyles and population growth rates is probably going to be the most rapid and compressed period of social change in history. I don't think we've yet begun to reckon with this possibility.

Robert McNamara of the World Bank has predicted that world population growth is likely to stabilize in about 70 years at a population of 11 billion people. He's also said that with concerted efforts we might be able to reach a stable population 15 years earlier, with a population of 8 billion. My guess is that as we begin to better understand the relationship between humanity and the biological systems on which we depend, and begin to acquire more information on the enormous pressure on these systems, the notion of 11 billion people will become very unrealistic. My own feeling is that the earth may not be able to accommodate even another doubling; that is to say, we could already be in the morning of the thirtieth day rather than the twenty-ninth.

DISCUSSION

FRED STROHBEHN, Iowa farmer and a member of Self Help, Waverly, Iowa: The political process is usually one of the slowest means for getting done in a hurry what has to be done--unless it's something like a war and the President declares war immediately. What is the fastest way to reach people who make decisions with the kind of news you've brought us?

LESTER BROWN: It seems to me that there are two important points involved here. One is simply acquiring the information, the understanding of the problems that are unfolding. As I look around both Washington and Academe, I'm upset by the extent to which, as knowledge has advanced, we've become so highly specialized, and therefore fragmented. Each of us is looking at only a tiny piece of the problem. What we do not have is a place where problems are being addressed in their own right. In the field of energy, for example, we have dozens of kinds of engineers. We have nuclear engineers, we have mechanical engineers, we have civil engineers, etc., etc. But if you try to hire an engineer whose specialty is energy, it's very difficult to find one. We don't train engineers to work on energy. We train them to work on other pieces of things.

In looking at the set of issues that I've just been talking about, I'm struck by the fact that political leaders around the world have so many economic advisors and so few ecological advisors. It seems to me that bridging the gap between the natural and the social sciences is terribly important. I think there's an obligation in the natural sciences to attempt to do that.

Once we get the information and have the analysis in hand, then the second stage, of course, is the political will. We know there's an energy problem now. We know we ought to be responding to it and we've known it, in a fairly graphic way, since the end of 1973. It's now early 1978, and we still haven't done very much on that problem.

I wonder if I have the opportunity to ask a question of the questioner. As a former farmer, I noted with interest that small four-wheel tractor that Self Help has on display. I note that it's being manufactured by a small local firm, as I understand it, not John Deere or International Harvester. What sort of distribution network do you have for it? How are you getting it into the developing countries where the farmer with 8 acres or 20 acres can use it, and what sort of a price tag does it have on it?

FRED STROHBEHN: With a diesel engine it sells for about $2300; the plow is another $170 and the planter is about $270. It has a 7 horse diesel engine made in Japan. Our long-range goals are to help other countries build the tractor and the equipment in their own countries and thus to lower the cost. The engine is lower priced in Honduras (where we're starting to build the tractors in a United Church of Christ school) because it is made in Brazil rather than Japan. Our present distribution is on a very small scale. We're not funded very heavily. We've only made about a 180 tractors in the last 15 years. Self Help was founded by Mr. Shield, an Iowa industrialist, who had the tractors designed specifically for small farmers in developing nations. The tractors are built to replace an ox team or mules and the components are designed to be very durable so that they don't need much repair.

WALLACE GRAY, Southwestern College, Winfield, Kansas: Mr. Brown, I've seen two positions attributed to you which seem inconsistent

6

to me. One of them, pointing back to The Geography of Hunger, maintains that "good nutrition is the best contraceptive." The second position comes from a summary of In the Human Interest. It claims that you pointed out that a number of countries have reduced their birth rates "without a large prior increase in their total GNP or per capita income." Could you comment on what seems to me two opposing positions?

LESTER BROWN: I think you've got some secondhand quotes there but, in any event, let me address the issue. There has been a great deal of debate in the population community in recent years as to whether the most effective way to address the population problem was through providing family planning services and population education on the one hand, or concentrating on social and economic development on the other. It seems to me that, like a lot of academic debates, this one is not terribly productive because it's not an either/or situation, it's not as though we were going to do one or going to do the other. We're trying to do both in most situations and to the extent we can do both, they will reinforce each other. The evidence in a great number of countries indicates that where social conditions improve, nutrition being one of the important ones, infant mortality drops, and when infant mortality drops then it's not usually too long after that before birth rates begin to go down. The reason couples have eight children is that they don't expect half of them to survive. Once they acquire that assurance through experience, then attitudes on family size change.

In some countries which have worked hard at both providing family planning services and population education and also improving social conditions, such as Taiwan, Sri Lanka and Mainland China, birth rates have come down very, very fast. They've halved the birth rates in a period of something like 12 to 15 years.

So, my general comment would be that it's not either/or. I think the statement that good nutrition is the best contraceptive is a reasonable one certainly. I would simply advise that we not get caught in that either/or situation because in the real world it's not an either/or question.

SURENDRA SINGH, Kansas Newman College, Wichita, Kansas: Where deforestation was done primarily for the purpose of making more agricultural land available, our experience has been that the land was not as good for crops as it was for forests. Do you think this experience will guide us away from the practice of deforesting in order to get more agricultural land?

LESTER BROWN: Perhaps we should have learned something from that experience but, in fact, it seems to me in great areas of the world the pressures for more farm land are still very intense. One of the interesting consequences of the rise in the cost of energy, and therefore the cost of fertilizer, is that dependence on energy

7

intensive techniques to increase output on existing cultivated area
has become more costly. The increase in energy costs has tended in
the last few years to cause the world at large to turn more to area
expansion than was the case between 1950 and 1972. I'm not sure
there are any easy solutions to this problem.

There's another interesting linkage between forests and farmland
in that, as deforestation progresses, villagers cannot get enough
firewood, and they begin burning animal dung for fuel for cooking
purposes. When this happens the manure that once went back on the
land no longer does, and soil fertility drops. So we have this interesting intersection between the energy crisis, if you will, in
the form of firewood shortage, and the food crisis. My guess is that
as we look ahead at the energy situation we're going to increasingly
see conflicts between the food sector and the energy sector for the
same resources.

In Brazil, for example, a well-developed plan is already under
way to produce alcohol from sugar cane or casava. They hope by the
end of the century that all gasoline will in effect be alcohol.
There are now service stations in both Rio and Sao Paolo that sell
an alcohol-gas mixture. In our own country we're seeing increasing
competition between energy firms and ranchers for scarce water resources in the Northern Plains. The coal mines will require water,
but the water is already being used by ranchers. Competition between the two sectors is, I think, going to be a very lively one,
and one deserving of a lot of research in the years ahead.

DANA LAROSE, Quaker School, near Philadelphia: In getting information out, how do we counteract consumerism and the almost hy-
sterical fear that people have in this country of cutbacks in production, causing unemployment?

LESTER BROWN: I think the response to consumerism is going to
have to be one of changing values. In looking ahead, some people
are very apprehensive about the possible slowdown in growth and all
the economic and social changes that may bring. I am probably less
so than some. The driving force behind our economic system at the
moment is materialism. One would have to assume that materialism
is the ultimate in human social evolution to be opposed to our moving beyond the present systems. I believe that as we make this accommodation we will find ourselves evolving toward a set of values
that are much more human than the ones we now have.

The second point you raised, the question of unemployment, is
going to be one of the most difficult ones for policymakers to deal
with for the simple reason that we've always assumed that the way
you get more jobs is through rapid growth and consumption. There
are a lot of areas in which we could create meaningful employment
while making the accommodation. One simple one is the recycling of
materials, for example. Recycling bottles, using entirely

8

returnable containers in the food and beverage industry, for example, would create a lot more jobs than we now have. It would save energy, it would reduce environmental stresses of all sorts. It's precisely the sort of thing we should be doing, but which we're not doing very well at the moment.

LENI BERLINER, University of Pittsburgh: When I first learned about carrying capacity, I was taught that one of the determinants of any population's carrying capacity was its pattern of distributing resources. I know that as far as fisheries are concerned, the overfishing you mentioned pertains primarily to fish high on the food chain, and the overfishing is a result of internal industry organization more than anything else, and some market forces. It's been estimated that an annual catch of 46 million tons (which is less than the current catch, as you mentioned), if properly utilized and distributed, could provide protein needs for 6 billion people. It is true that better biological information is necessary to determine the maximum sustainable yield for the effective regional arrangements you mentioned. But I think it's also important to realize that in some areas of endeavor in our biological research, we have more knowledge than we have thus far had the wisdom to use as far as distribution is concerned.

LESTER BROWN: As long as the global economic pie was growing rapidly, it was easy for politicians to say to the people at the bottom of the ladder, "Be patient, things are getting better, your lot is improving." But when that pie stops expanding it becomes very difficult to dodge the issue of distribution. In aiming at a sustainable society we're going to have to take into account political and social sustainability as well as ecological sustainability. If, in accommodating ourselves to some of the biological constraints, we do not take into account the distribution patterns both within and among societies, then I think we're going to create some enormous and probably unsustainable political stresses.

FOOD AND POPULATION: A CATHOLIC PERSPECTIVE

Rev. J. Bryan Hehir

Associate Secretary for International Justice and Peace
U.S. Catholic Conference

I would like to present a framework for understanding Catholic teaching on food and population.[1] For the purposes of this paper, I have chosen to include the food question under the broader rubric of development and then to discuss Catholic teaching on population and development. The argument of the paper moves through three steps:

First, I will situate a Catholic perspective on these topics within the spectrum of other major views.

Second, I will argue that it is an inadequate view of Catholic teaching either to characterize it as denying that population is a problem or to reduce its view on population simply to a discussion of the means of population control.

Third, I will propose a Catholic perspective on development and population which is a human rights approach to the topic.

I. Development and Population: Situating the Catholic Position

For the sake of initiating the discussion on development and population, it is possible to distinguish three broadly drawn positions; each position involves a definition of the problem, a target group within the problem and a means of resolving the problem.[2]

The first position argues that population is the problem. It treats population as an independent variable, then contends that if only one could deal with the population issue it would be possible to reduce poverty, hunger and perhaps even warfare. With this independent status accorded population, it becomes clear that the people who threaten the world are those having too many children, and in aggregate terms at least, this means people in developing countries where the aggregate growth rate is 2-3% as opposed to industrialized countries where it was 0.8% for 1975. Given this definition of the development-population problem, the solution for this perspective lies in a massive and direct attack on the population front, providing multiple methods of control accompanied by information, persuasion incentives, and, in some versions, coercion to induce the target group to alter its procreation habits.[3]

The second position argues that population is no problem. This position is the antithesis of the first, since it treats population entirely as a dependent variable. In this view, often depicted as a Marxist or a Roman Catholic position, poverty is the problem. If poverty can be addressed in depth, the population question will be cared for as a by-product. Given this definition of development-population, the target group which is "the problem" includes those who hold economic power in society, either internationally or within developing societies. The solution to the development-population problem involves radical structural change in patterns of political-economic control.[4]

The third position argues that population is part of the development problem. It treats the population issue as significant in itself, but not possible of resolution apart from the fabric of the broader question of socio-economic development. In this view there is not a single target group or a single set of measures which can deal with development and population. What is required is an integrated policy of development, involving multiple measures treating both poverty and population as interdependent variables.[5]

The third position, dominantly reflected in the U.N. Conference on Population at Bucharest (1974), is commonly referred to as the consensus position.[6] The supporting arguments for the position draw upon past historical success and failure in the population area. Negatively, it points to cases where a frontal but unilateral attack has been made on population and failed to produce the desired result of reducing population growth.[7]

Positively, it is argued that both the history of the demographic transition in the West as well as current cases where population growth has been curtailed have involved instances where the improvement of the socio-economic condition of the populace has resulted in a declining rate of population growth.[8] Three qualifications are needed to understand this argument. First, such an argument does not presume that the pattern of the demographic transition in the West can be simply replicated in the developing world.[9] Second, to argue that rising standards of socio-economic welfare contribute to declining population growth does not mean that it is necessary or possible to find a magic number of per capita GNP which must be reached before the impact will be felt on population growth. Such a number does not exist; rather, the more nuanced position holds that if people are given some sense of "control" over the rest of their lives (i.e., a minimal level of security regarding food, health care, education, employment) they will exercise "control" in the area of reproduction behavior. Third, this means that in assessing

the relationship between development policies and population, effective development strategy is not defined in terms of aggregate
economic growth or even per capita GNP, but are to be judged by what
Arthur Dyck has called distributive criteria aimed at improving the
distribution of income and social service in a society.[10]

This "developmental distributivist" position, as Dyck names it,
is substantively related to prevailing conceptions of development
strategy which are critical of the "trickle-down" theories of the
fifties and sixties for their inability to touch the quality of life
of the "lower forty-percent" of populations in the developing countries.[11] The critique of the trickle-down theories with their emphasis on massive infra-structure programs aimed at promoting rapid
industrialization and consequent "take-off" of the economy has produced a set of policy recommendations usually grouped under the rubric of a basic human needs strategy. This approach (which, like
take-off and trickle-down, has its own pitfalls if accepted without
qualification) would orient development policy precisely in the
direction of the "lower forty-percent" with the objective of satisfying, in minimal terms, their human needs/rights in the areas of nutrition, employment, education and health care.[12]

The significance of this third position for this paper is twofold.
First, it illustrates the growing conviction among analysts and policymakers that unilateral measures aimed either at poverty or population will not be effective; this judgment is made not in normative but
empirical terms, yet it coincides with one dimension of the Catholic
commentary on the development-population question. Second, it is
possible, I believe, to locate Catholic teaching on population and
development in this consensus position, one which takes seriously
both poverty and population questions and which seeks resolution of
both in terms of a strategy of social justice aimed at fulfilling
basic human rights of each person.

II. Development and Population: Stating the Catholic Position

An exposition of the Catholic position on development and population involves two levels of analysis. The "public tradition" of
Catholic social teaching focuses on the socio-economic context required for true human development. The "personal tradition," exemplified in Catholic teaching on the morality of contraception,
focuses on the means of population control. Too often Catholic
teaching is simply identified with the personal tradition, as if it
consumed the moral and religious wisdom of the Catholic tradition
on the complex development-population question. The reasons for
this lie both in the way analysts sometimes approach Catholic
teaching and in the way it is at other times presented by Catholics.
The argument here is that any analysis of the Catholic position requires attention to both the public and personal dimensions of the
tradition and that the relationship between the two dimensions admits

12

of more than one interpretation.

It is necessary at the outset, therefore, to distinguish two related but not identical moral questions in Catholic theological
ethics: the morality of contraception and the teaching on population
policy. In John Noonan's classic work on contraception, he identifies
moments in the history of the tradition when demographic trends affected the teaching of the magisterium, but these instances do not
stand out in his work as major determinants in the development of
Catholic doctrine on contraception.[13] Noonan's analysis illustrates
the complexity of the Catholic response to falling birth rates in
the late Roman Empire, in the medieval period and again in the 19th
Century. The Catholic position criticized the idea of restraining
population growth without asserting that procreation of children
should be fostered in a unilateral manner apart from other values.
The balancing factors in the Catholic position were the linking of
procreation to education and the high status accorded virginity in
Catholic life.

It is possible, therefore, to trace a relationship between contraception and population policy throughout Catholic teaching; until the 20th Century the dominant idea is the prohibition of contraceptive practices with the population issue treated as a minor
theme. Even in Pius XI's encyclical Casti Connubii (1930), which
Noonan describes as "a small summa on Christian marriage,"[14] the
population issue receives only indirect reference. A systematic
treatment of the morality of population policy as a distinct issue
in its own right is not evident in Catholic thought until the time
of Pius XII.[15] Beginning with his Address to Midwives (1951) and
continuing through the teachings of Popes John XXIII, Paul VI, Vatican II and the Synod of Bishops (1971) one can find an articulated
normative doctrine on population policy. The ethical teaching
responds to two dimensions of the contemporary population debate:
first, the renewal of the Malthusian discussion of the relationship
of population and resources; second, the move by governments to
design policies to affect demographic trends.

A. The Public Tradition

The public analysis is found generally in the social teaching
of the Church; the principal documents relating to population policy
are Gaudium et Spes (1965), Populorum Progressio (1967) and the
Addresses of Pope Paul on the occasion of the World Population Year
(1974) and the World Food Conference (1974). These documents mani-
fest a structural analysis of the population issue, seeking to place
demographic variables within a broadly defined socio-economic context. The tenor and style of analysis is exemplified in the following passage from Paul VI's message for the U.N. Population Year
(1974):

13

The true solutions to these problems--we would say the
only solutions--will be those which take due account of
all concrete factors taken together: the demands of social justice as well as respect for the divine laws
governing life, the dignity of the human person as well
as the freedom of peoples, the primary role of the family
as well as the responsibility proper to married couples.[16]

The perspective dominating all of these statements is that the
population problem is one strand of a larger fabric involving questions of political, economic and social structure at the national
and international level. While acknowledging the existence of a
population problem, this view asserts that it is morally wrong and
practically ineffective to isolate population as a single factor,
seeking to reduce population growth without simultaneously making
those political and economic changes which will achieve a more
equitable distribution of wealth and resources within nations and
among nations. To cite Paul VI's message to the World Food Conference: "It is inadmissible that those who have control of the
wealth and resources of mankind should try to resolve the problem
of hunger by forbidding the poor to be poor, or by leaving to die
of hunger children whose parents do not fit into the framework of
theoretical plans based on pure hypotheses about the future of mankind."[17]

The ethical categories used in this public analysis of the population problem are drawn from Catholic social teaching developed
principally in the papal encyclicals in the years 1891-1971.[18] The
foundation of the argument is an assertion of the unique dignity of
the person in the created order; the uniqueness of the person is
argued in both theological and philosophical terms. The dignity
of the person is the source of a spectrum of rights and duties articulated as claims upon and responsibilities toward other persons
and society as a whole. The distinguishing mark of a Catholic
theory of rights, setting it apart from a classical liberal argument,
is the assertion of the social nature of the person. Society and
state are necessary and natural institutions, presupposed and required for full human development.

The strong social orientation of Catholic political philosophy
holds that the way in which society, state and subordinate social
institutions are designed and structured is a moral question of
the first order. Society and state are not self-justifying; they
exist for the purpose of achieving the common good defined by Pope
John in Pacem In Terris in the following manner:

It is agreed that in our time the common good is chiefly
guaranteed when personal rights and duties are maintained.
The chief concern of civil authorities must therefore be
to ensure that these rights are acknowledged, respected,
co-ordinated with other rights, defended and promoted,

so that in this way each one may more easily carry out his duties.[19]

The central category used in evaluating the organization of social structures and institutions is social justice. This concept has roots in medieval Catholic teaching but has been developed and refined in the social encyclicals Quadragesimo Anno (1931) and Mater et Magistra (1961), as well as in the synodal document Justice in the World (1971).[20] As social justice is used in these documents, it serves to measure the role of key social institutions in procuring a fair distribution of wealth and resources nationally and internationally. In Pacem In Terris (1963) the normative prism for assessing social institutions is expanded beyond justice to include truth, freedom and charity.

At both the national and international levels the categories of common good, social justice and freedom of choice for individuals and families in society are used to define the population question. Among social institutions the family holds a unique place in Catholic thought.[21] It is regarded as the basic cell or unit of society and the Church. In the social hierarchy, reaching from the person through the state to the international community, no other association, save the Church itself, is accorded such status. The demands of the common good and the requirements of social justice are articulated in terms of providing the family and its members with those conditions of life which satisfy basic human needs, protect personal dignity and allow each the opportunity for human development through the exercise of rights and responsibilities in society.

High on the list of inviolable rights is that of marrying and having a family.[22] To protect this right for each person who chooses to exercise it, Catholic social teaching establishes two parameters: positively, it calls upon the society to guarantee a basic minimum of material welfare, and negatively, it prohibits the state from any significant interference in exercise of these rights. To summarize the public dimension of Catholic teaching, it accords primary attention to the context of the population question, focusing on the requirements of social justice which should be met as the first step in dealing with the relationship of resources and people. These requirements in specific form include questions of international trade, development assistance, agricultural reform, foreign investment policies, consumption patterns and the structure of social relationships within nations. Having accented these contextual issues in the population debate, Catholic teaching in the private dimension moves beyond them to the content of the procreative relationship.

B. The Personal Tradition

In contrast to the public teaching which focuses on societal structures, the personal tradition focuses upon the nature of the

15

conjugal relationship, and specifically upon the morality of the conjugal act. The principal issue involves analyzing permissible means of preventing conception. The personal tradition is rooted in the extensive Catholic teaching on contraception which has developed in a very complex and detailed fashion since the second century.[23]

The modern expression of the personal tradition is found in Piux XI's Casti Connubii (1931), Pius XII's Address to the Congress of the Italian Union of Midwives (1951) and Paul VI's Humanae Vitae (1968). The principal issues in the personal tradition include the morality of contraception, of sterilization and of abortion; in the magisterial tradition all are rejected as means of preventing conception or birth. The only means of limiting conception which is sanctioned is the rhythm method. In contrast to the state of theological discussion on the public tradition, there is a very significant division today between magisterial teaching on contraception and theological analysis of contraception. While the former forbids all forms of contraception, theological writings legitimate a variety of permissible means of limiting births.[24]

The personal tradition has public implications; it seeks to prevent any public policy which would either constrain or induce individuals to use contraceptives or would prevent them from choosing to have children. There are themes of coherence and consistency between the public and personal traditions: both view the procreative process as a uniquely sacred dimension of human relationships; both seek to preserve maximum freedom for the couple to determine when to exercise procreative rights; both stress that society and the state exist to serve their members and this relationship is articulated in terms of social justice and personal freedom.

III. A Human Rights Strategy: Resources in Catholic Teaching

The central question in assessing what the Catholic contribution can be to the development-population debate is how the public and personal dimensions of the tradition are to be related.

While it is substantively important to note the elements of continuity between the public and personal dimensions of Catholic teaching on population policy, it is equally important in interpreting this teaching to illustrate the tension which prevails today on these two levels. The tension can be exemplified by analyzing two principal texts: Populorum Progressio (1967) representing the public tradition and Humanae Vitae (1968) representing the personal tradition. Paragraph thirty-seven of Populorum Progressio is the most fully articulated and expansive statement of Catholic teaching on population policy.[25] The passage contains the following elements: (1) an acknowledgment that a population problem exists in the world; (2) an affirmation that governments have a

16

right and competency to deal with the problem; (3) a prescription that governmental action must be in accord with the moral law. This specific treatment of population policy is couched in the context of Paul VI's most detailed statement of the need for international reform in the political and economic order. Hence the paragraph presupposes that the social justice requirements are being addressed, and in that context it speaks to the question of measures to restrict population growth.

This passage is the clearest statement in Catholic teaching affirming the right of governments to intervene in the population question; left undefined, however, is the permissible scope of governmental intervention. The phrase which renders the policy ambiguous is that public intervention must be "in conformity with the moral law." In this area of public policy, what measures fall within the moral law? One way to clarify and specify the public tradition is to use Humanae Vitae as the guide for interpreting the moral law. The principal argument of the encyclical is that the moral law requires each and every act of intercourse to be open to procreation.[26] A supporting reason offered for this position is that any compromise on this point opens the way to unregulated governmental intrusion into the sacred doctrine of family life.[27] Presumably then, the conjunction of Humanae Vitae and Populorum Progressio would limit the scope of governmental intervention to supporting and fostering only that means of population restraint approved in Humanae Vitae.

Such a restrictive reading of the texts is not required by the principles of Catholic moral theology. The basic problem joining the two texts in this way is that it collapses the distinction between the public and personal dimensions of Catholic teaching on social morality. A characteristic feature of Catholic social teaching is its sense of the analogical structure of society. The state is distinguished from society and voluntary associations are distinguished from the state. Each principal part of the societal fabric is regarded as having a specific limited role to play.[28]

In an essay which is a classic because of its precision and clarity as well as its acute rendering of the Catholic natural law tradition in social ethics, the late John Courtney Murray, S.J. explicated the two principles of jurisprudence which flow from an analogical understanding of society.[29] First, there is no recognition that personal conceptions of morality cannot be directly translated into requirements for public policy; to attempt to do so ignores the distinct nature of social and institutional relationships in society and thereby "makes wreckage not only of public policy but also of morality itself."[30] Secondly, a recognition of two related but distinct levels of moral discourse, public and personal (or private), yields the jurisprudential distinction of moral law and civil law. While every human action and all human relationships fall under the moral law, only those which have a demonstrable effect on the public order and which are open to state regulation

17

without sacrificing other proportionately significant values are to be included under civil law or public policy.[31] While consistently affirming its right and obligation to teach on all dimensions of the moral order, the Church has not felt obliged to propose that the entire body of Catholic teaching be incorporated in the strict law or public policy of a society. In situations of moral and religious pluralism, in which highly controverted issues of morality are at stake, the determination of whether to attempt to bring all dimensions of public law or policy into accord with Catholic teaching depends upon a series of moral judgments and prudential calculations.

The moral judgments include the nature of the moral issue at stake (e.g., homicide vs. pornography), the intelligibility of Catholic teaching for those who are not members of the Church (e.g., should one try to incorporate a tertiary precept of the natural law in civil legislation?) and the authority employed in the teaching (e.g., conciliar statement, encyclical, papal allocution). The prudential calculations involve questions such as can the policy be implemented or will the law be obeyed? What is the balance of consequences between achieving the good the policy seeks and the harm which could occur in other areas of life touched by the policy? What are the results of past experience in trying to implement this policy? Is the civil law or civil government an effective agent to address the question at issue?

Behind these distinctions of the moral and legal order lie a carefully nuanced understanding in Catholic social teaching about the possibilities and limits of public law or public policy. Murray stated the case with his customary precision:

> Therefore the moral aspirations of law are minimal. Law seeks to establish and maintain only that minimum of actualized morality that is necessary for the healthy functioning of the social order. It does not look to what is morally desirable, or attempt to remove every moral taint from the atmosphere of society. It enforces only what is minimally acceptable, and in this sense socially necessary. Beyond this, society must look to other institutions for the elevation and maintenance of its moral standards--that is, to the church, the home, the school, and the whole network of voluntary associations that concern themselves with public morality in one or the other aspect.[33]

Using this traditional form of reasoning, I wish to argue a position which is a strictly personal view, based on my own theological reflection. It is not the position of the National Conference of Catholic Bishops and should not be so construed. It is, however, a theologically defensible view and I offer it as a means of both providing the general public with a framework for understanding the debate about development and population in the Catholic community and as a means of continuing that debate among Catholics and others

18

interested in the content of the Catholic position on these issues.

In the formulation of a public policy on the development-population issue the Church could use the natural law distinctions articulated above to relate the public and personal dimensions of her position in terms of a human rights strategy. Such a position would first argue for the primacy of a development strategy designed to insure a basic minimum of access to the physical necessities of life as well as a degree of participation in the social process which is called for in the political and civil rights enumerated in Pacem in Terris. Second, the means question could be stated in such a way that, save for the issues of abortion and sterilization, the public strategy of the Church would be to regard contraceptive practice as an issue of personal morality which it continues to teach for its members, but not an issue of public morality on which it seeks to affect public policy.

Justification for this position can be garnered morally from the style of recent Church teaching on contraception. While continuing to affirm a natural law argument against contraception, the arguments of Gaudium et Spes (no. 51) and Humanae Vitae (nos. 4, 11, 12) rely heavily upon the Church's right to interpret the natural law. While this point is not new, the emphasis accorded the authoritative character of the teaching in discerning the content of natural law renders it less useful for those in society who do not accept the teaching authority of the Church. If acceptance of Church teaching authority is so intrinsically linked to understanding of the rationale of the Church's position against contraception, there is moral reason not to seek to bind an entire society with the position. An empirical assessment of the possibility of establishing even minimal societal consensus on a prohibition of contraception policy reinforces this normative judgment.[34]

The logic of this position, while not ignoring the highly debated character of contraception within the Church, is not based upon the status of Humanae Vitae among Catholics. One can hold literally to the position espoused in the Encyclical for Catholics and still argue that we ought not to make that position the basis of our public policy. The public position on contraceptive policies could be a posture of a discreet silence. We could withdraw public opposition from contraceptive policies, leaving to the decisions of public authorities, within specified limits, the formulation and implementation of means questions.

The logic of the position being argued here involves a low profile for the Church on the means question in population policy. It does not involve a low profile on the substantive morality of population policies espoused by public authorities. The argument is to shift the emphasis of the moral case, not to eschew it.

Hence, a third step in this human rights strategy would be to

correlate a low profile on contraceptive policy with a strict, explicit, unyielding opposition to the employment of abortion as a
means of population control. Such a position against abortion
should be argued, as it can be, on human rights grounds. Fourth,
again on human rights grounds, the Church could and should oppose
sterilization as a tactic in a population policy because of the
possible abuses which can flow from placing this instrument in the
hands of public authorities.

To base our critique of population policy in terms of a human
rights argument allows the Church to take a systemic view of population policy, i.e., analyze the principles which guide the direction
and implementation of policy, and offers it an opportunity to join
forces with others who also have raised questions about the morality
of population policy here and abroad. The purpose of a human rights
evaluation of population policy would be to guarantee that any
measures adopted serve not only the common interests of the larger
society, but also respect the personal rights of individuals who
make up the society. The essence of the development-population
problem is the need to balance the aggregate interests of society
in maintaining a proper balance of resources and people with the
personal rights of the individual to marry and to determine family
size.

The style of systemic moral thinking which seeks to accord
proper weight to the "common good" while recognizing that the "common good is chiefly guaranteed when personal rights and duties are
maintained" (Pacem in Terris, no. 60) is part of the Catholic social
tradition as best expressed in modern papal teaching. To move from
a means argument to a rights argument on population policy is to
remain very much in a Catholic style and structure of moral reasoning. It is to move, however, from a particularistic to a univer-
salist mode of argumentation.

Dr. Arthur Dyck, in his discussion of the nature of the right
to have children, describes it as a "fundamental right" which an
ideal observer would recognize as being universally valid, "belong-
ing to every human being qua being human."[35] A human rights style
of argument places the Church in the service of all individuals and
thereby elicits the cooperation of others similarly concerned about
such fundamental rights. The shape of the argument defending such
fundamental rights against unjust intrusion by a public authority
would follow the lines of Pope John's discussion in Pacem in Terris
of the relationship between individuals and public authorities in a
state. The specifics of such an argument cannot be easily summarized,
but among the benefits of adopting such a style of moral reasoning
are the following: (1) it broadens the scope and basis of the
Church's moral reasoning on the population issue, speaking in defense of each person against unjustified restriction of a basic
right; (2) in this process it strengthens the defense of the Catholic conscience in the face of policies it might find particularly

20

offensive, e.g., sterilization; (3) it avoids the charge of a "sectarian" stance by arguing in categories and for principles which stand apart from any single faith perspective.

The need for such a human rights posture on development-population policy is evident both on the national and on the international levels of the debate. The pressure of the population problem tends to emphasize the need to stress systemic over personal values. The first to be affected by such thinking are often those in society without power to protect their rights. In evaluating the impact of incentives and compulsion as instruments of policy planning, Dyck finds that "Compulsion, like incentives, discriminates against the poor. Restricting the very poor to two or three children would render their lives much less hopeful and much more precarious. In less developed countries such restrictions for the poor mean economic losses in the form of reductions both in labor and in security for their old age."[36]

By adopting a human rights framework and strategy for its development-population policy, the Catholic Church would be using its strongest contemporary moral resource, an articulated social ethic, to join the public and personal dimensions of its teaching in coherent fashion. The adoption of such a strategy requires further debate in the Church, but not a drastic shift in its moral teaching. Because the move to such a position is ethically possible, and because the problems of development and population are so persistently present as a challenge to the human community, it is worth the effort in the Church to raise, debate and decide these issues in the style of ethical discourse which Murray used to call the tradition of reason in public affairs.

DISCUSSION

ADRIAN GIBBONS, Obloit Fathers Commission on Peace and Justice, Omaha, Nebraska: I've had numerous discussions about the theological sanction on abortion. The question is if the only argument against abortion comes from a theological position, how does that work into legislation? How do you switch from a theological to a moral-legislative point of view?

BRYAN HEHIR: I would say that the only argument is not made from a theological position. There is an argument against abortion from the theological position. There is another argument that is close to the theological argument, but that would not use any theological terms. The theological argument, most clearly stated, argues that God is the author of life; we are entrusted with life in terms of stewardship; and therefore we don't have the right to touch life once one identifies it as human life; the fetus is

21

identified as human life, and therefore the prohibition of any kind of abortion flows from that.

Another kind of argument is an argument that is made in public policy terms. This argument is made by Christian ethicists who are not Catholics, people such as Dyke from Harvard, Ramsey from Princeton, Potter from Harvard and Gustafson from Chicago. The argument is that what is at issue in the debabe about abortion is the question of what a society does when it is faced with the question of life. Now, immediately, someone says, "Well, what do you mean by life?" and then the debate starts about the fetus. The position of these Christian ethicists is that when there is a significant division in the society about whether you are faced with human life or not, it is not possible for a society simply to say, in laissez faire fashion, we will take no position on it. And, therefore, faced with that kind of question, one has to have some minimal grounds of public policy on which one will decide that issue.

Now, the argument then moves in several directions. Ramsey's argument is that once you get past eight days, there is no definable line that you can draw between that and death in which you can distinguish human life as coming into being as opposed to not being in being before that eight-day period. Then you move into more empirical arguments rather than normative arguments. But the essential argument is that society has, as a fundamental obligation, the protection of life. Since society is strongly divided over that kind of question, you have to have some kind of public policy debated and not simply decided by default.

PETER HUESSY, The Environmental Fund: I want to say that it's so good to hear that the Catholic Church is in favor of population control. I've always thought they were, but the means argument seems to cloud everything.

I'd like to comment on what I take to be the main assumption of your paper, that economic and social development will bring population into equilibrium. Many of us are concerned that this version of the Demographic Transition theory will not lead to a solution of the problem. Almost every senior geographer, ecologist, botanist, plant pathologist, tropical agriculture specialist, energy specialist and weather specialist that I know feels that the carrying capacity of this globe, at even a minimum decent standard of living (let's say a mid-European, Greek or Yugoslav level) is less than six billion, maybe seven billion, and certainly less than eight billion on a long term basis.

The Demographic Transition theory doesn't say anything about time. When are you going to stabilize it? Leon Tabah says 15 billion, Herman Kahn says 30 billion, Roger Revelle says up to 60 billion people can be fed on a U.S. diet.

22

The critical question, I think that this Demographic Transition theory does not address is that even if development brings birth rates down (and I think there is serious question as to the validity of the Demographic Transition theory, since it only applies to a small part of the world, historically), what if this brings us a world of 12 to 15 billion people and the ecologists are right? If they are right, then a world population of 15 billion people will result in the permanent denudation of the earth's carrying capacity, and the end result will be that perhaps only half a billion or a billion people can live and they can only live very poorly because everything is so poisoned and biological systems are broken down.

BRYAN HEHIR: First of all, I think you would be inaccurate to take from my speech that I said that the Catholic Church was in favor of population control, because that tends to be a code word. I said that the Church acknowledges population as a distinct problem, and that the Church has not said that everyone has to have as many children as they can have. It is said in Catholic teaching that the parents are to decide how many children they should have. So I want to be clear about that. I'm trying to represent an institution and represent a complex argument in addition to that.

In responding to your question, I'd make two comments. First of all, off the top of my head, I'm really not about to dispute the statistical analysis you've given. My understanding of the problem is that the statistics in this debate are remarkably fungible; that is to say, I look at Revelle's critique of some people's work and I look at Dyke's critique of what he calls crisis environmentalists, and I'm not sure anyone has made a demonstrable public argument which could be made the basis of public policy.

My second point is that public policy is always a mix of ends and means. About the means question, I would raise two points. First of all, if I understand the population debate, even if you put everybody in the room together and we said we were in favor of population restraint, period, no qualifications, no distinctions, we still don't know what motivates people to have or not have children. Therefore, to say that the aggregate environmentalist statistics can be translated into knowing what you ought to do seems to me to be a step that hasn't been demonstrated yet.

The second point is that some means are clearly regarded as objectionable by people. So even if you agree on the environmentalist position, the question becomes, "What's the cost of a public policy that is implemented where means are regarded as objectionable?" Here I would have to differ strongly with Representative McCloskey. My understanding is that people in the developing countries are not thrilled about the idea of the U.S. outlawing contraceptive techniques because of FDA standards and then using them in the developing countries. I just don't want any part of that argument.

I think the means question is a central question. I want to take the aggregate environmental data seriously, but what I'm saying is that it doesn't give you a policy.

JAMES GRANT, Overseas Development Council: Mr. Chairman, if I may at this moment, I'd like to put two broad sets of facts on the table, and then pose a question.

The Overseas Development Council has just completed a study of deaths throughout the world. Roughly 50 million people died last year, and of that 50 million people, some 39-40 million died in the developing countries. If the developing countries had had the life expectancy and the general health conditions that prevailed in the West, instead of there being 39-40 million deaths, there would have been 18-19 million deaths. In other words, roughly half the deaths would have been avoided if they had Western styles.

More significantly, if all developing countries had the health levels achieved by a few low income countries that really focus on basic needs and social justice programs, symbolized by, say Sri Lanka, which has per capita income of about $150 (or about half that of the U.S. in 1776), Taiwan, China and Kerala, if those death rates prevailed in the world, there would be approximately 15 million fewer deaths; one-half of those deaths would be children saved, with the great majority of those being infants under one year old. Now this is a big right-to-life issue.

An interesting footnote to these figures is that if all the developing countries had the same birth rates as those countries had when they achieved a death rate of 9, there would have been some 20 million fewer births every year. So there is a significantly greater savings in births in those social justice societies and interestingly enough, in each of those societies, the birth rate started down well before the introduction of major family planning programs. The major family planning programs then came in and accelerated the process. That is the factual context of what I would call 15 million readily avoidable deaths today.

Our study also carried the projection through to the end of the century. If you take the UN likely projections to the end of the century, and look at the death patterns likely to be prevailing, and compare those with the death patterns that would prevail if there were an effective address of basic needs in developing countries between now and the end of the century, the number of deaths which could be avoided each year by the year 2000 would be about 10 million a year. Now this is a rather monumental set of stakes that are involved.

This brings me to my second point, which is that we have in the Congress a revolutionary piece of legislation that Hubert Humphrey left behind to reorganize foreign aid to make it very clear for the

24

first time that our development assistance should be focused on addressing basic human needs for the poorest countries and the poorest people in the world. Senator Clark, one of the principal sponsors of that bill, has said it is a commitment to overcome the worst aspects of poverty by the end of the century.

After this long statement, Bryan, let me ask what sort of position the U.S. Catholic Conference is taking on the Humphrey bill? And, secondly, how do you feel about pressing the President for a far more active role in overcoming the worst aspects of absolute poverty by the end of the century?

BRYAN HEHIR: Testimony is now being written in my office which will strongly support the basic human needs strategy of the Humphrey legislation. There seems to me little question about this.

But, as I understand it, the development debate moves at two different levels. One level is this basic human needs strategy, which is distributionist in tone, which is aimed at the lower 40%, which emphasizes certain categories like health care and education and nutrition, and is aimed at overcoming the worst aspects of poverty on a mass basis. I'm heartened to see the shape of the Humphrey bill because I think it follows from the New Directions' mandate of the Congress and, from what I understand, there is public support for that kind of foreign assistance.

But I think it's fair to say that when we testify on the Humphrey bill, there will be another set of issues that we'll have to flag. These are the more structural issues of the relationship between industrialized and developing countries raised by the debate on the NIEO, the New International Economic Order. These more structural issues touching upon commodity pricing, trade relationships and restructuring the monetary system run into much more heat and flack than the basic human needs strategy. I am 100% behind the basic human needs strategy, but I think it is important to say that the U.S. position on these other issues will be of crucial importance. I hope that the basic human needs strategy is not looked upon as a way to deflect the debate from the more structural issues. This is a tougher issue with the Congress, and with the public generally, but I think it's an issue we need to deal with.

GODFREY ROBERTS, Livingston College and Rutgers University: We have spent a lot of time discussing the developmentalist position on population. But if we look at a human rights kind of question, I believe it is justified to say that a free choice in abortion should be perceived as a basic human right. I raise this in the light of the rights of a child after it's born. In the United States, for instance, although it's a highly developed society, we have a very high rate of child abuse. Life is even harder for many children in developing countries. In these conditions, how can we deny the right to abortion?

BRYAN HEHIR: I appreciate the question because it gives me a chance to clarify the issue. I really don't think I can give an answer that's satisfactory to everyone. I think that's intrinsic in the nature of the question.

A part of the difficulty in the abortion debate is that we don't agree on the question. When I read the editorials in the Catholic newspapers there are a whole series of presuppositions behind the editorials that are never articulated, and then a conclusion comes. When I read the Washington Post on the same issue, there are another series of presuppositions that are not articulated, and then the conclusion comes. And the conclusions pass each other like trains in the night.

The essence of the question, I think, is how you define the moral equation that you're trying to address. Now, in the U.S. Supreme Court decision, for example, the moral equation is defined in terms of the woman's right and the state's right or lack of right to intervene on her privacy. So it's a two-factored moral equation. The woman is involved, and the state is involved, and the question is, "Does the state have the right to restrict her freedom of choice?" Now, that's a debatable question. We use that moral equation for all kinds of civil rights issues. For instance, does the state have the right to tap my telephone? So I'm acknowledging that if you start with that question, then you move in a certain direction to an answer.

All I want to indicate is that from the Catholic position, and others who share that position, it isn't the argument about the answer that is so important. It is that we don't understand the question in those terms. The question, I would argue, is at least a three-factored question--the woman, the state, the fetal life. Now I've described it as fetal life. That is more restrictive than most people in the Catholic community would define it, but I'm consciously here trying to set some ground for dialogue. I'm simply saying that fetal life is an independent factor that has to be considered. Therefore, when one talks about the right to an abortion, in a three-factored equation one at least has to recognize fetal rights over against it, and then the state becomes a judicator, an arbitrator of that question. That brings me back to my first response when I said the essence of the question is that if one believes society is faced with the question of life in some form, and the state's role vis-a-vis life, at least you have a moral question you have to argue about. It's too simple a description to start with the presumption that abortion is a human right and to argue from the state of the child after he or she is born, because I want to argue about a prior right, and that's the right to be born. My point is the question is simply never defined clearly enough.

The way the Supreme Court decision was made preempted the question because the court decision clearly took one definition of the question from among several definitions that it could have taken.

26

But when you can't get agreement on the question, then you can't get a reasonable debate about the conclusion. Disagreement requires some prior degree of agreement in order to have disagreement.

STEWART MOTT, New York: As chairman of this session I'd like to make a few concluding remarks. One of Pete McCloskey's constituents out there in Palo Alto is the originator in Syntex of the pill. He once told me of new medical developments he was working on, including a little implant underneath the eyelid for people who suffer from glaucoma to replace the massive dosages of medication they now take internally. He said his search was to find a way of putting out a wastebasket on fire in the Empire State Building without bringing in a tidal wave; that is, go to the source and put it out right there.

I'm baffled as can be about the persistent debate as to whether or not population is the problem. It seems to me that when you first find an acre of land unable to support one person and then gradually two or three, and suddenly you get ten, that the land is not at fault, not the birds and the bees and the animals that habitate it; it's the number of people that are trying to divide it up. In our approach to what I perceive as the population problem, it seems to me that if we can find a way of addressing the problem with a fire extinguisher at the wastebasket rather than bringing in a tidal wave, then we are going to address the problem more efficiently. And, yes, of course, socioeconomic development should come along with our ability to address the population problem but, as those of you who hear from the managers of our AID program know, there are many, many ready acceptors throughout the world who do not have access to modern methods of birth control and others who find existing methods inappropriate. There is a great deal to be done in direct delivery of contraceptive services.

It's heartening to know that the United Nations Fund for Population Activities is doing a nation-by-nation survey of each country in the developing world, what they call their absorptive capacity study. And eventually we will have a bottom-line summing up of what is needed in terms of the ability of each country to absorb training programs for public health nurses, numbers of dozens of contraceptive units, jeeps, and other necessities for bringing that country's population program up to its absorptive capcity. We'll be able to get a world view, perhaps by the end of this year, of what year by year the developing world can absorb. That will give us, I hope, one definition, one goal, to strive toward. Pete McCloskey and his task force on reproductive research will provide us another objective.

The question is, how do we translate these objectives into reality? With $800 million going to cancer research, and $400 million to heart research, and with a Congress dominated by geriatric men, how will we raise the actual funding levels? I think one clear step is what Jim Scheuer and his colleagues have accomplished in the

House. The subject of population has been ignored far too long by the Administration, and now the Congress has a group of people who are willing to put in their time this year on this subject alone. I think that by the time they're ready to report out, and as they do so incrementally, it's up to those among us who believe in citizen action and political action to get behind their recommendations and make it the subject of a continuing large lobby during the coming year.

FOOTNOTES

1. For an overview of the issues discussed here cf: Theological Studies 35 (1974); The U.S. and World Development: Agenda for Action 1975, Washington: The Overseas Development Council and Praeger Press (1975); R. McNamara, Address on the Population Problem to the Massachusetts Institute of Technology, Washington, IBRD, (1977). Population Memorandum #3: Toward a Just Global Population Policy, Washington: The Center of Concern (1973); A. Dyck, Procreation Rights and Population Policy, The Hastings Center Studies, 1 (1973), pp. 74-82.

2. Limitations of time and space make it impossible to articulate in detail the several analytically distinguishable positions in the development-population debate. Two incisive summaries of how this can be done are found in M. Teitelbaum, Population and Development: Is A Consensus Possible?, Foreign Affairs 52 (1974), pp. 742-760; and A. Dyck, On Human Care (ch. 3: Ethics, Policy and Population Debates) Nashville: Abingdon (1977), pp. 32-51.

3. Teitelbaum describes this position as "The Population Hawk" posture; (pp. 752-53). Dyck's description of "The Crisis Environmentalist" position most closely accords with what I have called the first view (pp. 34-37).

4. Teitelbaum's description of "The Revolutionist Position," "The Over-Consumption Position," "The Accomodationist Position," and "The Social Justice Position" show them to be cognate views of this second position (pp. 751-52).

5. This third position is reflected principally in the view Teitelbaum calls "The Population-Programs-Plus-Development" position and in the position Dyck calls "Developmental Distributivist." In Teitelbaum's analysis the third view is also cognate with "The Social Justice Position."

6. Teitelbaum, pp. 754-758.

7. Dyck, using studies of Roger Revelle, John B. Wyon and John Gordon, points out the complex interrelationships of resources, consumption habits and population growth (pp. 41, 43, 44).

8. Dyck cites the examples of S. Korea and Taiwan; J. Howe and J. Sewell cite Sri Lanka, Singapore, Egypt and Barbados; cf: Let's Sink the Lifeboat Ethics; Worldview 18 (1975), pp. 13-18.

9. McNamara illustrates the complexity of factors involved in assessing the meaning of The Demographic Transition for developing countries today (pp. 19-21). Cf. also Teitelbaum, pp. 744-45.

10. Dyck, pp. 43 and 49. Cf. W. Rich, Population Explosion: The Role of Development, Communique, #16; Overseas Development Council, Washington, D.C. (1972).

11. The critique can be found in several places: R. McNamara, 1973 Address to the Board of Governors, Washington: IBRD (1973). M. ul Haq, The Poverty Curtain, N.Y.: Columbia University Press (1976), pp. 27-47; R. Hansen, The Emerging Challenge: Global Distribution of Income and Economic Opportunity, in The U.S. and World Development, op. cit., pp. 157-188.

12. Cf. ul Haq, pp. 57-75; R. Hansen, Major Options in North-South Relations: A Letter to President Carter, in The U.S. and World Development: Agenda 1977, cf. pp. 33-36; 60ff.

13. J. Noonan, Contraception: A History of Its Treatment By the Catholic Theologicans and Canonists, Cambridge: The Belknap Press (1965), cf. pp. 81-84, 275-78, 414-415, 514-516.

14. Ibid., p. 426.

15. D. Hollenbach argues that "Pius XII was the first of the modern popes to attend directly to the 'population question' as it is conceived today." The Right to Procreate and Its Social Limits, Unpublished Ph.D. dissertation, Yale University (1975), p. 394.

16. Paul VI, Message on the Population Year; Origins III, #43, p. 671.

17. Paul VI, Address to the World Food Conference, Origins, IV, #22, p. 351.

18. For a summary and presentation of this tradition cf: J. Calvez and J. Perrin, The Church and Social Justice, Chicago: Regnery, (1959); J. Gremillion, The Gospel of Peace and Justice, N.Y.: Orbis (1975); P. Pavan, Social Thought-Papal, New Catholic Encyclopedia, XIII, pp. 352-361.

19. John XXIII, <u>Pacem in Terris</u>, para 60; in Gremillion, op. cit., p. 214.

20. For an historical perspective on the development of this concept in Catholic teaching cf. W. Ferree, <u>Introduction to Social Justice</u>, N.Y.: Paulist Press (1948).

21. Cf. Hollenbach, pp. 295ff.

22. <u>Ibid.</u>, pp. 279-282ff.

23. Noonan.

24. The literature surrounding the contraception controversy is overwhelming; for an indication of the points of difference cf: R. Hoyt, ed., The Birth Control Debate, Kansas City: The NCR (1970); C. Curran, ed., <u>Contraception: Authority and Dissent</u>, N.Y.: Herder and Herder (1969); R. McCormick, Notes on Moral Theology, <u>Theological Studies</u>, 29 (1968), pp. 725-41 and 30 (1969), pp. 635-653.

25. The text reads:

> It is true that too frequently an accelerated demographic increase adds its own difficulties to the problems of development: the size of the population increases more rapidly than available resources, and things are found to have reached apparently an impasse. From that moment the temptation is great to check the demographic increase by means of radical measures. It is certain that public authorities can intervene, within the limit of their competence, by favouring the availability of appropriate information and by adopting suitable measures, provided that these be in conformity with the moral law and that they respect the rightful freedom of married couples. Where the inalienable right to marriage and procreation is lacking, human dignity has ceased to exist. Finally, it is for the parents to decide, with full knowledge of the matter, on the number of their children, taking into account their responsibilities towards God, themselves, and the community to which they belong. In all this they must follow the demands of their own conscience enlightened by God's law authentically interpreted, and sustained by confidence in Him.

26. The text reads:

> Nonetheless the Church, calling men back to the observance of the norms of the natural law, as interpreted by her constant doctrine, teaches that each and every

30

marriage act (quilibet matrimonii usus) must remain open
to the transmission of life.

For the full statement of the position cf. Humanae Vitae, para.
11 and 12; in Gremillion, pp. 432-33.

27. Humanae Vitae, para. 17, in Gremillion, p. 436.

28. The entire argument of this section of the paper rests upon an
     understanding of the distinction between public and personal
     morality and the legitimate use of this distinction in the
     Catholic ethic of natural law. There appears to be a surprising
     need to make clear the ground on which this distinction rests.
     The need is surprising because the idea is so central to a
     viable natural law ethic that one would hope those who are in
     the Catholic tradition would be adept in using it. Yet, the
     editorial in The Washington Standard (March 2, 1978) responding
     to this presentation manifests no awareness that the distinc-
     tion exists in Catholic thought: "Such a position simply has
     no place in Catholic doctrine or thinking." The Wanderer (March
     16, 1978) describes use of the distinction as "a cowardly cop-
     out."

     The distinction, as John Courtney Murray has noted, is as old
     as St. Augustine's De Ordine. Moreover, it flows from the very
     center of a natural law conception of society. Murray has
     stated the case in its best contemporary form:

          Society and the state are understood to be natural in-
          stitutions with their relatively autonomous ends or
          purposes, which are predesigned in broad outline in
          the social and political nature of man, as understood
          in its concrete completeness through reflection and
          historical experience. These purposes are public, not
          private. They are therefore strictly limited. They
          do not transcend the temporal and terrestrial order,
          within which the political and social life of man is
          confined; and even within this order they are not
          coextensive with the ends of the human person as such.
          The obligatory public purposes of society and the
          state impose on these institutions a special set of
          obligations which, again by nature, are not coexten-
          sive with the wider and higher range of obligations
          that rest upon the human person (not to speak of the
          Christian). In a word, the imperatives of political
          and social morality derive from the inherent order of
          political and social reality inself, as the architec-
          tonic moral reason conceives this necessary order in
          the light of the fivefold structure of obligatory
          political ends--justice, freedom, security, the gen-
          eral welfare, and civil unity or peace (so the

Preamble to the American Constitution states these ends).

It follows, then, that the morality proper to the life and action of society and the state is not univocally the morality of personal life, or even of familial life. Therefore, the effort to bring the organized action of politics and the practical art of statecraft directly under the control of the Christian values that govern personal and familial life is inherently fallacious. It makes wreckage not only of public policy but also of morality itself.

We Hold These Truths: Catholic Reflections on the American Proposition, N.Y.: Sheed and Ward (1960), p. 286.

29. Cf. "Should There Be A Law? The Question of Censorship," in Murray, pp. 155-174.

30. Ibid., p. 286.

31. The notion of "public order" and its distinction from "common good" as these terms came to be used in the Vatican II debate on religious liberty is a fundamental concept in understanding the relationship of public and personal morality.

32. Murray, We Hold These Truths, pp. 166-67.

33. Ibid., p. 166.

34. This empirical assessment would include recognition of the following elements: (1) significant divergence of emphasis, tone and content in the responses of the national episcopates to Humanae Vitae; (2) a documented split between significant sections of the theological community and the teaching of the encyclical; (3) statistically validated samplings of the Catholic community since 1965 which indicate widespread divergence between Catholic teaching and practice regarding contraception. None of these factors is meant to imply that in determining morality we are simply involved in a head-count. While the adjudication of the position within the Church on contraception has to take account of these various differences--which are qualitative (i.e., theological) as well as quantitative--the argument about public morality is not based on the internal standing of Humanae Vitae. The precise question being raised in this paper is whether it is morally or politically prudent to project as a public position of the Church for the whole society a set of prescriptions which the same society knows are under dispute among Catholics.

35. Dyck, Procreative Rights, p. 77.

36. Ibid., p. 79.

FOREIGN AID: WHAT SHOULD AMERICA'S NATIONAL INTERESTS BE?

Peter G. Bourne, M. D.

Special Assistant to the President

> My assistance program is part of an effort to combine
> support of our country's economic interests and se-
> curity with compassion for the impoverished millions
> of fellow human beings.
>
> President Carter's Message to Congress, March
> 13, 1977

One billion people are now surviving without adequate food,
shelter or health care, and yet, in the face of this world poverty,
it has grown increasingly difficult to justify our contributions
for foreign economic assistance to the American people. Recent
polls indicate that Americans believe our foreign assistance budget is relatively greater than that of other wealthy countries and
that the government is doing more than it should to fight poverty
in other parts of the world. Yet from 1965 to 1977, net U.S. official development assistance as a percentage of GNP decreased by
half, from .49% to .24%. This steady decline places us well below the UN suggested percentage (.7%); and we rank twelfth in
relative contributions among the 18 major industrial countries.
We spend six times more each year on alcohol than on official development assistance, seventeen times more on military defense.

Yet as our aid decreases, the developing world's problems are
growing. Food sources have only limited capacity to expand. The
world's readily arable land is reaching its limits; untapped supplies of fresh water for irrigation are shrinking; energy supplies,
and energy-intensive fertilizer, are becoming more costly. At the
same time, however, pressure on the food system is increasing at a
still-accelerating rate. If the present 3% population growth rate
of some of the most populous developing countries continues, they
will face a nineteenfold increase in population a hundred years
from now. World population overall is now doubling every 37 years,
a fact which will soon affect the U.S. and other industrialized
nations' economies as much as it affects those countries where the

33

increases occur.

Obviously, Americans and their governmental representatives have not felt any strong interdependency with the less developed countries (LDCs) in the world. The polls reveal that the urgency and the extent of global poverty are not recognized by most Americans, nor are the goals of our aid effort and the reasons behind it understood. One of the problems in selling foreign aid is that people do not see it as helping a starving child or curing disease. Responding to the initiative Congress took in 1973 to establish "new directions" for our development programs, President Carter has publicized our humanitarian commitment "to help poorer countries overcome the problems of hunger, disease and illiteracy." The Congressional debate is beginning on Senator Hubert Humphrey's last legislative proposal--a complete reorganization of our foreign assistance programs. The time has never been more appropriate to initiate a national debate on our relationship to the developing world, on our commitment to aid, and on the goals we as a nation would like to see it serve.

What is the extent of America's economic interests in the developing world? In these recent years of domestic economic crisis, the need to reduce inequities and improve domestic employment prospects has led to opposition to policies toward developing nations that run counter to narrowly-defined domestic interests. The transfer of productive activities overseas has been opposed by organized labor. Business and labor have supported protective trade barriers to screen out cheaper manufactured goods from the LDCs. People have argued that we are more certain to control an equitable distribution of our wealth here than if we give it to local elites in the LDCs.

However, there are also significant economic reasons for aiding the LDCs which deserve to have greater prominence in our so-called domestic debates. Our export sales ($40 billion this year) to the developing world surpass those to Europe and Japan, supplying millions of jobs for Americans. One out of every eight manufacturing jobs and one out of every three acres of farmland produce for export. The developing world is not only the market for our products, it provides us with the very raw materials essential to maintain our industrial economy. With only 6% of the world's population, we consume nearly 40% of its resources. By 1985 the United States will depend on imports for more than one-half of our supplies of nine out of thirteen critical minerals. Our oil imports are rapidly reaching 50% of total consumption. Senator Humphrey wrote in support of his assistance bill that "our own economic welfare depends to a large degree on an open world economy."

America's security interests have often taken account of this economic interdependence. In the recent past, our reaction to economic initiatives by LDCs that seemed to threaten our security

34

has included military confrontation, covert subversion and various kinds of intervention. Security and supporting assistance has also played a role in stabilizing potentially explosive situations, but, since it has seldom served development goals, it has not reduced many of the basic causes of instability. Regular development assistance, of course, serves to maintain our allies and there will always be this military justification for continuing aid. But what we need is a broader concept of our security interests, akin to what John Gilligan, Administrator of AID, recently expressed: "Nature's early warning systems tell us about population explosion, famine, depletion of resources, encroachment of deserts, environmental degradation and disease. No nation can afford to ignore these problems, and no nation as wealthy and powerful as the U.S.--and as involved commercially and politically in every corner of the globe as we are--can avoid their impact. If our military security should be breached, we have prepared a strong response to defend our interests. But our ability to deal with non-military threats, which can be every bit as devastating to our way of life, is dangerously inadequate."

Counteracting the widespread cynicism (and often ignorance) about the economics of foreign assistance, a growing popular desire to ensure human rights and demonstrate our humanitarian concerns by satisfying the basic human needs of the world's poor could form the focus for a renewed American commitment to world development. We have publicly committed ourselves to alleviate the worst aspects of poverty in a long series of international agreements (e.g., Charter of Punta del Este, 1961), but too often we have failed to translate our promises into adequate programs. The human rights issue has been used inconsistently, frequently as a political tool to further reduce the amount of resources we were willing to contribute to LDCs. Idealistic rhetoric, making the satisfaction of basic human needs our essential strategy, often detracts attention from the fundamental political changes such a strategy would require: land reform and the redistribution of wealth. As in our evaluation of the economic value of foreign aid, domestic debate on these issues has to take place in a broader and more informed context.

We do not influence the human rights policies of LDCs solely by our aid program. We must begin to examine all aspects of our presence in the developing world: our role as a political model, our military interests, our private presence as volunteer organizations and commercial enterprises. U.S. commercial interests in the LDCs have grown steadily larger; more money is now influencing development from private sources than governmental. Does the flow of private capital to developing countries have a beneficial development impact? How much does our private presence in an LDC influence or support the policies of its government? Developing countries encounter many obstacles for which we are responsible as they try to obtain a larger share of the gains from

35

their own production and trade. If our foreign assistance is truly to be in our national interest, we must search as widely as possible for the causes of social and economic injustice which threaten global security. If we are to be the world's human rights leader, we must be consistent in defining and accepting our social responsibility in the world.

Nothing the United States (or the developed world) does in its foreign aid program alone will solve the world's poverty problems. Even as we begin to reorganize and improve the administration and goals of our economic aid, we must be certain to educate the public that aid programs are just one aspect of our development policy in the LDCs. More political courage may be required to manage a national debate on these issues and to derive a policy governing all American presence in the developing world than would be needed simply to obtain an increased aid contribution each year. No lasting improvement in the global quality of life can be effected without significant reorientations of life styles and social goals. We need to discover what economic price we will have to pay to actually obtain some semblance of equity in the global distribution of wealth. We cannot continue to criticize the inequitable distribution of the benefits of growth within developing countries and not acknowledge a similar imbalance between our own industrial society and the rest of the world.

The debate in Congress on Senator Humphrey's proposed reorganization of our aid programs could be the first step toward a national re-evaluation of American attitudes about the developing world. His International Development Cooperation Act (IDCA) is designed to rationalize and integrate many related development programs and establish a permanent agency for foreign aid that would develop a consistent policy governing United States development policies overseas. Business groups, labor, voluntary organizations, interested citizens, and international institutions, would then have a focal point to work cooperatively with the federal government on development. A new constituency for foreign aid would be created. Congress would be able to oversee the new agency's work and expenditures more effectively (as matters now stand, this is impossible). The IDCA would provide for more effective administration of our policies, and ensure that our aid gets to those who need it most. Finally, it would create a spokesman for international development interests at the highest levels of government, enhancing the visibility and priority of development.

Everyone interested in development in America should take this opportunity to participate in formulating a new policy on foreign aid, one which is realistic and consistent with our moral principles and national self-interest. Senator Humphrey asked, in introducing this bill, "will we, by our positive efforts, help to affect and move this global upheaval in a direction consistent with our values and beliefs? . . . Will we design our future?" Merely

36

creating a new organization will not be enough to demonstrate our deep commitment to solving the problems of developing countries. The world must also witness an ongoing critical reappraisal of America's global interests and responsibilities. I believe that is what Senator Humphrey would have wanted his bill to accomplish.

DISCUSSION

FRED STROHBEHN, cattle-hog farmer with Self Help, Waverly, Iowa: I agree with you that self-help programs which help people to increase their own production are better than the aid given out by the State Department twenty and twenty-five years ago.

But how can we get through the bureaucracy to help people help themselves? Self Help has designed and built a small tractor which has been field proven for 15 years. Yet we're having trouble reaching through to some government groups. We do have a Midwest agricultural recruiter for the Peace Corps who's very enthused about the tractor, but it's still hard for some of us farmers to reach through even with our own Congressman. My question is, what's the best way for some of us outsiders to reach through the bureaucracy?

PETER BOURNE: This is a difficult problem because it's even hard for some of us insiders to reach through the bureaucracy. I think the approach you're taking is exactly what we would like to see. In the past we've been too preoccupied with transferring our own often inappropriate technology to the developing world, and what we need now is appropriate technology like your tractor.

The Peace Corps has changed its entire focus in the last year and is moving to become a development assistance agency (rather than a cultural exchange agency) specifically aimed at the development of village level appropriate technology. One of the difficulties we have is that when you change administrations you may change a few people, but in too many of our agencies we have people who have been there for 30 years with very fixed ideas and it takes time to change those people and make them responsive.

We will be happy to use what influence we have from the White House to help expedite your involvement. But, overall, I think it's going to be a very slow process. You've got to change people's attitudes, you've got to change their views, and you've got to see that new programs are developed in a way that's consistent with some sort of overall plan.

AUDIENCE: If birth rates are lowered, that slows the entrance of new people into the population pool. But if small pox and other diseases are eliminated, that slows the exit of people from the pool. Is anyone in the administration giving attention to how to cure disease or feed people without reheating the population problem. And if so, what kind of answers are they coming up with?

PETER BOURNE: This is an issue that's frequently raised. Are you saving people's lives from disease so they can starve to death? And obviously the answer, I think, overwhelmingly is that you're not.

In the first place, when you treat people's disease you're not just saving lives, you're improving people's general health. One of the most important payoffs from that is that you increase their productivity. Many diseases afflict people in ways which immensely reduce their agricultural productivity. For instance, the disease guinea worm, which has a cyclical recurrence in people, happens to strike coincident with the planting season in certain areas of Africa. At any given time during the planting season one-third of the population in some villages are incapacitated. The result, then, is that you have a dramatic reduction in food production. If those people were cured, apart from the fact that you would save lives, you would probably more than balance it with an increase in food production or overall gross national product.

The other thing which is very, very clear now is that as soon as you begin to reduce infant mortality, population growth goes down because people have traditionally relied on large numbers of children both to serve as social security in their old age and also to increase the labor force. Once people are convinced that they don't have to have ten children to have three survive, they voluntarily look to limit their families. And if they believe that they can have three children, and those three children are going to live, that's what people will have. In most instances, people don't want to have ten children, but the problem is that they just don't believe that those children are going to live.

So I don't see it as a question of compounding the food problem by saving lives. In the long run, if we save lives it will help the food problem and cut down on the population explosion.

JAMES DINNING, the University of Florida, Gainesville, Florida: Mr. Bourne, does the administration consider nutrition and food policy matters to fall within the province of health or agriculture?

PETER BOURNE: Well, they're not separable. One of the things that's very clear is that if you're going to deal with any of these problems, you have to deal with them on an integrated basis. You can't deal with food without being concerned about health. You can't deal with food and health without being concerned about general economic growth. One of the things we feel that is extraordinarily important is that we have a fully integrated approach in our development assistance programs. This has not been true in the past. There has been fragmentation between AID, Department of Agriculture, HEW, the State Department and a number of other agencies. We have looked at a number of reorganization possiblities that would try to pull these together in a more coherent way. The Humphrey-Case bill now before the Congress is another attempt to do the same thing. At a recent meeting the President was asked whether he supported the Humphrey-Case bill, and he said that he hadn't yet had a chance to read it but he could guarantee that he thought any reorganization would be an improvement over the present situation. We hope to overcome some of the traditional territorial problems that have prevented us from adequately integrating these areas. Obviously there are health elements to nutrition, though the fundamental aspect of nutrition is agriculture. But they really aren't separable. Rather than have HEW, Agriculture and AID each operating in isolation, I think that in developing nations one has to deal with the entire field in an integrated way and have some overall kind of plan.

BILL MARTIN, Slippery Rock, Pennsylvania: Mr. Bourne, your comments are very encouraging. I wish you good luck with them. Looking at past history, however, it seems to me that the United States has frequently been a negative force against underdeveloped, or Third World, or poor nations which were trying to improve living standards. Since World War II only a limited number of countries have made really remarkable changes in their living standards, in terms of food consumption, average income, and other aspects of a good economic life. Since the oil producing countries joined together in OPEC their per capita incomes have shot up. Also, at least as far as food consumption is concerned, China has experienced a rather remarkable change during the last 15 years. In almost all of these cases, rather than actively supporting this economic growth, as in the case, say, of the oil-producing countries, the United States government has actively opposed it, that is, by trying to keep the price of oil down. My question is, is the position of the Carter Administration radically different on this from the Ford-Nixon administration? Will they oppose efforts by suppliers of raw materials to come together, to "unionize," to raise the price of their raw materials?

PETER BOURNE: I think in general what you say is true though there are obviously exceptions. There are countries where remarkable development has occurred, where we didn't have conflicting interests, where we have encouraged that development. I can guarantee you there's a change because I don't think the commitment along the lines that I outlined in my paper was there in the White House previously. The question is: Can we translate that commitment into meaningful action that parallels what we say?

Here we run into difficulties because a lot of these issues aren't simple. For example, one of the really major problems for developing countries is the problem of tariff restrictions. The United States controls its own tariffs, but to change the world tariff structure to really help the LDCs develop the kind of capital and foreign exchange they need for their own internal growth requires lengthy negotiations with the whole community of nations. We are

39

making some progress in that direction, but it isn't something that is exclusively in the hands of the United States.

Another example of the difficulty the U.S. government has in translating a commitment to underdeveloped countries into practice is the role of multinational corporations. Though I think that the multinationals are capable of doing a great deal of good by mobilizing large amounts of capital into developing countries, it is true that they are immensely powerful. Multinational corporations, more than the United States government, end up making the kind of decisions that you're talking about, especially in setting the prices for oil and other commodities. You may be President of the United States, but that often isn't enough to really change some of what goes on with multinational corporations. One can try to use influence, one can try to convince them that it's in their own best interests to do things that would be beneficial to developing countries. We have tried to do this and I think there has been some success. Some multinational corporations are beginning to develop a social conscience. Not enough, but it's a step in the right direction. I think the Carter Administration is using a different approach, and I hope that a year or two from now you'll feel the different approach has paid off in terms of measurable accomplishments.

BERNARD ULOZAS, Carnegie Mellon University, Pittsburgh, Pennsylvania: In your speech today and in speeches yesterday, I was struck by the opposing positions in two areas. First, some have argued that we have the ability to handle problems associated with food and population, while others have argued that we don't. As an educator I'm interested in the second debate, that between those who say we can change people's attitudes and redirect the will of the people and those who say we can't. Now, to me, changing people's attitudes implies educational programs. I would like to know what directions your department or any other government department is taking in developing curriculum or even larger educational programs to address the problems associated with food and population?

PETER BOURNE: I think the issue of food sufficiency has to do with the potential to meet the food needs of the world, rather than actually having that food available at present. That is, if we fully utilized our ability to increase food production from currently cultivated land and we were able to bring under cultivation the remaining potentially arable land in the world, we have the potential to create a situation where we could have enough food for everybody. That doesn't exist right now. The other aspect of food sufficiency is that there is a major distribution problem because the countries that produce 60% of the food have 30% of the population.

I think the education element is very crucial. It's a question of how far the government can go in implementing the specifics of education. Visible public leadership from the government can have a very significant impact in educating people. Then too we might weigh the relative impact of having a five minute slot on Walter Cronkite against having a curriculum in schools across the country. It may be that five minutes on the evening network news does more to change people's attitudes than a lot of education programs in schools. But I think it's not really a question of either/or. We've got to do both.

I think conferences like this and other meetings help to disseminate information, to get interaction, to get people enthusiastic about going back home and enhancing their efforts in education. One of the major activities that the Presidential Commission on World Hunger will be involved in is enhancing education efforts. They will be in existence for two years and we hope that will be time enough to build interest in developing education programs at all levels. But I think we're looking for a multi-faceted approach in which traditional education in the schools and colleges is only one element in changing public attitudes.

THE POPULATION CRISIS:
A PLEA FOR PRESIDENTIAL LEADERSHIP

Charles M. Cargille

Population/Food Fund

In this paper I would like to briefly outline the nature of the problem with which we are faced and to develop a plea addressed to President Carter which is based upon an analysis of what I perceive to be the prerequisites for solution of the world problem. Then, based upon these prerequisites, I will sketch some options which are available to the President at this time for his leadership in developing an appropriate American national response to a world problem.

I begin with, not the assumption, but the fact that the response of the United States to the world population problem thus far has been inappropriate, insufficient, inadequate, and impossible for leading to a solution.

It seems perfectly clear to me that the rapid growth of populations at today's rates and at projected trends will lead to population levels which are unsupportable because they exceed the carrying capacity of the globe.

It is true for man, as for any other species, that he must live within the tough constraints of biological law. Those laws state that to exceed a carrying capacity leads to tragedy expressed in the die-off of the surplus population, if one uses that term to describe the number of individuals of any species in excess of the carrying capacity.

We have a historical record of the fact that past efforts to limit population size to supportable limits have failed. I think that we have failed because of four problems with the United States response to world population growth.

The first problem pertains to our goal. The United States has no population goal for the world.

The second problem pertains to the priority. The United States has no federal priority for this problem.

42

The third problem pertains to our plan. Population leaders, both in and outside of government, have no plan for stopping world population growth at supportable limits.

And the fourth problem is our funding. Funding for the population field in the United States and internationally is negligible. And because our funding is insignificant, the phenomenon which we are now observing is a true biological growth rate for human population, essentially unmodified by any deliberate effort at control by human intention.

Based upon that fundamental analysis of the reasons which explain our failure to date, I think that the prerequisites for an effective national response by this country become perfectly clear. There are four prerequisites, as there are four problems. The population problem, internationally, cannot be solved unless all four of these prerequisites are met. I think that all four are absolute necessities. If we are unable to satisfy any one of them, then we will fail in the necessity of controlling world population growth and catastrophe in the future cannot be avoided.

The first prerequisite is to develop a goal. A population goal for the whole world must be selected by the United States to guide its policies and its programs. Though this may seem harsh, I believe that the United States must develop such a goal as the basis of its national and international leadership, with or without the cooperation of other nations. The reason why I say this is not a political reason but a biological reason. We are dealing with biological law. Carrying capacity is determined by resources, by environmental impact, and by pollution absorption capacity (which is never discussed), just as carrying capacity is, itself, determined by social conditions and by political realities. But whatever the determinants of carrying capacity are, the upper limit is a finite and specific number of individuals for any species in any environment, and it is a finite number for the numbers of humans, under the conditions of today's social, political, and economic world structure.

I think that it's the responsibility of scientists to identify that number. Irrespective of political considerations, that number remains an upper limit for the supportable number of human beings under existing circumstances.

Economists and political leaders can indeed raise the carrying capacity by providing greater social structure, just as they can raise the carrying capacity by providing greater food resources and other needed resources for life support. But there is always a finite number, and that number is a consequence of biological law.

So I think we must have a goal because without a goal, programs cannot be goal-directed, comprehensive planning is impossible,

43

manpower requirements are unclear, systems methods are invalidated, time tables cannot be set, and progress cannot be judged. A world goal is necessary because the future of the United States is linked to a global ecosystem and a world economy.

One hundred and thirty-six nations were unable to agree on a target population objective at Bucharest in 1974. I think American scientists must research carrying capacity and provide that data as hard fact to the political community, both at home and abroad, because the carrying capacity defines the upper limit of population size, and that limit is not politically negotiable. I think it's the American scientific establishment which should do this, simply because our research institutions, university systems and federal agencies are best suited to do the kind of interdisciplinary biological systems research which will be necessary in order to identify the true limits on which a world population goal must be based.

The second prerequisite is a priority. It's mandatory that the United States have a high national priority to limit world population growth. My own opinion is that that priority should be the first ranking priority of the American government. I believe that it is a priority which deserves higher support than the priority of the defense establishment in the protection of American national security.

Why must we have a priority? I think it's perfectly obvious, because we have seen the population field go nowhere for 25 years for lack of a priority. Without priority, funding will continue to be inadequate, resources will continue to be lacking, manpower will continue to be deficient for addressing this problem. There will continue to be no Congressional support. Media outreach will continue to handicap the public because it will fail to bring the necessary public attention to these issues, and public education will continue to be deficient.

With priority, however, other nations can model their national response upon the U.S. response. Universities will emphasize rather than disregard population studies. And the nongovernmental organizations will be encouraged to focus their expertise and their staff support on the problem of world population.

The third prerequisite to an adequate response is a plan, a systems strategy, which we must develop if we are ever to achieve a steady state world population which is less than the carrying capacity of the global environment.

Why must we have a plan? Without a plan, agencies work at cross purposes. Research lacks direction. Public education is neglected. Key questions are missed as key questions have been consistently missed by the federal Population Research Program over a period of the last ten years. Time tables are irrelevant without a

44

plan, and the monitoring of progress becomes impossible.

With a plan, however, the newest, strongest technological tools become available to planners and program managers. Project engineering techniques apply if we have a plan. Technology assessment has never been applied to the population field, though it was called for by Dr. Seamans, former Secretary of the Air Force, in 1974 at the first meeting of the World Population Society, at which time Dr. Seamans was president of the National Academy of Engineering. He said perfectly clearly, "Technology assessment is an appropriate tool to apply to the population problem." That knowledgeable opinion, which was the first time an engineer had ever addressed the problem of world population in a public statement before an American audience, has been disregarded.

With a plan, funding, resource and manpower requirements can be assessed. And with a plan, there may be a hope of achieving a steady state world population which is within the limits of global carrying capacity.

The fourth, and unavoidable, prerequisite for solution of this world problem, is adequate funding. I have long been convinced that multibillion dollar funding must be provided for the support of what is likely to be a gigantic effort. In the past only General Draper has called for budgets addressing the world population problem in excess of a billion dollars. More recently, Lester Brown has called for this. These have been lonely voices. If one listens to testimony on the Hill, the issue is always whether or not family planning will receive 10% more or 10% less, which I think is an irrelevant question.

We have miscalculated the funding requirements for the solution of the world population problem by several orders of magnitude. Federal budgets, I am convinced, are at least 10-fold, and probably 100-fold, too low in addressing this problem. If one is funded at only 1% or perhaps 10% of the required costs of a project, I would maintain that it becomes immaterial how you spend so little money. You will fail, no matter what. It's like an admiral who's given $10,000 to build a battleship; whether he spends the $10,000 on a keel or on a blueprint or on a radio is immaterial. This ship won't float if it's underfunded because it will never be constructed. I think that's the situation we're in with the population field. Our funding, to this point, has been insignificant and it's impossible for the few persons who are working professionally in this field to accomplish anything of consequence.

The task of solving the world population problem is indeed immense. It is complex. It is global. It is expensive. Whatever agency takes this responsibility must be capable of an operation which meets those characteristics. The research to develop

45

the needed information, indeed the research to develop the strategy which has never been developed thus far, will be costly. The implementation of the plan will require vast manpower training because you can number the significant leaders and the full-time professionals in this field almost on a few hands. Indeed, the number of skilled full-time professionally trained manpower should be in the tens and hundreds of thousands. Massive public education will be required. Family planning services will have to be greatly expanded in most countries of the world. The figures which are quoted for the number of sexually active couples using contraceptives in the poorest of the Third World countries are often less than 5%. This is after 10 years of an American foreign aid population assistance program which is usually described by promoters as a success.

The task of designing a response to the world population problem will be more costly and far more complex than that of developing a new weapons system. Most weapons cost billions in terms of military research and development. Population solutions will be even more costly.

The President has options for implementing the above four prerequisites. Each prerequisite could be approached by several alternative strategies. I will mention only those which I would recommend at this time to the President.

The selection of a population goal for the world would best be done by the President with the advice of his staff and his chosen consultants. In the interest of time, he can identify a goal promptly. The goal that I urge him to consider is the goal which we urge from the Population/Food Fund for all organizations concerned about this problem: "to achieve a balance between population size and available resources for life support in a stable and healthful environment." I see no reason why the President of the United States cannot espouse a goal which is so drawn as to warrant the support of every nation, every political party, and every religious persuasion.

The task of assigning a high national priority could be established by the President or by the Congress or perhaps a Congressional commission. But the President, together with his Cabinet, has the authority, and I believe, should exert the leadership to assign the priority which this problem deserves.

The task of developing a plan is far more difficult. The obvious possibilities of delegating responsibilities to existing agencies such as the National Institutes of Health, the Environmental Protection Agency, or the State Department, would head the list. However, I think that it is already a matter of public record that these agencies have proven incompetent for this task. I would recommend the consolidation and the expansion of population activities from a variety of existing offices into some form of new federal

46

bureau, agency, or department.

The most difficult of all will be prerequisite number four, to provide the multibillion dollar funding and to implement the research, planning and education, as well as the program itself. To delegate such responsibilities to existing agencies of government, I think, is to ask the impossible of the incapable.

The numbers of options are limited. Among them are certainly a new population agency modeled on NASA under civilian control; a federal department which would combine population, energy, resource, and environmental management; or the delegation of this responsibility to the Department of Defense. Dr. Mumford will argue for the latter option during the debate on the Department of Defense's role in solving this problem.

If no action is taken by the United States, I think there are very clear cut implications for our national future and for the President. I think the President's inaction or his procrastination will clearly threaten our children (who will be in the prime of life in the year 2020) with an inexorable lowering of the quality of life. And for our grandchildren living until the year 2070, failure to address this problem will probably result in unimaginable disaster. The biological possibility is all too real for the extinction of man through mechanisms of which overpopulation will be the fundamental dynamic.

In contrast, if positive action is taken--decisive leadership by an American President to achieve a solution to a life-threatening problem common to all nations--this would be recognized internationally as a mark of statesmanship, vision, courage, and wisdom. Mr. Carter's greatest achievement, as President of the United States, could well be the gift of hope to a despairing humanity: the redemption of a future from the ominous threat of overpopulation which is poised like the sword of Damocles suspended by a single hair over the head of mankind.

DISCUSSION

GEORGE WALL, Lamar University, Beaumont, Texas: It seems to me that disagreements about carrying capacity come about because of a lack of clarity in the concept. I'm not sure we could come to such a clear conceptualization in five years, but it certainly needs to be done. In terms of setting goals, that seems to me to be a prerequisite which was not mentioned and which certainly needs to be met.

In your list of prerequisites, you seem to talk in terms of unilateral action on the part of the U.S. That strikes me as immensely naive, politically. As a matter of fact, there is somewhat of a paradox in your comments on this first prerequisite, since you mentioned something about a global ecosystem and a global trade policy. Well, it escapes me how anything like that is going to be accomplished unilaterally. So, when we talk in terms of goals, I'd like to know how your goals could be accomplished unilaterally by the U.S.? Of course, my position would be that this has to be done in concert with many other nations.

CHARLES CARGILLE: First, with regard to carrying capacity, the USDA computer system being demonstrated in the hallway, I am told, will return a bibliography with all of sixteen references on carrying capacity. Now that measures very little about carrying capacity, but it measures a great deal about the neglect of this area of research. We know very little about carrying capacity except that, whether we know it or not, it's a fixed biological maximum for any given set of conditions. We'd better find out what the maximum is very quickly.

I agree entirely that the only successful effort will be one of global mobilization based upon international cooperation of all nations. But in calling for American scientific leadership to discern what the carrying capacity is, I'm simply pointing out that someone must begin, and that leadership begins with an individual strengthened then by an institution, and then involving others in a cooperative manner. We don't need international cooperation to measure a physical parameter in a nuclear laboratory. We do not necessarily need international cooperation to identify a biological limit in a biological laboratory. We can provide that information to the international community as a set of objective facts based on research conducted by a single group.

I think that leadership in establishing an international consensus that we must have a world priority which places population control first above all other determinants of the future can also come from a single individual. And I can think of no task more appropriate for the American President than to exert that leadership. Clearly the success of the effort would be totally dependent upon the cooperation of other nations. But that cooperation can be achieved with the assistance of anthropologists, sociologists, political scientists, humanists and ethicists, who have keen sensitivities to the feelings of people in foreign countries and would know better how to achieve an atmosphere of cooperation for the future, I trust, than we have ever achieved in the past. Considering that this world is divided by global warfare every 25 years or so, I would say that diplomats in the past frankly do not have a very good track record for success in international negotiation and international cooperation.

48

STILLMAN BRADFIELD, Kalamazoo College, Kalamazoo, Michigan: I'd like to question your notion that we can specify a target population for ultimate carrying capacity.

You're making the questionable assumption that we now have reasonably perfect knowledge of the environment and that we have reached the technological limits. You're assuming that we know what the resource base is and there's no further technological improvements that can be made. Secondly, in trying to specify carrying capacity you're making a scientific answer to a nonscientific question. The question of how many people want to live, in what kind of style and at what level of consumption are all value questions which science has no way of approaching. I would suggest that in your own backyard you find the Hutterites with an average completed fertility of 10 per woman, and this varies widely throughout the world. There is no scientific question and no scientific answer to these inherently value and ethical questions, and yet it seems to me that your proposals assume that there is such a scientific answer.

CHARLES CARGILLE: I agree entirely that the choice of standards of living, which clearly determine carrying capacity, are based upon human values which are essentially political choices. But the social scientist takes human values as facts. They're difficult to measure, but they exist. And to some degree, they can be quantified, at least sufficiently so that the systems planner can take them into account in his estimates of carrying capacity. If we're going to further increase American affluence and per capita consumption, we will have a lower carrying capacity in the United States. If we all wish to live in tents, we can have a higher carrying capacity in the United States. Our standard of living must be taken into consideration in determining the carrying capacity of this country. And the same for India or Guatemala.

The estimate of carrying capacity cannot be deferred until we have perfect knowledge of the environment; there will never be such a thing. But the systems analyst and the systems modeler takes the best information available and uses that. If he lacks information, he makes the most plausible assumptions which he can, writing them down so that they're perfectly explicit, so that those who disagree can make alternative assumptions. But then he includes that assumption in the model, marked by a red flag so that all will know that it's an assumption and not a fact. In no other way can we describe a complete system. And unless the model is complete, it will not run on the computer. I do not assume no further technological improvement, but as a planner I must begin where we are now. As technology increases carrying capacity, we can adjust the numbers accordingly.

WALTER CORSON, World Population Society: Just two comments on a couple of your concepts--carrying capacity and funding levels.

Instead of conceiving carrying capacity as a biological law, it might be useful to think in terms of a sociobiological law. Nonhuman species have relatively fixed consumption levels and place relatively fixed demands on their environment, but humans' demands and consumption levels are almost infinitely expandable, and it's very hard to predict where consumption levels will be in 50 or 100 years. This makes it even more urgent to limit population since I think it's politically easier and more feasible to prevent future births than it is to limit consumption of people already born.

On the question of funding, I think if we consider population growth as a major threat to local, national, and world security, this could provide a justification for greatly expanded effort commensurate with the funding for military aspects of national security. At the present level, the U.S. population effort is less than a half of one percent of the money that's going into defense and military spending, whereas I think the threat from growth is commensurate with the threat from military factors. Yet our funding is just a tiny faction of that for military.

MOFAZZAL CHOWDHURY, from Bangladesh, now at Iowa State University: Bangladesh has been exposed to Malthusian theories for a long time. The British knew population was a problem. Nehru took action on it. We have been informed. And a lot of people have offered help: Sweden, the U.S., Russia, England, the FAO, the World Bank. All of them came with good intentions. But I feel that the approach has not been systematic. Sometimes there were so many cooks that all they did was spoil the dish.

In the United States pollution has become a problem, but this country has the resources to correct their mistakes. Let's say you made the mistake of investing trillions of dollars in automobiles and superhighways. You have the money to clean up your environment. But countries like Bangladesh and India can't afford to make costly mistakes. If there are too many cooks and one cook is a garlic fanatic and keeps dumping garlic into the dish, the whole effort can be ruined. So before people with good intentions come running in with their favorite solutions they had better make sure they're sound.

In regard to your idea of U.S. leadership in population, what do you think is the role of other powers, such as Russia, France and England, and what is the role of the United Nations?

CHARLES CARGILLE: The existing hodgepodge in the international community in attempting to help Bangladesh is the very problem that I am seeking to avoid by a single, sufficient, and systematic plan of international population growth control and aid assistance toward meeting the basic human needs of all peoples. I think that there's no difference between us at all. I'm not saying

50

how this should be done. I am saying that it must be done. Since we lack an overall strategy, our first task is to achieve a strategy. And I think the strategy is the very thing that you're asking for in advocating a very sound and systematic response to Bangladesh's problems.

With regard to the role of the United Nations, and of other nations, I think that this must be a part of the comprehensive planning, and I would make no more specific statement than that.

WALLACE GRAY, Southwestern College, Winfield, Kansas: I suppose we all would like to help rescue the world from the population explosion, and to receive a measure of gratitude for our initiative. But even well-educated persons have difficulty agreeing on what is the actual carrying capacity for a desirable level of life. Part of the challenge of overcoming the population tragedy is that the less educated do not identify population growth as the evil force in the tragedy. I once saw a motto in a book which read, "No one ever died of the population explosion." Most people see death being caused more directly by other things, and do not lay much blame at the door of the population explosion. How do we convince either the President or common people anywhere that there is an exit from the tragedy when we can't even agree on what the tragedy is, much less its cause?

CHARLES CARGILLE: I think we know sufficiently well to describe what the tragedy is and to describe its cause in many nations. The central role of population size can be identified as the source for such incredibly immense international problems in certain Third World countries as unemployment rates of 40% to 50%, deficient housing for the majority of population, widespread hunger, and illiteracy. We are well beyond the point of identifying the problem, particularly for a nation with the scientific capacity to go to the moon. We knew enough about the environment of the moon to support an individual in that location. I think we should be similarly capable of identifying the environmental characteristics on our own globe as to the number of persons which that environment can support.

KENNETH PIERS, Calvin College, Grand Rapids, Michigan: I have two comments about carrying capacity. First of all, I think any definition of carrying capacity is bound to be filled with arbitrary decisions. I'd be even more suspicious of such efforts if they were to be done by U.S. scientists. I find it hard to image that our scientists would include in their planning for, say, Mexico, a standard of living comparable to the standard of living we in the United States are now enjoying. Nor do I think they would plan a U.S. standard of living comparable to what people in Mexico now enjoy, which would change the carrying capacity quite considerably. I think that kind of option wouldn't even be considered.

51

Secondly, I think we can agree that we probably haven't reached the carrying capacity of the globe today. Yet, today there are many hungry people in the world. Until we start addressing the question of social justice, land distribution, the access to production methods and means, who consumes what and what are just levels of consumption, I think we've got the cart before the horse when we put population policy and control way out front.

CHARLES CARGILLE: I think we must give weight to the values and consumption patterns of peoples in other countries. The evaluation and the appreciation of those values is a part of the scientific evaluation of carrying capacity. There is already an international consensus that not only population control but meeting of basic human needs through effective development is also a necessity, that these two things are not alternatives, that the task must include both. But I think the one thing that's perfectly clear is that there will never be international development to any significant degree unless some damper is put upon the rate of international population growth by whatever means that strategy is devised to accomplish that goal.

MARTHA SAGER, American University: I'd like to say something about the phrase "carrying capacity." I'm an ecologist by trade, and I've been an ecologist since 1936 when it was most unpopular, when ecology was considered a generalist subject. We were all engaged at that time, scientifically, in specific enzyme study or a metabolic transformation process and those who knew all about a specific process knew about it inside, out and upside down, but were not interested in applying it anywhere. The term "carrying capacity" was built into ecology since the turn of the 20th Century. Now we like to bandy these terms about in our laws and regulations. We bandy about words like carcinogenic, terratogenic, mutagenic, and so on, without really paying attention to what they mean. I'm answering a number of you who were talking about carrying capacity in relation to a technological society. We need not worry about the limiting factor of space in a technological society like the United States because we are limiting our carrying capacity every day by dumping raw sewage into our drinking water. It may have been all right for the cavemen because the solution to pollution in those days was dilution, to fish off the front porch and you know what off the back porch, because it didn't make any difference. But we're still doing it. It makes a tremendous difference. The limiting capacity and the carrying capacity of technological societies will be not only organized but regulated by the debris and the waste products from our utilization of the natural resources.

THE EFFICIENCY AND EFFECTIVENESS OF
U.S. POPULATION ASSISTANCE

James H. Scheuer

Member of Congress from New York
Chairman, House Select Committee on Population

All of you are aware of the magnitude of the global population
problem. Our present 4 billion population is scheduled to hit about
6½ billion by the end of the century; by the year 2015 it will hit
about 8 billion, and it will probably not level off before hitting
11 or 12 billion and perhaps as high as 15 or 16 billion.

The implications of these figures are almost indescribable.
The stress on the environment worldwide, the excessive use of nonrenewable natural resources, the energy demands implicit in this
kind of population growth, for the production of food, irrigation,
heating and cooking, and moving people about--the consequences of
the population figures are awesome, and we haven't put the equation
together.

The United States and a number of countries in Western Europe
and Japan are concerned about the problem. Our country has given
approximately $1 billion over the last decade in foreign popula-
tion assistance. While this might not be as high a percentage of
GNP as many of us would hope, it doesn't loom so badly considering
a new awareness that we have enormous unmet needs in this country,
that we have finite resources in this country, that we do not have
an endless horn of plenty in this country. Foreign aid has been
somewhat affected by the growing realization, in Congress and
among the public, that we're taking a slice out of a pie that is
not constantly growing.

As you know, foreign aid has very little support from the
general public. When I go back to my district, people don't come up
to me and harass me for not pushing for higher foreign aid appropriations. Congressmen do not make points back in their districts by
voting for a greater percentage of the national GNP going into
foreign aid, and that's a political fact of life that we all have
to deal with.

Then, too, foreign aid today is different than what we were

53

involved in a generation ago. When World War II was over, we got
involved in the Marshall Plan and helped put France and Italy back
on their feet. These were countries that shared our mores, that
shared our values, that had a management infrastructure, that had a
tradition of free enterprise, that knew how to put that capital to
work, knew how to organize their manpower, knew how to tap world
capital markets, and knew how to produce a cost-beneficial application of the dollars that we gave them. The great example of that,
of course, is the dollars that we've given to Israel. They really
know how to fine-tune their use of capital and to give it a tremendous multiplier effect and make it work. The situation is not
quite like that in the developing world today. It is not quite so
easy for Congressmen to see taxpayers' funds used intelligently,
effectively, and thankfully. It's tough for citizens to see us
spending hundreds of millions of dollars overseas and being abused
for our pains. It doesn't mean we shouldn't do it; it just means
the political realities are tough.

From the point of view of cost-effectiveness, there are certain
things that we know will have an effect on fertility. In countries
where there are opportunities for women to engage in activities outside of the home and off the land, and where women have elementary
education and are literate, we know there is a marked and identifiable drop in fertility rate. We know that the status of women
is important, that when women are treated as chattel, as workers of
the farm and breeders of children they will act out society's per-
ception of who they are and what they are, and they will breed children. When they begin to see that society perceives them as something else than childbearers, then they will act out that role, too,
and they will begin to function as something else than childbearers.
Yet, we know that most of the countries in the developing world
have a real problem with the status of women.

We also know that when they get education monies, they do not
spend them bringing elementary education and literacy training to
the 75 or 80% of their population that live in rural areas. There's
more of a tendency to build another fancy post-graduate school for
the sons and the daughters of the elite. And when they get foreign
aid money for health purposes, they don't tend, normally, to build
tiny little one-room maternal and child health clinics with family
planning services out in the boondocks. They tend to build another
advanced hospital in a big city for the benefit of the elite.

I was in Nairobi last year, looking at population programs
across the continent of Africa, and it just so happened that the
time that I was there coincided with the beginning of the Jewish
high holy days. I went to the synagogue in Nairobi to attend services and one of the chaps standing next to me turned out to be
an Israeli. He explained to me that it was Israel's practice to
send rabbis to the developing world wherever there was a small
Jewish community, so that they would be able to have services over

54

the high holy days, even if they didn't have regular Jewish services throughout the year. There was a young fellow up front who seemed to be in charge of things, praying and chanting at a terrific pace, full of fervor and devotion. I said to the chap next to me, "Is that one of the young rabbis that the Israelis are sending around the world?" He said, "No, that's Dr. Jonah Epstein, of the University of Washington Medical School, who has just set up the first open heart surgery unit here in Kenya."

Now, I suggest to you that about the last thing that Kenya needs is an open heart surgery unit. Any of the elite in Kenya who need open heart surgery can fly to London, or they can fly to New York, or fly to the University of Washington. And I suggest to you that this is the kind of foreign aid grantsmanship on their part and giftsmanship on our part that is counterproductive, because it doesn't help them face up to the realities of life, doesn't help them begin to think about the kind of aid and the kind of programs that they are going to need that will really provide some basic impetus toward inducing women to lower fertility rates.

I think it's perfectly clear that where people feel they have a stake in society, where they feel themselves as people, they won't act out traditional roles that were there over the centuries when they were non-people. When there are fair land-owning policies, when there are fair tax policies, so the national government begins to have the resources from taxing its rich to spend for these programs, then I think people begin to feel better about themselves. And when they begin to feel better about themselves, and especially when women begin to feel their own identity as people and not as chattel, this will have an impact on fertility rate.

So then you get to the next step. What is our role? Do we place conditions on our foreign aid? Do we work the carrot and the stick? Do we say that if you don't do your part, there is no way that we can do our part? Do we tell them the story of the Aswan Dam? The Aswan Dam was built to produce more electricity per capita and to create more arable irrigated land per capita, and the Aswan Dam did everything that the engineers said it was going to do in terms of producing kilowatt hours and in producing "x" numbers of acres of arable land. But during the construction period of about 10 or 11 years, the population increase in the Aswan Dam Valley alone--not in all of Egypt, but in the Aswan Dam Valley alone--was so great that by the time the dam was finished, having fulfilled all of its predictions, there were fewer irrigated acres per capita and fewer kilowatt hours per capita at the completion of construction than there were at the beginning of construction. Is this the story that we tell to the Third World? And how do we let them know that with the limited amount of dollars we and other donor nations in the West have to spend at the present, we simply have to spend it where it works? We have to spend it where governments are providing enough leadership on their own in supporting thoughtful population-relevant development programs so as to prepare the way for specific population and family planning programs.

This is the dilemma with which many of us in Congress and many of you who are concerned about overpopulation are going to be wrestling for a long time. We have to sensitize our own people to the need for giving sums of a far greater order of magnitude for thoughtful foreign aid programs. But we also need to sensitize the governments, the decision makers, in the developing world that it is not just a one-way street, that unless they undertake significant population-relevant programs of their own which involve restructuring of many of their systems--their tax system, their land-holding system, their whole status of women which is infinitely complex and pervades every aspect of their lives--unless they do those things, history shows there is little they can do that will be meaningful in getting their exploding population growth rates under control. I think this is the major dilemma we're going to be dealing with in the coming years.

DISCUSSION

ASLAM KHAN, University of Washington, Seattle: I wouldn't emphasize the foreign aid part too much. Those of us from Third World countries--I'm originally from Pakistan--are aware that American foreign aid is a pittance when compared to your GNP. Except perhaps for Israel, the rest of the world isn't getting very much from the United States. Besides, most of the money goes to maintain the people in power. The American government really could help if they would help people to change the system in Third World countries.

JAMES SCHEUER: If the only major result of our foreign aid is to perpetuate the status quo, the existing inequalities, the existing structured inferiority of women that can only perpetuate high fertility rates, then it's a "catch 22." We'll be spending our money, but we'll be achieving nothing. I quite agree with you. And I also agree with you that there is enough evidence that our foreign aid isn't really working today the way it worked 30 or 40 years ago after World War II. The American people are not very supportive of vast improvements in the foreign aid program and, to tell you the truth, I'm not either. I would want to know that our foreign aid is really going to work, and I would want to know, on a country-by-country basis that the countries where we are investing our foreign aid are really making the structural reforms that have to be made in order for our foreign aid to be productive.

We know that in all parts of the world there are countries that have done very encouraging jobs. So, when I hear about

56

religious or tribal barriers to family planning, or ethnic, cultural
or nationalistic traditions that would militate against reduced fertility rates, I have to say, "Baloney," because there isn't a region
in the world where I can't point to countries that have done a job:
Singapore, Sri Lanka, Taiwan, Korea, Costa Rica, Indonesia. The
list is not endless, but it's significant. Most of them are small
countries where apparently they have channels of communication that
reach out to most, if not all, of the people. And, in sections of
larger countries where it's been tried--for instance in Bali in Indo-
nesia--they've gotten acceptors up to 50 and 60% of the women of
childbearing years. So I know it can be done everywhere. But you're
quite right. If all we're going to do is perpetuate the status quo,
I would have to wonder whether there's going to be enough public
acceptance of the foreign aid program in this country based on proven
results for it ever to be much of an order of magnitude larger than
it is now.

VIVEK BAMMI, Carnegie-Mellon University, Pittsburgh: I can't
agree with you about making conditions for aid. American aid cannot
start with the assumption that it will make structural changes in a
particular country. All your examples of successful family planning
programs are of small countries which perhaps have lesser problems
than more complex and historically more pluralistic countries, like
India, which is more tolerant of diverse attitudes and does not
wish to impose any such uniformity throughout the country, as perhaps Sri Lanka and other countries have done.

JAMES SCHEUER: I know of none of the countries that I have
named that have enforced uniformity. There is a certain amount of
peer group pressure. There is a certain amount of leadership from
the top. I agree, and I think that is wholesome and proper. I
didn't even mention Communist China which, of all of the countries
in the developing world, probably has the most effective family
planning system and has had the most effect on demographic growth
rates. But Communist China's system is the most Draconian in the
world; although they stop short of physically rounding up people
and taking them off to be sterilized, as Sanjay Gandhi apparently
did, the peer group pressure is intense, and the disincentive structure is Draconian--loss of jobs; long, long separation between husband and spouse; tremendous pressure against early marriages; tremendous pressure against larger than two-child families. That's
certainly a large country that's done it, and Indonesia has done
it in comparatively large areas like Bali.

VIVEK BAMMI: My general point is that if America sets long-
range social changes as a condition for giving aid, many countries
may refuse to accept American aid.

JAMES SCHEUER: You're quite right, and this is the dilemma.
We haven't found an answer for it yet, but it's not a new dilemma.
When the Alliance for Progress was organized about 13 years ago,

57

it was headed up by a very brilliant Puerto Rican by the name of Teddy Moscoso. He probably knew more than any American about development programs in underdeveloped societies. He went up and down Latin America, telling them that they had to create a more just society, that before we were going to have global tax programs, he wanted to see tax programs in each one of these countries, and fair land holding programs, and elimination of some of the tragic disparities in the distribution of wealth and resources. And almost everywhere he went, the ruling elite told him, "Get out. We don't need you. Take your foreign aid." He found that they were willing to do virtually nothing. And, of course, this is the dilemma.

One aspect of the dilemma is that the amount of dollars we're adding to the mix is not sufficient, really, to tip the balance. In each country it's a comparatively small percentage of their expenditures for social programs, welfare and the like. Perhaps if all the donor countries got together and spent $5 or $10 billion or more over a period of half a decade or a decade, they might have a little more clout in the decision-making process in the developing world. But as it is now, our contribution to each of these countries is not a sufficient incentive to get them to radically alter the structure of their societies, which in some cases is really long overdue and quite necessary.

RICHARD SCHWARTZ, the College of Staten Island: Congressman, your statement seems to imply that the population problem is located only in the underdeveloped world. I'd like to suggest that the most overpopulated country and the biggest threat to global survival is right here in the United States. In terms of the threat to life-support systems, pollution and usage of resources, there are estimates that each person here has an impact equal to that of 50 people in the underdeveloped countries. If you multiply our population by 50, you get 11 billion alone, which is close to the limits you say we might get to. We use about a third of the world's resources. We cause about half of the world's pollution.

Secondly, you've been talking mostly about aid. I wonder if there are other factors that should be considered in terms of a foreign policy. For example, can trade regulations be changed in order to give developing countries the opportunity to get a better price for their resources? Right now they get a low price for their raw materials and pay a great deal for our finished products.

JAMES SCHEUER: I agree that some changes are overdue in our trading posture. For one thing, this is the only place in the world where a highly-developed country sits cheek-to-jowl next to a developing country, along our 1950 mile border with Mexico. I think that we've got to provide a large package of incentives for the Mexican government to do what has to be done on population.

58

They've done quite a turnabout in the last few years, but they need a lot of help and they need to enlarge their program in many ways. And we also need their help in stopping the flow of illegal immigrants or undocumented aliens into our country. And one of the things I think we can tell them is that while we can't continue to absorb perhaps a million or more Mexicans a year into this country and give them jobs, we can provide more jobs for Mexicans in Mexico. I think what is long overdue is a fresh look at the barriers we place to Mexico's having access to our markets for their manufactured and agricultural products. Better access to our markets would create jobs in Mexico. It's bizarre to me that we keep out vine-ripened Mexican tomatoes that are superior in every way to the sawdust and paper-mache red dye product that we call "tomatoes." As a consumer, I resent the fact that I can't buy Mexican tomatoes that actually taste like a tomato.

In response to your first question, it's quite true that the developing world traditionally takes the position that we're the polluters, that we consume 40 to 50 times the energy per capita, that we produce 40 to 50 times the pollution per capita as a person born in the developing world where consumption of things that are wastefully packaged is virtually nonexistent. A child born in this country leaves a 75-year swath of disposables, plastics, cartons, tin cans, and bottles behind. You hear that everywhere you go in the developing world and a lot of it is true. We're trying to do something about it. Many of our counties and states are trying to ban disposable bottles. We're trying to get a handle on our energy consumption. But I suspect that very basic changes in our use of energy will have to be made. These changes won't be made out of sensitivity to Third World criticism, but out of absolute duress and lack of supply. It's going to be a hard and long time in coming.

BEE-LAN WANG, Wheaten College, Wheaten, Illinois: Representative Scheuer, you keep making references to the Marshall Plan and comparing the success of aid to those European countries during that time and the failures in the LDCs today. I think that perhaps to set things in perspective, we could look at some of the facts as to the amount of aid involved in those two instances.

In the Marshall Plan period, I understand, the total aid America gave out to just a few countries was between 0.75% and 1% of American GNP, and now the total aid package of the United States is down to 0.25% or less, and that aid is spread out among many more countries.

JAMES SCHEUER: That's absolutely true, although I didn't keep referring to the Marshall Plan, I referred to it once to make the very point that you're making. It was a very much simpler program. It affected only two countries which shared our traditions, our values, our goals, and had a management infrastructure and the

capability of using those dollars rather cost effectively. Today·
the dollars are spread out all over the developing world with far
larger population, with countries that are not very sophisticated
in how to manage programs and how to provide oversight, accountability, surveillance and review, and it's a very much more difficult problem. Because the results have not been terribly encouraging, and because some basic structural reforms are really going
to be needed before even comparatively liberal people like myself
could advocate a substantial increase in these programs, I think
we have tremendous problems. A major problem is to get these
countries to do the things that we feel confident they must do before our investments in development programs will be effective.
Do we attach harsh conditions? That's not politically acceptable
and I'm not sure we'd want to do that. Well, how do we do it?
How do we accomplish it without putting ourselves in an impossible
posture, without exacerbating the whole North-South dialogue?
Those are tough questions, and I think we'll be thinking them
through together for many years to come.

BEE-LAN WANG: Could I just make one comment? One of the
recommendations of the commission that was set up to investigate
AID policies was that foreign aid might change from emphasizing
efficiency, which is a very Western bureaucratic concept, to emphasizing effectiveness, and that effectiveness might come about if
we were willing to take seriously local grass roots development
initiatives.

JAMES SCHEUER: I think that would be efficient, too. I don't
know how you can be effective without being efficient. I think
working through local grass roots agencies and institutions and organizations is by far the most cost-effective way that we could
function.

BEE-LAN WANG: The problem is that American agencies are used
to ledger bookkeeping, and are not willing to take seriously initiatives from peasants who know what their life is and what they really
need.

JAMES SCHEUER: Well, I think the new AID administrator, Jack
Gilligan, and the new Assistant Administrator responsible for the
Population Program will be sensitive to the kind of thinking that
you're giving us. They're very imaginative people, and I think
they would be responsive to that kind of an appeal.

THE URGENT NEED FOR RESTRUCTURING THE
FEDERAL POPULATION RESEARCH PROGRAM

Paul McCloskey, Jr.

Member of Congress from California

By way of overview, let me mention that there is a new Select Committee on Population in the House of Representatives. We owe it entirely to the leadership of Jim Scheuer of New York, who initiated, organized, and now chairs that committee. There are 16 of us on it and, typical of this entire field, 15 of us are men and only one woman.

As I've gone around the United States the last two months trying to understand what is happening in the population field, I find that every institution, governmental and private, appears to be run by a triumverate of men at the top. Whether it's NIH or NICHD, the Ford Foundation, the Rockefeller Foundation, the Family Planning efforts, or the private drug companies that are primarily engaged in research on female contraceptives, these operations are being run almost entirely by men. A Congress made up primarily of men may vote to deny a poor woman the constitutional right of an abortion, but I wonder what would happen if the Congress were dominated by women and an issue came up of, say, a mandatory vasectomy for every man who had fathered two or more children.

The Select Committee has an immense task before it. It has to cope with the implications of what I perceive to be a real revolution which has taken place in the last three decades. Let me cite some facts which indicate that a "revolution"--and I use the word deliberately--has taken place. As late as 1950, in my home state of California

* it was illegal for a Caucasian to marry a Black person, a person of Oriental or Filipino descent, or a mulatto. Miscegenation was illegal;
* to obtain a divorce required a showing of fault on the part of the other party;
* as in most states, abortion was illegal;
* premarital intercourse was socially condemned;
* women's rights were subordinated to those of men;
* teenage pregnancy was relatively rare;

*population growth was not yet a matter of national and international concern;
* until 1960, the available methods of fertility control were coitus interruptus, the rhythm method, the condom, the diaphragm--all of them notoriously unreliable.

In the last 30 years, a revolution has occurred. The prohibition of mixed race marriages has been held unconstitutional. California, and an increasing number of states, permit no-fault divorces. Discrimination against a woman because of her sex was outlawed by the 1964 Civil Rights Act. And, subsequently, the Supreme Court ruled that a woman's right of privacy entitled her to an abortion within the first months of pregnancy. Premarital intercourse has become universally accepted. Development of the pill, the IUD, and the other contraceptive devices has created a whole new world of freedom of choice for women.

A 1973 study that was presented to our committee yesterday indicated that only 8% of married American women at risk of pregnancy were not using some form of contraception. And this included as high a rate of Catholic use as in the rest of the population.

It's significant that in the rise of the Communist Party to influence and power in Italy, the issues that are drawing young people toward the Communist movement are abortion, divorce and contraception. I think we are shortly going to see a change in the official positions of the Catholic Church, because the Church cannot stand the reaching of power of the Communist Party. Communism abhors religion, particularly the Catholic religion. In that confrontation in Italy, Spain, Portugal, and some other countries around the world, I think that the Catholic Church must change or lose an increasing number of young people who believe in the right of choice of contraception, divorce, and abortion.

Most importantly, last year over a million American teenagers became pregnant.

These changes in our society have occurred so rapidly that it is understandable that in both the medical and the political world we have been hard put to keep up and stay abreast.

At Bucharest in 1974 the nations of the world, including the United States, agreed that a new basic human right had come into existence--the right of every individual and couple to choose the number and spacing of their children. If the United States foreign policy of the late 1970s is, indeed, as President Carter has said, to be predicated on leadership in the human rights field, we certainly owe more than lip service to this concept of freedom of choice, both here and abroad.

Basic to the choice of how many children you're going to have

62

and when, is availability of information and materials which are necessary to the exercise of that choice. Yet the facts today do not bear out that that choice exists. Not all women in the United States have access to contraceptive information and materials.

Our basic research knowledge of the human reproductive system is still in the horse and buggy stage. Compared with space age or weapons research, for example, we've expended an almost pitiful amount for research in this area despite the tremendous impact on all of our daily lives. There is still no truly safe or fully effective contraceptive.

A study received yesterday by our Select Committee indicated that the pill had a 2% failure rate; the IUD, 3%; diaphragm, 10.3%; the condom, some 6%; the rhythm system, 9.5%. The most effective contraceptives, the pill and the IUD, have undesirable health effects on many women.

In 1972, 13% of all births conceived by married couples were the result of unplanned or unwanted pregnancies that occurred while the woman was using a contraceptive method. One woman in three in the United States today will have an unplanned or unwanted child as a result of our lack of knowledge and ability to safely and effectively contracept.

Under those circumstances, it's almost appalling how little money we are spending on the Federal research effort in this area. If you look at comparative statistics of the National Institutes of Health, where we're spending almost $3 billion this year, the amount for contraceptive research and development is a paltry $56 million. This affects the freedom of choice of nearly every American and, as we have led the world in other respects, perhaps it affects the freedom of choice of women throughout the world.

I think it is time to tremendously expand this research program. Of the 11 institutes at NIH, for example, 10 of them have intramural research facilities, where people can do on-campus work in the field of their specialty. The single institute of NIH which has no such facility is the National Institute of Child and Human Development which includes the Center for Population Research.

Every scientist I have talked to in the last several months agrees that until we have a basic center for the focus of intramural research in this field, until we have substantially increased funding for basic reproductive system research, there will be no breakthrough in the development of safe or better or more effective contraceptives.

I would guess that we could double that $56 million we are spending this year and still not approach what our obligation is to our people, particularly our women and our children, and the world.

In the Greep Report of 1976, a group of leading research physicians suggested that we should be spending this year $400 million merely for an <u>adequate</u> exploitation of the opportunities and the information that is available for us for research in the reproductive system. They suggested that $600 million this year would be appropriate if we were to give a high priority to research and to the development of contraception.

But what is missing, I think, is a sense of what this revolution really is: that women have equal rights, that they cannot exercise those equal rights and freedom of choice without this kind of research. We're spending nearly $1 billion on cancer, and a substantial amount on heart disease. While it is true that cancer and heart disease affect older people in this nation, they are not generally of a material impact on younger people. When you look at the impact on women and the impact of unwanted children, it seems to me that it calls for an incredibly substantial increase this year, and a whole restructuring of the Federal drug research program.

I've not touched on the area of FDA drug regulation and the laws that have grown up with respect to inhibiting research in the private sector. It's significant, I'm afraid, that none of the modern contraceptives were developed through governmental action. The pill and IUD were essentially developed by private enterprises competing in a profit market, stimulated to some extent by private foundations such as the Ford and Rockefeller Foundations. That research which was done in the past is no longer possible today because of a combination of circumstances--the length of time required for the drug testing procedure by the Federal Food and Drug Administration, the fact that incredible amounts of capital investment are required over long periods of time. Further, the risk involved in the political circumstances have not led private industry to invest their money in this kind of long-term research because of the uncertainty of regulation that pertains to it.

A few years ago when we were spending $30 million on contraceptive research, the bulk of that was done by private industry. Today we can't identify more than $5 million being spent by private industry in contraceptive research. There needs to be competition in this field, there is real need for stimulation by the government of contraceptive research by private industry. It may take a change in our patent laws; it may need a sharing of revenues from research that is done partly with governmental funding; it requires review of our entire regulatory system and the FDA system of drug approval, if we are to give this the priority I think it deserves.

For example, Depo Provera, an injectable which can cause people to become non-fertile for as many as six months, has not been approved by the FDA. I would feel more comfortable with that lack of approval if I was not aware of the fact that it stems from political intervention by members of Congress who contacted the FDA and asked the director of the FDA to override the advice of his own advisory committees which had approved Depo Provera. And while Depo Provera might not be as safe as would be appropriate for American women, population planners and health ministries in the developing countries would plead with us to make it available to their people and plead with us to let our Food and Drug Administration standards be more appropriate to the risks of death from pregnancy in their countries.

That's a brief overview of some of the information our Committee has received. Each day we are hearing new witnesses who bring in new facts and new judgments that are affecting the committee's decisions as to priorities. Under our new Congressional procedures we've got to come up with funding priorities within the next month or two. I'd be happy to answer questions for a few minutes before I get back to the committee hearings.

DISCUSSION

GEORGE WALL, Lamar University: I was interested, Congressman, that you noted that the Bucharest Congress declared that there was a new human right. My question has to do with the whole concept of a right and what correlative obligation goes with it. We could say that a person has a right to fly, and he had that right, you might say, in the 19th Century. The question is what obligation is imposed on another person because of this right. Similarly, with the right to limit one's family, the essential question which you addressed is the obligation of the government. Should it support better contraception, which I think is the back you're taking, or should it, let's say, attempt to take a more indirect approach which, according to the material that I have read, seems to be more effective; namely, improve the economic level of those who are having problems with their family.

PAUL McCLOSKEY: I don't think we have any quarrel about the need to improve the economic level all around the world. If you look at the expenditure of resources the United States has given to improving the situation in developing countries, it's immense compared to what we have spent on contraceptive research. I don't suggest that in contraceptive research we abandon the efforts to assist the developing countries to improve their standard of life. I think it's absolutely clear that the best means to give people the freedom of choice is to increase maternal health care, lower infant mortality and improve the standards of living in those countries. But the means of exercising the freedom of choice for people who want to do so is presently not there.

When I look at the research budget of NIH or the Defense Department or any of the other departments of our government, as related to the gravity of the problems that those institutions address, I find that we have not caught up in our government with this almost incredible revolution that's occurred in the last 28 years. I mean, we have materially changed the law of this country, and we've materially changed social conduct that is acceptable. It seems to me that, with contraception being practiced so widely, we really can't abide the fact that the present contraceptives both fail and are unsafe. I find no philosophical problem that the government undertake that particular facet of giving people freedom of choice. The one philosophical principle on which I understand everyone to agree is that the freedom of choice of the individual and the couple to decide how many children they want is absolute. If there's any philosophical disagreement that people shouldn't have that choice, I haven't heard it.

GEORGE WALL: I have.

PAUL McCLOSKEY: Well, I'd like to hear a discussion on that. Is there some philosophical argument which holds that people should be denied the right to choose how many children they bring into the world? I can't think of a more basic human right than the right of a child to be wanted and loved by two parents.

PETER HUESSY, The Environmental Fund: I would say that most of the research at NIH and the research in this country that's population oriented is contraceptive oriented. I think also that most of the research in this field has been devoted to means and not ends. We constantly talk about the way to get from A to B, which is contraceptives. But we never talk about why it is that people have large families. People want large families in the Third World. American women wanted close to four children on the average in 1958, and that's why we had the baby boom.

What I'm trying to say is that I support your efforts in the area of better contraceptives, abortion rights and women's rights. There can be no question there. But shouldn't we start looking very seriously at how you bring desired family size down, both in this country and the Third World, to two children or less? It's my feeling that we must bring desired family size down, Congressman, because I don't think people have a right to bring more than two children into this world.

PAUL McCLOSKEY: Well, you see, there we disagree. We might reach the point, at some future time, when we did not want to permit people freedom of choice. At the moment, the governments of Germany and France are even inclined to favor more children rather than less. I think freedom of choice includes the right to have more children rather than less.

In December, 1977, 17 members of parliament representing 11 political parties from Japan, Canada, Great Britain and the United

66

States, met in Berlin and discussed this question. The principle that was unanimously adopted was that, consistent with the right of choice, we should make contraceptive technology available to the developing countries which desire it but that we should not impose it on anyone.

We have a slightly different kind of problem with Mexico. I'm not so sure that the United States should be as free in welcoming illegal immigrants to do our menial labor as it is. As long as illegal immigrants coming to this country with the tacit acquiescence of government, management and labor contribute to the Mexican gross national product, we are, in effect, telling Mexico that not only can their surplus population be absorbed in our country but also that it can return benefits to Mexico. This situation presents the Congress with an unholy political problem. Are we a nation now, as Marx said, where capitalism can only survive by trying to exploit cheap labor?

In any case, I don't think under any circumstances we can deny the right of people in other countries to choose the family size they wish. I think the evidence is clear that as people increase in affluence and in a standard of living which does not require large families, they will voluntarily choose to have fewer.

I was impressed by Dr. Satar from Bangladesh, which probably has the gravest population situation, who described the voluntary willingness of men in Bangladesh to undergo sterilization because it really meant survival in their country. But that again is freedom of choice.

LOUISE CHUBB, writer, Alexandria, Virginia: Congressman, you asked whether anyone was proposing a limit on the freedom of choice to have as many children as you wish. I suggest that we should start thinking about the carrying capacity of the world for people in a civilized life, and that we should establish the present population, or as soon as people agree on it, the present population then, as a ceiling and make a random limitation of total births a requirement. This would be random in the incidence on individuals and families so there might be some families with more than two. By the way, there have to be more than two children for replacement levels because not everyone has children. But I do suggest we have a limit.

PAUL McCLOSKEY: At some time in the future we might very well reach a situation where we want to think about limiting population. At the present time, however, I think it would be unwise and impolitic to try to impose on this field even the concept that government could tell people to limit their family size. Government is the art of the possible. Your proposal is worthy of debate, but it seems to me in attacking this problem, for a government to suggest to any person, as Mrs. Gandhi did in India, that you must limit this choice is wrong.

As a Republican, I'd like to go back to what Lincoln once said: "Everybody ought to be free to do whatever they want, as long as no one else is hurt." I don't yet see that anyone is hurt by exercising this choice. I believe that even in the poorest nations of the world, women don't necessarily want to have large families. There are some that do. There are some in this country that do. Some of our most impoverished people feel that a child is the only asset they might bring into the world, particularly in some of our teenagers. But I think, given the choice, that women will exercise this and hopefully men might also have the means to exercise it.

HARBANS SINGH, Elizabeth, N.J.: Most contraceptives, especially pills, are designed to fit in with the nutritional and housing patterns of this country. Now, would you ask your experts on the Select Committee what type of nutrition people in underdeveloped countries should take while they are on the pill or on some other chemical contraceptive?

PAUL McCLOSKEY: Your point about nutritional patterns is absolutely accurate. We have developed our pills and other methods essentially for a U.S. market. For the companies which have developed contraceptive pills--Upjohn, and Syntex in my own Congressional district--there is basically no profit to encourage them to put time into marketing the kinds of dosages and the kinds of uses that might fit other countries' needs. One of the options the committee is considering is that we fund the World Health Organization's research in this area because it is proving far easier to approach many countries through international organizations than it is through even the most enlightened people in AID (which doesn't have the best record in this field.)

JANET HUBER LOWRY, Hamilton and Kirkland Colleges in New York: How exactly does the Select Committee define this area of population? I've heard you speak very strongly about contraceptive research, and I have also heard you talk generally about such things as illegal immigration. Is the committee concerned with those issues and hearing testimony about them, or are you going to more narrowly define your interests as dealing with the reproductive systems of individuals rather than their social values and the social causes of population problems?

PAUL McCLOSKEY: There are sixteen members on the committee and we would probably have sixteen areas of disagreement. We have Catholics on the committee who do not want to tough the abortion issue. We have people who do not want to touch the immigration issue. We have people who don't want to touch sex education or

68

teenage pregnancy. There's one thing about being a politician in a democracy--you have to worry about the tightly organized narrow special interest groups that can beat anyone in the next election. And if you have 20%, or even 10%, Right to Life in a Congressional district that switches sides by 3%, you have an understandable reluctance as a politician to be engaging in a field of inquiry which is viewed to be morally wrong.

Each of us on the committee would probably define the scope of population programs and problems differently, and I think that part of our problem is going to be defining the scope of our inquiry and what areas we go into. Quite honestly, I would probably put the status of women at the head of the list. And yet, that is not yet a source of defined inquiry by our committee. We've had to fight to get women on the staff. We've had to fight to get women witnesses before the committee. How we define it is up for grabs.

CHARLES CARGILLE, Population/Food Fund: Congressman McCloskey, in 1977 the Population/Food Fund initiated a series of occasional papers entitled "Population/Food Fund Papers." The first was entitled "Should the Federal Population Research Program Be Administered by NIH?" I was the author of that analysis first presented at the 1976 Capon Springs Population Policy Conference.

The paper examined the reasons for NIH's failure to provide the research leadership necessary for solving this global problem. I was forced to conclude from that analysis, based originally on the Republican Task Force on Population Growth and Ecology report in 1972, as well as my own experience as a senior investigator at NIH from 1966 to 1974, that NIH is simply institutionally incompetent to direct our social science research program in population.

My conclusion was that social science research must find another base in government, whether that be a NASA-type agency, or a change to an existing agency. But I think it is clear that in a biomedical institution you will not have the research necessary to solve the world problem.

PAUL McCLOSKEY: Dr. Cargille, I would have to say, after my limited study of the last 60 days, that I would have to agree with you on the record of NIH in the past. But when you look at the problems of governmental reorganization, how long it takes a new agency to get under way, to be organized, to become effective, I'm inclined to think that a strong Congressional mandate to NIH with clear directions as to priorities would be more beneficial than any other method that we might set up. I wouldn't take the past record of NIH as indicative of what we might do with a strong Congressional mandate because the Congressional mandates in the past to NIH have essentially been to inhibit the research into, say, contraception, which has not been a politically acceptable area of research in all areas--sex education, teenage pregnancy. Some

69

of my colleagues quiver up, turn into little pretzels when that situation comes back. There is no issue at home more explosive politically
than who ought to get sex education and at what age. And when you've
got a million teenagers pregnant, the very real issue comes up, at
what stage do you give them sex education which will inhibit the
birth of unwanted children and at what stage will sex education
stimulate their conduct which leads to the children. For people
under the age of 18 government has not yet been willing to take a
clear position on what the parents' rights were and what the government's rights were. So, reluctantly, I would say that NIH is the
proper place to try to expand this research effort.

POPULATION AS A NATIONAL SECURITY ISSUE--
OPENING PUBLIC DEBATE

Resolved, that the Department of Defense be named
the Executive Agency for managing the world population problem.

PRO: Stephen D. Mumford, author of <u>Population Growth Control</u>

CON: Everett Lee, University of Georgia

DISCUSSANTS: Peter Brown, Director of the Center for Philosophy and
Public Policy, University of Maryland

J. Philip Wogaman, Dean of Wesley Seminary, Washington,
D.C.

PRO: DR. STEPHEN D. MUMFORD, Research Group Leader,
International Fertility Research Program,
Research Triangle Park, North Carolina, and
author of <u>Population Growth Control</u>, Philosophical Library (1977)

The idea of world population growth as a national and international security issue is relatively new. In April 1977, Robert
McNamara, president of the World Bank, devoted part of a speech at
MIT to acknowledging world population growth as a national and international security issue and implied that it was <u>the</u> most serious
threat to security.

In October, Dr. Lester Brown, director of Worldwatch Institute,
published a lengthy paper on this subject titled "Redefining National
Security."

In December, Dr. Brzezinski, the U.S. National Security Advisor,
spoke at length in a press briefing on the subject of "The Demographic Explosion That Is Transforming the World's Population."

His office has just completed a study on this subject which I understand will not be made public.

Population growth as a threat to security has only emerged in the last decade or two, and its recognition has only begun to surface in the last few years.

There is now a school of thought that believes world population growth has emerged as the single greatest threat to U.S. national security, having already surpassed the threat posed by Russia. But the financial, political and moral commitment to managing this new threat is but a tiny fraction of that now made to counter the Russian threat.

The world is currently programmed to add 2-1/2 billion people over the next 25 years. In order to avert enormous food shortages it would be necessary to increase world food production by 60% over the next 25 years. It is unrealistic to assume this will occur. A 30% increase in food production during this period would be a more realistic hope.

A 30% increase in food production is an enormous expansion, but such an increase would still mean a shortfall equal to the total food requirements of one and one-quarter billion people, a number equal to nearly one-half the population of a not very well-fed developing world today.

A critical factor in the security of any nation is social organization. Social organization is the very basis of national security, yet no other phenomenon is more disruptive of social organization than hunger. The realistic possibility of widespread disruption of social organization makes world population growth a serious security issue.

It should be made absolutely clear at this point that world population growth is the number one U.S. national security issue because it is the most serious threat to the security of every single nation. It is inevitable that U.S. security will be affected when security is lost in countries upon whom we are dependent. We are all aware of the fact that the U.S. is dependent on a large number of countries and that this dependence continues to grow rapidly. An excellent example of this dependence is in the area of essential industrial raw materials. As the disparity between population size and food production increases in countries which supply the United States with essential raw materials, we cannot expect that these raw materials will continue to flow to the U.S. as social organization is lost in country after country. Internal security abroad will give way to social chaos resulting from hunger. The internal security of the U.S. will be seriously threatened.

The gravity of the problem is now beginning to be recognized and acknowledged. With the passing of a few more years, the extreme seriousness of man's predicament will become common knowledge even in America.

Once the gravity of the situation has been acknowledged, it seems to me that the next order of business is the selection of an organization to lead the world population growth intervention effort. This selection is the most important single activity that we now face. We must make the right selection the first time around. We do not have a decade to decide we chose the wrong organization or combination of organizations and then hurriedly make another selection. In the next decade we will have added 1 billion people to the world's population and deterioration in social organization will have already become evident.

Even if man's best effort is brought to bear on the population problem there is still a risk of failure. World population growth is a problem of enormous dimensions and complexity, and its solution will also be of enormous dimensions and complexity. Solution of the problem unquestionably will be the most complex undertaking ever attempted by man. There will be no guarantee of success but we must not build failure into our effort by failing to choose the best organization to lead the effort.

The U.S. must prepare itself to provide assistance to other countries in their population growth control efforts. We must provide the necessary leadership and lead by example. We must provide the resources no matter what the costs, even though these costs may run $10 to $30 billion a year, or 2-6% of next year's U.S. government budget. We can afford these resources because we must.

This year only about one-half of the requests for population assistance are being met. It is likely that if all requests were being fulfilled today, the level of requests would be even higher. But we must look down the road a few years--perhaps even 10 years-- and make an assessment now of what requests for assistance will look like then. As the disparity between number of people and food supply grows over the next decade, requests for assistance will multiply enormously, and may approach a level 100 times that of today.

We must make the assumption today that these requests will be forthcoming in the years ahead. We must begin preparation now by readying an organization to provide this assistance. If we wait until requests reach the predicted level before we assign this task to a capable organization, we are risking failure of the intervention effort and the loss of U.S. security. We do not have a decade to spare. We must begin preparing this organization now. We can be assured that more requests for assistance will be forthcoming.

Let us now examine some of the essential characteristics that this organization must possess. Above all else, this organization

73

must have influence. We will be placing enormous demands on this organization, and it must possess the influence to marshal the commitment and all of the resources necessary to meet these demands. It must possess influence both in the U.S. and abroad. It must be a respected organization, one in which all concerned will have confidence--confidence that what must be delivered,will be delivered.

Second, this organization must have a tremendous organizational capacity. The world population growth control effort may require 10 million full-time employees or more, and the U.S. component of this effort will need to be at least several hundred thousand strong. The organization must be of sufficient capacity to bring together whatever resources are necessary and to distribute these resources whenever and wherever they are requested.

Third, it must be highly responsive to a chain of command for two important reasons. Time is critical and this organization must be capable of responding to requests with all deliberate speed. The second reason for responsiveness to a chain of command deserves a moment of discussion. Widespread hunger causes social disorganization and, as was said earlier, social disorganization is our major concern. But there are other phenomena that can cause social disorganization besides hunger. One of these is the imposition of coercive population control programs upon people. We must ensure that social disorganization induced by hunger is not replaced by disorganization induced by coercive population control programs. Responsiveness to a chain of command will ensure that over-zealous members of the assistance effort do not attempt to encourage coercive population control programs in countries requesting assistance.

Lastly, the personnel of this organization must be highly dedicated. Every person in this effort must deliver whatever is demanded with his or her best effort. Nearly every organization has some people who perform in this manner, but high level dedication and performance must be universal in this effort.

These are the four characteristics that are absolutely essential to the organization assigned the intervention effort. Any organization that is not highly influential, does not possess a vast capacity to organize, is not highly responsive to a chain of command, or is not highly dedicated, will ultimately fail.

I examined each of the U.S. and international organizations currently involved in the population assistance effort and found none which had these four characteristics. Other existing organizations were then examined, since the urgency of the situation demands that we use an existing organization. The only organization found to possess all these characteristics was the U.S. Department of Defense.

We cannot ignore the fact that the DOD is the most influential organization in the domestic U.S. It has more influence with respect to securing what it needs to carry out its mission than all of the other U.S. Departments and Agencies combined. We cannot ignore the fact that it is the most influential organization on the international scene. Though many Americans may disagree, the fact is that the DOD is far more influential internationally than the State Department.

General Draper used his military background very effectively in advancing population programs in the developing world. Let me cite an example. AID was having trouble helping the Philippines get their population program off the ground. General Draper visited General Romulo of the Philippines, a long-time friend. His message was simple: "Your nation is faced with a serious problem and I would like to talk with you about it." The program got off the ground immediately thereafter. And let's not forget that 80% of the developing countries have as their leaders present or former senior military officers, most of whom have worked with the U.S. military in the past.

We cannot ignore the fact that the DOD is one of the largest and probably the most complex and sophisticated organizations man ever created. It has a history of success with the design and management of vast and intricate programs of many kinds.

We cannot ignore the fact that the U.S. Department of Defense is the only organization that has extensive experience in almost every aspect of the needed assistance effort. It has organized and delivered the world's largest research effort. One-fourth of all U.S. scientists are currently involved in this effort. It conducts the largest worldwide training programs ever to exist. It has developed and currently maintains the world's most sophisticated and efficient communication, supply, and transportation systems, which are literally capable of reaching every square foot of the earth's surface. It is the world's largest supplier of services and its experience and record in service delivery is unsurpassed.

These facts cannot be ignored in the selection of the organization that will be assigned the task of the U.S. assistance effort. Before skeptics remove the Department of Defense from contention, they must find a suitable alternative. I have been unable to do so. Clearly, failure to deliver our best effort toward solving the world population problem entails great risks to U.S. and international security.

In summary, the U.S. must make the economic, political and moral commitment to manage this newly emerging and most serious threat to U.S. and international security. Merely increasing the economic commitment utilizing existing organizations is not enough, since existing organizations lack essential characteristics and will continue to be inadequate. An organization that has the necessary characteristics for effectively managing the solution must be selected and

assigned the task of the U.S. assistance effort. I believe our only
alternative is the U.S. Department of Defense.

          CON: DR. EVERETT LEE, University of Georgia

     I must say I don't stand quite so much in awe of the Defense
Department. I suppose that, having seen it from the point of view of
a first lieutenant, I was never quite so sure they were as well organized as my colleague seems to think. (Laughter) In fact, I think
that the worst possible agency we could choose for directing a program of population assistance--or, more accurately, population con-
trol--for the underdeveloped parts of the world would be the U.S.
Defense Department.

     I don't think it would be quite so bad for the developed coun-
tries because they have already made an enormous sacrifice for the
rest of the world in that they have, indeed, reduced their levels
of population growth to where they will soon, not too long after the
turn of the century, have reached zero population growth. Indeed,
for most of the developed world, including the United States, the
character of the debate will soon turn to whether or not we should
increase our birth rate or admit more immigrants from underdeveloped
countries simply to keep the population from falling. The developed
countries are perhaps most in need of low population growth rates because for many of the most crucial resources, including energy, the
U.S. consumption per person (and at about half that level in the rest
of the developed world) is anywhere from 500 to 1000 times that of
most of the people in the underdeveloped world.

     The problem of population growth is an enormous one. It requires
a vast amount of re-education, first, of ourselves and also, frankly,
of the world's underdeveloped countries as well. The vastness of the
problem is complicated by the fact that there are so many countries
involved. I wonder if Mr. Mumford's faith in one agency with worldwide experience does not stem from frustration with the necessarily
fragmented nature of population control programs. On the one hand,
the five largest underdeveloped nations have 44% of the world's population, a figure which suggests that efforts might be concentrated
on these countries. On the other hand, 56% of the world's population
is distributed among the other 156 countries of the world and such
a spread is difficult to deal with. The median population size for
all countries in the world is only about 5 million, and the median
area for all nations in the world is only about 78,000 square miles,
or roughly the size of Montana. So I do agree with Mumford that
there is a problem of great magnitude in getting the message across
and in supplying the needs of all these developing nations. The
question is, however, whether we should entrust our efforts to an
agency which does not have, and indeed never can have, the trust of

the rest of the world.

Let me just look at this from another point of view. I can very
well picture Idi Amin, for example, thinking that indeed the country
in the world which above all others should reduce its birth rate is
the United States. Perhaps he might include the Soviet Union, too.
And he would like very much to send a mission to the United States
which would have the mission of helping us reduce our birth rate. He
might choose one of his more faithful generals, give him enough
money and send him to Harlem or elsewhere to bring down the U.S.
birth rate. This example is a reductio ad absurdum, but I really
mean to indicate that that is probably the way we would look if we
sent our generals to some of the smaller countries which are engaged
in controversies with their neighbors or are caught up in the kind of
cat and mouse game which the Soviet Union and the United States play
with each other by advancing small countries against each other.

And that is the image of our defense establishment abroad. By
and large, it is not seen as a group which comes in to help you out.
Oh, it may give you some arms this year, but next year it may be giving arms to your neighbor. In every case Defense Department assistance is given for the benefit of the United States as it is seen
by the United States at the moment--usually wrongly, in my opinion.
As most people abroad perceive the role of the Defense Department, it
is not the kind of organization which we could expect to gain acceptance in the underdeveloped parts of the world. It is certainly
true that all countries of the world, especially the United States,
need to be aware of the population problem and the need for immediate
action to reduce the threat not just to our security, but to everybody's security, which is posed by runaway population growth. I believe that thinking people in all countries accept that and almost
everybody who can think rationally about such problems are agreed
that something has to be done. Of course, in most cases what is
thought is that it is the other country that should reduce its birth
rate. For that you can get agreement almost everywhere. To do it
within your own country is a little more difficult.

Very often the people in a country seem to be willing, even
anxious, to find ways of reducing birth rates, but they run up against
two major obstacles: one is the government itself, which may have the
idea that its strength depends upon the size of its population (and
when you consider the median population size you can understand this);
and the other is that in many countries influential ethical or religious leaders are opposed to birth control and they exert a great deal
of pressure upon the government. In many cases, leaders of religious
groups have to be won over before a reasonable program for limiting
population growth in a particular country can be effective. I do
not believe that the U.S. Defense Department is especially well
equipped to talk with ethical and moral leaders within a country or,
in general, with those people who are most effective in changing the
policies of countries.

Let me now take up the point of social disorganization. The
fact is that in an enormous number of developing countries there is
already a great deal of social disorganization. Even the very smallest countries usually have two groups which are very much opposed
to each other. Take the little country of Djibouti, for example,
which is divided between two tribes and indeed might well have a
civil war of its own even if it were not pulled in one direction by
Somalia and in the other direction by Ethiopia, with the connivance of
some of the larger world powers who would like to have a special role
within the horn of Africa. Thus the existing social disorganization
brought on by competing power groups is helped along by our own (and
Russia's) Department of Defense, the very agency that Mumford claims
will diminish social disorganization.

Hunger is a problem in many of the countries of the world. And
hunger indeed does create disorganization. And hunger may, sometimes,
lead political leaders to try coercive methods of reducing population
growth. I think we have seen this on a fairly large scale in India.
(Actually, the results were not very large-scale but the effects were
large-scale in changing the government). Imagine if we had had our
Defense Department assisting Indira Gandhi with her population program.
And I might ask what is the natural feeling of somebody who has been
trained to take immediate effective action with people who are a
little reluctant to do what they've been told to do, or what we want
them to do. Now, it's my opinion that the Defense Department might
very well have put itself solidly behind Mrs. Gandhi, made her programs doubtless more efficient, but on the other hand the feeling
which was aroused against Mrs. Gandhi by people to whom this came in
the wrong way and perhaps at the wrong time, would then be transferred to our Department of Defense, and through our Department of Defense, to the United States as a whole.

I have an alternative suggestion to the one Mr. Mumford makes.
I think it is time that we stopped withdrawing from international organizations when something happens which doesn't please us very
much. It's time we stopped the practice of not paying our dues to
UNESCO. It's time we began working as closely as possible with as
many international organizations as possible and, for purely diplomatic reasons, letting other countries take the lead, even though
ours must be the most important financial support. If there is to
be a worldwide program for the reduction of births addressed particularly to the underdeveloped countries, then it must come from a co-
alition of countries--not just from the U.S. or from the Soviet
Union--led by an agency which already exists, and including in its
councils in very important positions and among those who go out into
the countries to lead the efforts, the underdeveloped countries themselves. This is not the time for us to appear as the nation, which,
above all others, wishes to do something to limit population growth
in other parts of the world. This is a time for us to coordinate our
efforts with the other nations of the world, not as a danger to our
national security, but as a threat to the whole world, us included,

but only as a part of the world.

And then let us put our best foot forward, which is not the Defense Department, by any means. Let us be content to not take the leading role, except financially, but let us finance well the international organizations which are already set up to lead such an effort. Let us then not pick up our marbles and go home the first time something happens which doesn't suit us too well. If they give aid to a Communist country, or if they give aid to one which, for the moment, doesn't seem to be a friend of ours, well, so what! If it's for population control, and if they're not a friend of ours, I can't see that we're going to be very much hurt.

Above everything, the United States must, in this whole context of international diplomacy and international aid, quit trying to carry the burden by itself and, above all, quit linking the aid which we're giving to considerations of American national security. There is absolutely no way in which we can tell the Mexicans--just to take a neighbor, for example--that they must reduce their birth rate and we will send down several tons of condoms and other useful items and have our military establishment distribute them throughout the country so that indeed they do not constitute a threat to the internal security of the United States. Let's raise our aims a little; let's recognize that population growth is a threat to everybody, those in both the developed and the underdeveloped world. None of us can do it alone, and it really doesn't matter who takes the lead. We're not going to have an efficient organization all at once, but no organization is efficient when it begins. Perhaps, in this particular area, the aim is not necessarily the greatest efficiency but the greatest acceptance. I think I can assure you that the United States Department of Defense, no matter how efficient it happens to be, does not have a high degree of acceptance in other countries of the world, and, I regret, because it's dangerous to us here, it doesn't have the highest degree of acceptance within the United States itself.

REPLY BY DR. MUMFORD

Dr. Lee has made many good points which can't be dealt with in the time we have. I think it will take many months, perhaps several years, to fully explore the proposition of this debate. Let us respond to just a few points.

First, I'd like to say that Dr. Lee's Mexican example is not at all what is intended. My book, Population Growth Control: The Next Move is America's, goes into this in a lot more depth than I can now.

One essential point on which Dr. Lee and I disagree is the ability of the United Nations to lead the population control efforts.

79

I contend that they are not capable of leading. And, whether we like it or not, world population growth is going to be recognized as the number one U.S. national security issue. I do not see Americans placing their security in the hands of the United Nations over the next 25 years. I just don't think that's going to occur. I fully agree with Dr. Lee's idea that this has to be an effort of cooperation among all countries, including all developed countries. What I'm proposing is that the United States take the lead and hope that the other developed countries will join the United States in the effort. The experience of the past 10 to 15 years shows us that there has to be a leader. I think the United Nations model is not quite mature enough for it to do so.

We have to look fifteen years down the road. We're pretty certain we're going to see a billion to a billion and a half people added to the world's population in the next 10 to 15 years. Some of the objections to the Department of Defense assume that current attitudes will continue forever. But we've got to look down the road a little bit. How will people in developing countries look at assistance efforts by the military as the disparity between food supply and numbers continues to grow?

REPLY BY DR. LEE

As you can see, we don't quarrel over the necessity for reducing the rate of growth of the world's population. However, there are wide differences of opinion between countries as to where the reduction should take place. That, I think, is inevitable. Thus, as a practical matter, it seems to me that the apparent leader is going to incur an enormous degree of enmity from many countries of the world. This is particularly so if that leader is a country which has so much of the world's riches, and if it puts its foot forward by letting its army follow its trading vessels. Under these conditions we could find ourselves not accomplishing what we wanted and not accomplishing what most of the developing countries themselves want. It simply isn't the way to do it.

DISCUSSANT: DR. PETER BROWN, Director of the Center for Philosophy and Public Policy, University of Maryland

While agreeing with both speakers in viewing the world population problem as extremely serious, I'd like to point out some of the ambiguities of Dr. Mumford's thesis and to suggest places where I think more conceptual work is needed. I don't intend to agree or disagree with what he said; rather, I hope to show what sorts of work would be needed to determine whether or not what he is saying is correct.

In addition to the rather serious problem of the DOD's institutional credibility mentioned by Dr. Lee, it seems to me there are at least three areas where further work is needed. The three areas that I think are in need of conceptual clarification in this argument are: first, the question of what it means to have something be a threat to your security; second, I think a definition is needed of excess population growth that is nation-specific; and third, I think we need to examine some of the institutional assumptions that underlie the food requirement projections that Dr. Mumford relied upon so heavily.

Let me start with the threat to security. As I was listening to his remarks it occurred to me that there were probably a variety of definitions of this idea--threat to security--and, just to point to that problem, I would note at least two such definitions. One is a definition which has been used by the Supreme Court, that security is threatened when there is a clear and present danger to your nation, when the enemy ships are lying just over the horizon, when there's a very serious threat to your large population centers. I don't think Dr. Mumford is using the notion of threat to security in this sense. He's using it in a much broader sense, and I think a much weaker sense, that your security is threatened when the raw material sources of your nation are threatened. And this looser, weaker sense of threat to security removes some of the moral persuasiveness from his argument. I would also point to an empirical problem that not all major suppliers of raw materials to this country have, or are likely to have, rapid population growth. Not all the OPEC nations have large populations now, nor are they likely to be overpopulated in the near future.

The second problem I want to mention is that we haven't been given a very clear definition of what constitutes excessive population growth. An intuitive notion which seems to lie behind what Dr. Mumford is saying is that excess population growth occurs when population is expanding more rapidly than resources. The problem with this is that it fails to offer any standard by which one could appraise whether a nation had its fair share of the world's resources. There's been a lot of talk around recently about each nation growing its own food supply and becoming self-sufficient. But there's practically no nation in the world that's self sufficient, and the resources on which a nation relies for growing food are very much dependent upon its position in world markets for petroleum, fertilizer, seed, etc.; the amount of these resources that a nation has are very much dependent on human institutions, largely human financial institutions. We can increase the share of resources that a nation has through various forms of resource transfers and there's no reason to take a nation's particular resource base at any time, which is an historical accident, as the resource base on which it should depend. So I think that we need to have a clearer definition of what

81

constitutes excess population growth before we can decide on the merits of this case.

The third thing I think we need is to examine some of the institutional assumptions in the food requirement projection that Dr. Mumford makes. As world income rises, it's almost universally the case that grain consumed through meat is substituted for grain consumed directly. The more effective development efforts are at increasing income, the more likely it is that there will be greater pressure on the grain supply. The projection of enormous food requirements that Dr. Mumford relied upon assumes that we will continue to accept this pattern. It assumes, in a word, that we will continue to accept normal market allocations of grain supplies in the world. However, we don't have to continue to accept this in its present form. We can, for instance, just to give an example, create incentives so that people's desire to consume grain in the form of meat is retarded, so that the enormous food requirements that he projects would no longer be of that order of magnitude.

In summary, I don't think you can tell whether or not his institutional proposal is correct without clarification of at least these three conceptual problems.

DR. J. PHILIP WOGAMAN, Dean of Wesley Seminary, Washington, D.C. and co-author of Qualify of Life in a Global Society, Friendship Press (1978)

This is an interesting kind of question. I find myself thinking a little bit whimsically of what it's like to live in Washington and to witness the difficulties through the years of relating human value concerns, morality, to political policy considerations, politics. It's such a rare thing when what is good morally makes an immediate linkage to something that is also wise, prudent or shrewd politically. It's a very rare synthesis. It's a somewhat less rare synthesis to have something that is immoral, unrighteous, and shortsighted in terms of values linked with something that is politically naive or stupid. That's a less rare synthesis, as one might reflect, in recent years in Washington. Now I think Mr. Mumford has come close to that kind of synthesis. (Laughter)

I want to say, first off, that I think Mr. Lee has all of the right side of the debate insofar as this is a debate. Clearly, first of all, because the policy proposal made here would fly absolutely in the face of every sensitivity about the world. Some of you may have attended the Bucharest Population Conference, as I did. You will recall that on every hand we were told that to be concerned about the population question is to be a neo-Malthusian imperialist. It's all wrapped around the American flag. Even news about this debate, much less publication of the book or expressions of serious interest in the proposal, would be beautiful ammunition all over the Third World. It would be seen as one more piece of evidence that the United States is trying to push its neo-Malthusian imperialistic designs through the population field. To link population control with the Department of Defense--well, I think it's important to observe the canons of propriety and politeness in such a case as this, but in truth I think the point needs to be stated very bluntly--I would be appalled if the debate continued very long. (Laughter)

Now that's on the practical, political level. On the moral level I would be a little more generous because I suspect that the concern really is broader than the category in which it has been phrased. But the category is a national interest category--what is in the national security interest of the United States. To champion this category would be a step backwards from the finest humanistic traditions rooting clear back to Cicero and Seneca, the great Stoic thought, Jesus and St. Paul, the great Christian thought, Mohammed. Great figures in virtually every one of the high religious and philosophical traditions have emphasized not national interest or group interest but the human interest of the whole human community. We're in a time where the erosion of a value commitment to the unity of the whole human family is the most serious ethical problem facing any of us. To formulate a problem in national interest categories today is to take a moral step backwards at a time when there is urgent need to take a moral step forward.

My own values as a scholar and, I hope, a practitioner of ethics, simply won't fit into this kind of moral category. We are talking about the human interest, the whole human family, and that would seem to suggest that Dr. Lee has been very wise, not only practically and politically, but also morally, in saying that the real steps ahead are those steps which involve commitments to international institutions and ways of doing things. We are, after all, in a time when the great challenges facing human kind--population, energy, food, ecology--all require global cooperation if they're to be solved. They cannot be solved unilaterally or even within a basically nationalistic frame of reference. For that reason I have been appalled at some of the nationalistic attitudes toward the Law of the Sea Conference, currently under way. Wherever there is an opportunity to be international, to use international institutions, to give them the kind of strength which carries credibility with it, we must surely seize those opportunities and use them.

My final word is to those present who are not U.S. citizens. Please don't take this too seriously. (laughter and applause)

AUDIENCE QUESTIONS AND COMMENTS

STAN DEGLER, The Bureau of National Affairs, Inc.: This isn't a question but an observation which I'm making in the spirit of the last comment about not taking this thing too seriously. A couple of days ago the Beetle Bailey comic strip had Beetle Bailey and another private solder looking at the bulletin board, and Beetle said to the other soldier, "Which one of us do you think is going to be promoted first?" And the other soldier said, "Why, Zero, of course." "Zero?" said Beetle. "Oh, yeah, I forgot. This is the army."

WALTER CORSON, World Population Society: I think this debate misses a major issue and that is the problem of mobilizing resources. The population problem is probably less a problem of identifying the right organization to implement population activities and more one of establishing leadership commitment to allocate the necessary financial and physical resources to population activities. In many countries it's really a question of authorizing necessary funds and resources and this probably can't be done without shifts in public opinion and public understanding.

DANA T. LAROSE, Wallingford, Pa.: I have a question for Mr. Mumford. After these last two days of speeches and debates I don't think that there's any question that population is a problem. But social justice is also a very pressing problem. And would not the threat of population growth to our national security be quite a bit less if resources were more equitably distributed?

STEPHEN MUMFORD: This is one of the places where we run into the problem of not having the full argument stated. It's a very complex argument, which can't be presented in fifteen minutes. The population growth assistance effort I'm talking about does not rule out the redistribution of resources.

As those who have lived in developing countries know, the resource that hungry people are most concerned about is food. As I said earlier, it is the growing <u>disparity</u> between food and population growth that makes population growth a threat to national security. So the assistance effort I'm talking about would pay as much attention to food production as it would to the mechanics of population growth. In so far as food is the central resource needed by the poorest countries, I think the assistance effort I have in mind would speak to the question of resource distribution.

I would also like to say that my involvement in population came from the moral end. But people are not responding to the lower ranking ethical values. People tend to respond best to the number one most highly prized ethical value, security-survival. And that is one reason we must acknowledge overpopulation as a national security issue.

84

PETER HUESSY, The Environmental Fund: What I have to say here does not necessarily reflect the views of my organization. First of all, I would like to congratulate Dr. Mumford for having a great deal of courage. I don't believe the Pentagon is the right place to take on the effort (although they could give some assistance), but I think that's immaterial. The population debate has generally assumed that there are only two ways to reduce population growth: one via the compulsory sterilization method used by India, and the other through completely voluntary approaches. The voluntary approach is divided into two programs: one, providing people with contraceptives, and turning around and praying that some day they may bring their desired family size down to two; or through development efforts which are by and large swallowed up by population growth as soon as you get funds into an area. I would like to suggest that both approaches--development efforts and family planning efforts--have missed the boat. I'd like to address myself to the issue of whether world government or international organizations are the proper place to begin this effort.

I would suggest that the U.N. is not capable of leading, in any way, in population matters. They are set up to either do family planning assistance on request or they're set up to do development on request, and the money they have is quite small. But I would suggest that there is an organization which could be created to take the lead on population matters. It must be an organization of member states which agree on the rule of law. Let me propose that all of the world's democracies--including Japan, New Zealand, Canada, Australia, all of Europe and the United States--join together in what has been called the Atlantic Union. These countries could do the following:

1. Stabilize their own population almost immediately;

2. Reduce their population growth, which is well within possibility if the fertility rate stays at 1.7, which is where Europe is at;

3. Concentrate on reducing our consumption of non-renewable resources and conserving these resources;

4. Join together in a massive, all-out development effort in the Third World on the model of Singapore, Sri Lanka and Kerala in India. Incentives and disincentives are what these countries have decided they want. Korea has now joined in this type of an incentive program by providing scholarships to people if they have two children or less, and Indonesia is contemplating a similar move.

Such a union of democratic nations could not be seen as an imperialist plot from the United States; this is what developing countries want to do. I think we're missing the boat unless we concentrate on the real problem, which is bringing desired family size down. It is not a debate between population and development. You can combine the two.

One last comment. In the last three months, George Kennan, Lester Brown and Dr. Brzezinski have all cited population growth in this country and overseas as the gravest threat to our national security. It is not a weak argument. Secondly, there's no such thing as excess population growth. Pretty soon population growth in any form is going to be excess.

I'm sorry I've taken this much time but most of the speakers today have been opposed to Dr. Mumford. I don't feel that it's a laughable matter. I think Dr. Mumford has a great deal of guts because he's joined an issue that should have been joined long ago. We have very little time left. I want to congratulate you, Mr. Mumford, on a book that puts the crisis in its proper perspective, even though I may not agree that the Pentagon is the right place for solving it.

J. PHILIP WOGAMAN: Let me say something about humor here. One of the high functions of humor is to spare us taking either ourselves or absurd ideas too seriously. Now, I really have rather strong feelings that for the United States to lead out, symbolically and actually, with that agency in our government which is most directly and clearly identified with the American military presence, American excesses in power, all over the world, to lead out in a constructive area of population would be a very bad mistake. Of course I take the whole area of population and food seriously. All of these issues are of desperate importance, but they're far too serious for us to approach on a purely nationalistic basis.

KENNETH PIERS, Calvin College: I, too, don't think the subject is a laughing matter, although when one hears recommendations for DOD supervision of population control it does conjure up images of television cameras in bedrooms throughout the land to see whether or not we're engaging in intercourse appropriately. But that is not my question.

You said in your presentation, Mr. Mumford, that widespread hunger causes social disorganization. I would say that social disorganization and social malformation causes widespread hunger.

STEPHEN MUMFORD: I think that the idea that social disorganization does cause hunger is a very important point. In the book, I talk about the implications of social disorganization for food production. As social organization decreases, food production decreases, which further reduces social organization. A downward spiral is set in motion. One feeds on the other. I think you're making a very important point.

LOUISE CHUBB, writer from Alexandria, Virginia: I also think that it was great for Dr. Mumford to be concerned about population. I wish the government as a whole were more concerned. My feeling is that the effect of this conference is blunted somewhat by the emphasis on food. We have a number of fine ideas for improving food production but of course they may decrease the amount of trees, increase the amount of floods, increase the amount of pollution from insecticides, and so on. I wish therefore that the conference had been solely or primarily dedicated to the problem of population. It seems to me that many of the remarks made suggest that what we need is agreement that population should be stabilized worldwide. May you please have your next conference on this issue. If we could agree, here in the United States, we could then ask the other nations to agree too. I'd like for us to be the leaders but I'd like for it to be a worldwide agreement that population should be stabilized. With such agreement surely we could develop a somewhat more democratic method than seems to be implied by Dr. Mumford.

CHARLES CARGILLE, Population/Food Fund: Miss Chubb, I'll respond to that. As the organizer of the conference, I'll never hold another conference only on population. The Capon Springs Series began in 1976 with 40,000 invitations mailed to the academic community. Only ten individuals responded with a policy paper concerning population. That does not speak to the disregard for the subject, but simply to the fact that the support level for population is so low that, with the exception of a few individuals you could count on two hands, academics are not performing research today on population policy. Secondly, we have chosen not to isolate population because it is inextricably linked to food, resource and environmental policy.

LOUISE CHUBB: A committee of The National Academy of Sciences a few years ago said, "Population control is the absolute primary essential without which all other efforts are nullified."

CHARLES CARGILLE: I agree with you entirely that it's the central driving determinant of the global system.

SARA H. SCHMINKEY, graduate student, University of Pittsburgh: During this debate several people have argued that the choice of the Department of Defense as the agency which should manage the world population problem is wrong. I certainly agree, but I feel that most speakers have avoided the real substance of the causes of hunger. They've said that widespread hunger causes social disorganization, creating the greatest threat to U.S. national security. It seems that what the speakers feel is being threatened is a style of life which they believe must be preserved at all cost. But all the speakers so far, pro and con, have ignored the fact that this style of life, or this system, is the major cause of the hunger and population problem. What is needed is a restructuring of the system to allow for distributive justice. Unless such changes take place, the population and hunger problem will never be dealt with effectively. The discussion so far has dealt only with the symptoms and not the causes. The debate proposal, and the responses made, indicate an intense fear of change; that is, change which would threaten the lifestyle and institutions which currently are being maintained in this country. I have not heard any expression of concern or consideration for the interests and problems of the Third World, which is essential for any program that deals effectively with the population and hunger problem. (Applause)

WIN BEST, population consultant, Chapel Hill, North Carolina: In agreement and disagreement with Dr. Wogaman, I would say that we should continue the debate, but with all deliberate speed. And I would say that my friend and colleague, Dr. Mumford, is simply calling a spade a spade when he talks about population as a national security issue.

This country has invested about a billion dollars in population aid abroad already, and by whatever name you call it, it is in the self-interest, as well as the altruistic interest, of this country. I think it is a humanitarian investment; at the same time, it's an investment in self-interest. In population and other fields we often do the right things for the wrong reasons, and that may get us into a philosophical discussion of whether the ends justify the means.

A good example of this mixture of good and bad is the investment domestically in family planning programs that emerged from the Tidings Bill, the Family Planning and Population Research Act of 1970. Those of us who were involved with seeking to enact that legislation felt that research was the best foot forward because it was the most benign. And yet, I think anyone connected with that legislation, and with the hundreds of millions of dollars that resulted from it being invested in family planning programs, recognizes that Congress did not enact that bill for humanitarian reasons simply to help the deserving poor, to use an old-fashioned expression. They enacted it to cut dependency costs. They sought to save tax funds. They, indeed, liked the idea of helping the poor, helping those who were denied contraceptive services because they didn't have private physicians, but their primary motivation was to reduce tax dependency, and, if possible, to have fewer of the poor rather than benefiting them in a humanitarian way. That's really what Dr. Mumford is doing in calling a spade a spade.

All this is just a preamble to proposing a compromise. While Mumford favors DOD involvement in helping other nations reduce their rampant population growth, and Professor Lee opposes such a role for the Pentagon, both have already expressed their agreement that the United States is investing not nearly enough in its own self-interest and in the interest of all mankind, in helping deal with the world population dilemma. So if the DOD turns out to be unacceptable, for all of the reasons given, as the primary agency charged with providing population program assistance abroad, what about this compromise: that Congress enact the principle, and provide the funds to back it up, that whatever agency administers population aid--whether it be an international agency, a consortium or an agency of the U.S. government--be given funds equal to either 1% or 2% of the

88

Defense Department budget.

DOD's budget for the next fiscal year is likely to be about $130 billion. Present population funds for international assistance administered by AID are at the level of $150 million a year. So if, through the compromise formula I've suggested, population assistance funds were required to be just 1% of the Defense budget, this would elevate them promptly to $1.3 billion, more than an eight-fold increase in current U.S. overseas population investment. Of course, spending this amount of money effectively in the immediate future poses another challenge. The escalation of investment would need to be gradual. But, again, I would use the phrase, "It must be done with all deliberate speed."

My formula may not satisfy Dr. Mumford but it may seem more feasible and acceptable to Everett Lee.

EVERETT LEE: I certainly would like to see funds for population research and for whatever things are needed for population limitation increase greatly. I said so yesterday to the U.S. House of Representatives Select Committee on Population, and I believe that very strongly. It's extraordinary that, even when we agree that the implications of population growth and redistribution are enormous, we do so little to find out what it really means or to help people who would like to limit population growth do so. I agree with Mr. Best on the need for increased funding.

I would object to tying it to the Defense Department budget, however. For one thing, I would hope, as an idealist, that some day our Defense budget should go down. I doubt that but, at least in real terms or in proportion to the national income, I hope it would go down. At the moment I think that would be a very bad thing to have happen with whatever funds you're giving to population. On that score I agree with Dr. Mumford. Those funds need to go up, no matter how they are allocated or distributed.

DAVE ROBINSON, University of California: Mr. Chairman, the only reason that I'm here at the microphone is to thank Dr. Lee and Dr. Wogaman for the reassurance that the subject of the debate is a facetious one. I've been terrified by the twist this conference has taken this morning. It began with Dr. Cargille's suggestion that the President of the United States should lead the drive to curb world population and then proceeded to the suggestion that the Department of Defense should be the mechanism by which this is done.

I would like to strongly support the young lady who preceeded me at the microphone and say almost exactly the same thing, but perhaps in a different way. The reason why I think the President of the United States and his Defense Department would be least capable of pioneering this venture is because of the vast credibility gap in the way that the rest of the world views these two particular agencies.

89

During the course of this conference we've heard the term "nutritional need" and "effective economic demand" used in relation to food. And we've learned that calculating nutritional needs is quite useless because, in fact, _effective_ economic demand is the thing that swallows up the food resources, even when that effective economic demand comes from a cattle feeder who wants to feed feed grains to livestock. No one seems to have applied the same logic to population. There are two ways of calculating population: you can calculate it by head count, or you can calculate _effective_ population, that is, a person-equivalent in relation to the resources available. The biological resources that Dr. Cargille has stressed so much are presently monopolized by a very small segment of the world's population. If we were to look at the effective population, or the person-equivalent, there is one outstanding villain in the world, and that's ourselves in the United States. The U.S.A. does not have a population of 200 million; it has an effective population of 10 billion, in terms of the resources that are utilized. We've heard at this conference, for example, that even people in our own nation, the Hutterites, can survive quite well with ten children; but they do so at a much lower use of biological resources. We've heard from some young people from Tennessee who can live on a dollar a day here in the United States.

My question is: Suppose the United Nations took charge of this venture, rather than the President of the United States or his Defense Department; what would happen if the United Nations then suggested to us that we modify our lifestyle to bring it into line with the biological resources? In the debate it's been claimed that population is a national security threat to the U.S.A. I would like to suggest that the world at large views the U.S.A. as a threat to the rest of the world's population. We've heard over and over again in this conference that the most effective contraceptive is a rise in socio-economic status, not condoms or any other contraceptive method. But nothing so decreases the rest of the world's ability to raise its economic status as the monopoly of resources by one small segment of the world's population.

CHARLES CARGILLE: Let me say something about population as a national security issue and also something about Presidential leadership. In the first place, the National Security Council has already discussed this at the highest levels of government. Its reports are not available to the public because of the sensitivity of these issues, although limited portions have already been released to the press and discussed by leading columnists in the United States over the past sixty days.

Secondly, I would remind you that in 1969 the only Presidential address ever given in the history of the United States to the Congress on the subject of population was delivered by President Nixon. In that statement he recognized that the effectiveness with which this nation responds to the threat of global overpopulation, more than

90

any other single factor, will determine the future of our nation, and that we will be judged at some point in history on the basis of how effectively we have solved or have failed to solve this problem. Since the leadership of President Nixon in 1969, there has been a shocking silence from the American presidency for nine years. I personally believe that that statement to the American Congress was the finest act of the Nixon administration.

GODFREY ROBERTS, Rutgers University: Dr. Mumford's position essentially seems to be that there should be a sort of "war" against childbearing. I think it's important to look at the experience of specific countries which have made a crisis, war-time kind of response to the problem of population growth. Specifically, I'm referring to the mandatory sterilization program in India which seriously set back one of the oldest family planning programs in the world. Other countries in the same region, namely Sri Lanka, Hong Kong and Taiwan, have been referred to in this discussion as examples of countries which have successfully brought about declines in birth rate. But if we look at these countries it was basically development efforts which brought down their birth rates. I was surprised when the gentleman from the Environmental Fund referred to Sri Lanka's success in family planning as being essentially an incentive program. I worked in Sri Lanka's family planning program and it's fairly clear that it's based on education, health and other kinds of development experiences. I think we have to be cautious about making a war-time response to population because, instead of having a positive effect, it might backfire, as it did in India.

My second brief point is that instead of locating a U.S. attempt to coordinate world population in a defense agency, perhaps a development setting, such as HEW, would be more appropriate.

STEPHEN MUMFORD: What's being proposed is a humanitarian effort using the skills and abilities of the Defense Department. It is not a military effort that I'm proposing.

HARBANS SINGH, Montclair State College: I think the implicit reason for putting population programs under the Defense Department is that it is by far the most generously funded agency in the federal government. But I do not think we need to house population programs in the Defense Department. The real question is whether we can get the funds to implement the population programs we think necessary. A NASA-type agency which has been very efficient and highly organized, would be very desirable for implementing this program and it would be more acceptable to the general American population.

FRAN HOSKEN, Women's International Network News: How are you going to fund this, and who is going to vote for it? I think that settles the whole issue. I cannot visualize any U.S. citizen voting for this to begin with.

Secondly, the yearly statistics of the Swedish International Peace Research Institute (SIRPI) tell us that the U.S. is the largest exporter of arms by far and that the U.S. increase of armaments exports to developing countries is the largest in the world, nearly twice as large as Russia. So they have the money! If this money would be diverted to development, we would have all the problems solved on population and everything else.

One final observation: It is women who have babies, but the military establishment is 100% male in every country. Your proposal to control the reproduction of women by an all-male coercive military establishment is the most obscene proposition I have ever heard.

NANCY ERWIN, Jackson State University: I hope Dr. Mumford will end by defending the Defense Department in some logical way. Let me say personally, I was an anti-war demonstrator, my graduate studies were disrupted, I lost a job, my husband got blacklisted; this all came through the Defense Department. You don't have to go to Third World countries to find people who do not want to see power extended to the Defense Department. I've also worked in Latin America, and I have dealt with some of the military people who run those countries. I don't want to see them supported any more than necessary either. So what I'm asking you is how are you going to convince us that it would be pragmatic, efficient and effective to put more power in the hands of the people who gave us Viet Nam?

STEPHEN MUMFORD: It seems to me that one of the reasons why we haven't seen much response to the world population problem and the distribution of resources is that thus far we've appealed to ethical values that are low ranking in most people's priorities. For me, personally, these low ranking ethical values would be more than enough justification to act on these problems. When I came back from Asia, I did a great deal of work to find out what we're doing now, and where we need to go. I was appalled at how little we were doing and how poor the prospects were for doing a great deal more. Because of my own religious background I was extremely puzzled by this. After a year's thought, it occurred to me that appealing to these lower ranking social values was the problem, and that we were going to have to appeal to the highest ranking social value: namely, security-survival. It's unfortunate, but it's this way. Ms. Hosken asked, "Where's the money going to come from?" I believe that if the money comes, it will be only for one reason, and that's because we appealed to the highest ranking ethical value: security-survival, the security-survival of Americans. It's unfortunate, but this is the way it is.

With regard to Ms. Erwin's comments, I agree that the image of the military in the United States is a problem. But over the next few years, as we come to realize that world populaton growth is the number one U.S. security issue, I think we'll begin to view things differently. The image of the military can change. And when you start looking for workable alternatives, I don't think you're going to find any.

THE PATH TO ZPG

Sharon Frink

Zero Population Growth

The options for population change in the U.S. over the next 50 years vary from an increase of 28 million to 115 million people, depending on policies and programs adopted by our government (see Fig. 1). After careful examination of the options, ZPG has selected a course which will result in a peak U.S. population of approximately 243 million in about the year 2008, about 28 million more people than there are today. This goal can be met through balanced reductions in both fertility and immigration rates, with the emphasis on lowering legal immigration quotas and curtailing illegal entry.

The objectives of this policy call for a decline in the U.S. total fertility rate to an average of 1.6 children per woman by 1985, continuation of that pattern into the 21st century, and reduction of total immigration to an annual average of 150,000 during the same period. ZPG believes that this reduced fertility level can be achieved entirely through voluntary actions of U.S. citizens. Stricter policies will be required to cut total immigration to a manageable level.

The proposed balance between fertility and immigration was selected by ZPG in order to permit maximum freedom of choice for individuals in selecting their preferred family size and also to reduce stresses both here and abroad caused by immigration to the United States. Since World War II, the United States has actively promoted the "brain drain" of skilled persons throughout the world by encouraging their immigration. This policy has sapped the human resources of developing countries and has contributed to retarded economic and social development in areas where development is essential for slowing population growth.

The flow of illegal immigrants into the United States, estimated by ZPG at 800,000 annually, aggravates unemployment and contributes to increased costs of social welfare and education programs. It also takes pressure off other countries to cope with overpopulation. Allowing this situation to continue is neither wise nor humane. The proposed curtailment of illegal immigration and the reduction of legal quotas will help the developing countries to more

93

Figure 1

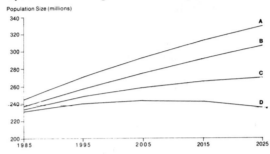

Options Concerning Future U.S. Population Size

Series A--assumes a total fertility rate (TFR) of 1.8 children per woman and annual net immigration of 1,200,000 continuing from 1975; present fertility and immigration levels assuming 800,000 illegal immigrants annually.
Series B--TFR of 2.1 by 1980 and annual net immigration of 400,000; assumes slight increase in fertility and elimination of illegal immigration.
Series C--TFR of 1.8 and annual net immigration of 400,000 from 1975; assumes no change in fertility and elimination of illegal immigration.
Series D--TFR of 1.6 and annual net immigration of 150,000 both by 1985; ZPG's recommended path which assumes a slight decrease in fertility and a substantial reduction in immigration.

effectively handle their own social and economic programs. The new quotas will permit the United States to continue its important role in providing asylum for refugees, homes for orphans, and the reunification of immediate families.

The following programs represent the primary tools which will bring a stable population through the informed and voluntary participation of citizens. The emphasis is placed on broader access to family planning information and services, the removal of restrictions affecting individual decisions, education, increased research, and effective governmental administration of policy goals and programs.

PROGRAMS TO END GROWTH

These programs are designed to end population growth around the year 2008. As national goals are established and modified in light of changing circumstances and future research, individual programs can be adjusted.

I. Fertility

Universal Family Planning Services. Family planning information and services should be available for all citizens by 1980 in order to permit individuals to make informed decisions concerning family size and timing. This will require a renewed commitment, together with sufficient appropriations by Congress and state and local governments.

An estimated 4.6 million low- and marginal-income women and 2.0 million middle- and upper-class teenagers were denied family planning services in 1975, because the services were simply not available. Although the number of women in their childbearing years continues to increase, funding for family planning services has stagnated at roughly half the level required to meet the needs of low- and marginal-income women.

Increased spending for family planning services results in almost immediate tax savings. For each dollar it spends now, the government will save two dollars next year in Medicaid and welfare payments. Further savings will continue for many years through reduced costs for food, housing, education, and medical care for the children of low-income families.

Contraceptives for Teenagers. Legislation is required at the state level to guarantee access to contraceptive information and services for teenagers and for the removal of existing restrictions.

The personal crisis and significant social problem of teenage pregnancy must be dealt with intelligently rather than encouraged by existing taboos and restrictions on the availability of contraceptives. One of five U.S. births is to a teenager, and teenagers account for half of all out-of-wedlock births and a full third of all abortions. An estimated four million teenage women (15-19) needed family planning services in 1975; only half were able to get help. Continued restrictions on the availability of contraceptive services (24 states have not yet confirmed the right of unmarried minors to obtain contraceptives), contribute to the health risks, limited educational and employment opportunities, and major social disadvantages faced by teenage mothers.

Availability of Contraceptives. Existing restrictions on contraceptive advertising, sales and display should be removed in order to provide individuals the opportunity to practice family planning. The Federal Communications Commission should play an active role in modifying the broadcast industry ban on radio/television contraceptive advertising.

Twenty-two states prohibit the sale of some or all contraceptives, 23 prohibit commercial advertising of contraceptives, and 27 prohibit the sale of contraceptives from vending machines. The result is that most states officially encourage millions of their citizens to have unwanted children, to spread potentially fatal diseases, and to relinquish the individual's right to plan family size.

Voluntary Sterilization. The individual should have the right to choose sterilization without restriction but with sufficient information concerning procedures, health risks and consequences for informed consent.

The lack of regulation and the fear by many physicians of liability in the absence of clear regulations have resulted in many unnecessary restrictions on the individual's right to choose this option.

Abortion Services. Under the guidelines established by the U.S. Supreme Court, state and federal prohibitions and restrictions should be removed in order that all women, regardless of income, can choose to have an abortion. Hospitals receiving federal funds should be required to meet the need for abortion in their areas. The current difficulties experienced by poor, young and rural women should be removed through federal action. In 1975, between 260,000 and 770,000 women needing abortion services were unable to obtain them.

Contraceptive Research. The federal government should encourage and adequately fund increased research and the development of new, safer and more effective contraceptive techniques.

The Commission on Population Growth and the American Future recommended a minimum annual funding of $150 million for reproductive and contraceptive research; in FY 1976, the total appropriated was $11.8 million. Private drug companies have reduced contraceptive research and development as a result of federally imposed pre-marketing tests and limited patent periods, and the public is now being faced with controversies concerning the safety of popular methods without being provided alternatives.

II. Immigration

Immigration Goals. ZPG recommends that immigration goals be established and reviewed in conjunction with national fertility progress. In order to reach zpg by 2008, ZPG recommends that total legal and illegal immigration be reduced to a five-year net quota of 750,000 by 1985 with future adjustments as needed. Immigration policy should protect developing countries from the loss of skilled workers and should continue to provide for the reunification of

96

immediate families and asylum for refugees.

Legal Immigration. The United States accepts the largest number of legal immigrants of any country in the world. According to the Census Bureau, the current annual rate of 400,000 would add 13.4 million people by the year 2000 and 48.8 million by 2050. Immigration is generally selective by age and influences the age structure of the total population; those admitted contribute to the total number of births and the demand for both skilled and unskilled jobs.

As highly skilled persons from throughout the world are drawn to the United States, developing countries lose the essential expertise required for advancement in such fields as engineering, medicine and economic development. This skill drain slows the progress of these countries which in turn further encourages the unskilled to seek illegal entry to the United States.

Illegal Immigration. The United States should move toward eliminating illegal immigration by providing economic aid and expertise for development programs in the countries of origin, by restricting employment opportunities of illegal aliens in the U.S., and by strengthening national border surveillance.

Between 1960 and 1975, the yearly number of illegal aliens apprehended in the United States has increased tenfold, from 70,684 to 766,600. The Immigration and Naturalization Service estimates there are between 6 and 8 million illegal aliens currently in the United States and another 500,000 to 1 million enter each year.

Since illegal aliens leave their native countries to seek greater economic opportunities here, the solution lies in assisting those countries with further development while removing work opportunities for illegal aliens in the United States. Combined with increased border surveillance, this approach will prevent illegal aliens from competing unfairly in skilled and unskilled labor markets, reduce educational and medical expenditures in cities where they congregate, reduce national welfare costs, and improve the U.S. balance of payments.

III. Education, Social Change, and Administration

Education in Population Dynamics. Nationwide curricula changes are required to include increased information on the implications of population dynamics, human sexuality, contraception, family life, parenthood and alternative non-parenthood roles. Adequate funding is required to implement these changes in all school systems.

Increased public awareness of population/resource trends is necessary for active, informed public participation in formulating and adjusting a long-term population policy. The limited funding allocated for these purposes falls far short of meeting the demand for information materials and technical assistance.

Research Commitment. Increased funding is required for behavioral and social science research concerning population issues and for demographic research necessary in tracking the progress of a national population policy.

The relationship between population phenomena and economics, resources, environmental quality and government services is an area requiring substantially increased emphasis if we are to understand personal fertility motives and implement effective programs meeting individual needs. Timely and accurate demographic statistics are essential in order to evaluate progress and determine the need for future policy modifications.

Equality of Women. The right of women to exercise free choice in selecting roles and lifestyles should be a basic component of a national population policy.

In addition to the many social and personal benefits of women's equality, substantial progress toward zero population growth can be made simply by permitting women to freely choose their roles rather than being consigned automatically to the role of motherhood.

Governmental Organization. Changes within the federal administration are required to ensure a coordinated, effective approach to the national population policy and to avoid problems of duplication and omission.

ZPG endorses the following recommendations of the Commission on Population Growth and the American Future aimed at improving the federal capacity to implement and coordinate various public programs affecting population trends:

--Organize a separate Institute of Population Sciences within the National Institute of Health;

--Establish central coordination of existing urban and rural development programs;

--Establish coordination of all population-related activities through a Population Growth and Distribution Office within the Executive Office of the President;

--Add demographic experts to staffs of related councils, such as the Council of Economic Advisers and the Domestic Council.

DISCUSSION

LUKE LEE, Department of State: You've outlined a very interesting national policy for U.S. population programs. Does ZPG have any position in regard to international policy?

SHARON FRINK: We're a nonprofit national organization dedicated to stabilizing U.S. and world population growth. Because we are a domestic organization; because as registered lobbyists we can be most effective with the U.S. Congress, we're concentrating on the much needed problem of a U.S. population policy, although we do have stands on world population.

RICHARD SCHWARTZ, College of Staten Island: Sharon, I agree with most of the things you said. But I wish your group was called ZPIG--Zero Population Impact Growth. I think if we were far less wasteful in America we could probably sustain more people.

My second comment is that I'd like to see something come out of this conference. It's good that people have a chance to express their ideas, but we've got to go beyond conferences to impressing upon our leaders how serious the situation is. The population is growing too rapidly, we're running out of oil, 50% of our petroleum is from foreign sources, pollution is increasing rapidly and we're more aware of the poisonous materials in it . . . the least we should do at a conference like this is to endorse resolutions on which we can all agree and see that they get to the public and the government. I'd even recommend that instead of continuing the discussion session everyone walk over to the White House to demand new policies to end the incredible wastefulness in our society. We can't keep doing business as usual.

SHARON FRINK: In response to your first suggestion that we form a ZPIG--Zero Pig--organization, I'd certainly endorse a spin-off group of that type. I hope you'd consider being its chairman.

About your idea of doing more than sharing ideas, I hope everyone here will endorse the concept of a national population policy for the United States. ZPG's recommendations, by the way, are not dissimilar to the recommendations of the National Commission on Population Growth and the American Future. I hope too that you'll join the National Alliance for a Population Policy which is now being formed.

KENNETH PIERS, Calvin College, Grand Rapids, Michigan: Ms. Frink, when I read your recommendations, I can't help wondering whether the contours of your program are far too narrowly drawn. It looks to me like you have sized up the U.S. lifestyle, the resource consumption system, and said, "Now we have arrived, and we want to maintain this. So we're going to restrict immigration policies."

This essentially says that poor people may look at us, but can't touch us. If this is true, it's both an arrogant and an indefensible position. It's indefensible because, in fact, our present lifestyles in this country have been extracted at the price of exploiting many of the poorer nations in this world, practices that we are continuing to do.

I think your project has got to get much more at basic structural reforms in our society rather than just saying, "Cut off population growth, and we'll try to maintain a quality lifestyle" (from which I gather you think we have one).

SHARON FRINK: I have no disagreement with what you said. The programs that I outlined are those which, after studies by internationally renowned scholars, were thought to be the most economically, socially, environmentally, and most of all, politically feasible to accomplish very quickly. Now you notice my programs talk about being instituted by 1980, so that within two generations we can stop our population growth. But, God knows, I don't think. population is an isolationist issue. The reason for slowing population growth is to make our other problems more manageable. Your concerns are absolutely valid, and I think everybody at ZPG--the staff, the membership, the board of directors and the sponsors-- shares them.

LUKE LEE: One of my functions is to brief American ambassadors about U.S. population policy. Recently, the Ambassador-designate to Gabon came to our office and asked, "What is the U.S. population policy in Gabon?" Now Gabon's population is about 525,000, one of the sparsest populations on earth; and yet, at the same time, it has some of the richest mineral natural resources on earth. The problem that Gabon faces is not overpopulation, but underpopulation which stems in part from infertility due to disease. What would ZPG's policy be in Gabon?

SHARON FRINK: ZPG has no policy on population in Gabon, but our basic position is akin to Congressman McCloskey's: reproductive freedom and higher quality of life for all. If a woman cannot conceive and she wants a child, then all means should be taken to give this couple what makes them feel happy. Reproductive freedom means just that, that those people who do not choose to have children should not be forced to, and those who do choose to have children should have the ability, the means, to do that. Unfortunately, I don't believe that's our problem in the U.S. That's why we concentrate on our problems here.

LUKE LEE: As a footnote to this, my answer was that the U.S. should help Gabon increase its population by sending medical assistance to eliminate the diseases which are the main cause of infertility. The name of your organization, Zero Population Growth, seems to oppose an expansion of population where it might be sensible.

100

ASLAM KAHN, Seattle, Washington: Miss Frink, during your speech you said there were 6 to 8 million illegal aliens in this country. I'd be interested in knowing the source of those figures.

SHARON FRINK: The Immigration and Naturalization Service.

ASLAM KAHN: Okay, now let me question that. The former Commissioner of Immigration, General Chapman, was asked the same question--"where did you get these figures?" He said, "This is what I hear in the press." To a person from the Third World like myself this talk of illegal aliens is very disturbing. To me it has racial overtones, especially for the Chicano population. I just can't accept the figures you gave of 6 to 8 million illegal aliens.

SHARON FRINK: Your point is well taken. There is no way that I know of to take an accurate census of people who are entering the country or living here illegally. We use whatever figures there are from reasonable people who try to gauge this. There have been estimates that illegal immigration is as high as 3 million a year, but we don't go that high. Just because we don't have absolute certainty doesn't mean there's no problem. And it's not going to go away if we ignore it.*

As far as racism is concerned, population people have always been accused of being racists or genocidal. It may be true about some of the zealots, but you're not going to find it at ZPG. For us it's not a question of who you are, it's a question of how many. I don't know if there were any other population groups represented in Congress last year when they were proposing an unequal distribution of immigrants allowed from the Western Hemisphere compared to the Eastern Hemisphere. ZPG testified that you've got to equalize it, that everyone has to have an equal chance to get into the U.S. So I beg to differ with you; ZPG just isn't racist.

SHIRLEY BAWDEN, Rockwell City, Iowa: I think your group must have started out in Iowa, and I'll tell you my reasons.

Iowa is mostly rural but we do have a few big cities, and a couple of weeks ago we **read** that Des Moines was going to close ten

---

*The issue of estimating illegal immigration into the U.S. was raised at the 1976 Capon Springs Population Policy Conference. Cynthia Green of ZPG cited Commissioner Chapman's hunch that 8 illegal aliens get into the country for every 1 who is caught. Since about 100,000 were caught in 1975, the estimate was that somewhere between 800,000 and a million had entered. Paul Bente, then of the Council on Environmental Quality, added that an independent consulting firm had made an analysis of illegal immigrants and concluded that the Commissioner's figures were essentially correct. See Key Issues in Population Policy (University Press of America: Washington, D.C., 1978), pp. 180-181.

elementary schools. Now, I know a lot of people at this conference
are educators. Pretty soon this is going to catch up on the university level. Has your organization thought about the impact of fewer
children on education?

SHARON FRINK: That's why we organized. Many of the problems
we face today are those which, ZPG feels, could be more easily dealt
with if we had a stable population. As demographers are fond of
pointing out, the baby boom is like a goat working its way through
a boa constrictor which has swallowed it. At each point you can
see the bulge as it moves from beginning to end. The baby boom babies
put an incredible crush on the baby food industry 20 years ago. Then,
as they grew, new elementary schools, new high schools, and new college buildings had to be added to keep up with them. It was harder
and harder to find work for all of them. And then, even though the
average number of children per family has declined, there were so
many more baby boom adults having children that another boom can be
expected. In another few years the pressure on the health care system as baby boom kids retire is going to be immense.

We believe that if the population is more stable you won't have
the major dislocations which cause so many social, economic and
political problems. We organized precisely to stop the boom and bust
cycle in population in the United States and to work for a stable
base for all our other decisions.

THE POWER OF FOOD

Mark Andrews

Member of Congress from North Dakota

More than 75 years ago, the U.S. reluctantly became a world power. The 20th Century saw us become the most productive nation in the world. The American farmer, particularly, through his labors and technical expertise, has made our ability to produce an abundance of food one of our greatest achievements. We produce food and fiber well beyond our domestic needs and are therefore in a position to help feed a world with serious food deficiencies. With our growing influence and leadership in the international community came additional responsibilities and obligations to pursue goals of global assistance and cooperation.

The specters of starvation and malnutrition have stalked the world since the beginning of time. But in the last quarter of the 20th Century, millions of people in the U.S. are still underfed and malnourished. With all our abundance and technology, it defies all logic that half a billion people throughout the world still live on the razor's edge of existence.

Logical or not, the problem is real. Fifteen to 20 million of us die each year as a consequence of hunger. Three-quarters of these are children. And at least 400 million people on our planet are seriously malnourished.

It's not much use to talk about solving the problems of hunger in the world unless we look first at ourselves. The foremost responsibility of our government throughout our history has been to defend our nation and provide for our national interest. In the complex world we live in, national and international goals often pull in opposite directions. Even when the basic goals are shared, there remain differences on plans of action and priorities.

During 1978 our country will face a multitude of policy decisions, both domestic and international, which are related to food production and distribution. This is of special interest to me as a life-long farmer and, of course, as a member of the House Appropriations Committee on Agriculture that has to set the funding level for that department. I certainly don't know all the answers to the complex

103

issues facing us, but I did benefit from some insights as a delegate
to the FAO in Rome and through subsequent trips to the Soviet Union
and the People's Republic of China.

As you know, the FAO is made up of 141 member nations, most of
which are food-deficient Third World countries. The opportunity to
have frank and open discussions with representatives of these nations
gave me an important and different perspective on the critical role
of food in the world today. It's one thing to sit over here, both
as a farmer and as a Congressman, and ponder our problems--prices,
production, operating costs, and all the rest--and quite another to
listen to people from all over the world who tell you that a loaf
of bread or a bowl of rice is the stark difference between life
and death.

I returned home from the FAO conference more convinced than
ever that if our nation has the wisdom, the compassion, and the will,
our food can be a more effective instrument in forging an enduring
peace than any military might we may conceive. We can't overlook the
fact that dozens of nations and millions of people desperately need
our food. Hungry nations are restless nations, often volatile and
potentially explosive. We've proved time and time again that food
is good peace insurance, far cheaper and more effective than planes,
tanks, and guns, and a lot less of a burden on the American taxpayer.

I make these positive points in favor of a sound farm export
policy knowing full well that any world food policy isn't worth
talking about, and not even possible to implement, if it's not firmly
rooted in a sound agricultural policy. It's sheer folly to talk
about delivering good nutritious food to American consumers and sharing our abundance with the rest of the world if American farmers don't
have the economic ability to produce that food, and produce it in
abundance. It's on the land and on our farms that any national and
international food system has its origin.

If American consumers expect to get a constant supply of food;
and if we continue to expect our food exports to keep bailing our
nation out in paying for imports of oil; if we expect to use our food
abundance as an instrument to create world cooperation and peace,
then the people and the nation must share the responsibility to
maintain a viable, productive and economically sound agriculture.

American taxpayers may not be aware of it, but they're subsidizing food consumption at the expense of agricultural production.
Although this might not be the intent of our policy, it's the effect
of it. For example, during this fiscal year, the USDA will spend
over $9 billion on domestic food programs, with only $3.7 billion
going for agricultural programs for farm research and conservation,
for investments, if you will, to build up the plant to nourish the
goose that lays the eggs.

Our national investment in agriculture has, over the years, given American consumers the best food bargain in the world. In most of the rest of the world wheat costs far more than $5 a bushel, and consumers spend a larger portion of their take-home pay for groceries.

In the meantime, our farmers have been encouraged to increase the quality and quantity of their food yields because of the government's commitment to cheap food for our consumers. And because of the fear expressed by thoughtful people in sessions like this all over our country that we couldn't keep up with the demand for food in a world that was getting smaller and smaller, we have a responsibility as a government and as individuals concerned about nutrition throughout the world to follow through and do something to address the economic stress now felt on our farms because of this call to produce. If we don't, not only farmers, but consumers as well will be sorely affected.

This is what's been happening. In the last ten years funding for agricultural research has not even kept pace with inflation. As a matter of fact, for fiscal 1979 the Administration has requested a reduction in funds for the Agricultural Research Service. This research is badly needed to increase crop yields and produce disease-resistant crops, and to study human nutrition. In the past two centuries in this country, and in other countries around the world, we've learned more about how to nourish pigs than how to nourish people. We simply haven't put the proper inputs into this all-important field.

At the University of North Dakota, which I'm privileged to represent as a member of Congress, we have the only ARS Human Nutrition Lab. The second one is going to be established in Tuskegee because our committee has been emphasizing this. In research done at the Human Nutrition Lab, they found that bran from hard spring wheat not only gives you the benefits of fiber in the diet but, for some strange reason not known yet, it reduces the serum cholesterol in your blood--if it's from hard spring wheat. They don't notice this from other winter wheats.

Just scratching the surface of things like this can make a vast amount of difference in the future for tens of millions of people all around the world.

And if you say, "Why should we be doing this?", let's contrast ourselves with the other super power. When I was in Moscow I talked with their minister of trade, their minister of agriculture and the deputy chairman of the Supreme Soviet. They're frank to admit that they've been putting their emphasis on agricultural production. They say, "We can't understand why your country seems to take it for granted." They're spending 28% of their government wherewithall for agriculture. They're going to bring 12 million new acres into irrigation by 1982. We're spending less than 2% of our government budget. If one super power thinks it's all that important, then why do we sit back and sleep and fail to realize that this is really where the future of this troubled planet is going to lie in the next two or three decades?

We also have to take a close look at needs abroad. We know we can't maintain a peaceful world, free of war, riot, and turmoil, when one-third are rich and two-thirds are hungry. We must use food as an instrument of peace. A starving Oriental child needs high protein wheat for sustenance, not a fifty caliber machine gun bullet. We need to raise food priorities and recognize food as our most powerful tool for peace.

As a responsible member of the Global Community, the United States must decide what its trade objectives are, how to implement them, what criteria to establish for food aid, and to what extent U.S. food should be used as a "diplomatic tool." I must say I get pretty tired of hearing our food spoken of as a diplomatic tool. I think far better would be the word "example." Our food productivity, the genius of our American farm families, is the best example we have to show that the American system works better than any other system around the world. In the slums of Latin America, as my wife and I found 12 to 14 years ago, when you're talking eyeball to eyeball with a mother of three or four children who are suffering from malnutrition, they're not too impressed with a man on the moon. And they could care less that we've got the atomic capability to knock the world out three times over. But they are impressed that we've got enough food to feed ourselves and quite a bit left over. I think that rather than using food as a tool or a weapon, we should use it as an example of what's best about our country, an example that we've really overlooked and failed to stress.

Since 1972 U.S. agricultural trade has become increasingly important to our country and food importing nations. American farmers produce far more food than our nation can consume. The farmer must export his surplus to maintain his income, and our entire society benefits from abundant, cheap food supplies and the favorable trade balance.

The statistics tell us, for instance, that for every billion dollars worth of food we export, we create 54,000 new jobs in the United States. And that makes an awful lot of difference to people living on the Eastern seaboard who don't know a steer from a heifer. It makes a big difference in our overall economy as well, not only because of the earnings overseas that pay for our imports, but because of the job opportunities right here at home.

Our exports of farm commodities are important not just to farmers, but to the viability of our nation itself. Agricultural exports have gone from $7.2 billion in 1970 to $24 billion in the last two years. Because of the importance of agricultural trade to the national treasury and the American public, U.S. policy should be focused on promoting exports and reducing international trade barriers. We need to see better, more aggressive international salesmanship of our agricultural products. There's really been too much talk and too little action in this field. Despite the importance of agricultural exports to our economy, the Administration has budgeted only $28 million for agricultural trade efforts this year. The same amount is budgeted for our industrial trade efforts.

Last year we exported $4.7 billion in industrial goods--the hardware, the jet aircraft, tanks, and all the other things--and we exported $24 billion worth of food products. I suspect that this indicates that it isn't our salesmanship that's moving the food products and probably we ought to put more emphasis on that side than on the other side.

As a member of the Appropriations Subcommittee that funds the State Department, I've been calling for greater efforts to expand foreign markets. I've also called for promoting our agricultural attaches to consular status in our embassies throughout the world. Most of the time when members of Congress go to embassy briefings, the Ambassador is flanked by military attaches, political attaches, economic attaches, what have you. But the agricultural attaches are generally kept out of sight, despite the importance of agriculture to the American economy.

The point I want to leave with you is that we've been granted a number of things over which we have no control--by the Lord, primarily; by the people who came before us to locate in this country; because of the type of climate and soils we have--we've been granted an abundance of food that we've taken for granted for far too long.

I think we may be entering a new era, an era where we don't take our food production for granted, where we are proud of it, where we set it out as one of the great gifts that the system that is America can share with the troubled world. If this gift is shared in the proper way, it can serve as an example to bring better understanding and closer cooperation among the nations of the world and lead to a better life for all of us in the future. I think this is the challenge that faces us. In facing that challenge, let me again emphasize, don't overlook the producer, the man on the land, because if he's not in a sound economic position, the food supply will not be there to stimulate discussions about how we're going to distribute it.

DISCUSSION

SURENDRA SINGH, Kansas Newman College, Wichita, Kansas: Congressman Andrews, I greatly commend you for your ideas. I very strongly believe that we have to go this route. However, I would like to ask you how much support you feel you have for using food as power instead of guns and tanks?

MARK ANDREWS: Our biggest problem comes in the apprehension the American consumer has that if we export wheat we'll somehow or other drive up the price of food here at home, and the American consumer is going to suffer.

Three years ago at the height of the Russian and Chinese wheat sales--actually our Asian friends bought more from us than the Russians did--there was a lot of publicity about the need for export controls. As a matter of fact, the pressure of public opinion forced the imposition of export controls, which I think was a tragic mistake. During that time you may remember seeing the head of the American Bakers making a statement on the evening news to the effect that "if these exports continue, a loaf of bread is going to cost $1.00." Well, I picked up the phone and called him and I said, "Now look. You know before there's a dollar's worth of wheat in a loaf of bread, wheat has got to sell for $65 a bushel. There's only 1¢ worth of wheat in a loaf of bread for every dollar a bushel that wheat's worth." He said, "That's right, Congressman." But he said, "You know we've got problems in our industry. The cost of the wrapping is going up, the cost of ovens is going up, labor is going up, the cost of delivery trucks is going up. We're going to have to raise the price of a loaf of bread, and we just thought that with all the publicity going to these overseas shipments we ought to kind of mention it now while the mentioning was good."

Well, this is part of the problem. I would suspect that, at the time of our exports to Third World powers and also to the Soviet Union, the PRC and Japan, that 95% of the consumers on the East Coast wanted an export embargo. They didn't know why. They didn't know really what the true cost-price relationship is, but they were demanding an embargo. That's why this type of a conference is worthwhile because public opinion has to be changed so that they do understand the economics of food production and food export policy, and how exports benefit them.

We're getting more sympathetic understanding from urban members of Congress, from both political parties, today with the American Agriculture Movement marching because suddenly they're beginning to think that maybe things aren't all right down on the farm. But it's been a long time coming. And farm organizations have been doing a whale of an awful lot more to confuse than to convince members of Congress by going off in seventeen different directions. You've got the super conservatives. you've got the super liberals, and you've got the moderates; and some are interested in merchandising grain, some are interested in selling insurance, and very few are really interested in a food policy. These are the farm organizations that for years have been speaking for farmers and for farm policy. So, we've got a problem, but it's one of public relations and better understanding.

108

CHARISSE HUTTON, Augustana College, Sioux Falls, South Dakota: I'd like to address a question to you about food as a diplomatic tool. When you speak of agricultural exports, I'm concerned because it seems that you're implying that exporting food for peace is good for U.S. trade only if it's economically advantageous for farmers. Do I understand you correctly?

MARK ANDREWS: No, I said that we ought to use our food to show that the productive genius of our system does work well; and, that we ought to make it available to all comers, but that there wouldn't be enough food if farmers were bankrupt and not able to produce. I think we need to realize two things: one, that a proper food export policy can pay great dividends in better understanding around the world; and two, that unless producers are kept in a viable, healthy condition, we're not talking about availability of food, we could be talking about a shortage of food.

CHARISSE HUTTON: But isn't this understanding of agricultural exportation still using agricultural exports as an economic tool?

MARK ANDREWS: You have to pay for the product you export. We can use our Food for Peace program to provide food at low interest, long-term loans to countries that can't otherwise afford it. But this is, again, one of the myths of food exports that ought to be examined and thoroughly discussed. Wheat, today, in the United States, brings $2.50 a bushel. In virtually every other nation in the world, it brings $5 or more a bushel. Fifteen years ago in Latin America, I was shocked when I found that corn, which is the basic food of the peasants in Latin America, cost three times as much in Latin America as it did back in the United States. It hasn't been the fact that food is high priced in America. Food is invariably low priced in our country, and it only begins to approach the price it commands in the rest of the world when there's a shortage.

I think we have to get out of this roller coaster type pricing system because each time you go down into the trough--with the American farmer producing below the cost of production, with farms becoming highly leveraged today, and the farm debt load higher than ever before--you come out of the troughs with a little bit less productive capability, and the overall supply of food in the world suffers because of that. Somehow or another we've got to address ourselves to getting an adequate price, maintaining the plant, and worrying about the terms under which we sell our food overseas based on the use of PL-480 and the rest. So, yes, I do make an economic plea for the American farmer, a plea that he not be selling below the cost of production because they're only 5% of us, and they can't afford to carry on their backs the cost of maintaining the only dependable food reserve in the world.

JONATHAN J. LU, geographer, University of Northern Iowa, Cedar Falls, Iowa: When I first read the title of your paper, I did not

think I wanted to hear it because of the idea of "food for power."
But after listening to you, I think you are moving in the right direction. I'm glad that you end up with the thought that we mustn't
forget the man in the field. Now, my question is, many farmers today
are facing very difficult situations--farmland prices are rising
rapidly, input costs are skyrocketing, some farmers are forced to give
up farming; what policy does the government have toward alleviating
these problems?

MARK ANDREWS: One of the biggest problems I think we've got today is how to pass the family farm on from one generation to another.
Farmland has been used for something new in the last decade, as a
hedge against inflation. USDA figures show us now that on the farm
the return on investment is about 1½%. Fred Richmond, a Congressional colleague of mine from New York, is on the House Agriculture
Committee which is concerned about the plight of the farmer. He said
he was all for low interest loans but when I asked him what interest
he thought would be fair he said 5 or 6%. I said, "Fred, there's no
point loaning young families money at 5% or 6% when they're only making less than 2% return on their investment. They'd be going behind
each year."

We have to address ourselves to this problem, but we have to do
it carefully. We can't do it by setting a $300,000 exemption on farm-
land transfer because people say, "Oh, gee, that's a fat cat."

I think what we ought to do is address our Finance Committees
and Ways and Means Committee with this suggestion: Why not value a
farm as we value an automobile dealership, a hardware store, a drug
store, or any other small business. When you sell from one generation to another, when the father sells to the son or the father dies
and the son inherits, the IRS figures that a small business that's
functioning well should produce a 13-14% return on investment, so
they say 8 times your net over the last 5 years is the value of the
property for an inter-family transfer. With farmland they don't do
that. And that's why the farm family is becoming the only family
that can't have continuity. If we move from a farm family type agriculture to a corporation type agriculture over the next 10 to 15
years because of high valuation of estates, we're going to have a
tremendous problem in getting an adequate food production.

Dad died in 1938 when I was 12 and those friendly bankers came
and foreclosed the mortgage. The only reason we've still got the
farm is because it wasn't worth what was against it, so they gave
mother back a contract for deed because nobody wanted it for the
mortgage against it. Now, that was a different situation. It was
typical not only in our family, but in a lot of other families all
through the upper Midwest. Today, suddenly the farm is worth more
parceled out than as a going entity, and if we're not wise in our
tax policy, we're going to find a single generation of farmland
owners who've turned into millionaires and no farm family tradition

at the turn of the next century. And that would be bad for America.
It's something we have to address and address quickly.

JOHN COATE, The Farm, Summertown, Tennessee: Since more protein
can be derived from an acre of soybeans by people eating the beans
directly rather than running them through the cow first, could world
food availability and U.S. food exports be increased by de-emphasiz-
ing eating animal protein as recommended in the U.S. Dietary Goals.

MARK ANDREWS: There's no doubt that more grain would be available if the world ate less meat. But you have to remember a number
of things. First, the beef animal can utilize an awful lot of roughage from a lot of land that can't produce soybeans and grains and
most of the protein we get in meat comes not from soybeans but from
roughage. Secondly, a lot of people in the world want to eat meat.
When I visited the Soviet Union I was told that their goal was to
provide a broader and a better diet to their people, and that meant
more and more meat. In fact, the reason they're buying feed grains
from us is to increase their production of meat.

I agree with you that we may come to a point where the arithmetic of world population growth and increased standards of living
may force us to do what you suggest. We know that the world's population of 4 billion people is going to double by the year 2010 or
2015. And we know that half the people in the world are eating the
equivalent of 700 pounds of grain per capita per year, while we in
the United States eat the equivalent of 2100 pounds per person per
year. We know that people in the underdeveloped countries are looking for a better and broader food supply, not a second automobile or
a second TV set. So if you increase the consumption of food in the
underdeveloped countries just to the point where they're eating half
as much as the average American, you've increased the food intake of
half the people in the world by one-third. Add to that the demands
of a doubled population by the year 2015 and you may come to a point
where it will be necessary for us to eat grain directly.

But the desire of people for a broader diet, for meat proteins
is still strong. As long as our choices are ruled by consumer preference, I think we'll have an animal agriculture. When the arithmetic of population vs. food supply presses in on us, when we can
no longer afford to feed animals grain, then we'll have to reevaluate.

111

POPULATION, FOOD AND ECONOMICS FROM THE
FARMERS' VIEWPOINT

Tony T. Dechant

President, National Farmers Union

The next world food crisis may be only a year or two away. I
say this even though world food stocks are now large enough to depress farm prices to levels which are causing a great deal of justifiable protest. It does not take much in the way of excess supplies to destroy farm prices.

World food stocks, indeed, are only moderately larger today
than they were before we got into trouble in 1972. Either a major
crop disaster somewhere in the world, or an unexpected rise in food
demand, could wipe out the current margins of safety and turn apparent surpluses into distressing shortages.

For four years now since the World Food Conference we have
been talking about a world food security system, but it exists yet
only in theory. We do not have a cushion against disaster and farmers in most nations are in precarious economic situations.

By allowing farm prices to persist at levels well below the
cost of production, the United States and other governments are taking grave risks on the adequacy of future food supplies. If the
U.S. government and others do not take measures to raise farm prices
and income above the cost of production, today's farm disaster will
turn into disaster for consumers as soon as the next year or two.

The population/food crisis could take a sudden and disastrous
turn by 1980, not at some far-off date 20 or 50 years from now. If
this disaster takes place, it will not be because we have reached
the limits of our resources or of our physical environment. It will
be because we have destroyed the chances for farmers to continue
producing the food products which the people of the world need.
Such a calamity, if it happens, will be due to lack of a comprehensive
food and agriculture policy.

We are presently doing a miserable job of feeding and nourishing the four billion people who inhabit our planet. A half billion

112

of our people are in varying stages of starvation, another billion are poorly nourished.

Certainly this gives credence to the doomsday prophecies which we hear from time to time. But we ought to make a distinction between calamities which are self-inflicted and therefore avoidable and those which can in no way be escaped.

Let me be clear about this. We recognize that we live in a finite world. We recognize that there are "outer limits" to our natural resources and our physical habitat. There will be a point at which resources cannot sustain a greater population under conditions tolerable to the human spirit. But our difficulties in the next several years, if they happen, will not be attributable to our having reached the outer limits.

The widespread hunger in the world today has not come about because we are constrained by lack of land, water, energy, labor or other resources. Those may someday be the constraining factors, but they are not at the present moment.

The constraints upon food production are political. They involve such policies as how societies treat their farmers, the economic and social arrangements in food production, distribution and trade, and the national policies relating to employment and purchasing power.

Presently we are using only about half the world's arable land for crop production. While most of the best land is probably already in use, some land could be brought into cropping if prices and returns provided a sufficient incentive.

Certainly, under optimum conditions, food output could be greatly expanded, on existing lands and on lands brought into crop use.

Some contend that the world can potentially feed a population as high as 30 billion. Others see fearsome difficulties if the population grows to 16 or to 11 billion. My own concern is whether we can overcome the formidable problems we may have feeding 7 billion people by the year 2000.

But my viewpoint has been colored by doubts more about the political will of nations and governments to cope with the hunger problem, rather than sheer lack of resources and physical capacity to feed ourselves.

Over a period of 32 years, I have had the opportunity for personal contacts with farmers and farm leaders from more than fifty nations around the world. I have had this opportunity through Farmers Union's participation in the International Federation of

113

Agricultural Producers, a global association of farm and cooperative groups. These contacts began in the post-World War II era when the IFAP was formed and have continued to these recent years in which I have had the honor of heading the international organization of farm producers.

Although there may be considerable differences in farm structure and agricultural technology around the world, farmers everywhere have similar problems, particularly as regards economic policies of their governments.

Two things hold back agricultural output around the world: the lack of effective food-buying power on the part of consumers, and the lack of a remunerative return to producers for farm and food products placed on the market.

Almost universally, farmers have a low priority with their own governments, even though adequate food production is recognized as an important goal.

It is popularly supposed, here and in many of the developing countries, that all that is needed is to increase food production in the food-deficit countries. But if nothing is done to augment the food-purchasing power of the population, the production of additional surpluses for markets that are already demoralized will accomplish little if anything.

It is not shortages of food which account for a half billion people in the world starving and another billion being malnourished.

The production of additional surpluses will not feed hungry people anywhere. The real and compelling reason that people are hungry is that they lack money to pay for the food they need.

Unless parallel steps are taken to provide remunerative employment for the citizens of the developing nations, efforts to expand food output will simply create even more desperate conditions for local farmers.

To increase effective food purchasing power, particularly to transform the food needs of the hungry and malnourished into cash demand, will require a combination of policies:

1. International economic reform which specifically raises and stabilizes the prices of raw materials exported from the less-developed countries.

2. International trade reform which permits more open access of labor-intensive manufactured goods from the developing countries to the markets of the industrialized countries.

114

3. Concerted public works and full employment measures in the less developed countries and in other countries having serious employment problems.

4. Aid transfers from rich countries to less developed nations in the form of loans, capital grants, technical assistance and food aid designed to stimulate economic development and employment.

To the extent that we can use these measures to create cash demand for food, we will ease the food/population relationship. Effective cash demand for food in the hands of the people of food-deficit countries will cause the needed food to be produced within that country or imported from elsewhere.

The real race in which we are engaged in this world of ours is a race between food production and food demand, rather than between food production and population.

For most of our lifetimes, food demand has run behind food production, and even further behind productive capacity.

Population growth in itself does not create food demand. In the less developed countries, it creates food needs, but it only creates food demand to the extent that the people have spendable income.

We face a dilemma, of course, if the economic measures to spur employment and purchasing power are not adequate or not successful.

If the poor, the jobless and the destitute continue to be in that situation, they will not have access to food even if it is available and plentiful, unless it is given to them as food assistance or on some concessional terms.

If we cannot reorder the world economic system so that the people of the world are able to earn their own basic food needs, there are two possibilities ahead, neither of them tolerable:

1. One is massive hunger and starvation.

2. The other is a world-wide feeding program of such a magnitude as to stagger the imagination. While current food aid programs help tens of millions of people each year, it is hard to conceive of the possibility that a global welfare feeding program could take care of the 500 million now in various stages of starvation, nor the millions more that will join the ranks of the world's poor in the coming years.

As a practical matter, it will probably not be possible for the major food producing countries to feed all the hungry of the world. It will take stronger food demand to bring forth the food

115

production which the world will need. As long as food purchasing power is lacking, it is pointless and futile to expand food output here or elsewhere.

My comments to this point have been rather negative about the hopes that the world will be able to satisfactorily feed itself.

But, supposing that a new world economic order or some other form of economic cooperation brings about a revitalization of the world economy and bring the poor people of the developing world into the economic mainstream. What will the prospects then be for the world to feed itself?

Obviously, with 70 million people a year being added to the world's population--the equivalent of another United States every three years--mankind has to be mindful that there has to be some ultimate limit. Eventually, the world's population will have to stop growing. But we could put off the ultimate crisis perhaps for several decades.

I have no doubt that under optimum conditions, with the needed incentives to farmers and strong food demand in the hands of con- sumers, we can double world food output in the next ten years and double it again by the end of this century.

Assuming that we will make some new breakthroughs in farming and food technology--and in solar energy technology--we can push back the time of doom for an undetermined number of years.

But I am not going to worry about the year 2025 or the year 2050. I think we ought to worry about humanity getting through the rest of this century. My major concern is that we are going to bring the ultimate crisis down upon our heads much sooner than it needs to be.

We are compounding the problems of mankind by the lack of farm and food policies, by the lack of enlightened trade policies, and the lack of positive employment measures.

There is still time to establish national and international farm and food policies. There is still time to launch a new era of international economic cooperation.

We can buy ourselves the time during which economic and social improvements can level off the population growth rates.

There are some inconclusive signs that the pace of population expansion may be slowing down. Part of this is attributable to family planning programs, but perhaps a large share to rising liv- ing standards.

116

But, even if we were to reduce population growth to a replacement rate, we are bound to grow in numbers before the total global
head-count peaks out at perhaps 10 or 11 billion people.

Through intelligent farm and food policies, we can buy the
time to make the population adjustment, to bring growth rates
within a manageable level.

Bringing down the population growth rate to acceptable levels
will also ease the pressure upon our food producing and distribution systems.

The International Food Policy Research Institute has made some
projections of the food deficit by 1990 in the market-economy developing nations.

The Institute projects that there will be a deficit of 142
million tons in terms of market demand and 185 million tons in
terms of quantities needed for dietary standards.

That total of 185 million tons is more than the entire current
volume of grain handled in world commerce. It is doubtful that
transportation or distributions systems will exist to handle such
a volume either of trade or of concessional shipments.

These estimates are based on the medium variant in world population projections. But, if the low variant is used (5% lower
than the medium variant), the food deficit would be as much as 18
to 20 million tons smaller.

In summary, a new and shattering world food crisis is in the
making. Surely, it is avoidable. But it will not be avoided if
we continue on our present course.

We recognize that it is vital to be working in every helpful
area; population planning, environmental protection, preservation
of soil and water resources, and reducing our dependence on fossil
fuels.

But, honestly, I cannot imagine that these problems will ever
become manageable until we have an effective farm and food policy.
And that has to start with the people who are to produce the food
if it is going to be produced--the farmers of the United States
and the world.

DISCUSSION

FRAN HOSKEN, Women's International Network News: I was delighted to hear you say that the problem of hunger is not a question of supply but one of demand; the poorest people are unable to buy the food they need to survive.

But to get at the real cause, I think we have to look at the ways in which we undermine subsistence farmers in developing countries. All the efforts made by the organized agricultural sector are directed towards the cash crop farmer. When you do this, you increase the problem of surplus and destroy the markets for food that is produced on a small scale by individual subsistence farmers who sell next door or in a local market.

Few people realize that, in Africa, for instance, 80% of the food that is eaten--as opposed to exported--is grown by women subsistence farmers. The women are now being pushed off the most productive land by cash cropping, which is to a large extent financed from abroad. Men do the cash cropping, women do the subsistence farming. The imbalance in local food consumption can be directly attributed to the fact that women are not given the tools, the training, or the assistance to increase their production. As cash cropping increases, women are being diverted away from the subsistence farming needed to feed their families in order to work, without pay, for their husbands.

This growing neglect of subsistence farming in developing countries is then translated into a decrease in nutritional standards among the poor. This vicious circle has generally been ignored, although the Protein Advisory group at the United Nations has recently published a report, "Women as Food Producers, Food Processors, and Food Growers," which I recommend.

TONY DECHANT: Your points about subsistence farming and cash crop farming are well made. In order to get balance of trade payments, some developing countries are forced to rely on cash crops for export. Part of the reason for this is that developed nations have raised the highest trade barriers against the one thing that developing countries have most of--labor intensive goods. If they could trade with us on a comparable basis, they would be selling their goods here and earning money. What would they be doing with this money? They would be buying food and they would be buying small machinery to increase production.

The world just isn't working at full capacity and that's why we're in a recession. After World War II we invested in Europe and Japan and we set off a great wave of trade. We can't do it alone this time, but we have to provide leadership to the other developed nations to coordinate a program that will mean full employment in both developed and developing nations.

UKO ZYLSTRA, Calvin College, Grand Rapids, Michigan: I want to express my appreciation for your remarks. They pointed to the real source of social problems in the world. I think it's a mistake to treat population as the source. It's not food vs. population; it's food production vs. food demand. What this means is that social justice, rather than carrying capacity, has to be the central motivating force of any policy that hopes to deal with the world's problems. We can't go ahead with specialized, scientistic, piecemeal approaches-- such as population control--when what we need is an integrated response to social injustice.

DALE BAWDEN, Rockwell City, Iowa: Dr. Cargille has spoken of having a goal for world population, but I think you have to learn to walk before you can run. If we concentrate on population control, I feel we aren't going to achieve a world in which all hunger is dissipated. They say that 500 million people are hungry. From what I've heard at this conference it seems like we have the ability to eliminate hunger if we work at it. Do you think it would be feasible to set the goal of diminishing hunger by, say 10%, in a given time?

TONY DECHANT: Of course we should have a goal of trying to eliminate hunger. When we met four years ago in Rome at the World Food Conference we set a goal of dealing with the most extreme hunger by setting aside emergency supplies. But, as I indicated in my remarks, that's still in the theory stage four years later.

We really have not yet come to grips with creating the kind of inventory that would get the job done. The truth of the matter is that even in the United States we do not have a food policy. In past years we've had a boom and bust policy of going all out in production and hoping to find a market for our goods. My biggest argument with Secretary Butz over the years is that he had no plan for dealing with good crops worldwide. The result is low prices in the U.S. and excess supplies. We haven't any place to put the food because there's no effective demand, and you can't create effective demand if there's no purchasing power. So if we are to reduce or eliminate hunger, it takes more than good wishes. It requires effective demand for our food and an effective way to get it where it's needed.

I think also we ought to be concentrating on the real problems of the world instead of the games some countries are playing of putting too much emphasis on military aspects. As Ms. Hosken pointed out, many small nations are concentrating on cash crops. Why? To buy military supplies. Why? To get into the endless race that goes nowhere, the weapons game in which the biggest developed countries pawn their outmoded military hardware onto the smaller nations.

119

We ought to be concentrating on the awesome challenge facing us between now and the year 2000 of how to accommodate another 2 billion people on this earth. There's no doubt in my mind that we've got the resources in the world to go 50 years and billions more people, but it means harnessing these resources and planning for the future now instead of drifting along.

STILLMAN BRADFIELD, Kalamazoo College, Kalamazoo, Michigan: In famine after famine it's the rural people who always do the starving. Whether it's a socialist or capitalist system, there's always been a tendency to tax the rural people by subsidizing food consumption in order to keep wages and the cost of living down in the urban areas. Financing industrialization by keeping food prices low seems to have a very high priority in underdeveloped areas. The political realities are that the urban poor are the ones who can organize to bring down a government, while peasants generally don't have that power. So politicians worry about keeping the prices of basic goods down no matter what happens to the farmer. Do you favor a policy of slowing down the rate of industrialization in order to get food prices up and keep more people in agriculture, or should we continue to subsidize urban consumers?

TONY DECHANT: I'm opposed to continuing what we're doing because it isn't working. We have 6% to 7% unemployed and 3% underemployed. The problem in this country as well as worldwide is a lack of purchasing power

But I don't think we ought to slow down one sector of the economy at the expense of the other. The National Farmers Union has always advocated that farmers should be on par with other segments of society. And that calls for 100% of parity. I reminded President Carter last week that the six non-war years out of the last 35 years when farmers were at parity were the best ones for America. There were adequate supplies of food for the consumer at reasonable prices, farm costs were managable, and America was working. When you have a cheap food policy that makes the farm segment of the economy pick up the costs of inflation for the industrial sector, sooner or later things are going to go out of kilter.

CHARLES FLUEGEL, Lutheran World Relief, New York City: I wonder if I might make a general comment about some of the prophetic proposals I have heard at this conference. First, I think we need to be much more explicit about carrying capacity. As far as I can tell we just do not have much good information about the actual limits of either population or resources.

Secondly, I'd like to challenge the thesis that the problem is all over there. I think the problem is right here in the United States. Unless we take steps to set population and food policy targets here, we have no business addressing world population and food policy. If we are to make any suggestions to President Carter, I think we ought to start with food and population policies for the United States. Then some of the models which we work out for ourselves may become models which could be used for world population and food policies.

120

FAMILY FARMS AND A FULL, FAIR PRICE--TWO PILLARS OF AMERICAN FOOD POLICY

Ann Bornstein

National Farmers Organization

We here in the United States are extremely fortunate that by accidents of history, timing and placement on this earth's surface, our country developed in a manner that was not only unique, but absolutely ideal. Our populations in the early years of the country were small. We had endless land and resources. Many of the early settlers in the country turned to agriculture and tilling the land in such a manner that our country has never, in its entire history, really known food shortages of the type and scale that are experienced in regular cycles in many parts of the world.

Through the years, farming in our country has changed with the times. It's become more mechanized. We have, in turn, become much more dependent upon fuel, fortunate enough that, until very recently, the livelihood on America's farms was good, and it provided our country and many parts of the world with abundant and good quality food.

Boom and bust cycles, cycles of export demand, and price fluctuations are not new to the American farmer but, in recent years, there have developed patterns of these cycles which are relatively new and which are very difficult to cope with, especially in terms of developing an overall food policy for the United States.

In the spring and summer of 1972, during a time of temporary short crops in many parts of the world, temporary and localized droughts in the Dakotas and elsewhere in our own country, and long-term changes which were taking place in northern Africa, in the Sahel, and other places in the world, two situations developed simultaneously which have a very strong bearing on the feelings of farm people that are being vociferously expressed now.

First, we had the Russian grain sale, an unprecedented single sale in our country to another single purchaser. More than 12 million tons of wheat, approximately one-quarter of our total supply, was sold to the Soviet Union in 1972. Prices for wheat and coarse gains skyrocketed as a result. The farmers prospered, and while

121

there has been criticism of the Nixon Administration for encouraging farmers to plant fence row to fence row, the bottom line--the reason why farmers responded with bumper crops between 1973 and 1976-- was because the price situation was good. The incentive was there. Land which had not been arable for years was put back into produc- tion, extra money was spent on more fertilizer to make this land pro- ductive. Much of it was marginal land; much of it still is marginal land. But the American farmer felt that it was worth it at the time.

What we know today about world population growth was given a great deal of coverage, and most American farmers felt that the need for food would not die, that demand would not decline, that all they could produce would be needed and sold throughout the world.

The second thing that happened around the same time was the oil embargo, which simply underlined a growing crisis condition in the availability of fuel reserves and fuel resources. Although farmers felt its immediate impact, it is only recently coming home to roost as far as the farmer's cost situation is concerned.

Fertilizers and all other costs of farming that were related to fuels or petrochemicals of any kind increased greatly. Fertilizers, which had cost $85 per ton in 1971, cost $175 in 1974. Anhydrous ammonia went from $79 a ton in 1971 to $229 in 1974. As long as the farmer's price for his product was good, he could bear those costs, still earn a living, and everything remained relatively evenly balanced until about a year ago.

Even in the face of continuing world population growth, even in the face of the continuing need for food, we saw a decline in the demand for our crops. Other countries' food production increased. Bangladesh had a record rice crop 2½ years ago. Almost all countries which were normally food importing countries for the first time in years had sufficient supplies of their own, so that while our far- mers in the United States had been producing record crops, demand slumped. Their tremendous production costs, which had been an un- easy but relatively hidden burden during times of good prices, came home with a vengeance. Land prices had escalated during that peri- od at an unheard of inflationary rate. The American farmer's debt load has risen to the point that many bankers are concerned that the amount of equity farmers now have is too low. For the farmers bor- rowing through the Farm Credit Administration, which is not the total farm population, but for that particular sample group, recent figures show that the average age of borrowers is approximately 47-48 years old, and that their equity and their holdings is only about 46%. The farm debt that they're bearing now is over $800 billion.

It is an uneasy situation because while the farmer has been more and more exposed to marketplace pressures of boom and bust cycles, they are less and less protected on the built-in costs of doing their business--growing food. Some have criticized the farmers' purchaases--buying new equipment and more land--back in the period of 1972-73-74. However, at the time these things were done, it appeared that such purchases were well justified. I think that time will prove that indeed they were justified. Eventually, the world will need all of these supplies and more. But now these supplies of grain bear down on our Administration, our Government, our Treasury, and our individual farmers as an excess burden, as a financial handicap. It will take time even if demand picks up to work off the supplies that we now have on hand. We have approximately a full crop and a half--in the neighborhood of 192 million metric tons--in storage on farms in what we call the pipelines right now, being paid for by farmers, by the American Government, the taxpayer of the United States. It is a heavy financial burden.

Now, how do we extricate ourselves from this particular quagmire so that the second pillar, the fair price to the farmer, can be reinstituted and so that our production of food can continue unabated without fears that their very production will drown them in debt?

I recall that when Bob Bergland was before the Senate committee for his confirmation hearings as Secretary of Agriculture, he made a statement in answer to one of their questions that I thought was something we need to bear in mind. "The need for food in the world is tremendous. It will grow. There is no doubt about that. But need is not equivalent to market demand. And that market demand and the price that the market will return to the producer is the incentive which will draw forth the continuing needed supplies of food." At that time Bergland stated that one of his chief goals as Secretary of Agriculture would be to develop as many programs as possible to translate that need into market demand.

I feel that the current Administration, many groups, many parts of our economy, are working together in order to solve the problems of food, price, and population. Some of the answers are in the Food and Agriculture Act of 1977 and in programs that are now on the books. While the cost-price squeeze is at a negative low right now--they are paying more out than they are getting in--even with the programs already on the books that situation may ease a good deal over the next eight to ten months. The 1977 farm bill's provisions need time to work through the system. The 1976 loans will expire at the end of February. Crop loans for 1977 are now being made, and as a matter of fact, the Department of Agriculture will soon have figures on how much of the new crop was put under loan and put into the three-year reserve program.

I would anticipate that a great deal of the 1977 crop is under loan. The program that was instigated for the three-year farm owner controlled and farm-stored loans is a very critical issue to be considered by those concerned with future supplies of food because if indeed the low price cycles now experienced by farmers are going to

123

bring on shorter supplies, which would be the normal process, then the fact that some of the 1976 and 1977 crop is going to go under a three-year storage program will be essential to supply food at a time when it will be desperately needed; and in three years' time, it very well could be.

The way the program is set up, much of the storage cost is borne by the Government, but it should secure and reassure the world and the American population that our supplies are in hand and available when we need them.

Higher farm support prices contained in the new 1977 farm bill are just beginning to be felt by the American farmer. Payments for last year's crop went out within the last 30-40 days. The President has directly resisted recent efforts to raise those support prices. The fear is that it is a known quantity, that if those support prices are raised even a little, retail food prices will go up. There is no doubt about it. It's happened too often in the past. We know what will happen; justified or not, that's the way it goes.

By denying these requests, the Administration has alienated many farmers. Unfortunately, that will not keep retail food prices from going up. The prediction is that for the coming year of 1978, our food prices at retail levels will rise between 4% and 6%. [Editor's note: In April, 1977, USDA revised the figures to 8 to 12%.]

The other avenue to pursue is the promotion of export sales. Just recently the United States Department of Agriculture put out a release on the measures that they have taken to increase our export sales, to bolster the demand for farm products. We do know that our earlier midsummer estimates of the rest of the world's crops were wrong. They were too high. The rest of the world has not produced as much as we thought they would, especially Russia and Australia. Much of their crop was damaged or the quality was considerably lowered by weather conditions at the time of harvest.

One measure the USDA has recently taken to increase overseas sales is to double CCC export sales financing to close to $2 billion. The other measure that is being taken is increased pressure during world trade negotiations to assure that prices set for agricultural products will have some chance of returning a fair price to the person who produced them.

We have had, in the past, negotiated rates of exchange for agricultural products. They do not exist right now in our country in a similar manner to what was once known as the International Wheat Agreement. Every effort is being made at the current time to put something similar to that old International Wheat Agreement into effect.

In recent negotiations, efforts are being supported to once again set ceiling prices and floor prices for wheat and other food grain products that are traded on the international market. Unfortunately, in trade negotiations, agriculture often gets the bottom rung of the ladder and the least consideration. We have no assurance that these efforts will be successful. Most American farmers in our organization, at any rate, seem to feel that it is essential that these negotiations be successful.

Aside from these measures, the one thing that most of our members have constantly reiterated over the last four or five years is that before public officials and others make speeches about how many bushels of wheat we have to sell on the open market and how much food production we can supply the world, we must remember that it belongs to the farmer at this point and that it must be bought from them first.

Many of our members, and most farmers today, would remind us, I think, that the core of charity is justice and that there cannot be charity without justice. With just and fair prices to the farmer, we will ensure the solidity of the foundation of the family farm structure and the increased food production which farmers are capable of rendering to our country and to the world.

DISCUSSION

FREMONT REGIER, Bethel College, North Newton, Kansas: I want to thank you for your excellent presentation and ask two questions about the future of the family farm in America. Would you comment a bit on the relationship between the increasing indebtedness that our family farmers are experiencing and their future. Who finally will actually own the farming production in the country if indebtedness continues to increase at the rate it has? Secondly, would you comment just a bit on the efficiency of the small farm versus the large farm in terms of manpower, production per acre, production versus energy and employment concerns.

ANN BORNSTEIN: If you don't mind, Mr. Regier, I'll answer the second question first because it's the easiest. The single-family farm is the most efficient production unit that we have in our country. Two or three years ago the United States Department of Agriculture put out a very good summary on this point, "The One-Man Farm." Any further economies realized by larger units are simply economies of scale. They are not real economies.

Some short term economies of production, which I view as false economies, can be achieved by what we call "deep pocket financiers," who can afford to produce food at a loss for other reasons. But in the long term that is not an efficient process for producing food. Most of these are extremely large corporations which control resources, supplies, distribution, retail outlets and processing plants in two or three different major product lines throughout the country. Such corporations as Greyhound Bus and Sun Oil own and operate farm land. They do make economies of size because they also own their own oil and build in only a 2% margin when they buy from themselves instead of the 8% that you or I would have to pay. But these are short term economies; if the corporate structure prevails over the single-family structure, then ultimately they will no longer provide us with that false economy of scale, and we'll pay the difference.

As to who will own, it's a toss-up. The family farm system is under pressure. Many businesses may not want to buy land for production of food, but simply as land investment. I don't know who will own the nation's farmland in the future.

KENNETH PIERS, Calvin College, Grand Rapids, Michigan: Ms. Bornstein, you referred to the demand for American food in the marketplace and contrasted that with the demand that there actually is, what we might call the biological demand for food. Now, my question is this: Is not the increasing reliance on capital and energy-intensive agricultural practices in the United States guaranteeing that economic demand for our food products will be limited to the other wealthy nations in the world, thereby removing our food from the grasp of the most needy nations in the world? I guess I question the assumption that the American food system is the best bargain that the world has.

ANN BORNSTEIN: You're quite right that, because of our higher labor and production costs, we do risk being too expensive for many other countries. But it's the same problem with all of our products in international trade, not just agriculture.

In regard to energy intensity, the demand for more and more food in the world requires a certain amount of dependence on fertilizers and mechanization. But even now the cost of fertilizer, machinery and petroleum is already driving many farmers to alternative production methods. Wealthy California vegetable growers, for instance, are already consulting very high priced people to come in and tell them how to get this bug to eat that bug.

GINA COLETTA, the University of Pittsburg: You were talking about higher support prices and putting pressure during trade negotiations to get higher prices for the export products. As a point of clarification, I was wondering why these are the things we hear all the time when the farmers are having difficulty; why is their quarrel never with agribusiness? Is it because it's easier to tackle the Government than a corporation that takes the product and distributes it?

126

ANN BORNSTEIN: Yes, I think that is exactly the reason. It's even easier for farmers to tackle the Government than it is for Government to tackle agribusiness. I think farmers believe they can make the greatest impact on the political system.

I didn't make any kind of an organizational pitch here because I didn't believe it was the proper forum, but the National Farmers Organization differs from other farm organizations in that we do not feel a fair price should come solely from the Government. We believe that farmers themselves have an obligation to themselves and all other farmers to organize in such a way that they can begin to apply the traditional market pressures to get what they feel they need, from agribusiness or whoever their normal purchasing channels are. For the past 23 years we have been organizing farmers in a method somewhat similar to labor's organizational methods, in the sense that we have tried to collectively bargain for our products--for wheat, milk, barley, oats, whatever--so that we can get prices which reflect what we had to pay to produce these products. In some regions, it has worked. We have some very good contracts with regional slaughter houses and packing plants. Our milk programs are very, very solid and going very well. Grain is the traditional problem and probably always will be, and it is the problem to which I addressed myself most today, because it is basically these farmers that are hurting so much right now. Most other prices are not as bad.

UKO ZYLSTRA, Calvin College, Grand Rapids, Michigan: I'd like to pursue that last question a bit more. I guess I was a little bit surprised that you didn't really address yourself to what seems to me the most basic problem of the small family farmer, namely the competition that he has from agribusiness contract farmers and corporate farmers. Price supports and the other government programs really don't benefit the small farmer; in actuality most of that goes to the corporate farmers. So it seems to me that your organization should push the government to tackle the problem of the influence of the agribusiness and contract farmers on the farmer's situation.

That leads me into another related area which ties in with Lester Brown's comments. He pointed out a number of stresses on our croplands, one of the most dangerous being loss of soil fertility. Even though right now we are extremely productive in the United States, the fact is that our top soil is rapidly being lost. Iowa, for example, which used to have 12 inches of top soil, now has 6 inches and is likely to have 3 inches twenty years from now. This loss in soil fertility is, to some extent, attributable to the farming methods (cash crops, monoculture, excessive use of fertilizer, etc.) which are promoted by the corporate type of farming. It seems to me we have to come to grips with a different kind of policy which more directly than what you've outlined supports the

127

existence and the continuation of the family farm, especially since it is the most efficient. So my question is, are we simply interested in making more money or are we really concerned about food production and the maintenance of a way of life? In other words, we have to begin to assess the role of farming in our society.

ANN BORNSTEIN: In our organization I try to avoid the term "small farms" when I mean a family farm because the question of small versus large, profit-making versus nonprofit-making (whether that's intentional or not), is an area that is difficult to define and understand.

I do not believe that a euphemistic attitude toward farming as a way of life is going to sustain family farms. The livelihood must be there to support the way of life.

I don't know how else to address some of the questions you raised. I believe that the soil fertility problem is a serious one. I must say that for a number of years the extension services and the land grant universities have not done the ordinary, moderately sized commercial farmer who makes his living at farming a great deal of justice in the type of incentives and programs they have developed. I feel that it will be addressed and will turn around. These things do take time, but I believe the trends are in place which are forcing farmers to be aware of the problem.

Another big problem that is even more closely tied with population than soil fertility is land use, and the amount of good arable land that is being used for housing tracts, airports and shopping centers, and that is a serious problem. We will address and we will improve our soil fertility problems long before the nation will have either the political guts or the understanding of the problem to attack the larger issue of land use. And, unfortunately, there are many farmers themselves who do not understand some of the dangers that they suffer by not having a reasonable land use policy.

ELIOT GLASSHEIM, Population/Food Fund: You spoke of organizing farmers to get better prices for their goods. Is there any practicality in organizing farmers to get direct contracts with consumers rather than going through middle men? Is that simply impractical or could a slow change in our whole distribution system actually help farmers? Couldn't I, as a consumer, make a yearly contract with a farmer, give him more money, and save me some money from my supermarket price? Or is that impractical?

ANN BORNSTEIN: Because we did not think it was impractical, three years ago NFO had what we call "direct meat and cheese sales." We had some here in Washington. We had some around the country. I'm sure Des Moines had one. About 120 cities all told had them, many of them very small towns in New Jersey, upstate Maryland,

128

upstate New York. I personally handled a lot of the red tape involved in selling an agricultural commodity on the streets of Washington, D.C. by unlicensed people to the general public. And it
wasn't any fun. It took two weeks of intensive effort, but the
positive response on the part of the general public was almost mili-
tant in nature. It was a wonderful response.

The problem is that there are very few commodities which a farmer could sell directly without going through certain processing,
grading and safety standard inspections. Most of us as consumers
would not want to bypass many of these points in our food chain.
We would see resurgence very quickly of many of the health problems
that have long since been eradicated from American life. When I
was very young I lived on a military base in Trinidad for a year
and we were not allowed to buy food outside the military base.
It had to come from the United States. Diseases of all types were
very prevalent down there. I personally knew people who had lost
three and four children because of ignorance and negligence on the
part of their system.

Aside from health and safety, another big problem is that farmers need a large and steady volume demand on the other end. But I
frankly believe that it is feasible to deal with such operations as
the Cherry Dale City Consumer Coop outside Washington. Those people
buy in large quantities. Chicago also has a self-help group of
mainly very low income people which buys truck loads and semi-loads
of fruits and vegetables from the South during the winter. I do
think it's feasible. I don't think many people understand the tremendous amount of coordination and work that would be involved in
the middle, no matter how you structure it. There are a lot of
nitty gritty problems. But once these are overcome, I think there's
a tremendous untapped market for farmers.

POLICIES AND DEVELOPMENT OF THE
UNITED NATIONS FUND FOR POPULATION ACTIVITIES

Joseph A. Cavanaugh

Population Consultant, Bethesda, Maryland

UNFPA has its roots in the past work of UN units concerned with demographic statistics, training, technical assistance and research. These functions were very important, because they called to attention and evaluated an emerging and serious imbalance between population numbers, distribution and resources necessary to maintain and improve standards of living.

In 1967, a trust fund was established by the UN Secretary-General for support of additional demographic activities. The Trust Fund began with a contribution of $100,000 and grew in a year to a million dollars. The Trust Fund was then transferred to UNDP with resources of $2.5 million. Governments were invited to make contributions and, in late 1972, 52 nations participated. UNFPA was changed to a semi-independent fund of the General Assembly and government council of UNDP, subject to policies of the Economic and Social Council.

The policies, aims and purposes were:

(1) to build up capacity to respond to population and family planning needs;
(2) to promote awareness of population problems;
(3) to offer, at a country's request, technical assistance;
(4) to play a leading role in coordinating projects among the UN participating agencies, WHO, UNICEF, ILO, etc.

The objectives included a new dimension, not previously employed by the UN, i.e., family planning assistance. This was apparently a recognition by the UN that growth rates were dangerously high and that it should encourage efforts to lower them by attempting to change the demographic structure of less developed nations.

However, in its declaration of objectives, alteration of the demographic structure, especially lowering growth rates, has never been considered a strong objective. Thus, subsequent goals of UNFPA have been expressed as a "recognition of population problems, promotion of population planning and policies, promotion of family planning in the interests of health and well-being." Admittedly, UNFPA has had many constraints, including the sovereign right of each nation to determine its own population policies and assistance needs, a forced neutrality by UNFPA in respect to population policy, and freedom of choice by any family to have as many children as they wish. These constraints have greatly diluted implementation of the policy of reducing fertility and population growth rates.

While UNFPA is an efficient and well-run bureaucratic organization under the direction of Rafael Salas, its ability to affect fertility rate reductions and population growth rates in the developing nations is seriously limited. This stems from basic philosophies and policies which underlie the conception of population problems held by most underdeveloped nations and the leadership within the UN specialized agencies.

Growth rates and fertility levels in the Third World are still high. Some have increased sharply within the past ten years, depending on what statistics one is willing to accept. The overall crude birth rate in some other developing nations has remained virtually unchanged over the past decade, with the exception of a few small countries and islands where birth rates have declined. UN data indicate that crude birth rates as well as growth rates in some countries may have been increased, especially in some countries in Africa, Latin America and Eastern Europe. More importantly, the absolute number of people being added to many countries of the world is now greater, with a few exceptions.

Current efforts to assist in solving the population problems are complicated by emphasis on only "acceptable" projects which are usually health related. These activities often rely on (1) family planning associated with maternal-child health programs and (2) overall "development." Both are based on erroneous assumptions for reducing growth rates. Voluntary family planning, i.e., the provision of contraceptives and birth control information to couples, does little to reduce desired family size, which among Third World people remains at its traditional level of between 4-6 children and more than 6 in Africa. Should family planning be "100% successful," the world's population growth rate and crude birth rates would result in a population problem almost as serious as ever because family planning, under the current UNFPA definition, is voluntary and allows couples, rich and poor, to have as many children as they want, whatever the reason.

Development is a long process requiring tremendous capital output by both developed and less developed countries. Dependence on "development" for population growth rate reduction is a dubious solution because of the uncertainty of the result and the great increase during the period of development. In at least one country, Mexico, development has occurred without subsequent decreases in rates of growth.

UNFPA needs to take advantage of its strategic position and capitalize on past experience and reputation to move into a radically new assistance phase. It must redefine and more clearly state its objectives from those that "promote awareness of population problems and family planning" to those that are much more directly related to rapid changes in the rates of growth. UNFPA must eliminate contradictions in its own policy formulation.

It must insist on strong national population policies for reducing population growth as a prerequisite for receiving assistance. UNFPA should require that their funds, of which about 25% are USA contributed and 95% American and northern European, are for alleviating population pressure and not for improving maternal-child health or other developmental infrastructures. Any beneficial side-benefits are welcome but incidental to the central objective of reducing growth rates. UNFPA has constantly stated that project requests outstrip available funds. This is because some country project requests are only marginally related to reducing population growth. It is very possible that the existing fund ceiling is sufficient if only those projects are approved that definitely relate to changing the demographic structure.

The funding of health programs where family planning is merely an appendage should be reexamined and evaluated. There is always a possibility that funds intended for population activities become so commingled with the promotion of improved health that it is difficult to know what is used for health vis-a-vis population, even if one accepts the dubious proposition that family planning will contribute to reduced growth rates.

UNFPA assistance policy provides for maternal-child care and reduction of infant mortality as a condition for subsequent fertility decline. No research findings thus far support this theory. Thus, it finds itself supporting a policy with millions of dollars that has little scientific merit for reducing fertility.

Although the effects of migration on growth rates are receiving more attention by UNFPA than previously, very few resources are being given to this problem, which some countries perceive as more important than high rates of natural increase.

UNFPA has spent too much of its funds and resources on family planning programs and reducing infant mortality. It has not taken the lead in warning us all of the problem of population growth--both in rich and poor nations; it has not initiated or proposed programs

132

for reducing desired family size; it has not clearly spelled out--in stark economic terms--the catastrophic consequences of continued population growth that await many countries in but a few short years. Its task is immense. In reality, it cannot do more than its member nations want to do themselves. But it can take the lead in showing us the way. If nations will not follow, UNFPA can do little more.

THERE IS NO PLAN FOR SOLVING THE WORLD POPULATION
PROBLEM--A CRITIQUE OF THE TRADITIONAL
A.I.D. POPULATION STRATEGY

Charles M. Cargille and Eliot Glassheim

Population/Food Fund

The Agency for International Development is the leading population control body in the United States and in the world. One would
expect to find a carefully detailed plan published by AID for bringing world population growth within supportable levels.

Strangely enough, no public documents specify AID's plan. But
there are several sources from which one can piece together AID's
goals, objectives and strategies. The first is a one-page note published in 1969 by Dr. R. T. Ravenholt.[1] This is still the clearest
statement of many aspects of the AID strategy.

Based upon that publication, the goal of the AID program is to
improve the health, well-being and economic status of people in
the developing countries. Its objective, taken from this text,
appears to be that of improving the conditions of human reproduction
in these socities by support of broad gauge population and family
planning programs. Its strategy is "To make family planning information fully available to all elements of these societies," and the
same for family planning services. In this initial statement there
is no time table, budget or manpower estimate.

Somewhat greater detail is reported more recently by Dr. Ravenholt in his 1975 address to The World Population Society.[2] In that
text, the strategy described is to provide essential international
assistance for population and family planning for about 10 years at
a total average cost of about $1 per capita over the entire period
of ten years, during which time the following objectives would be
achieved: (a) appropriate population policies within each country;
(b) country-wide availability and use of fertility control; and (c)
decline in birth rates to the mid-20 range. The timetable in this
report is provided within the context of a 20 year plan. Ravenholt
stated that essentially United States population program assistance
on a global basis "could be accomplished during the twenty years
from 1965 to 1985"--twelve years of this period have already trans-
pired--"if the United States Congress provides steadfast and strong

134

support for this program during the second decade of its operation as it has during the first decade."[2]

Dr. Ravenholt's statement is one of the most specific assurances that objectives of an international program in population can be accomplished, that it can be accomplished within a time frame that will end by 1985, and that it can be accomplished within the level of political and financial support already provided by the Congress over the past twelve years. It's all the more remarkable because most workers in the field view the level of Congressional support since 1965 to be no more than a spit in the ocean.

In terms of a timetable, Ravenholt claims that "It should be feasible to bring the world birthrate below 20 and world population growth rate below 1% by 1985." This is estimated to result in a total world population of 5.5 billion by the year 2000. That would be a very encouraging figure, if it were true. Even this figure, though, is not an equilibrium level, but merely the level in the year 2000 under the optimistic conditions. Nowhere in the text is a projection made as to the ultimate equilibrium population if this plan were to be implemented within this time frame and on this budget. So we don't really know what the ultimate world population size would be or if it would be within the global carrying capacity.

The budget provided by Dr. Ravenholt is a request for support at the level of $250 million per annum for a number of years. If we allowed that that was for the period from 1977 to 1985, Ravenholt is asking for a total of $2 billion over 8 years. He does say that the total cost from 1965 to 1985 according to this budget would be less than $3 billion and that takes into consideration the fact that in the first eleven years of the AID program total population program assistance amounted to $732 million. So with an additional $2.2 or $2.3 billion over the next eight years the AID program would be within the $3 billion figure.

Unfortunately, in such a brief report, there is no basis provided to support these budget estimates, except citation of the figure $1 per capita for the "total average cost." We interpret that to mean $1 per capita for the population which is served, let us say approximately 2 billion people a year for a period of eight years. If you divide this $1 per person over 8 years, the program cost would be about 12¢ per person, per year.

As a critique of this proposal we must point out the following:

(1) The cost estimate of $1 per capita for the entire ten year program is certainly unsubstantiated and sounds much too low. One can compare that to the figures which the United Nations Fund for Population Activities has published to the effect that the cost of providing family planning services on a per capita basis (per capita to the entire population) is 50¢ to $1 per year,[3] but not

135

for 10 years.

(2) The goal provided is not stated in terms of an equilibrium population size. If one wishes to take seriously, as I think we must, the harsh warnings of geographers and ecologists, that global carrying capacity is probably less than 6 billion people, then we must know what the ultimate population equilibrium would be before espousing any programs. Although a figure was not cited in The World Population Plan of Action, some of the State Department members of the American delegation to the Bucharest Conference projected that, if implemented with 100% perfection, the World Population Plan of Action itself would result in a population of greater than 8 billion at equilibrium. It is very risky to take a point in time such as the year 2000 and say that 5.5 billion is acceptable when we don't know to what figure that will ultimately grow. Even if Dr. Ravenholt's aims were to be accomplished, the population would still be growing at 1% by the year 2000. If the population size is less than the carrying capacity, then 1%, on a temporary basis, may be an acceptable level of growth. If the population size is over the carrying capacity 1% would be a disaster.

(3) The plan is not based upon any scientific assessment of carrying capacity. That seems to be consistently true for all population planning.

(4) The AID plan states that United States aid can be withdrawn when birth rates drop to the mid 20s, thus assuming that further declines in birth rate down to the level of 9 to 14, as will be required in order to match the death rate and stabilize population size., must be accomplished without United States assistance. It is pure speculation to imagine that an undeveloped country with American assistance can lower its birth rate perhaps from 35 to 25 and then, on its own, without any further assistance or consultation, continue those programs to the degree of effectiveness required to lower the birth rate all the way to 10 or 12.

(5) The plan does not allow for any higher costs to reduce birth rates from the level of 20 down to 10 than to reduce the birth rate from 40 down to 30. However, the law of diminishing returns would suggest that a higher cost would be incurred for each additional reduction of birth rate as the rate itself is reduced. If American assistance is terminated as the rate reaches 20 to 25, then there would be virtually no international assistance for the additional and rapidly increasing costs of finishing the job.

(6) The costs of research on motivational factors and the costs of any necessary public education do not appear to be included in these budgets. Such projections have never been made because such programs have never been designed.

(7) A similar comment applies to economic determinants of

fertility and the costs of incentives and disincentives. These are not known and are probably not budgeted.

(8) There is no evidence available to show that desired family size will drop to low enough levels in such large and poverty stricken countries as India and Indonesia to allow an annual growth of only 1% or ultimately a reduction to a population equilibrium. The stated AID intention is actually to withdraw from a number of countries--including some rather large and rapidly growing nations-- by about 1978. This presupposes that our programs have been sufficiently successful to allow American assistance to be withdrawn. Since those birth rates are still quite high and the family planning structure certainly has not yet reached completion in these countries, it seems sensible to question whether the withdrawal of such aid might not in fact be premature.

(9) The AID proposal places primary emphasis upon the delivery of contraceptive services and it appears to assume that universal availability would solve the problem. But very few professional workers agree with this. Most believe with Dr. Roy Prosterman[4] that basic improvements in nutrition, literacy, health, housing, and social security will be required if contraceptive acceptance is to increase substantially. But none of these essential factors are included in the budget projection.

(10) The full details of the plan are simply unpublished. Supporting research is completely absent; there is no substantiation by any consultant or management scientist outside of government.

The strategy of the American AID Population Assistance Program is a plan of obvious international importance. AID is the most important source of population funding in the world. Its goals and strategies should certainly be well documented and should be impartially supported by independent managers and scientists.

(11) The accuracy of census statistics showing fertility reduction in countries which have been aided by AID's population assistance program have recently come under serious question. The United States Bureau of the Census had not, at the time this was written, published its data for 1975 and 1976, which reportedly show declining fertility in response to AID family planning programs. The Environmental Fund has published higher figures for population growth based upon data which they have selected from international organizations and other sources. This data[5] in turn has been challenged by responsible statisticians. There is, in fact, a controversy and what the resolution of that controversy will be is unclear at this time. It appears to be a fact, however, that the principal source of statistics which favor the AID position concerning their program effectiveness is from other federal agencies paid for by AID. A part of the controversy revolves around the question of whether AID should or should not publish data and conclusions which have been arrived at

by other federal agencies which AID itself is unsatisfied with. One wonders why in fact there should be a question as to the objectivity and the accuracy of data from the United States Census Bureau. Both the Population Reference Bureau and the Environmental Fund publish data sheets with rather markedly differing statistics for population. Although we are unable to resolve that controversy, it is important to point out that not all of the statistics are to be believed. Therefore, it is important to know which figures are under question.

In summary, the AID proposal to solve the world population problem at a cost of less than $2.5 billion over the next ten years is unbelievable. The current plan is to provide more of the same. There is no new strategy or planning which appears to hold any promise for fulfillment of the AID objectives.

DISCUSSION

CHRISTIAN HERTER, JR., Corporate Policy Services, Inc.: How is it scientifically determined what the carrying capacity of the earth is?

CHARLES CARGILLE: I think it's safe to say, at the present time, there is no established method for determining carrying capacity. That's not to say that it would be technically impossible. It's only to say that no one has tried because there's no money for this research. An examination of the Directory of Federal Population Research over the past eight years would indicate that in the judgment of the National Institutes of Health, which is the coordinator of the entire federal research program, carrying capacity is irrelevant to population. I cannot agree with that judgment.

CHRISTIAN HERTER, JR.: Well, if this is true and nobody knows what carrying capacity is, how do you develop a plan that's related to carrying capacity?

CHARLES CARGILLE: I would begin by finding out what the carrying capacity is, with research funding. In the absence of hard facts, one must go to far more subjective information. But I think it's generally recognized that the limits which are closest to all of us, with regard to putting an upper limit on carrying capacity and population growth, are limits of resource scarcity and environmental impact.

Now, there are experts in resources. The relationship between resource bases and population support is a field of inquiry called geography. In asking geographers what their best professional judgment is on this issue, I have consistently obtained estimates, subjective indeed, but nonetheless knowledgeable estimates, of carrying capacity at 6 billion or less, based upon an evaluation of resources.

With regard to environmental impact, those specialists who do research on the relationship of any population to its environment, are
called ecologists. Without exception, those ecologists with whom I
have talked, and who have reported to me the consensus of their colleagues, agree with the geographers that, with regard to environmental impact, the global carrying capacity is 6 billion or less.

I find this deeply troubling. Economists consistently estimate
10, 15, 30 billion people with particular concern for either resource
scarcity or environmental pollution. But they do not possess expertise in either of these areas.

I'm very deeply concerned by a population projection which almost
guarantees us a global population level in excess of 8 billion when
the true carrying capacity according to the professional judgments of
the ecologists and the geographers is no more than 6 billion, and
perhaps 5. The difference between the population size and the upper
limit of carrying capacity could be called "surplus people," for want
of a better term, and I find that a very frightening concept.

AUDIENCE: If you go about developing a budget for population
planning in given countries, and you try to assess the carrying capacity of the individual countries, how do you make transfers to account for a Saudi Arabia or a Bermuda, which make the carrying capacity of a breadbasket country both greater and less. You have to
add into the carrying capacity of their breadbasket neighbor the imported petroleum, but if you then were to assume the petroleum products
were not available, and that the exports of food stuffs from the neigh-
boring country were not available to be sent to Saudi Arabia, after
going through all the pluses and minuses, where do you come out? Do
you assume no import and export, or do you assume all the import and
export at the present levels? Any given nation is so interdependent,
especially the two I named, that I don't see how you could arrive at
a standard for carrying capacity of either of those two countries, for
example.

CHARLES CARGILLE: It would certainly be necessary to make estimates of reasonable import-export relationships. Quite truly, we're
already inseparably interdependent. That would be one of the soft
areas and the difficult areas to deal with. There are certain limits,
however, which I think could certainly be placed as reasonable maxima.

In dealing with carrying capacity, one can err in either one of
two directions. One can estimate carrying capacity too low and
level off population at a level substantially below the true carrying capacity, an error on the low side. In that case, one has what
is called "resource abundance." And, if there are too few people,
you can change your fertility motivations and policies, and encourage more.

However, if you err on the other side, and you exceed carrying capacity, you are dead. The biological law which describes the relationship between populations which are too large for the carrying capacity says that when the environment is degraded, if not sooner, then later, the surplus individuals and that species die off.

REPLY TO DR. CARGILLE BY R. T. RAVENHOLT, A.I.D.

I'm very happy to have additional people helping to increase our budget, which Charles is quite right, has ordinarily been too small, and smaller than we have wished it to be. But, as many of you know, it is not easy to suddenly get all the money that one might wish to have for a program, even one as important as the world population program. So, during these years, we have ordinarily worked very hard in trying to get the monies and then to use them to the best possible advantage.

As Charles has indicated, along the way we've made certain judgments and, indeed, he cited the main strategy of the program, which is to assist the developing countries to convert what has been a paper statement of human rights--that every couple shall have the fundamental human freedom to have the knowledge and the means to control their fertility as they wish--into an actuality by providing such assistance as we can to many countries.

Our goal is a fairly simple one, that of helping to ensure that all couples in the developing countries do have the information and the means to control their fertility. We also provide assistance to help governments of developing countries with improvement of their policies, and we provide substantial assistance for measurement of demographic status, evaluation of programs, and so forth.

During the past decade the Agency for International Development, through fiscal 1977, had provided $1 billion of assistance to the developing countries. You might find it of interest just how these monies were spent. First of all, $146 million of this billion went to the United Nations Fund for Populations Activities to assist them with their program, which is a very multifaceted and far-reaching program. About $82 million of the monies went to the International Planned Parenthood Federation in London to support their family planning associations in more than 80 countries. Some $180 million dollars, or 18%, was spent for contraceptives and surgical equipment, commodities for control of fertility. Just about $300 million went for support of family planning and population programs as a form of bilateral assistance in the developing countries. And we spent about $50 million for research and development of improved technology, new means of fertility control. A little more than $100 million went for training, a little over $100 million went for all kinds of informational and demographic activities, such as the World

Fertility Survey. And the balance went for administration.

Now, which of these items would one wish to change? $146 million for the UNFPA? Some say that's too little, some say it's too much. It turned out to be that for a whole host of reasons. Many people participated in these judgments of how much should go for any one of these items. $180 million for contraceptives? Some say that's too much, some too little. 18% of the budget spent for contraceptives? I don't know; what should it have been, 25%, 30%, 10%? Any of you could, perhaps, have your own figure.

We've gained quite a lot of experience in the last decade with respect to how rapidly programs move or don't move, and indeed the experience of the world is heterogeneous. Some continents have moved a long way: others have not. The most rapid progress has been in East Asia, where there's been a revolution in fertility status, in the availability of services, and rapidly decreasing fertility. In Latin America quite a lot has happened, but much has not yet happened. Some of the major countries, particularly Mexico, only recently began to provide services and Brazil is just beginning. Some of the smaller countries have gone a long way. Africa has not moved much yet for a whole set of reasons, including political sensitivities in many quarters, and lack of resources. Indeed, during 1974, 1975, and 1976, our budget was decreased each year rather than increased at a time when we should have been enlarging the support for Africa. Our budget is now once again on the increase but, in real terms, our budget is still less today than it was (in constant dollar worth) in 1972.

With respect to carrying capacity, which Charles mentioned, I don't think anyone has an exact fix on this. All of you can make your own calculations, and think of where it should be or might be. I think it depends greatly upon the various kinds of energy which are available to the world. If we get nuclear fusion energy, that's one scenario. If we have to depend upon simply nonrenewable and then also renewable resources (sun, and so forth), that's another scenario.

Our orientation is that the population of the world is already very large and increasing at an unhealthy rate, and that we need to do everything we can to curb the undesirably rapid increase in world population as quickly as we can. And this is what we're bending our efforts to. I do think from what we see that considerable progress is occurring. The change in the world demographic status is quite profound in the last decade. In 1965, when the world population was approximately 3.3 billion, the average birth rate was approximately 34 births per thousand population and the death rate about 14 deaths per thousand population, for a difference of 20 per thousand, or a 2% growth rate. The increment in world population in 1965 (2% times 3.3 billion) was about 66 million people.

Now, many actions have gone forward, and the demographic situation has improved. Keep in mind the demographic

141

data lag--ordinarily at least 2 years goes by from the time something changes out there until it is measured. Our most recent information is mainly relating to 1975, at which time the world population was about 4 billion, the average world birth rate had dropped from 34 to approximately 26.6 and the death rate had dropped to about 11.2. The difference is about 15.4 per thousand, for a 1.54% growth rate. There are additional data in for 1976 indicating that the average world growth rate probably fell below 1½% in 1976, whereas in 1965 it was about 2%. If we use 1975 figures (1.54% times 4 billion) we get an increment of world population that year of about 62 million, only down from 66 million in 1965.

But the trends have changed substantially, and the maximum increase probably occurred about 1970 when there was an increment in world population of about 70 million. Already, then, this has fallen from 70 million in about 1970 to 62 million in 1975.

Looking ahead at the trends we see now in motion, I think it is reasonable to expect that the average world birth rate will be below 20 by 1985, and the growth rate below 1% by 1985. This will still leave a very huge problem because by that time the world population will be about 4.5 billion, and 1% times that is still an increment of 45 million. So we're not going to suddenly run out of the need for additional agricultural productivity.

That's our scenario. If this happens, then I think it's reasonable to expect that the world population by the year 2000 will be under 5.5 billion. This is still a substantial increase, but had the 1965 annual increase of 2% continued unabated from 1965 to the year 2000, the world population would have been 6.7 billion. So there's at least that much change in the outlook; the world population by the year 2000 may be about 1.2 billion less than if we had not intervened to attempt to lower the birth rate.

As far as monetary needs, as Charles has indicated also, having spent $1 billion and gotten some feel for how this goes, I still believe that the great bulk of the needed U.S. foreign assistance for solution of the world population problem can be done in the next decade for another $2 billion; in other words, a total expenditure of about $4 billion from 1965 to 1985. So this is our feel for this.

I would say there are some very heartening elements in the scene. China is the most heartening. China does have, no doubt, the most powerful population policy and family planning program, or as they call it, planned birth program. I was happy, just a month ago, to get a report form a woman who had lived in the People's Republic of China since 1946. She stated that she visited some of the ministries and other organizations in Peking, just before leaving there in early January, and she was told by the Women's Federation of the PRC that the average birth rate for all of China for 1976 was 12. Now this is the first time that we've gotten a specific birth rate for all of China for 1976. You can doubt it if you wish. I wouldn't from what we see of the effectiveness of programs in other places.

Probably the best of any of the programs we support in the world
is the Indonesian program, where they have implemented a remarkably
effective program. The birth rate in Bali for 1977, from everything
we know, was less than 20, despite the fact that this is still a rural,
agrarian, poor, and considerably illiterate society. The birth rate
in Java is not that low, but it is falling rapidly, and the Indonesian program is going forward very rapidly. Many programs do not go
so well. Programs in South Asia have not gone so well. There are
many problems of government and the implementation of progress. So
it's a heterogeneous scene with some countries making very rapid progress; and others, medium progress; and some, very little progress at
all yet. There's still a great deal to be done, but I think the job
is doable.

CHARLES CARGILLE: The statement that I must take issue with is
the statement that AID is "reducing fertility as quickly as we can."
The AID budget estimate for 1978-1985, a $250 million per year figure,
is $1.75 billion.

Stephen Mumford has published his estimates in Population Growth
Control that $140 billion are needed from 1978 to 1985. That's based
on an estimated cost of $20 billion per year, which equals 0.67% of
gross world product.

Now the difference in judgment is virtually a hundredfold.   I
think such a difference should be resolved by hard nosed, third party
management reviewers. My personal hunch is that Dr. Mumford's estimates
are closer to the true costs, if indeed world population can be controlled at all.

FOOTNOTES

1. R. T. Ravenholt, Science, 163:124, 1969 (January 10).

2. R. T. Ravemholt, in Since Bucharest and the Future, International
    Population Conference of the World Population Society, November
    19-22, 1975, World Population Society, Washington, D.C., 1976,
    p. 43.

3. Lester Brown, In the Human Interest, Norton, New York, 1974.

4. Roy Prosterman, in Glassheim, E., C. M. Cargille and C. Hoffman
    (eds.), Key Issues in Popualtion Policy: Problems, Options, and
    Recommendations for Action, University Press of America, Washing-
    ton, D.C., 1978.

5. S. Baum, in Glassheim, et al., ibid.

143

AGRICULTURAL DEVELOPMENT AND POPULATION POLICY
IN PUERTO RICO

Kent C. Earnhardt

Department of Biostatistics
University of North Carolina

Puerto Rico is a Caribbean Island of almost rectangular shape, 100 miles by 34 miles in size (3,421 square miles) with an estimated mid-1977 population of 3.3 million. This combination of relatively small size and large population presents Puerto Rico with an over-all population density of 965 persons per square mile, a density which greatly exceeds that of almost every comparable population in the world and is sixteen times higher than that of the United States.

Puerto Rico has been politically associated with the U.S. since 1898; since 1917 they have been demographically integrated with the U.S. in the form of U.S. citizenship, which facilitated the well-know, economically motivated mass migration of Puerto Ricans to the U.S. mainland in 1945-1970. This migration served to greatly reduce both population growth and population density in Puerto Rico, as a variously estimated 1.5 to 2.0 million (or about one-third of all Puerto Ricans) now live on the U.S. mainland.

Puerto Rico had one of the world's highest rates of population growth--around 3% per year--until reduced first by the massive net out-migration of 1945-1970 and then by a substantial real fertility decline in 1940-1975 and especially in 1960-1975; the total fertility rate was 5.9 in 1940, 5.4 in 1950, 4.8 in 1960, 3.3 in 1970, and 2.8 in 1975. Present birth and death rates per 1,000 population however are 23 and 6--yielding a relatively high rate of natural increase of 1.7% per year, as compared to 0.6% in the U.S. or 0.4% in Europe.

Since Puerto Rico has been politically associated in one form or another with the United States since 1898, various policy developments in agriculture and population cannot be fully understood without taking into account both the socioeconomic and political relationship between the mainland and the island. For example, from 1898 to 1948 the government of Puerto Rico was administered by the U.S.-appointed Governor in rather close conjunction with U.S. Government Executive Agency policies--although the elected

144

Legislature of Puerto Rico provided additional and sometimes differing policy inputs. Then, after 1948, the Government of Puerto Rico was administered through an elected Governor with relatively more political autonomy from Washington policies, especially after 1952 when the U.S. Congress made Puerto Rico a U.S. Commonwealth instead of a territory. As a result of this relative transfer of political control from Washington to Puerto Rico, and the concomitant increase of political power and nationalism in Puerto Rico, agricultural and population policies among others underwent significant change.

The past U.S. policies with respect to agriculture and population in Puerto Rico were perhaps most fully developed in the mid-1930s by the Roosevelt Administration. In March 1934, U.S. Assistant Secretary of Agriculture Rexford Tugwell--who in 1941 was to be appointed Governor of Puerto Rico by President Roosevelt--journeyed to Puerto Rico in order to help formally develop a "reconstruction plan" for an island which had been devastated not only by the Great Depression of the 1930s but also by two hurricanes of 1928 and 1932. Following Tugwell's visit, three high Puerto Rican officials were named to a "U.S. Puerto Rico Policy Commission," to develop the reconstruction plan for Puerto Rico. This Commission convened in Washington in the U.S. Department of Agriculture, where it developed a plan which was announced by President Roosevelt himself during a visit to Puerto Rico in mid-1934. This plan came to be known as the "Chardon Plan."

The Chardon Plan emphasized that the basic economic problem of Puerto Rico was an imbalance of high population density and rapid population growth on the one side and low economic productivity on the other. For the short run it suggested the multiple solutions of (1) industrialization, (2) emigration, and (3) increased agricultural productivity through land reform; and for the long run (4) birth control policies (but not emigration policies) were more or less attempted by the Puerto Rican government in the mid-1930s.

One early reaction to the Chardon Plan and to its initial implementation came in a resolution approved by the Legislature of Puerto Rico in March 1935, addressed to President Roosevelt and the U.S. Congress. This resolution stated that the Legislature was "not against" either "birth control" or government-assisted but voluntary emigration but, however, favored "modern ideas" such as increasing agricultural production in Puerto Rico--which through modern science, new techniques, and the "positive economic value" of high populat-on density might, it said, support a population of over 20 million (compared to the then population of 1.7 million).

From 1941 to 1946 Tugwell served as the U.S. appointed Governor of Puerto Rico. He emphasized that Puerto Rico suffered from underproduction rather than overpopulation, during his administration somewhat utopian plans for greater economic production through public planning for industrialization were launched, and some real but limited economic success was achieved.

During his reign as Governor, Tugwell worked more or less closely with the rising political leader in Puerto Rico who was later to serve as a four-term elected Governor from 1948 to 1964, Luis Munoz Marin. In 1946 Munoz stated that Puerto Rico was already overpopulated by 500,000 people--as an agricultural country; thus, he concluded that "industrialization" was the "only answer" for Puerto Rico. This policy prevailed until 1970 when a later Governor announced official support of Family Planning programs both as a health service and for their desired and presumed demographic impact. In the meantime, of course, the mass out-migration to the U.S. mainland of 1945-1970 had served to greatly reduce population pressures in Puerto Rico in spite of an officially neutral external migration policy.

In the span of less than 40 years, the Puerto Rican economy has been transformed from a traditional agricultural economy into an industrial and service oriented economy based on manufacturing, commerce, construction, tourism, government and other services. Agriculture, the predominant sector in 1950, employed about 216,000 people (36% of total employment) and contributed $149 million (25%) of the Island's total income. By 1976, agriculture was the smallest of the major economic sectors, providing employment for only 6% of the labor force and accounting for only 5% of the total net income. During the last 40 years, of course, Puerto Rico has become increasingly and markedly dependent on food imports.

As of 1978 the agricultural development of Puerto Rico in relation to its population represents a fundamental and extensive imbalance between the production and consumption of agricultural products. As a result, the large majority of foods and food mass consumed in Puerto Rico are imported. In addition, the economic development of Puerto Rico in relation to its population is so insufficient that unemployment and poverty are very high by U.S. standards. The cost of food, however, is generally higher in Puerto Rico than on the United States mainland. This imbalance between employment and economic production in relation to economic income needs for the purchase of food in Puerto Rico is also largely alleviated by import via a massive net economic transfer payment from the U.S. Treasury in the form of the U.S. Food Stamp Program. Approximately 70% of the population of Puerto Rico now qualifies to receive--and over 50% do receive--USDA food stamps to support their food consumption needs, resulting in a food stamp transfer payment which is much higher per capita in Puerto Rico than in the U.S. nationally or in any U.S. state. As a further result, Puerto Rico thus receives a disproportionately large share (in relation to population) of the total food stamp transfer payment in the U.S. economy.

In 1946, the political leader of Puerto Rico argued that it

146

was overpopulated as an agricultural land and, thus, that only industrialization could solve an acknowledged population problem by generating the economic production and income necessary to pay for food and other necessary purchases. By 1978, Puerto Rico was also overpopulated as an industrial land and seriously needs increased agricultural production. Fortunately, the government of Puerto Rico now recognizes that industrialization is not the "only answer" and is committed to increasing agricultural production and reducing food imports in Puerto Rico.

THE APPLICATION OF VALUE-ANALYSIS TO POPULATION POLICY: THE CASE OF IRAN

R. Kenny Burns

Population Studies Center, University of Pennsylvania

The analysis of national policy by a structured, systematic framework has been applied to many areas: international conflict, world trade, international communications. This paper does two things: (a) selects some concepts for a framework of policy analysis, and (b) applies this framework to population policy in Iran.

A Framework for Policy Analysis

Population policies are the results of complex, often non-demographic and non-scientific enterprises of individuals and coalitions that try to cope formally and explicitly with demographic change. In this perspective, policies are defined as results of social processes in which participants, seeking the realization of private or public values, act through institutions to make actual these values in the public domain.

Values are desirable end-states of well-being which influence actions insofar as values, as final "causes" or goals, help determine how a society makes its choice of means. In the Lasswell framework, principal values are power, enlightenment, well-being, wealth, skill, affection, respect, and rectitude.

Institutions are collections of individuals which allocate scarce resources to activities and thus embody values in social organizations. Institutions may embody implicit or explicit values. Where coalitions have values in conflict, policies are termed "inconsistent" or even "irrational."*

---

*For example, parts of the U.S. government support danger warnings on cigarette advertising and a ban on mass media advertising, seeking the value of public health (or well-being), while other government legislation provides agricultural subsidies for tobacco growers, supporting economic values (or wealth). "Inconsistency" or "irrationality" in national policy is probably more characteristic in a developed society with a diffusion of power than in a developing one where power is concentrated at the center.

Policy outcomes are the activities in which preferred values are expressed by organizations; such activities are intelligence gathering, promotion, appraisal, prescription of norms and others explained by Lasswell (in Ilchman, 1975).

Application of the Framework to Population Policy in Iran

Support for Iran's current policy on the control of population growth is traced to the current monarch, Mohammed Reza Pahlavi, since Iran formally adopted a pro-control policy in 1967. The Shah has endorsed the concept of rapid fertility decline, assigned family planning as a mandated service for the National Health Corps, and called for a national network of clinic planning services. The Shah has stressed three values in order to justify population control: food, water and literacy. First, the food theme or value of well-being (Ministry of Health, 1970):

Many of our brethren in all corners of the world are dying of hunger. The world's population is rapidly increasing. If we do not give thought to this fact now, starvation will dangerously increase day by day.

The food theme was repeated in the 1974 message to the U.N. Secretary General as part of the Declaration on Food and Population (Shah Pahlavi, 1974):

Priority must be given by governments to implementing sound population control and environmental protection policies, to devising methods of increasing food production, especially that of grains, to encouraging increased cooperation between developing and developed countries in order to provide aid for population control and food production programs, and to making provisions for sufficient food reserves to guard against famine.

Iran is a country of enormous mineral and geological resources, but without great water reserves; the Shah also underscored the water theme (Ministry of Health, 1974):

. . . therefore the number of people who live in this land must be consistent with the natural bounties of this country. . . . What use will it be, for example, if there are 200 million people in this land who are condemned to die of thirst.

In 1975, the Shah issued a statement on the elimination of world illiteracy and the obstacles that rapid population growth presents to reaching the objective (Shah Pahlavi, 1975).

Princess Ashraf Pahlavi, twin sister of the Shah, has importance in the social policy of the regime, as is illustrated in the expert

149

ranking technique of Zonis (1971) which placed her as one of the four
most powerful persons in Iran. As head of the Iranian delegation to
the Bucharest Conference, and president of the Iran Organization of
Women, she has endorsed legislation to change the former religious
divorce codes to the more modern Family Protection Law of 1976 (Ashraf and Sadeghi, 1976). In her Washington, D.C. speech in 1975,
she cited the economic supports for high fertility which might characterize the rural sector of Iran (Ashraf Pahlavi, 1975):

> The major obstacles to population control are, first and
> foremost, those socio-economic structures and cultural
> values unfavorable to an effective population policy. Where
> children constitute the backbone of the family economy, as
> a source of energy and cheap labor, attempts at birth con-
> trol sometimes go in direct opposition to the economic in-
> terest of the heads of families, and might appear irrele-
> vant to their most pressing problems.

> Without a patient and long-range policy of restructuring
> the socio-economic relations of society, the redirection
> of a population trend becomes an almost impossible task.

Princess Ashraf's call for a long-range policy with emphasis
upon social change, not merely birth control, was issued at the same
time as a World Bank consultant team recommended restructuring and
elevation of organizations responsible for population policy. However, in the three years following the consultant report no basic
changes were made in organizations responsible for policy.

Policy Outcomes: Intelligence Gathering

The principal sources of demographic intelligence have been the
national census series in 1956, 1966, and 1976. The censuses have
been characterized by increasing competence in skill and organization
and have created major awareness of the growth of population. The
census efforts have yielded data on gross size, but have not included
measures of demographic growth components, namely fertility and
mortality (Tofigh, 1977). For unclear reasons, the 1976 national
census schedule omitted use of Brass-type questions for indirect
measure of fertility and infant mortality in spite of the defective
state of most rural vital registration systems (Brass, 1975).

What was lacking to policy makers in the 1967-76 period was adequate knowledge of the demographic determinants of fertility, such
as age of entry into marriage, the effects of marital dissolution,
widowhood and remarriage, lactation and infant mortality, as well as
the emerging social characteristics of literacy, education, work
patterns, and nuptiality patterns of the youngest cohorts of Iranian
women who will principally determine the trajectory of Iranian fertility.

Due to the age structure defects in the 1956 census, the possible disproportionate underenumeration in both 1956 and 1966 and, most importantly, the marginal rate and pattern of mortality decline since WW II, the use of stable models provides only approximate estimates of crude birth and death rates.* Since neither vital records nor reliable birth histories have yielded fertility trends prior to 1973, my opinion is that no evidence supports the thesis that the birth rate has fallen, as set forth by others (Zanjani, 1977; SETIRAN, 1976; and the first report of the PGS, Plan and Budget, 1976-77). Further, the PGS data suggest no decline in marital fertility, the central indicator of a longer term "transition" in the European cases. In my opinion, the case for a time-series decline in the Iranian birth rate has no empirical basis until the rigorous and objective analysis of PGS and WFS birth histories is conducted.

Policy Outcomes: Policy Appraisal

Iran appears to have the ingredients for the successful pursuit of a policy of stabilizing and modernizing fertility in concert with mortality. Policy appraisal, crucial to the process for Lasswell, is "the analysis and reporting of the degree to which policy goals have been achieved, and the allocation of imputed or effective responsibility for results" (Ilchman, 1975). Appraisal relies on a feedback process that reviews the fundamental questions of goals, trends, conditions, projections, and alternatives. Appraisal is future directed so that "as information becomes available during the future, it is possible to appraise the previously adopted goals and priorities" (ibid.).

Writing in general of his own role as monarch, the Shah has said

But it is one thing to issue an order and another to see that it is carried out. .... Remorseless following-up is required, and this alone demands many contacts. (Mohammed Reza Pahlavi, 1961, p. 325).

Applying the framework to Iran, three conclusions emerge: First, there is no clear focus of responsibility for policy appraisal within

*On the basis of data from the National PGS (Population Growth Survey), the author has applied the South Regional Model family (from Coale and Demeny, 1967) to intercensal estimates over the two decades (1956-1976) and reached estimates of RNI (rate of natural increase) for 1956-1966 of 2.6%, and 3.0% for 1966-1976. Crude birth rates for the periods were estimated at 46.0 and 43.5 with corrections for quasi-stability. Under assumptions of greater duration of mortality decline, the adjustment for quasi-stability would necessarily produce higher CBR and a less apparent "fall."

the current organization of population agencies in Iran. A statistical bureau collects data; a ministry of health provides clinic-based family planning, over twenty non-government and private agencies provide services. However, no highly placed organization has responsibility for overall policy appraisal.

Second, the major macro-planning efforts in Iran, the Fifth Development Plan (PBO, 1973-78) and the National Spatial Distribution Plan (SETIRAN, 1976), have proposed scenarios which assume a European-like transition of fertility within a 20-year period. However, major research on the European decline has emphasized both the irregular pace of decline and the specific cultural factors that make decline possible--such as the European nuclear family. Iran --which is Islamic in religion, Persian in culture, with extended kinship family structures, very high marital universality--has few, if any, cultural ingredients of 19th Century Europe. These assumptions of a European-like transition suggested in the first PGS report have never been critically examined in the appraisal process.

Table 1, using the standard Coale indexes (I_g, I_m, I_f), compares Iran (in 1974-75) with three "median" transition European countries at the beginning of their fertility decline. Iran's index of nuptiality (I_m = .82) is nearly twice as high in comparison with the I_m of England and Wales, Finland, Denmark, and 10 other countries of the Van de Walle and Knodel study (1967) that have I_m in the transition zone of .44-.54. Professor Coale has speculated, on the basis of partial data of marriage patterns in pre-19th Century Europe, that there were two demographic transitions: one from early marriage (high I_m) in medieval Europe to relatively low I_m at the time of Malthus; two, the secular decline in the 19th to 20th Centuries that was essentially a fall in marital fertility (to lower I_g). With the very short time-series evidence on Iranian fertility, there is an indication that urban women (Plan and Budget, 1976, 1977) have married later than urban women in 1966, but no evidence of a decline in marital fertility (I_g) among urban women.

Third, policy appraisal has not examined the critical relationships of demographic growth and self-sufficiency in food production. Rising per capita food consumption patterns and incremental population growth have contributed to a shortfall in agricultural productivity. Iran has adequate national revenues to purchase a volume of basic foodstuffs like wheat, dairy goods, and meat on the international market, principally from the U.S.A., but it is unclear if the country can achieve self-sufficiency in food production under its current trajectory of rate of natural increase.

The conflict has been set between the values of near term self-sufficiency in foodstuffs and the values of continued high population growth. Given the fragmented process of current policy appraisal in Iran, it is uncertain how this conflict will be resolved.

TABLE 1

Indicators of Comparative Demographic Transitions
for Iran and Select Transition Countries

	Index of Proportion Married I_M	Index of Marital Fertility I_g	Index of General Fertility I_F	Infant Mortality (per 1000)
Urban	.77	.49	.38	60.4
Rural	.85	.74	.60	123.7
Total Iran (1974-5)	.82	.64	.53	105.4

Thresholds for Select Countries
at Onset of Decline*

Finland (1910)	.46	.70	.31	114
England and Wales (1892)	.48	.68	.31	149
Denmark (1900)	.47	.68	.32	131

I_M = index of universality and age of marital unions. If all women 15-49 are married, I_M = 1.0.

I_g = index of actual marital fertility to standard of biological maximum; for Hutterite women: I_g = 1.0.

I_F = index of actual fertility to biological potential of all women; for Hutterites I_F = .7.

*Median Values

Selected from 14 European countries (excluding Ireland) at year of beginning of decline based on deviation downwards of 10%. E. Van de Walle, J. Knodel (1967).

Note: All indexes for Iran are based on calculating women "ever married." Thus, complete remarriage is assumed and the indices are probably biased upwards.

REFERENCES

1. Ashraff and Sadeghi, in Jacqz, Jane W., ed. Iran: Past, Present and Future. New York: Aspen Institute for Humanistic Studies, 1976.

2. Brass, W. Methods for Estimating Fertility and Mortality from Limited and Defective Data. Chapel Hill: University of North Carolina, 1975.

3. Coale, Ansley J. and P. Demeny. Regional Model Life Tables. Princeton: Princeton University Press, 1967.

4. Ilchman, W., et al. Policy Sciences and Population. Lexington, Mass.: D. C. Heath & Company, Lexington Books, 1975.

5. Ministry of Health, Iran. Summary Statement on Iran's Population for the Bucharest Conference. Tehran, 1974.

6. Pahlavi, Mohammad Reza Shah. "Declaration on Food and Population: A Call to Governments and People for Action by Concerned Citizens from Many Parts of the World." Paper presented to Secretary General of the United Nations Kurt Waldheim on April 25, 1974. Washington, D.C.: Population Crisis Committee.

7. _____. Shahanshah's Message on the Occasion of the World Campaign Against Illiteracy: Anniversary. Etela'at (Persian), 17th Shahrivar, 1354 (September 1975). Translated by James Saliba.

8. _____. Mission for My Country. London: Hutchinson & Son, Ltd., 1961.

9. Pahlavi, Ashraff. "Population, Women, and the Quality of Life." Address by H.I.H. Princess Ashraff Pahlavi at the International Population Conference, Washington, D.C., November 19, 1975.

10. Plan and Budget Organization of Iran (PBO). Fifth Development Plan 1973-1975. Tehran: PBO, 1973.

11. _____. Population Growth of Iran: Tehran 1976, 1977, First Survey Year 1973-1974. Second Survey Year 1975-1976.

12. SETIRAN. National Spatial Strategy Plan: First Stage Final Report. Tehran, 1976.

13. Tofigh, F. "The 1976 Population and Housing Census of Iran." A paper presented at the Fifth Population Census Conference, Honolulu, Hawaii, January 31-February 4, 1977.

14. Van de Walle, E. and J. Knodel. "Demographic Transition and Fertility Decline: The European Case." Proceedings of the Conference on Population, I.U.S.S.P., Sidney, Australia, 1967.

15. Zanjani, H. "Evolution de la Population Iranienne a Travers des Recensements." Population, No. 6, November/December 1977.

16. Zonis, M. The Political Elite of Iran. Princeton: Princeton University Press, 1971.

PROGRAM BUDGET ANALYSIS OF A.I.D.

William C. Binning

Youngstown State University

This paper has two objectives: first, to identify the rhetorical changes in A.I.D. policy; and second, to identify the budget changes in A.I.D. programs.

Changes in Rhetoric

The rhetoric of A.I.D. changed significantly with the development of "New Directions" in the 1973 A.I.D. legislation. The rhetoric of A.I.D. from its founding in 1961 had focused on the development of democracy under the symbol of "national security." The focus of program assistance in the 1960s was on urban centered large capital projects.

Support for the symbol of "national security" was eroded with the Viet Nam experience in the 1960s. The reduction in support for national security weakened the support for A.I.D., which, because of entanglements with short-term U.S. policy objectives and a multiplicity of programs was without a sense of mission.

In the early 1970s A.I.D. policies have undergone significant changes largely free of executive intervention, without high visibility and with the involvement of relatively few actors. One of the more significant actors in reshaping the direction of A.I.D. has been the international assistance community. The Development Assistance Committee, part of O.E.C.D., has made a strenuous effort to standardize and coordinate all western assistance activities. Additionally, other international forums concerned with specific problems are major forces in shaping the direction of aid policy. The World Population Conference and the World Food Conference are examples of the attempt by international forums to focus the policy of bilateral and multilateral donor agencies. In response to this new emphasis on international aid policy, A.I.D. has completely forsaken its former emphasis on capital intensive projects and has shifted its attention to population programs and, more recently, agricultural programs.

The House Foreign Relations Committee has been very influential in changing the direction of A.I.D. policy. A.I.D. policy is

156

currently labeled "New Directions," which means:

> Future U.S. bilateral support for development should
> focus on critical problems in those functional sectors
> which affect the lives of the majority of the people
> in the developing countries, food production, rural de-
> velopment and nutrition; population planning and health,
> and education, public administration and human resource
> development.[1]

This legislation specifically directed A.I.D. to move away from the
previous effort emphasizing infrastructure and capital development.
A.I.D. was now to give attention to rural development.

The thrust of "New Directions" has filled the mission void of
A.I.D. New Directions recognizes that western economic growth patterns cannot be replicated in the less developed countries. The
scarcity of resources scenario reinforces this position. The challenge for the less developed countries is to develop modes of production that meet the basic human needs of their population. A.I.D.'s
emphasis is on labor intensive, rural agricultural techniques.

The problem of technology in less developed countries is particularly acute since the goal of western technology is to minimize
the use of labor in production. A.I.D. is searching for technologies
that increase both production and demand for labor. This is a useful approach because labor is the most abundant factor of production
in less developed countries. The policy seeks not only new technology but also is directed towards rural areas in an effort to stabilize migration to urban areas.

Budget Analysis

A.I.D. has only recently prepared its budget programmatically.
Budgets, particularly program budgets, are quite useful for policy
analysis. As a means of relating policy rhetoric to actual policy
output, the tables on the next page attempt to organize early A.I.D.
budgets, so that they are comparable to current program budgets.

The impact of the political changes in 1973 is apparent in
Table A which indicates the shift from large capital programs to
education and agricultural development. The most evident shift is
from industrial, mining and finance to an emphasis on agriculture.
Table B indicates a shift in assistance to the poorest countries,
but it is not as dramatic as the rhetoric of "New Directions" suggests. Despite changes in project funding, Table C indicates few
trends in the distribution to geographic regions with the exception
of Africa which has continued to experience increases.

A.I.D. has developed a mission that is autonomous from the
short-term policy shifts of the United States. A policy of

A.

Distribution of A. I. D. Loans and Grants by Category

CATEGORY	1965	1969	1973	1977
Transportation	10	7	8	—
Industrial Mining & Finance Industrial	52	24	6	—
Agriculture	13	40	32	55
Power & Communication	12	—	7	—
General Government	5	12	12	6
Health & Population	2	6	25	16
Education	7	10	10	23

B.

Distribution of A. I. D. by Level of Development

	62—65	69	73	77
Low-Income Countries	47	53	57	40
Lower Middle Income Countries	11	32	28	55
Upper Middle Income Countries	18	15	15	5
High Income Countries	24	—	—	—

C.

Regional Distribution of A. I. D. Loans and Grants

AREA	62-65	1969	1973	1977
Near East & South Asia	51	43	29	42
Latin America	20	27	32	24
East Asia	8	16	22	12
Africa	11	14	17	22

self-sufficiency in LDCs should contribute to a decoupling of dependency relationships and a reduction of tension. Congressional evaluation of U.S. assistance programs should focus on the impact of specific aid projects in assisting the poor rather than on the short-term effects on the political behavior of political elites. Basic human rights should not be placed in conflict with the basic human needs of the world's poor.

FOOTNOTES

1. U.S. Congress, House of Representatives, Committee on International Relations, New Directions in Development Aid, 94th Congress, 2nd Session (Washington: U.S. Government, 1976), p. 1.

DATA SOURCES FOR TABLES

1. Sewell, John and the Staff of the Overseas Development Council. The United States and World Development Agenda 1977. New York: Praeger, 1977, pp. 160-171.

2. U.S. A.I.D. The Foreign Assistance Program Annual Report to Congress: 1965.

3. U.S. A.I.D. The Foreign Assistance Program Annual Report to Congress: 1969.

4. U.S. A.I.D. U.S. Overseas Loans and Grants and Assistance from International Organizations Obligations and Loan Authorization July 1, 1945-June 30, 1975. Washington: U.S. Government, 1976.

5. U.S. A.I.D. Population Program Assistance. Washington: U.S. Government, Dec., 1972.

6. U.S. Congress, House of Representatives, Subcommittee of the Committee on Appropriations. Foreign Assistance and Related Agencies Appropriation for 1974. Part 2, 91st Congress, 1st Session.

7. U.S. Congress, House of Representatives, Subcommittee of the Committee on Appropriations. Foreign Assistance and Related Agencies Appropriation for 1978. Part 2, 95th Congress, 1st Session.

PERSONAL OBSERVATIONS ON "BIRTH PLANNING"
IN CHINA--1977

Jessma Blockwick

Department of Population Problems
United Methodist Church

In the fall of 1977 I went to China with what we understand was
the first American people-to-people group specifically interested in
the subject of birth planning. We were family planning directors,
clinic directors, demographers, and I work with a church department
of population. I must make the usual caveat that, of course, we saw
a very small portion of China, and my observations are going to be entirely non-scholarly and non-scientific.

Before going to China I had read a good deal about China's population policies and their family planning program. The elements that
are usually mentioned are the Chinese stress on late marriages; having one child, probably within a year after marriage; having a space
then of four or five years, followed by a second child; and then,
ideally, sterilization for the woman or the man.

The first observation I would like to emphasize is that it is
simply impossible to understand the pervasiveness of this program until you experience it on the spot. We are so accustomed to our own
medical and health care system in which we need to be motivated to go
out and seek some kind of service. But virtually nothing is left to
that kind of chance in China. I had the feeling that we were never
more than 20 feet away from somebody who was responsible for family
planning. Every work brigade on a commune, every workshop in a factory, every unit of a neighborhood lane, has a person or persons who
are responsible for the family planning program. We always asked
about family planning even when we were doing the usual tourist kind
of things, and once during a tour of a lacquer ware factory we asked
our interpreter to take us to the person in that workshop who was
responsible for family planning. She immediately took us over to a
young woman who opened her work bench drawer, and there she had a box
of condoms and two kinds of pills. She did not prescribe them, but
she kept them on hand for people who forgot to take their pill or some
other special circumstances. The clinic and the factory, or the clinic
and the commune, keep the menstrual records and the contraceptive

records of women and couples. There's simply no way of not taking your pill, and not having someone know about it.

Having read that abortion is easily available in China, I was quite interested to find out that, in fact, they do frown upon more than one. If a woman becomes pregnant because of contraceptive failure, and that should really be the only excuse, she can have an abortion. But if she becomes pregnant twice, when it's not her turn or when she's not supposed to, she is lectured very severely on her carelessness (this was the term they usually used) and they would probably recommend that she be sterilized.

The full range of family planning services of pills and condoms, the IUD, sterilization--any kind of contraceptive service--is free, even though there are fees for all the other kinds of health care, which also somewhat surprised me. Even a tubal ligation in a hospital is performed absolutely free of charge.

But the pervasiveness extends far beyond the availability of services. Mao said over and over, and we heard over and over, that family planning, or controlling population growth, is not a matter of technology, it's a matter of ideological and political work among the masses. And here again, I don't think you're ever more than 20 feet away from somebody who is charged with that responsibility. It was even difficult to quite get a picture of the structure of family planning services because there were so many overlapping units that could and would deal with the question. There's a family planning committee in every factory and every commune; the Women's Federation does a lot of work in this area; and the Revolutionary Committee of the Party is responsible for seeing that all these other units are doing what they should to propagandize people. The propaganda is personal--about why you will benefit if you have a smaller family--as well as why it is important to the nation in building the new socialist society. There are posters all around stressing population control. Our interpreters frequently pointed to posters hanging on buildings that said, "We cannot build our society and achieve our goals unless we control population."

We often asked for examples of how this all worked, and I remember one story they told about a mother-in-law who was still possessed by Confucian ideas and thought that men were superior to women. Her daughter-in-law had had two daughters, and wanted to be sterilized, but the mother-in-law thought she should keep trying to have a son. The peer pressure began with a visit from a group of women from the family planning association, followed by a visit from a barefoot doctor. They would sit down with her and talk about what old China had been like, and the fact that she herself had had eight children of whom five had died. This happened to be a commune that specialized in growing fragrant blossoms for tea, such as jasmine; in old China women were not even permitted to irrigate because so contemptible

161

were women that their presence might blight the tea blossom. So they pointed out to this mother-in-law that now her daughter was educated and could work with the tea blossoms and had a future in the society. And eventually, the mother-in-law agreed that two was enough, even if they were girls.

So while in many ways there's no choice in this matter in China, there's a constant effort to have people understand why there is a necessity to control their growth.

I was also interested to observe the extent to which women still control practically this whole system. They have worked so hard and have really done incredible things. I still don't quite understand how, in such a short time, they have raised the status of women as much as they have, which was really from the level of a beast of burden in old China. In all of the communes or factories I visited the family planning committee is made up entirely of women. Even though all of this propaganda is directed at men as much as at women, and couples always sit down together to be told about family planning means, it seemed as though the women had more feeling for what it had to do with their lives, and they wanted to keep control of it. I don't think we ever heard of a man who was on a family planning committee in any of the communes or factories. Perhaps as a result, tubal ligations are about seven times more frequent than vasectomies in China.

One thing that interested me was that we were told that population policies do not apply to minorities since China is very anxious for them to be upgraded because they were the lowliest of the low. There is, however, beginning to be some resentment on the part of the Han majority that the minorities are not expected to participate.

And one last word. On this trip I really became aware of how obsessed Americans are with statistics. We found it very difficult to break out of the pattern of asking that everything be quantified, which I think the Chinese very often found puzzling. But when we went into a local factory or a commune, they always had exact statistics on how many women were using the pill, how many women were using the IUD, how many couples were depending on the condom. Though it's hard for Americans to accept, I believe them when they say they do not have national population statistics; the only figures they're collecting are the ones they need for planning at the decentralized units of commune and factory.

DISCUSSION

SHARON LYNN, The Environmental Fund: I'd like to know a little bit about your itinerary since the reports we're getting out of China have an enormous variety in them. Could you tell us a little bit more about your trip route?

JESSMA BLOCKWICK: That's why I put in the caveat about not being scholarly. Basically, the areas we visited were Peking, Souchong, Nanking, Canton, and Shanghai. We never met anybody who made claims beyond their own area--that's the reason I stressed that we got strictly local statistics--and they always pointed out that they were doing much better in the cities than in the countryside. We were told by an official in Peking that their goal is to get down to a 1% growth rate. When we asked when they were aiming to achieve that, he said they didn't know, but a woman looked up and said, "Well, as soon as possible." So, when I speak of the pervasiveness, obviously there are differences in quality and in how effective it's being, and I don't think they ever misled us as to that. But I see no reason to question that they're putting this into position as rapidly as possible, and it seems to be as effective a system as you could probably come up with.

ALAN ACKERMAN, Navajo Community College: In another session, Mr. Ravenholt, director of the AID population program, said that he had information which indicated that China's crude birth rate on the national level was now 12. I find this a little difficult to believe. I have also heard him say, on another occasion, that the Chinese have established a policy of a one-child family. Did you find any evidence of movement toward a one-child limit, and do you have any nationwide data about either the crude birth rate or the growth rate in China?

JESSMA BLOCKWICK: No, we never found any Chinese official who would make any statement about that, except as to their goal. I think that Leo Orleans and others are probably right in saying we just really do not know what's going on inside of China as far as the total. The Chinese claim they do not have the statistics themselves. Some people think they're just concealing them, but I don't really know why they would. As far as anybody knows they haven't taken a census for some time. Americans find it hard to believe, but I think they gather what they need to gather in order to achieve their immediate goals, and not simply to collect statistics. So I don't know where Mr. Ravenholt got his figures. We had a meeting with the staff of the American embassy there, and they didn't feel there was any good information on that. I think you pay your money and take your choice.

We never heard anything about a one-child family. We did ask if there were cases of women who chose not to have any children or not even to get married, and we were told that that is still very rare. It seems to me that China has built a whole new system on a very old system. Everything still is very much family centered and even intergenerational centered. Most young couples would still choose to live near or with their in-laws. Of course, in the old days it was always with the husband's in-laws, but we were told that now they'll choose whichever one might be better for babysitting purposes, which I thought was a very American concept. But they still are very apt to be centered on home and family, and, apparently, it's still quite rare for

163

a Chinese couple to choose to have fewer than two children. The children are, obviously, still very much at the center of society. We had a number of doctors with us who were quite impressed with the health and the care and attention given to children, including by the fathers. We would notice, for example, when we went to a clinic in a hospital, there would be as many fathers with their children waiting in line to see a doctor as there would be mothers. So, while there have been changes in the sharing of nurturing roles and the child care roles, I think it would be a rare Chinese who would not want children.

JOHN CONROY, Arlington, Virginia: Were you able to observe whether or not there was such a thing as an unwanted child in China?

JESSMA BLOCKWICK: I don't think we ever asked a question quite that way. We did ask if there were adoption, and they said it's really very rare. They insist that there is virtually no premarital sex in China, and I think that's believable in terms of the difference in the media, and the lack of privacy, the constant education to serve the people, and all of that. They don't claim there isn't any, but there would be no onus about the child of an unmarried couple. We were told that the young woman could either have an abortion, or could give up the child for adoption. I think it would be rare to encounter unwanted children in China simply because all the services are so available and there's no moral stigma about having an abortion. If you became pregnant and didn't want the child there'd be no problem with having an abortion. The problem would be if you repeated that pattern, and then they would want you to be sterilized. So it would be very hard to think of circumstances in which anybody would have to have an unwanted child, except, perhaps in the rural communes way out west where medical services are not quite as available as they are in the cities.

PETER HUESSY, The Environmental Fund: What's irritating is to hear you describe this program as "family planning;" in fact, it drives me up a wall. It is not family planning. You can plan to have a hundred kids. It is population control. And I think all the difference in the world lies in the distinction between those two words. The family planners say you can have as many children as you want. In China, as you've pointed out several times, "They" want you to be sterilized after two or three children. I feel it's terribly important that this distinction be made.

JESSMA BLOCKWICK: These are my perceptions and my use of terminology, Peter. You may have yours. I think we all use terms as we mean them to be used. I did make a distinction between the fact that they have family planning services, and they do have population control goals. I simply don't think the use of the term "family planning" per se implies that you can have a hundred children.

PETER HUESSY: But I think that's what's very confusing to

people. I don't think it's birth planning. It's birth control or population control.

JESSMA BLOCKWICK: Well, that's the term we were told to use in order to get approval to come to China. We were told to come as a "birth planning" group and that's the reason we called ourselves birth planners.

CAROLE GOLDMAN, National Organization for Non-Parents: It seems to me that China has emphasized the motivational aspects very heavily while in the United States we're still very involved in the techno-logical aspects. We don't look enough at why people are having chil-dren or why people want large families. Is there some lesson we can learn from China about motivating people to choose their own behavior based on their own personal goals and values without moving into the population control stage?

JESSMA BLOCKWICK: I think we have to say just one more word about "control." Control of population growth is the ideal, the goal to which China is working. There obviously are people in China who are still choosing to have four and five children. We talked to a woman on a commune who had four children, and she's not an outcast. This is not controlled in the sense of being in force except through motivational means, and an awful, awful lot of peer pressure on the young people. But, since China has not achieved its growth goals, there clearly are people who are having more children still.

RICHARD SCHWARTZ, College of Staten Island: As I see it, there are two ways to approach population: one is in terms of sheer numbers and the other is in terms of the impacts of the people on resources and environment. For example, some people have pointed out that one American has an impact equal to fifty people in the underdeveloped world. Could you comment on what China is doing in the area of not wasting, cutting down on use, recycling.

JESSMA BLOCKWICK: We didn't look specifically at that because we were pretty concentrated. If you look back at what Mao said, the motivation for controlling population growth was that they could see ahead the problem of resources and feeding the people. We were told that what they're working toward is some kind of balance between re-sources and the problem of feeding everybody. However, if you read this past week about the trade agreement they signed with Japan, China is desperately anxious to industrialize and to modernize. We were on communes where they said they had thousands of dollars saved up in order to buy tractors, which are simply not available because, up till now, China has made a great effort to be self-reliant and self-sufficient. One evening I had a long discussion with some Westerners who had been in China for many years. I told them it sounded to me as though China was on the same course as the United States, of facing employment, resource and inflationary problems as they mechanize. Their response was "Well, you know, China has so many needs right now, they won't think about that until they get there, which might be fifty years or so." Fifty years didn't sound very long to me, but whenever we raised that question that was the level of the answer. Presumably, somebody in the government is working on it, but the whole drive is on better standard of living. There's a tremendous amount of construction going on every place. I see Tang wants a television set for everybody. We hear so much in the United States about how beautiful it is, all the labor out in the fields, but China is now anxious to mechanize as fast as they can. I never heard anything in terms of being frugal or conserving simply in order to save resources, but only because they have to right now.

PREVENTIVE CARE AS A PUBLIC HEALTH POLICY ISSUE--
A SURVEY OF FAMILY PLANNING AND FEMALE CIR-
CUMCISION IN EAST AND WEST AFRICA*

Fran P. Hosken

Publisher, Women's International Network News

This paper is based on a study trip in February/March of 1977
through seven countries in East and West Africa: Sudan, Egypt,
Ethiopia, Kenya, Ivory Coast, Upper Volta and Senegal. The purpose
was to survey health conditions of women related to reproduction,
to update my investigation of female circumcision, and to learn about
the impact and progress of family planning.

My objective here is to identify preventive care options and
activities in which women on all levels can participate as agents,
educators, and deliverers of services, as well as consumers. Participatory self-help by and for women will improve health and reduce
the need for acute care services.

I would define preventive care as the prevention of unwanted
pregnancies (child spacing) and the prevention of damaging repro-
duction-related practices such as female circumcision. A preventive
package should include all the essentials of life, such as food,
nutrition, environmental sanitation and prevention of disease. Such
a package should be addressed to women and should include women in
planning and delivery, since women are responsible for children,
water and food--the essentials of life.

My thesis is that channeling scarce resources to preventive
care and health education--where they have permanent results--is
much less costly and more productive than financing mostly curative
care, as is done now. China has developed one alternative to the
Western hospital-based system with the barefoot doctors.

I would like to outline another option here which is based on a
women-to-women preventive care approach, using existing traditional
birth attendants and midwives in most of the developing world and
especially in Africa. This should be backed by an all-out effort
_____
*The complete 15-page paper on which this condensation is
based is available from the author at 187 Grant Street, Lexington,
Mass. 02173.

in self-help health care and health education. Such a preventive, self-help and health education approach should be backed up by para-medical personnel with mobile health units and/or rural clinics, and finally by the existing medical research and hospital system in the cities.

Except for Egypt, family planning has been quite recently intro-duced in the African countries I visited, but services tied to the curative Western medical system are available only in the modern sector. Female circumcision practiced by the traditional health system continues almost unaffected by the modern health system, which ignores these practices.

The traditional birth attendants that exist in villages all over Africa can form a health delivery base. Most of the women can be taught new methods, and can take over the distribution of contraceptives and the teaching of birth control. In addition, young women from each community should be taught, as has been done, for in-stance, in the Sudan for some time. The Sudan has a highly developed midwife system.*

A training program for traditional birth attendants exists in Addis Ababa. The International Confederation of Midwives held semi-nars all over the world, including two in Africa ("Restructuring Midwifery Training Curricula"), and recommended that traditional birth attendants should be included. In Egypt one successful village program operates on a women-to-women base. Teaching traditional birth attendants modern skills will integrate them into the modern system and eliminate traditional, often unsanitary, and damaging practices which operate in opposition to modern health care.

Developing countries need to start extensive health education programs--multi-media presentations in preventive care, self-help and basic information on reproduction and sex--to provide all women with the basic information they need, since women make the basic health decisions for their families.

Our Bodies Ourselves, a book by women for women, has become an important tool for women forming health groups in the United States. Similarly, women in Africa must be given the opportunity to learn about the functions of their own bodies. Only when women have some control over their own bodies and lives will family planning be accepted in Africa. This knowledge will dispel old myths and thus the practice of excision will be abandoned. Health education pro-grams will also acquaint women with modern health care and what it has to offer.

*"The Training and Activity of Village Midwives in the Sudan," by Ahmed Bayoumi, M.D., Nairobi University Medical School, Nairobi, Kenya. Tropical Doctor, Vol. 6, No. 3, July 1976. (Article summar-ized in WIN NEWS 3-1 p. 24, available from WIN NEWS, 187 Grant Street, Lexington, Mass. 02173).

Self-help health and participatory health education should be publicly financed so as to reach those who are left out of the curative services. Family planning programs should obviously be part and parcel of a self-help health policy. In developing countries especially self-help health programs could fill a very large gap. Women are responsible for the welfare of children and therefore a women-to-women base for self-help health delivery is a logical answer.

Such preventive care packaging plus self-help and health education is much less expensive than building hospitals and clinics, reaches many more people and is self-perpetuating: it is an excellent investment and will have permanent results.

Survey of Family Planning and Female Circumcision in East and West Africa

Sudan--Population Growth 2.5%

Sudan recently began government supported family planning with a Family Planning and Infertility Clinic located in the Khartoum Civil Hospital. A private organization affiliated with IPPF has existed for several years. Family planning reaches only a few women in the modern sector and most women want as many children as possible. Decisions on child bearing are seldom made by the women who bear the children.

The Vth Congress of Obstetrics and Gynaecology in the Sudan which I attended had a panel discussion on female circumcision; a resolution was unanimously passed urging that "Female circumcision in any form should be abolished." Female circumcision in its severest form (infibulation) is practiced throughout the Sudan, except in the southern-most area, and statistics show that it is only marginally decreasing.

The Ministry of Health and Social Welfare sponsored the Congress and the inquiry into circumcision in order to find ways to abolish this practice. A World Health Organization - assisted study of the epidemiology is currently ongoing, including a questionnaire seeking to find out why people continue the operations.

Egypt--Population Growth 2.5%

Family planning in Egypt is fully supported by the government, with all health facilities participating. There are many private family planning clinics as well, sponsored by the Egyptian Family Planning Association. Nevertheless, the population is expected to double in the next 30 years. Circumcision, which used to be performed on all young girls up to about the 1920s, still continues in the villages, according to the Ain Shams University Gynaecological

169

Hospital. The operations are done mostly by village midwives as in the past. The village population is reached neither by family planning nor by information on reproduction and health.

Ethiopia--Population Growth 2.5%

The Family Planning Guidance Association has 182 clinics all over the country. The Ethiopian Women's Welfare Association has a birth attendant training program. This activity and other private health activities are being taken over by the government. Circumcision is universally practiced by all people of Ethiopia except those of Gojjam. Infibulation continues in Eritrea and in the border area of Sudan and is practiced by all Somali population groups (Ogaden). Family planning and modern health care reaches very few people.

Kenya--Population Growth 3.4 to 3.5%

Kenya has internationally supported family planning programs organized by the government as well as a United Nations-supported Program for Better Family Living. Female circumcision continues to be practiced by most population groups except the Luo and has been advocated by President Kenyatta ("No Kikuyu will marry an uncircumcized girl.") Fatalities are reported occasionally in the newspapers but the Health Department does not consider female circumcision a problem.

A woman's status depends on having many children. Basic health education in reproduction does not reach even young people in Nairobi. Circumcision continues to be widely practiced and family planning is not acceptable to the vast majority.

Ivory Coast--Population Growth 2.8%

Family planning is a private concern. There are no government programs at the present time. According to the Hospital in Treichville,*excision is widely practiced.

Upper Volta (Population Growth is Negative)

There are no family planning programs at the present time. Contraceptives are available to those who can afford to buy them in the cities. Female circumcision has been universally practiced in most of Upper Volta; up to 70% of the girls today are subjected to excision.

Senegal--Population Growth 2.7%

Family planning is a private matter. Most women want more children and infertility is their greatest concern. Excision is practiced in many areas in Senegal. Though it is widely advocated that

170

male circumcision should be done at clinics to prevent infections, nothing is said about female circumcision which continues in traditional ways without any sanitary measures.

The absence of family planning and the continuation of female circumcision are closely linked. Failure to promote basic health and reproductive education will ensure continuation of the practice of circumcision and the low rates of acceptance of family planning.

A health education campaign addressed to women and the support of a women-to-women health care and self-help system could remedy both, and should be internationally supported.

*Centre Hospitalier et Universitaire d'Abidjan, Hopital de Treichville, Maternite, Abidjan, Ivory Coast.

OBSTACLES AND ALTERNATIVES IN SUCCESSFUL IMPLEMENTATION OF FAMILY PLANNING PROGRAMS IN LDCs

Faisal M. Rahman

Division of Business and Accounting, Quincy College

The weight of evidence suggests that high rates of population growth are perhaps the single most important obstacle to economic growth. However, delays and difficulties in transforming abstract principle into positive reduction in population growth have proved formidable. The problem of reducing population growth rates can be subdivided into four aspects: (a) Technological advances and their impact on mortality rates; (b) Economic development and its effect on fertility rate; (c) Technology of fertility reduction and its acceptability, and (d) Birth Control Programs-- obstacles and alternatives.

This paper deals with the fourth and final aspect, since everything else proves meaningless if this part is inadequate. The most difficult job is not developing techniques of birth control but turning them into a successful program. The main obstacles to implementation of successful family planning programs in any LDC may be listed as follows: (a) illiteracy; (b) ignorance of family planning methods; (c) lack of communication between husband and wife; (d) the desire for children (especially sons) for political, economic and social reasons; (e) early marriage; (f) lack of alternatives for women; (g) few small family models to emulate; (h) invisibility of social support; (i) peasant resistance to change and (j) remote and problematic reward for successful action.*

The nature of the problem--as evident from this long list of obstacles--is far more complex than ordinarily understood. The prerequisites to any successful program are: (1) Creating attitudes favoring small families; (2) Creating attitudes favoring the use of birth control; (3) Increasing the knowledge about birth control programs; (4) Inducing the acceptance of some methods of birth

---

*B. Berelson, "On Family Planning Communication" Demography, 64b, 1, 94-105.

control, and (5) Inducing the effective use of the method.*

The key lies in education. Among all variables, a 1% change in the index of education exerts the largest absolute influence upon age specific birth rate, as shown in the following table:

EDUCATION LEVEL	NUMBER OF CHILDREN PER WOMAN		
	Ghana	Jordan	Chile
No Education	5.7	8.7	4.9
Elementary Education	5.2	7.3	1.3
Secondary Education	2.5	4.5	1.7
University Degree	0.5	4.0	n.a.

Source: Milbank Memorial Fund Quarterly, July, '68 and Population Bulletin of UN Economic and Social Office in Beirut, July, '73.

The message of family planning can be sent across through any of the following methods: (a) mass media; (b) mailing; (c) group meetings; (d) home visit and (e) local representation. The media and mailing materials may create an atmosphere conducive for adoption of family planning techniques but the last three measures are most effective with poor and uneducated people.

Studies of past and existing family planning programs suggest that population problems cannot be solved in isolation by promoting a variety of contraceptive services. An alternate population policy for the LDCs should be an intersectoral approach not only aimed at lowered fertility rates through birth control measures but accompanied by steps in the areas of child care, mass education, rural and urban community development and social welfare. The objectives of the policy should include: (a) Establishment of a small family norm of not more than 2 children; (b) Conception control in line with religious teachings (if possible); (c) Restriction of marriage by fixing minimum age; (d) Tax and other laws designed to encourage smaller families; (e) Regulation and direction of migration, and (f) Change in family relationship and the woman's role in the family.

Coordination of action by various government and private agencies to achieve these objectives should stretch from effective policy decisions, to creation of a psychosocial milieu to proper administration.

What is needed is a process of total communication coupled with a program of mass education. The higher the literacy, the lower the rate of population increase. This is even more true if female literacy is higher. The communication process in most previous family programs in most countries was woefully short in perspective and did not reach the relevant strategic groups. The communication process must deal with the following issues:

*S. Tangri, "Lessons from Successful Family Planning Programs," Studies in Economics, Heath & Company, Boston.

1.   Establishing the view that individuals and families, for their well-being, should have the right of access to contraceptive services, paralleling the rights of access to a minimum living, health care, education and work opportunity.

2.   Reaching the poor and the illiterate with birth control rationale and services.

3.   Influencing family relationships which are not character- ized by male domination, absence of reproductive knowledge, irres- ponsible parenthood, etc., and which play an important role in determining attitudes toward fertility.

4.   Getting the government officers, politicians, and mem- bers of elite groups to become concerned about the population prob- lem and to participate in population control efforts.[*]

William Rich, in his book, Smaller Families through Social and Economic Progress, puts forward almost the same argument sug- gested by this author:

> In a number of poor countries, birth rates have dropped
> sharply despite relatively low per capita income and
> despite relative newness of family planning programs.
> The common factor in these countries is that the ma-
> jority of the population has shared in the economic
> and social benefits of significant national progress
> to a far greater degree than in most poor countries.
> Combining policies that give special attention to im-
> proving the well-being of the poor majority of the
> population with large-scale, well-executed family
> planning programs should make it possible to stabilize
> population in developing countries much faster than
> reliance on either approach alone.

The problem of transmitting abstract principle into posi- tive reduction in population growth remains the main problem for most countries. The requirements are many--money, time, trained manpower, sincere leadership, active cooperation of everyone; the availability of some or all of these are limited in most LDCs.

----

*Ahmadullah Mia, "A Population Program Is More Than Family Planning," IDR 1973/4, pp. 17-21.

VILLAGE COUNCILS AND POPULATION CONTROL
IN BANGLADESH*

M. Rashiduzzaman

Political Science/Economics Department, Glassboro State College

Importance of local participatory institutions: There is a growing realization that population control cannot be achieved in the developing countries without community consciousness and active support of local participatory institutions. Union Parishad [Village Council] is the lowest elected institution in Bangladesh whose leaders could be harnessed for an effective population control program. This article is based on a study of 51 sampled village councils selected through stratified random sampling techniques.

Emerging rural leadership: One of our hypotheses was that a younger generation of village leadership has emerged which might be more receptive to population control programs and exert influence in the rural areas. Our hypothesis has been vindicated to the extent that 73.63% of the recently elected village councillors, according to this survey, do come from the 30 to 49 age group. More than 10% of our respondents were even below 30. It appears that most of our selected leaders were landowners and fairly affluent businessmen. Most of our surveyed leaders had literacy up to high school level. About 11% of them had up to college level literacy and only 2.48% of them were without any formal education.

Awareness of the Population Problem: The rural leaders are overwhelmingly aware of the fact that Bangladesh is overpopulated. They have also expressed their willingness to support government programs for fertility control. The elected village leaders offered a variety of suggestions for solving population problems in Bangladesh. Such overwhelming support (99%) for population control provides a sense of legitimacy to those who are involved in population policy making and implementation in Bangladesh.

Local Government Ordinance 1976 gave the village councils formal responsibility for helping to implement official population

*This paper is based on a research project in Bangladesh conducted with a grant from the Pathfinder Fund.

175

control policies. Numerous official exhortations called upon the elected local leaders to cooperate with population control policies and programs. It is believed that the new multisectoral community oriented population control programs will substantially depend on the elected local leaders and rural institutions. Although most of our respondents were aware of their new responsibility to help implement population control programs, only about 10% of them gave top priority to this new assignment. A variety of other functions (agriculture, cooperatives, village roads, etc.) were rated more important. Most of the rural leaders suggested some kind of integrated family planning program associated with different development activities. This is a significant input for the population policy makers who are thinking in terms of an integrated population control strategy.

Role of the Village Councils: The government seems to be using the local councils more as a sounding board for their policies. It is felt that the Union Parishads [village councils] in Bangladesh should be harnessed for the actual implementation and administration of programs. Numerous policy statements confirm that Bangladesh authorities were delegating some administrative and supervisory responsibilities to the village councils. It is impressive to note that more than 91% of the interviewed leaders were willing to accept further responsibilities and supervise local family planning programs. We have found that most of our surveyed village councils did not have adequate resources to take an effective part in family planning programs in their areas. Most of them wanted trained personnel and financial strength for the new responsibility in population control. They also asked for more legal authority to play an effective role in population control.

The need for financial resources could be met by allocating additional funds. Other resources needed are: trained personnel, transportation, and family planning clinics. Further extension of authority may include the right to hire and fire local family planning officials, report job irregularities and recommend follow up.

We found that villagers usually seek the advice of the rural leaders about birth control and contraception. Although it is difficult to assess the actual influence of the local leaders, the majority of our respondents (52.77%) felt that the villagers usually accepted their suggestions. Most of the interviewed leaders recommended voluntary family planning associations at the local level. They recommended that voluntary organizations could be used to distribute contraceptives and provide birth control information.

Our respondents offered their help in motivation campaigns. Most of them (70%) agreed to introduce family planning workers in their respective communities. They also offered definite

176

suggestions about the supervisory role they can play. A good percentage of them recommended joint supervision of population control activities by the village council and some informal leaders: i.e., teachers, local Matbars, the Ulema, etc.

We wanted to find out if the government actually seeks cooperation of the Union Parishad in implementing family planning programs and, if so, what the nature of such activities was. We were not really impressed by the frequencies of official requests for local council cooperation in family planning. More frequent meetings and coordinated activities between the Union Councillors and family planning personnel are needed.

Conclusion: The government of Bangladesh may delegate more supervisory functions and some controling authority to the Union Parishads for implementation of family planning programs. This may be done gradually by transferring limited controlling authority and supervisory functions initially. Subsequent expansion of such authority can be made after careful evaluation of powers already delegated to the Union Parishads. Delegation of power should be specific; otherwise it will generate a clash of personalities and confusion, which will be counterproductive to population control programs.

Union Parishad members and chairmen could be more vigorously involved in official campaigns for family planning. Two women members have already been nominated to fulfill the family planning responsibilities of the village councils. It should, however, be a specific obligation of all the members and chairmen to extend necessary cooperation for family planning campaigns. An effective training program could be launched for this purpose.

FAMILY PLANNING ATTITUDES OF TRADITIONAL AND ACCULTURATED NAVAJO INDIANS

Alan Ackerman, Klara B. Kelley, Joyce Shohet Ackerman and
Katherine D. Hale

Navajo Community College

The Navajo Indians live primarily in the Navajo Nation, an area of about 25,000 square miles, covering a large portion of Arizona as well as parts of New Mexico and Utah. Until the 1930s, most Navajo households lived off the commercial and subsistence products of sheep herds. During that decade the U.S. government cut the Navajo livestock population in half to reduce a serious overgrazing situation. Since then, wages and public assistance have been the main sources of income (8,9,10).

The Navajo population has grown greatly since the livestock reduction, though the Reservation area has received few additions since about 1920. The population of the Navajo Nation in 1930 was around 35,000 (7) and is now about 130,000 (6). Crude birth rates are currently in the high 30s and infant mortality rates are about 20. The overall mortality rate is slightly higher than the national rate and life expectancy is rising toward national levels. These figures suggest that Navajo people are in a state of socioeconomic transition toward industrial development. In this context, the Navajo Nation can be seen as a region of the United States with many characteristics of a developing country.

A small number of studies give information on the attitudes of Navajo people toward family planning. The earliest of these is Bailey's study (1) of sex practices and beliefs in Navajo communities based on interviews in the early 1940s. Bailey's informants had little use for family planning. They looked favorably on contraception only when having children would endanger a woman's health. They valued children to help around the house, especially as the parents grew old. Their knowledge revealed little discussion between men and women on sex practices in general. Many believed that conception occurred during menstruation.

Kunitz (5) has analyzed attitudes of Navajo people in 1972-73 in communities around the northwest Navajo Reservation, including both rural and industrializing communities. As with Bailey's informants, the older women in this survey considered contraception justifiable only to preserve the health of a woman, but younger women were more interested in learning about contraception. Women whose husbands favored family planning were more likely to use contraception. Kunitz also suggests that spouses living in "traditional" extended family residence groups are less likely to discuss family planning with each other than are spouses living in "modern" nuclear households. Mean number of pregnancies per woman increases with age, of course, but decreases with education among women under 50. Mean number of pregnancies for women over 50 with no formal education was 13.

Kunitz' analysis indicates a difference in attitudes between older and younger women and between women living in "traditional" and "modern" circumstances, with the younger and modern women favoring family planning more. This may suggest that attitudes become more favorable as educational levels rise and industrialization proceeds. Another study by Kunitz in 1976 (4) suggests that the practice of family planning may increase as development of the area proceeds. The eastern Navajo Nation is more industrialized now than the western area. Both mortality and fertility rates in the eastern portion are lower than in the western area, though they are still above the national average. However, Kunitz also shows that, for the reservation as a whole, birth rates remain high while death rates (especially among infants) are dropping (2,3).

In order to learn more about the attitudes and expectations of a highly educated group of Navajo people, we administered a questionnaire survey at Navajo Community College, which is owned and operated by the Navajo Tribe. The student body is 90% Navajo, 5% other Indian, and 5% non-Indian. We discarded all questionnaires from students who indicated that neither parent was Navajo. The survey included questions on such indices of acculturation as respondent's age at first marriage, first language learned in childhood, percentage of life spent in the Navajo Nation, educational level of parents, number of siblings, type and location of schooling, occupational preferences, income sources, voting behavior, religious practice, and degree to which respondent considers him or herself "traditional" or "modern" along several dimensions. Also included were questions on attitudes toward limiting family size, responsibility for family planning, value of children, acceptability of abortion, and traditional beliefs on conception and pregnancy.

The questionnaire was administered over a two-day period in eight of the largest classes at NCC. These included required courses and other courses taught in English or Navajo, to obtain a representative sample of the student body. Ninety-nine students returned questionnaires and 85 of these were retained.

The final sample of 85 includes 53 women (62%) and 32 men (38%). The mean age for the entire sample is 23. Mean age at first

179

marriage is 19 years (18 for women, 21 for men). About 34% have at
least one child (49% of the women, 20% of the men). Respondents
with children had an average of 2. The parents of respondents had
an average of 7 living children.

The first language learned in childhood was Navajo for 60%,
while 32% learned English first and 7% learned both languages simultaneously. The majority of the respondents have spent 100% of their
lives in the Navajo Nation. About half the respondents have registered to vote. Forty percent of the respondents have gone to a traditional medicine man for treatment in the last two years.

The Navajo people in this survey appear to hold attitudes towards family planning quite different from their parents and grand-
parents. Whereas most of the women over 50 in Kunitz' sample favored family planning only to preserve the health of the mother, the
majority of the respondents (50% of the men with 37% neutral, and
75% of the women with 17% neutral) agreed with the statement that a
woman should have the opportunity to limit the number of children
she wants.

While the majority of women in the sample knew that the maximum
risk of pregnancy occurrence was not during the time of menstruation,
25% of the women in the sample did agree that intercourse during a
monthly period carries a high risk of pregnancy.

While abortion as a method of birth control was not considered
acceptable (50% did not favor it), 20% did agree with abortion and
30% had no opinion. The students in the sample do not appear to
feel that people want children to help around the house (as labor)
or for security as the parents get older (social security in children). Conversely, the majority feel that limiting family size to
increase the standard of living is good, and that limiting family
size allows each child to have more attention. In general, the
composite attitude of this young educated population would seem to
favor the availability of family planning services.

The students at NCC are a young and relatively well educated
group living in "modern" circumstances. They are younger and have
more years of education than Kunitz' informants, and live in more
modern circumstances than Bailey's. Therefore, we would expect them
to be more sympathetic toward family planning than the informants
of Bailey or Kunitz. The results of this survey confirm this ex-
pectation.

The students tend to agree that women ought to be free to limit
the number of children and that one should limit the number of children to provide each with a better standard of living. They tend to
disagree with the statement that it is important to have many children. Furthermore, the ideal numbers of children they specify for
both Navajos in general and themselves are below those of Kunitz'

younger informants. And these ideal family sizes are certainly
well below the 7 children that their parents have had. However,
nearly half the women in our sample have children already, even
though their mean age is only 23. In order for these students to
achieve their goal of limiting family size to three children, they
will need access to more birth control information and devices.
Data collected here indicate that information discretely provided
to younger people on family planning would be more useful than a
general education campaign aimed at the entire Navajo population.

REFERENCES

1. Bailey, Flora L. Some Sex Beliefs and Practices in a Navajo
   Community. Papers of the Peabody Museum Vol. 50 No. 2. Cambridge: Harvard University, 1950.

2. Kunitz, Stephen J. Demographic Change among the Hopi and Navajo
   Indians. Lake Powell Research Project Bulletin No. 2. Los
   Angeles: UCLA Institute of Geophysics and Planetary Physics,
   1973.

3. _____. Factors Influencing Recent Navajo and Hopi Population
   Changes. Human Organization 33:7-16, 1974.

4. _____. The Relationship of Economic Variables to Mortality
   and Fertility Patterns on the Navajo Reservation. Lake Powell
   Research.Project Bulletin No. 20. Los Angeles: UCLA Institute
   of Geophysics and Planetary Physics, 1976.

5. _____. A Survey of Fertility Histories and Contraceptive Use
   among a Group of Navjo Women. Lake Powell Research Project
   Bulletin No. 21. Los Angeles: UCLA Institute of Geophysics
   and Planetary Physics, 1976.

6. U.S. Commission on Civil Rights; Hearings, Window Rock, Arizona,
   Oct. 22-24, 1973. Washington, D.C.: U.S. Government Printing
   Office.

7. U.S. Department of Commerce, Bureau of the Census. Fifteenth
   Census of the United States, 1930. Vol. 3. Washington, D.C.:
   U.S. Government Printing Office.

8. Wistisen, Martin, Robert J. Parsons, and Annette Larson. A
   Study to Identify Potentially Feasible Small Businesses for the
   Navajo Nation, Phase I: An Evaluation of Income and Expenditure
   Patterns, vol. 2. Provo: Brigham Young University Center for
   Business and Economic Research, 1975.

9. Young, Robert. The Navajo Yearbook 1958. Window Rock, AZ:
   Navajo Agency, 1958.

10. _____. The Navajo Yearbook 1961. Window Rock, AZ: Navajo
    Agency, 1961.

INTRODUCING AN ASSESSMENT POINT AS A FIRST STEP TOWARD EVALUATING FAMILY PLANNING PROGRAMS

Chia-Lin Pan

United Nations Social Affairs Officer (Retired)

Due to vigorous efforts in medical research on family planning techniques, it is now feasible for nurses in developing countries to administer most contraceptive treatments. This includes the injection of Depo Provera in liquid or solid (silastic implant) form for an effective contraceptive period ranging from 18 to 60 months, as an alternative to the pill, diaghragm or IUD. Early pregnancy treatment by means of menstrual induction (dosaged diethylstilbestrol) or early abortion by means of prostaglandins (either by injection or as a vaginal suppository), vacuum aspiration (with curettage for checking) and dilation curettage, can be performed by a nurse on the recipient as an out patient procedure within the first trimester. These new techniques have the potential to make contraceptive services widely available in the Third World.

There are some 15 countries and areas where family planning services have achieved fairly concrete results. Table 1 lists these countries and areas, showing their 1975 population, average birth rate for 1970-75, the calculated ratio of women in childbearing age groups to total population for 1970 and 1975, the average ratio for the period 1970-75 or its estimated value, and the period average level of total fertility rate.

The 1970-75 period average level of total fertility rate ranged from about 0.1000 in Hong Kong, Singapore and Barbados to 0.1560 in Republic of Korea and Jamaica. Since the average fertility level referred to the midpoint of 1970-75, it is reasonable to assume that the present level of the countries with even the highest total fertility rate would have dipped to below 0.1500. In order to have some assessment point against which family planning programs can be evaluated, we have, therefore, arbitrarily selected the 0.1500 level as an indicator of implied effective motivation for family planning on the part of recipients of the services. Table 2 shows 31 countries and areas where some family planning service has been in existence, classified by population, ratio of women in childbearing age groups to total population and total fertility rate for the 1970-75 period with a calculated standardized rate for comparison. In these countries, making

182

progress in the area of new acceptors of family planning services and in that of enhancing achievements of accustomed acceptors is crucial to improving their living standard, particularly in those countries with limited natural resources.

Defining total fertility rate at 0.1500 as an indicator of on-par mutual effort-making (by the recipients as well as the service renderers) is a first step toward evaluating field work performance in some concrete terms.

TABLE 1

COUNTRIES AND AREAS WITH ACHIEVED RESULTS IN FAMILY PLANNING, ON THE BASIS
OF AVERAGE TOTAL FERTILITY RATE FOR 1970-1975

Country or Area By Continent (1)	Population in 000's, 1975 (2)	Average Birth Rate for 1970-75 (3)	Ratio: women at childbearing age/total population			Average Total Fertility Rate 1970-75 (7)	Period Rating on Family Planning Motivation (8)
			1970 (4)	1975 (5)	Average 1970-75 (6)		
Africa							
Mauritius (isle.)	858	27.0	*	*	.210**	.1290	above par
Reunion	493	29.1	*	*	.210**	.1390	above par
Asia							
Republic of Korea	36,245	33.3	.211	.218	.215	.1560	near par
Republic of China	16,076	26.1	.220	.226	.223	.1170	above par
Sri Lanka	13,728	28.7	.203	.227	.215	.1340	above par
Hong Kong	4,339	19.5	*	*	.210**	.0930	above par
Singapore	2,251	21.5	*	*	.210**	.1020	above par
Macao	277	(25)	*	*	.210**	(.1200)	above par
Latin America							
Chile	10,595	27.5	.201	.212	.207	.1330	above par
Jamaica	2,065	32.7	*	*	.210**	.1560	near par
Costa Rica	1,967	30.7	.202	.219	.210	.1460	above par
Trinidad & Tobago	974	25.5	*	*	.210**	.1220	above par
Guadeloupe	352	28.5	*	*	.210**	.1360	above par
Martinique	351	25.0	*	*	.210**	.1200	above par
Barbados	232	21.5	*	*	.210**	.1030	above par

Note: "Above par" (column 8) signifies above par motivation effort in practicing family planning on
the part of recipients of contraceptive services in the community at large.

*Due to effects of international migration and shifting relative proportions of age groups, calcula-
ted ratios are not adequate for approximating the total fertility rate.

**For approximating total fertility rates, the ratio .210, which has been derived from empirical
models based on ranges of factor variation, is used.

TABLE 2

COUNTRIES AND AREAS WITH SOME FAMILY PLANNING SERVICE BY
POPULATION, RATIO OF WOMEN AT CHILDBEARING AGE, TOTAL
FERTILITY RATE AND STANDARDIZED RATE, 1970-75

			1970-75 Period Average	
Country or Area (1)	Population In Millions 1975 (2)	Ratio: Childbearing Age Women/ Population (3)	Total Fertility Rate (4)	Standardized Rate (5)
Africa				
Nigeria	63.0	.215	.2300	.2300
Egypt	37.1	.210	.1850	.1850
Sudan	18.3	.215	.2500	.2500
Morocco	17.5	.192	.2500	.2300
Algeria	15.7	.192	.2500	.2300
Kenya	13.6	.200	.2500	.2400
Tunisia	5.8	.197	.1890	.1850
Botswana	0.6	.207	.2200	.2200
Swaziland	0.5	.213	.2400	.2400
Asia				
India	614.0	.210	.1900	.1900
Indonesia	139.4	.210	.2050	.2050
Bangladesh	80.6	.210	.2200	.2200
Pakistan	69.3	.210	.2100	.2100
Philippines	43.4	.210	.2000	.2000
Thailand	42.4	.201	.2000	.1900
Turkey	40.3	.213	.1850	.1850
Iran	34.9	.200	.2300	.2200
Nepal	12.6	.210	.2100	.2100
Malaysia	12.4	.205	.1800	.1750
Syria	7.4	.190	.2500	.2300
Yemen (San'a)	6.6	.210	.2350	.2350
Yemen (Aden)	1.7	.210	.2350	.2350
Latin America				
Mexico	59.2	.209	.2150	.2150
Colombia	25.8	.210	.2000	.2000
Venezuela	12.8	.210	.2000	.2000
Ecuador	7.0	.210	.2100	.2100
Bolivia	5.4	.214	.2100	.2100
Haiti	5.1	.220	.2000	.2050
Dominican Republic	4.9	.210	.2200	.2200
El Salvador	4.1	.206	.1950	.1900
Honduras	3.2	.210	.2250	.2250

Note: The listed countries and areas refer to those with a population of half a million or more. The standardized total fertility rate assumes that the ratio of chilbearing age women to total population be .210.

UNWANTED FERTILITY AND POPULATION POLICY

Robert H. Weller

Center for the Study of Population, Institute for
Social Research, Florida State University

The extent of unwanted fertility is crucial to the proper formulation of policies to reduce fertility levels. If a substantial
proportion of births is unwanted, then the elimination of unwanted
childbearing would result in a significant reduction in fertility.
However, if only a small portion of births is unwanted, then the
elimination of unwanted childbearing would not affect current fertility levels very much. In the first case, suitable policies of
reducing fertility levels would be directed toward increased distribution and use of birth prevention techniques. In the second
instance, deliberate attempts to alter levels of fertility might
be most effectively aimed at reducing desired family size and the
level of wanted childbearing. This line of reasoning has led Ryder
and Westoff (1972) to state: "The extent of unwanted fertility is
at the core of the debate over the kind of fertility policy necessary to achieve replacement."

Direct information on unwanted childbearing is not available
for less developed countries. However, data collected in a number
of less developed countries show that completed family size is
usually larger than desired family size and that most couples with
3 or 4 children do not want more (Berelson, 1966, pp. 658-662).
Thus people in these countries are having more children than they
desire and the provision of birth prevention services, supplies, and
knowledge would facilitate lower fertility.

However, even if realized, desired family size in these countries would still be considerably higher than replacement level
fertility and non-family planning approaches to reducing fertility
are also necessary.

In the United States a surprising proportion of births are unwanted. Women ages 15-44 in 1973 reported they would have had 14
million fewer babies during their lifetime if they had borne only
the children they wanted at the time they became pregnant. Average
family size would have been 2.1 instead of the 2.6 CEB actually observed. On a cross-sectional basis, almost 10% of all births in

1973 to ever married women were reported by the mother as "not wanted."

If no unwanted births occurred in the United States, the birth rate would be considerably lower and the rate of population growth would be reduced. For example, if no unwanted legitimate births had occurred, the amount of population growth would have been reduced by 20.7% in 1968, 17.9% in 1969, and 14.5% in 1972 (Weller, 1976).

Table 1 contains the cumulative fertility (including current pregnancies) of currently married, once married women interviewed in the 1973 National Survey of Family Growth. Each birth is classi- fied by wantedness and timing status and by its mother's race. The role of unwanted childbearing in producing racial differentials in cumulative fertility is clear. Blacks average .55 more children ever born than whites. This is entirely a function of the fact that blacks are more than three times as likely as whites to have had an unwanted birth. If only wanted births (including timing failures) are counted, then whites would average 1.91 live births and blacks would average 1.93 live births. Blacks also average more timing-later failures and less timing-sooner failures and births "wanted then" than whites average.

TABLE 1

Average Number of Live Births by Wantedness Status and Race

Wantedness Status	Whites	Blacks	Ratio of Blacks to Whites
All births	2.14	2.69	1.26
Unwanted births	.23	.75	3.26
Wanted but later	.54	.76	1.41
Wanted but sooner	.21	.10	.48
Wanted then	1.16	1.07	.92
Other	.00	.01	---
No. of wives	24,489[*]	2,081[*]	

[*]Numbers of cases are rounded off to the nearest 1000.

Source: Weller and Hobbs (1978).

187

Unwanted childbearing has several negative consequences for society, the child, and the child's family. Combining these with its demographic effects suggests that eliminating unwanted childbearing should be given a very high priority by national governments.

1. The costs to the family of raising a child to age 18 ranges from $77,000-$107,000 (Espenshade, 1977). Incurring such costs may result in financial hardship for the parents and reduce the amount of money available on a per capita basis for expenditure on the unwanted child's brothers and sisters as well as on improving the family's standard of living.

2. The groups that generally have the least financial resources-- the poor--have the most unwanted childbearing. Thus unwanted childbearing not only perpetuates poverty, it increases it.

3. Children resulting from unwanted pregnancies are more likely than other children to be socially and mentally maladjusted.

4. Considerable costs to governments in terms of direct expenditures for welfare, medical, and social services and lost tax revenues occur. For the 250,000 unwanted births in 1973 only, it is estimated that the costs to the federal government by the time they reach age 19 will be almost $2 billion. This is for 1973 births only. It does not take into account costs incurred by unwanted births from other years. It does not take into account costs to local and state governments (Weller, 1978).

There are two things that could be done to reduce unwanted childbearing in the United States:

1. Improve the contraceptive practices of all segments of the population. The extent and accuracy of beliefs and knowledge of currently existing contraceptive technology should be studied. The reasons some segments of the population are apparently unable to control their family size successfully while other segments of the population are able to do so should receive high priority. Is the explanation motivation, education, communication, and/or distribution? For some segments of the population such as teenagers and the poor it may be necessary to develop and use a completely different communication and distribution system than currently exists.

2. Socially and economically nontraumatic abortions should be made available to all segments of the population. At the present time, abortion is not readily available to the poor and to persons not living in metropolitan areas. The United States is on record to the effect that it is a basic human right for a couple to decide the number and spacing of their children. This right should not be denied to people just because they are poor, or black, or don't live in a large metropolitan area.

REFERENCES

1. Berelson, Bernard. "KAP Studies on Fertility." In _Family Planning and Population Programs_, Bernard Berelson et al., eds. Chicago: University of Chicago Press, pp. 655-668, 1966.

2. Espenshade, Thomas J. "The Value and Cost of Children." _Population Bulletin_ 32 (April), 1977.

3. Ryder, Norman B. and Charles F. Westoff, "Wanted and Unwanted Fertility in the United States: 1965 and 1970." In _Demographic and Social Aspects of Population Growth_, Charles F. Westoff and Robert Parke, Jr., eds. Washington: Government Printing Office, vol. I, pp. 467-487, 1972.

4. Weller, Robert H. "Number and Timing Failures Among Legitimate Births in the United States: 1968, 1969, and 1972." _Family Planning Perspectives_ 8 (May/June), pp. 111-116, 1976.

5. _____. "Family Size Goals and Their Realization by American Women." Testimony presented before the Select Committee on Population, U.S. House of Representatives, 1978.

6. _____ and Frank B. Hobbs. "The Differential Attainment of Family Size Goals by Race." Paper presented at annual meeting of the Southern Sociological Society, 1978.

189

ANXIETY STATE-TRAIT LEVELS IN FEMALES ACCEPTING AND RESISTING CONTRACEPTIVE METHODS FOR CONTROL OF FAMILY SIZE

Robert D. Towell

Medical University of South Carolina

In earlier research efforts this author has investigated anxiety levels between parents and children, parents and parents, parents and hemophilia children, couples in marital and sexual therapy, and delinquent families (Towell, 1976a, 1976b, 1976c, 1977a, 1977b). The results of these studies have been published or reported at various conferences in the United States and Europe.

The test instrument selected for these studies was the State-Trait Anxiety Inventory; the STAI form X-1 and X-2 for adults and, in two of the studies, the STAIC form C-1 and C-2 for children. The STAI form and the STAIC form consist of separate 20-item self-reporting rating scales for measuring state and trait anxiety. The STAI and STAIC A-scale requires people to describe how they feel at a particular moment; the STAI and STAIC A-Trait scores reflect relatively stable individual differences in anxiety proneness that are impervious to situational stress (Johnson and Spielberger, 1968; Spielberger, et. al., 1970).

The present study sought to measure anxiety levels between couples that were participating in the family planning clinic of the Spartanburg Public Health Center and couples who came to the center who had refused, for one reason or another, to use contraceptives in family planning. The design was to give the wives copies of the STAI form X-1 and X-2 which they filled out upon their visit to the Public Health Center, assisted by one of the public health nurses. The male form was given to the female to take home to her sex partner if she felt he was willing to fill out the form and mail it in a self-addressed envelope. However, the mail response was very poor, with only 11 out of a potential total of 80 responding. Therefore, it was decided to use just the female data in determining if there were any differences between the groups.

The statistical treatment of results indicated that there were no significant correlations between either of the groups. There were no significant differences between the means of each group on either the X-1 or the X-2 form (Table I and II).   In other words, there was no difference between the anxiety levels of the women in family planning and those not choosing to be in family planning. Anxiety is not a factor in their choice.

TABLE I

N=32

	Form	Mean	Standard Deviation	Standard Error
Family Planning Females	X-1	44.81	13.19	1.33
	X-2	45.21	12.61	1.11
Non-Family Planning Planning Females	X-1	45.91	13.47	2.35
	X-2	44.42	13.54	1.68

Table II

Correlation Coefficients of STAI Forms, X-1 and X-2

N=32

Form	Correlation Coefficient	Level of Significance
X-1	r = .1659	N.S.
X-1	r = .1940	N.S.

BIBLIOGRAPHY

1. Johnson, D. T. and Spielberger, C. D. The Effects of Relaxation Training and the Passage of Time on Measures of State and Trait Anxiety. _Journal of Clinical Psychology_, 1968.

2. Spielberger, C. D., Grosuch, R. L. and Lushene, R. E. _Manual for the State-Trait Anxiety Inventory_, Palo Alto, California: Consultants Psychologists Press, 1970.

3. Towell, R. D. "Anxiety State-Trait Levels Between Parents and Children in a Family Practice Clinic," _Stress and Anxiety_, Vol. 4, edited by C. D. Spielberger and I. G. Sarason; Hemisphere Publishing Co., Washington, D.C., distributed by John Wiley & Sons, 1976.

4. _____. "Treatment of Child Abuse." _Victims and Society_, edited by Emilio Viano, Visage Press, Inc., Washington, D.C. 1976.

5. _____. "Anxiety Levels Between Hemophilia Children and Parents." A paper presented to National Hemophilia Foundation, Chicago, Illinois, May, 1976.

6. _____. "Treatment of Delinquent Families." Paper presented to International Seminar on Comparative Criminal Justice, West Germany, July, 1977. To be published in proceedings.

7. _____. "Anxiety State-Trait Levels Between Couples in Marital and Sexual Therapy." Presented to Fifth International Congress of Psychosomatic Obstetrics and Gynecology, Rome, Italy, November, 1977. To be published in proceedings. Spring, 1978. (Academic Press).

SOME HINDRANCES TO COMPREHENSIVE POPULATION/FOOD POLICY IMPLEMENTATION

William R. Kornsey

Department of Psychology, Yeshiva University

Basic to an understanding of the population controversy is the realization that by the year 2000 the world's population will be 6 to 7½ billion; that a quarter of all the people who have ever lived since the dawn of history are alive today; that of the present population in the industrialized countries, 27% is under 15 years of age and the corresponding figure for developing countries is 42%; and that, no matter what political measures one envisages regarding population, it is probable that the world's population will have reached 12 billion within our children's lifetime (8). Moreover, it is theorized by many that population size will be reduced somehow because the present imbalance is too extreme to be maintained much longer.

Sometimes there is value in just being able to point out some of the difficulties in the nature of a problem. To this end, this paper lists a number of hindrances to be encountered in the design of comprehensive policy relating population to surrounding environmental conditions, especially food resources.

Conceptualization of the Problem

Many of the conceptual difficulties in developing a complete population/food/resource policy stem from the increasing polarity between two major factions contributing most of the literature on population. The minority view states that mankind will best be served by employing a "holistic" or ecologic approach to the analysis of man-environment relations. The ecologic method attempts to link man with the total environment. Here, researchers from many disciplines work to understand and control a host of complex variables at different levels of complexity in solving the problems of living.

Within the second group, the vast majority of writers dealing with population issues are "reductionists." Implicit in their work is the notion that population problems are reducible to simple causal factors, or a specific etiology, and often require a singular solution (e.g., immediate involuntary sterilization, massive dispersal of foreign aid, etc.). Further, the solution for a problem more often than not will come only from their specific discipline and, even more alarmingly, at their working level of analysis or expertise. There is little integration and agreement to be found in reductionistic writings; they are not interdisciplinary in nature. In extreme reductionism, the population dilemma is broken down into many fragmented conceptualizations. Often confused with a scientific approach, this "pigeonholing" leads to great confusion in the attempt to link man to his environmental surroundings since a unifying theme is lacking.

Some chief examples of this conceptual difficulty resulting from extreme reductionism are those who (1) point only to the lack of food production (volume-amount) as being the chief cause; (2) promote the belief that failure to achieve proper food distribution (sharing-caring) is the root cause; (3) are concerned only with kinds of food (types-nutritional value) being produced and distributed; and (4) deal with both amount and kinds of food being produced without regard for any other aspect of the population dilemma (behavior, economics, politics, technology). These first four kinds of conceptual reductionism are solely concerned with food; they believe that simply producing more and/or nutritionally more desirable foods will solve the problem.

Further conceptual hindrances are: (5) failure to take into consideration the earth's carrying capacity, the idea that the planet might have exceeded or will soon exceed its ability to properly support people in relation to resources; (6) failure to realize that maintaining present carrying-capacity might require extensive resource [ab]use and excessive pollution since there is little time for conversion to more efficient food and energy sources; (7) prematurely fostering massive decreases or increases in population without firm scientific determination of what carrying capacity really is (Ehrlich, in Pohlman, 1973, p. 17, asserts that the population of the United States should eventually be reduced to well under 50 million and that of the world to an absolute maximum of 500 million; Clark, also in Pohlman, 1973, p. 163, finds the world capable of supporting 28 billion people); (8) too little attention to the population distribution issue (since 1800, the influx to towns has increased at a colossal rate; compared with a three-fold increase in total world population, urban population has increased forty-fold).

Other voices in the conceptual debate are: (9) Those who rigidly adhere to the belief that the problem is ultimately reducible to the notion of "class struggle," i.e., that the issues are merely political and economic. (10) Those clamoring for an "attitude change" on the part of the underdeveloped countries concerning

194

family size. (11) The moralists who refuse to consider the problem because of "the sensitive nature" of population issues. Here a great number of educators, politicians, and religious members hide out. (12) Those promoting scientific study and technological intervention without regard for cultural differences, moral-ethical considerations, and aesthetic issues. (13) Those furthering "humanistic" concern and baldly deploring any use of science and technology, believing that science is "to blame," and a back-to-basics approach is the only salvation. (14) Those who solely intend to fix responsibility or blame, but who are unconcerned about actually ameliorating the crucial problems of starvation and pollution. (15) Those who make the serious error of assuming that because birth rates in some areas are decreasing that this resolves the issue and that overpopulation will not be a concern for the future. (16) Finally, perhaps our most dangerous misconception is that environmental, urban, and behavioral problems resulting from too rapid population growth are <u>not</u> <u>real</u>, that nobody dies of overpopulation, that there can be no such thing as overstimulation and dysfunction of the central nervous system with resultant behavioral and physiological pathologies due to population size or density.

Disagreement on Facts

An additional block to development of comprehensive population policy is extensive disagreement on scientific facts and the inferences which can be made from these findings. Some of these areas are:

1. Confusion over population figures (demographics) and trends.
2. The "limits to growth" controversy (especially demands for increase in the GNP ad infinitum).
3. Confusion over the present carrying-capacity of spaceship earth in relation to food and other resources.
4. The amount of land area available worldwide which is suitable for agricultural purposes. (The literature on this issue is incredibly varied. Ehrlich and Ehrlich, 1970, 1972, p. 113, cite a 1967 report of the President's Scientific Advisory Committee estimating the amount of potentially arable-farmable land on the earth to be 7.86 billion acres; Clark, in Pohlman, ed., p. 163, claims that the world possesses the equivalent of 77 million sq. km. of good temperate agricultural land. Ehrlich's figures are equivalent to approximately 31.8 million sq. km., less than half of Clark's estimate. Such glaring disagreements on critically important data are commonplace in the literature on population issues).
5. Limits to the "green revolution" issue (future agricultural production from dramatic improvements with high yield crops, fertilizers, pesticides, etc.).
6. The failure to separate hunger from malnutrition (starvation from proper or desirable nourishment).
7. Severity and latency period of overall environmental

195

degradation from too rapid population growth and resource abuse.

8. Consistent failure to recognize and accept the links between high population density and the resulting behavioral, physiological, and social pathologies.

9. Lack of consensus on the desirability of creating technological controls to replace naturally occurring controls.

10. The presumptuous notion that science and technology are limitless and, that given enough time, scientists will spontaneously generate solutions to all our problems (e.g., use of interstellar transport vessels to wisk our excesses of humanity away to colonizable worlds).

11. Decision-making on the optimum population for earth (taking into consideration the "quality of life" issue).

12. Has food production been keeping up with increases in population? From the Ehrlichs (1972, p. 109): ". . . in 1968 the average country in Africa and Latin America grew less food per person than it did 12 years before. This situation has obtained in spite of substantial increases (roughly 30-35%) in absolute food supplies in these areas during that period."

13. The possibility that we cannot continue to absorb massive population increases without unprecedented economic and political upheaval (especially in India, Pakistan, Latin America, and Africa).

14. Arguments on the state of technology concerning acceptable means of birth control, perhaps on a massive scale.

15. The mistaken belief that only in high numbers is there strength. That the higher the population, the greater the world power. As Clark (in Pohlman, ed., 1973, p. 285) states, "The facts of world power and of population are inescapably connected." The simple realization that about 16% of the world's population possesses nearly 80% of the world's wealth should explode the myth of power in excessive numbers.

16. The unchallenged belief that each woman should have the number of children she wants, under the assumption that if she has this number this will automatically curb population growth. Because a high proportion of the total population is at present under 15 years of age, the number of couples in fertile ages will increase dramatically within a few decades whatever the outcome of population planning. It seems clear that the world--saving an unforeseen disaster--will face a rather dramatic rise in population density during the next 50 years.

Incentives to Change

For any changes in human behavior (increased emphasis on food production, more equal distribution of food, decreased reproductive activity) there must be sufficient motivation. Behavioral changes are brought about through increased incentive or by substituting reinforcers. Some problems relating to change are:

1. Stubborn resistance to change in all human societies.
2. How to change the lifestyles of the wealthier peoples of

196

the world or, What incentives does one offer the wealthy to share their wealth--to sacrifice something?

3. Setting up specific stimuli to ensure a more equitable distribution of goods and services. Something explicit beyond pleas for virtue, sacrifice, and sharing.

4. The abandonment of short term profit for the altruism of long term good for the most amount of people.

5. The possibility of government sponsored incentives and programs to limit population size.

6. The tremendous problem of apathy--getting people to do something for future generations when the general attitude seems to be "What did posterity ever do for me?"

7. Resolving the moral dilemma for those who want to have more than the average number of children or more than they can adequately provide for. Here the possibility of ridicule and even prosecution might enter the issue. Is having a child when one is not prepared to provide for it a form of child abuse? What does an additional birth impose on society and the ecosystem?

8. Can education to the seriousness of the problem (the potential for suffering) offer enough incentive for responsible reproductive conduct?

9. The desirability of offering incentives for less family-oriented pursuits.

10. A possible qualitative change in our involvement with the family unit itself.

11. The realization that more people are lobbying for increased spending for military-related programs than health programs and, that the salaries of a great many Americans are directly or indirectly dependent on defense funds. It would seem that more people are working toward the destruction of mankind than the saving of it.

12. Exposing the false dichotomy set up between a past of so-called reproductive laissez-faire and a future of reproductive prohibition or brutal coercion. The issue concerns social control over reproductive motivation and behavior as separated from individual volition (where many reproductive controls are implicit and decentralized). Both forms are under the control of reinforcers; it's just more obvious under some controls than under others.

13. Population policy must include reward systems which are clearly understood, as opposed to simply resorting to rhetoric about attitude change. It must deal with the "costs" involved in deciding whether or not to be a parent.

14. Policy must account for the manner in which decrements in population or reproduction rates come about.

15. One should realize that no one introduces legislation and no one follows directives, unless there is some advantage in doing so.

16. One significant incentive we fail to make clear is that without changes in population size and distribution there is the serious potential for suffering and destruction. What does the future hold for a child in an overpopulated, hungry, polluted,

anxious and divided world?

17. We must recognize that continued experience with circumstances perceived to be beyond the control of one's actions leads to a condition of "helplessness" (9) where one may simply give up. This damage may be irreparable even with high incentives working to offset this condition.

18. The failure of present economic structure, in which the world's present technology is almost entirely based on extracting concentrated resources from the earth, processing them, and using them in such a way that the useful elements are dispersed so widely as waste products that we cannot, with present technology and will not under current economic practices, reuse them. Even if science and technology can save us, economics and politics will not permit it to under present incentive conditions.

Rewarding Action

We must break away from the pattern of simply "monitoring" the situation and begin to act and make over the world. It is less important to tell us whether in 1995 the U.S. will have 296 or 302 million people, or that the world might have 6.8 or 7.1 billion. Even knowing what the population is and what the problems are, we refuse to do something now. Action is needed, not more monitoring.

Population policy should attempt through education and technical services to make every birth the result of deliberate choice. As opposed to enforced sterilization to prevent births, or the punishment of unwanted births, changes in reproductive motivation and behavior can be brought about through the use of explicit reinforcement contingencies. We can create social change more effectively by outlining and rewarding what we want than we can through punishment or involuntary control of what we don't want.

The issues of serviceable or optimum population (in number and distribution) rest on much more than biological demands. With the added factors of culture and quality of life, the idea of what number of people is ideal is determined by a compromise between social and physical factors. This number is relative and open to change; it can be revised to meet changing conditions and is therefore evolutionary.

Note: This paper excerpts a portion of a much longer paper which finds in the population-food-resources literature some 123 primary hindrances to implementing a comprehensive population, food and resource policy. Reprints of the longer paper are available from the author at 5657 East Wister Street, Philadelphia, PA 19144.

BIBLIOGRAPHY

1. Berelson, B. "Population Policy: Personal Notes." In Pohlman (ed.), Population: A Clash of Prophets, A Mentor Book,
   New York, 1973.

2. Borgstrom, G. The Hungry Planet: The Modern World at the Edge
   of Famine. Collier Publishing, New York, 1972.

3. Clark, C. "World Population." In Pohlman (ed.), Population:
   A Clash of Prophets. A Mentor Book, New York, 1973.

4. Ehrlich, P. and A. Ehrlich. Population. Resources, Environment. W. H. Freeman and Company, San Francisco, 1970, 1972.

5. Ehrlich, P. "Playboy Interview." In Pohlman (ed.), Population:
   A Clash Of Prophets. A Mentor Book, New York, 1973.

6. Guest, A. "Defusing The "Population Bomb": A Humanistic Alternative to the Arguments of Dr. Paul Ehrlich." In Pohlman
   (ed.), Population: A Clash of Prophets. A Mentor Book, New
   York, 1973.

7. Kornsey, W. "Population-Related Policy: Future Cost For
   Continued Nondecision." Presented at the Second Capon Springs
   Public Policy Conference, February 22-24, 1978, Washington,
   D.C.

8. Levi, L. and L. Andersson. Psychosocial Stress. Spectrum
   Publications, New York, 1975.

9. Seligman, M. "Helplessness." On Depression, Development,
   and Death. W. H. Freeman and Company, San Francisco, 1975.

10. Skinner, B. F. Beyond Freedom and Dignity. Knopf Publishing,
    New York, 1971.

A SURVEY OF SOME ECONOMIC THEORIES OF POPULATION*

Scot A. Stradley

Department of Economics, University of North Dakota

In surveying the history of modern economic theories of population dynamics, one finds a broad difference in basic method of approach between the Classical and Marxist schools.

The mainstream of the Classical school and the father of the Neoclassical school both viewed population growth as subject to natural laws, especially the limitation imposed by the natural law of the land. Ricardo even extended this analysis to draw the conclusion that the perpetual tendency of the laboring population to overbreed and thus press against the means of subsistence would eventually result in the collapse of capitalism and the arrival of the stationary state. Malthus' economics essentially agreed with Ricardo's analysis. Sensing the profound implications of this argument, John Stuart Mill advanced the entire package--Malthusian population law, Malthusian law of the land, and Ricardian economic consequences--and accepted fully the eventual stationary state. Horrified by the implications, Mill deduced the need for practical reform and became an outspoken advocate of measures such as the control of births and increased rights for women, which would aid in adjusting to the stationary state.

Alfred Marshall, the founder of the Neoclassical school of economics, accepted the Malthusian Theory of population and land, but because of obvious historical developments in the productive powers of the world, he placed the Malthusian aspects at the edge, or made them the boundaries. According to Marshall they were still very relevant, but human productivity had forced the development of another natural law--the law of increasing return. Increasing return is strictly a social phenomenon because it develops as a consequence of internal and external economies of scale. The latter are all products of human industry and, collectively, these forces have overcome the niggardliness of nature. Thus, the actual lot of the laboring class has improved. But, Marshall notes, this

*This paper presents the conclusion of the author's more extensive analysis. The longer paper on which this summary is based may be obtained from the author at the Department of Economics, University of North Dakota, Grand Forks, N.D. 58202.

improvement could be lost because of the fact that resources are limited; the presence of the law of diminishing returns is a real force to be cognizant of. Consequently, Marshall believed it was essential that premature and improvident marriage be avoided; he especially warned against a rapid growth in population (that is evil in its effects). To this end, Marshall emphasized foresight on the part of the laboring population, a foresight that aims at providing a better life for your offspring than you yourself had.

Characteristic of mainstream English economics is an emphasis on brutal natural laws to which mankind is subjected. Relief from the immediate operation of these laws may be obtained by prudential restraint and industrious activity. However, human restraint and activity can only postpone the inevitable operation of natural laws, and this fact is especially severe in its implications for the working classes.

Marx's approach represents an opposite methodological approach which is at the base of the difference between the economics of the Neoclassical school and the Marxian school. Marx argued that no abstract law of population holds for humanity because the size of the population is subject to limitations imposed not by the means of subsistence, but by the means of employment.

Marx maintains that mankind has been progressively separated from Nature and this process peaks during the phase of human history ruled by capital. Capital further separates humanity from the means of production, including both the earth and productive equipment. The commodities that result from productive activity are also separated from the producers, leaving the proletariat with only their labor time to use for acquiring an existence. Labor power is purchased by the capitalist for only one reason: its capacity to yield a surplus product. In other words, employment is regulated by accumulation which is, in turn, regulated by profit or, more generally, surplus value.

The implications of this general law of accumulation for the laboring classes are examined at length. The influence of accumulation on the population of the bourgeoisie is not examined, probably because Marx viewed the bourgeoisie as transitional and therefore unimportant. The laboring population is regulated by the absolute growth and the relative growth of the variable constituent of capital. The growth of the variable constituent relative to the growth of the total capital is emphasized because Marx's economics rests on his theory of alienation. Because of this and because of the competitive struggle that mandates productivity increases, Marx concludes that the trend of the variable constituent must result in a relative decline as a part of the whole capital. This process is exaggerated at times because of the competitive struggle for industrial or national supremacy that necessitates rapid advance in productivity. This means that machines come to the forefront

201

as the source of production, to the relative diminution of labor. The result is that labor appears superfluous, or what Marx termed the relative surplus population.

Marx concludes that the campaign for birth limitation is extremely destructive to the future of the laboring classes vis-a-vis capital. This seeming paradox is due to the fact that if population declines relative to the total capital, wages may advance with the consequential bourgeois drive for labor-saving machinery. What seemed to be the key solution for Mill becomes fraught with morbid potential in Marx. Further implementation of labor-saving machinery means throwing living labor out of production and further increasing the industrial army. This, of course, is an excellent condition for the bourgeoisie, but the consequences for the proletariat are dismal since the lower sediment of the industrial army consists of the poor. Thus, it is likely that the general law of accumulation (the normal activity of bourgeois production) will result in an increase in numbers of the poor.

To summarize the essential difference between mainstream and radical political economy is to distinguish between natural law arguments and real arguments. Finally, it should be noted that, contrary to popular belief, Malthus' work contains both of these kinds of argument. The natural law argument is contained in his Essay on Population, and this is the argument that all his followers devote their attention to. However, his Principles of Political Economy contains the positive or real argument, which Malthus' followers seem to ignore altogether. But Marx was totally aware of it, and must have derived substantial insight from it. Marx notes in a footnote that in the Principles of Political Economy "Malthus finally discovers, with the help of Sismondi, the beautiful Trinity of capitalistic production: over-production, over-population, over-consumption--three very delicate monsters indeed" (K. Marx, Capital, Vol. I, p. 634).

ON MAKING RATIONAL MORAL RESPONSES TO OVERPOPULATION AND FOOD SHORTAGES

George B. Wall

Department of English, Lamar University, Beaumont, Texas

Food-population problems are profoundly moral. Getting an adequate handle on the moral issues within a short paper is, however, a formidable task. I choose to focus on one of many moral models, namely, utilitarianism. Utilitarian morality may be stated as follows: An action is right if and only if it results in no less value than any alternative action.

The main point that I wish to emphasize about utilitarian theory is that it demands rational decision making--a value goal is highly unlikely to be realized unless it is pursued rationally. The demand of rationality, whatever else it may be, is a demand for action based on an accurate appraisal of the real situation. In the case of food-population problems, the complexity of the real situation makes accurate appraisal a task of overwhelming proportions.

Yet the search is not altogether hopeless, for on some issues an informed consensus already appears to be present or forming--a sign that a degree of understanding may have been reached. For example, there seems to be agreement that the earth could provide enough food to easily meet the demands of population growth through 2100. Robert Loomis maintains that if one considers simply the natural factors of biology, soil and climate, one can say that with the present base of arable land, with a largely vegetarian diet based on yields that should be achieved with present knowledge and human effort, the world could support a human population of at least 50 billion.[1]

On the other side of the food-population equation, the worst-case projection developed by Tomas Frejka is for a population of just over 15 billion in 2100. If population growth were to follow present trends, the more likely projection would be a population of 8.4 billion in 2100, with population growth then leveling off.[2]

Obviously, what the earth <u>could</u> produce is not what the earth <u>will</u> produce. Just as obviously, what is produced will not necessarily be adequately distributed. However, the point is that information concerning potential food supply in relation to reasonable population projection suggests hope rather than bleak despair.

In the area of proposals for action, a degree of consensus may also have been achieved. For example, a generally received view today is that the best hope for underdeveloped countries lies, not in rapid industrialization, but in the rapid improvement of agricultural activity in rural areas.[3] The value of this approach is that it takes cognizance of the actual situation of underdeveloped people. It is a solution which at least attempts to tailor its proposals to the conditions present. No other kind of solution is rational; therefore, no other kind of solution can be moral. A solution which blandly assumes that underdeveloped countries must be crammed into the technological-economic clothing of the developed countries has not met the first condition of rational morality. Such a solution is unlikely to work; worse, it inevitably accepts in an uncritical manner the economic-cultural values of developed countries and tries to clothe the underdeveloped countries with these values. Uncritically accepting one's own values is an egregious lapse from rational procedure, exceeded only by the uncritical attempt to clothe other societies with one's own value.

In addition to a consideration of where people are, socially, economically and culturally, a rational appraisal of the real situation requires a consideration of what people are doing or plan to do. In other words, reaching a moral decision requires that an agent take into account the actions of other persons who are or will be affecting the total situation. In the case of food-population problems this requirement translates into consideration of the actions of recipient nations. If a nation refuses to adopt policies consistent with a reasonable solution of its food-population problems, then the moral decision may be to withhold assistance. The decision becomes especially anguished when an unrepresentative clique is in power in recipient nations. The decision is only slightly less anguished when the government is truly representative but the cultural values are in conflict with a solution of food-population problems. Respect for life is clearly a prime value, but so is respect for freedom. Respect for freedom may require permitting a country to proceed on a path which only aggravates its food-population problems.

Decisions which affect other people significantly are moral decisions. The first requirement of utilitarian morality is that moral decisions be rational. The aim is really doing good, not do-goodism. The difference is as profound as the difference between an actual and an attempted rescue.

FOOTNOTES

1. Robert S. Loomis, "Agricultural Systems," Scientific American,
   September, 1976, p. 105. A slightly different estimate is made
   by Roger Revelle in "Food and Popualtion," Scientific American,
   September, 1974, p. 168: "If 10 percent of . . . potential gross
   cropped area were set aside to grow fibers and other nonfood
   products, and if technology and purchased inputs of production
   . . . equivalent to those used in Iowa corn farming were applied
   to the remainder, a diet based on 4,500 to 5,000 kilocalories
   of edible plant material could be provided for between 38 and
   48 billion people."

2. Tomas Frejka, "The Prospects for a Stationary World Population,"
   Scientific American, March, 1973, pp. 20-21.

3. Sterling Wortman, "Food and Agriculture," Scientific American,
   September, 1976, p. 36. Wortman says that "the only real
   solution to the world food problem is for poor countries to
   quickly increase the production of crops and animals--and
   incomes--on millions of small farms, thus stimulating economic
   activity.

FAD AND PREJUDICE AS OBSTACLES TO SOLVING
POPULATION AND FOOD PROBLEMS

Wallace Gray

Southwestern College, Winfield, Kansas

When shapers of opinion such as news commentators or preachers exhibit faddism, prejudice and ignorance, the public is prevented from overcoming its confusion and inactivity.

But when scientists and other specialists contradict themselves and each other and sound as dogmatic and sure of themselves as any barber, preacher or news commentator, that means that the source of objective data and cautious judgment is in danger of drying up. It is to protect and, if possible, rejuvenate that source that I am issuing this brief alarm and suggestion.

I first noticed the phenomenon of faddism in church circles. The very ministers who, one year, would take the population explosion with extreme seriousness in their thinking and speaking would ignore it or downplay it the next year. In several church or church-related settings my wife proposed that effective birth control strings be attached to all donations of food. Her proposal was called immoral, unchristian and genocidal. Times change and preachments do, too, for recently a bishop, no less, has said that as a condition of aid, "Vasectomies should go along with the groceries."[1] At the expert level, biologist Garrett Hardin states:

> As a matter of method, let us grant ourselves the most malevolent of motives: let us ask, "How can we harm India--really harm her?" . . .

> Quite simply: by sending India a bounty of food, year after year.[2]

The vicious circle of hunger = more people = more hunger might be broken by the swift and efficient application of modern methods of birth control. Paul Ehrlich in The Population Bomb did much to nourish that idea. Recently, however, he has ridiculed it (at least in its more simplistic forms) as a "'condoms from helicopters delusion'--a psychological condition that is rampant among well-meaning upper-middle and upper class Americans." I understand

Ehrlich's recantation is based on his realization that poor people of the world see the need to have many children for their future security and are unlikely to buy family planning in their present social and cultural settings.[3] When an eminent authority changes his mind, the public--and sometimes even more knowledgeable disciples and critics--are apt to neglect the reasons for the change and leap to extravagant conclusions.

One of the reasons for the on-again off-again stance of some scientists and leaders concerning the importance of curbing population growth by persuasion and coercion is the recent revival of the "demographic transition theory" presented in the 1950s by Josue de Castro in The Geography of Hunger. An implication of the theory is that until nutrition needs are met, population growth cannot be expected to level off. Such authorities as Roger Revelle and Lester R. Brown go so far as to say that "good nutrition is the best contraceptive."[4]

"Lester Brown nevertheless is cognizant of a number of nations which have proved exceptions to the theory, noticeably reducing their birth rates and population growth without a large prior increase in their total GNP or per capita income."[5]

The important concession Brown makes leads to the first of my short list of suggestions:

1. Let responsible opinion-shapers and scientists always list important exceptions or qualifications to their favored theories and distinguish more probable from less probable conclusions.

2. Let leaders distinguish programs which are more or less experimental from ones which have some basis in history or experience.

3. Let scientists, technologists and others look at food or population problems in a systems-context of food, energy and population.

4. Let advocates of more or less unlimited growth debate the limits-of-growth proponents in settings such as national TV and food and energy conferences.

In conclusion, I would like to hazard a guess related to my last two suggestions. In general, I would expect a broader and sounder perspective from a demographer, ecologist, or biologist than from a food or energy expert for the simple reason that the former has been trained always to take the latter into account, whereas a food or energy expert may not have had to face such a total picture of population, environment, etc.[6]

What we have been discussing here is an integrated and adequate perspective on food, energy and population problems. It is not that simple answers can be found to complex problems but rather that all specialists, generalists and laymen concerned with the issues need to pursue vigorous inquiry and debate. The debate of such issues will necessarily be confusing, but at least dogmatism and premature conclusions should not be allowed to add to the confusion.

FOOTNOTES

1. Cited without name by Joseph Fletcher, "Feeding the Hungry: an Ethical Appraisal," Soundings, Spring, 1976, Vol. LIX, No. I, p. 52. This special issue of the interdisciplinary journal Soundings is devoted to WORLD FAMINE AND LIFEBOAT ETHICS and has been re-published under the same title by Harper & Row (1976).

2. Garrett Hardin, "Carrying Capacity as an Ethical Concept," Soundings, op. cit., p. 125. A somewhat complementary thesis is that of Frances Moore Lappe and Joseph Collins in "Food First!" (a broadsheet distributed by four Protestant denominations, including United Presbyterian Church U.S.A., Hunger Program, Room 1268, 475 Riverside Drive, New York 10027, and based on the book Food First published by Houghton Mifflin Co., Boston: 1977, $10.95): "Escape from hunger comes not through the redistribution of food but through the redistribution of control over food-producing resources." Surprisingly, Lappe and Collins argue with some cogency that the key to solving world hunger lies in justice for the small farmer. Only once is their argument flavored by the kind of overstatement protested against in the present article: "It is not, then, people's food needs that threaten to destroy the environment but other forces. . . ." If this sentence were rewritten to read, "It is not only people's food needs . . . ," my objection would be met. The title "Food First!" is itself a catchy oversimplification of a highly complex problem in which there truly may be no "first" item except the human ecological system itself.

3. Arthur Simon, in Bread for the World (New York: Paulist Press and Grand Rapids: 1975), p. 27, citing Paul and Anne Ehrlich, "Misconceptions," The New York Times Magazine, June 16, 1974.

4. George R. Lucas, Jr., "Political and Economic Dimensions of Hunger," Soundings, op. cit., p. 18, citing Lester Brown, In the Human Interest, (New York: W. W. Norton, 1974), p. 119.

5. Lucas, op. cit., p. 19.

6. Anyone interested in a more controversial, more fully argued version of this article, send $1 for duplication and mailing to

Wallace Gray, Southwestern College, Winfield, Kansas 67156.
Perhaps most pertinent to the present article is my claim in
the longer version to have discovered a new disease, PCD or Population Control Denial. My suggestion as to possible causes is
sixfold:

1. Many Western leaders have discovered their inability to sell
    measures of population control, even the mildest and most
    voluntary kind.
2. Third World leaders, noting the high per capita consumption
    of food and energy by Western or developed nations, see an
    ulterior motive even in scientific pronouncements about
    population growth.
3. Population experts have been abandoned by some church and
    state leaders who have too many other fights on their hands
    to continue this "expendable" one.
4. Christians and leaders from other world religions may re-
    flect their scriptures' concern for feeding the poor and
    healing the sick, and overlook population pressures which
    those scriptures knew nothing about.
5. The slowing of our own U.S. population growth may have lulled
    many citizens and leaders to sleep.
6. Experts cannot always clearly agree on the top priority
    human need, much less its magnitude or cure.

There are also six values influencing our action or inaction. The
first five are inappropriate or at least inadequate to meet the crisis.

A phrase or sentence will usually betray a faddish or superficial
response to a crisis like the need for food:

1. "It's easy to sell" (salability).
2. "It feels good."
    If gifts to "solve" world hunger give the donor a good feel-
    ing inside then hunger "must be" the top priority (emotionally).
3. "Today's program is the most important" because it is today's
    (bureaucratic time-lines and opportunism).
4. "Avoid high cost solutions at any cost" (short-range economics
    and psychological security).
5. "No matter what the real priorities for survival are, people
    will do what they please, so keep your thoughts to yourself
    and maintain your cool as a leader of the crowd" (cynicism,
    popularity, personal power).
6. The situation is truly difficult, people are slow to change,
    full and systematic answers elude us, and time is running out.
    Nevertheless, we believe solutions may be found if enough of
    us become concerned enough, informed enough and ingenious
    enough (faith, truth and love).

RELIGION, ETHICS AND POPULATION POLICY

Harmon Sherry

New City, New York

A current definition of religion goes as follows: "Religion has traditionally been comprised of three main branches called cosmology, epistemology and ethics. Cosmology is the study of the Universe. Epistemology is concerned with the nature of truth or knowledge. It is the function of ethics, using the results of the first two, to formulate codes of behavior which will best fit Man into the Universe."

That religions have failed to produce an adequate universal ethic is obvious. While our problems today stem in part from a lack of knowledge, a major factor has been the failure to develop value judgments and ethical systems which are consistent with what knowledge we have. Without these, our efforts at problem solving take on the aspects of treating symptoms while ignoring the disease. Until we have developed universal values and ethics we will continue to squabble over solutions, thus minimizing the effectiveness of our efforts.

The more important reasons for the failure of religions to develop an adequate ethic seem to be:

1. The acceptance of the teachings of one or a few men as Absolute Truth.

2. The building of immutable dogmas around these "truths."

3. The maintenance of these dogmas in spite of contrary evidence.

4. Using these dogmas to gain power and control over other men, while passing the responsibility to God.

Clearly Science has given us the most complete and accurate cosmology the world has known, although there is much left to learn. But Science has also developed an "epistemology," or, more accurately, General Semantics. It is what I believe Bronowski meant by "science itself." It is an epistemology in the sense that, given that science is a body of knowledge, it asks how scientists know what to add, what to delete and what to modify within this body of knowledge? That Science has accomplished this with considerable success is apparent; with sufficient success at least that we can confidently adopt their methods.

Conceptually, this scientific "epistemology" is simple. It consists of two main points and an attitude. First it assumes that there is no such thing as Absolute Truth, with the practical consequence that no one man is ever entirely above critical review. Second, it requires that everything be published in the open literature where it is available for criticism by anyone who cares to. The attitude is the tradition of objectivity. Scientists try to be objective and expect the same of their peers, while severely criticizing lack of objectivity.

It is tempting to carry this analogy between science and religion to the end and expect science to develop an ethic. This would be a mistake because the scientific community is far too narrow a base for this most important final step of developing an ethic. Scientists should and will remain cosmologists and they should participate in the building of an ethic. But this task is the concern of all of us, of as many qualified people as we can muster.

A necessary but not sufficient condition for the establishment of a viable, long-range population policy is a thorough restructuring, in the light of modern scientific knowledge, of our value judgments and the ethical codes to support them. Our present religions are based on premises which far predate the scientific revolution; they have failed to revise their dogmas to be consistent with the new knowledge. Thus, before any population policy can be successfully elaborated, a new religion is needed which

(1) is consistent with scientific knowledge;

(2) is based not on a few prophets, but on the work of as many qualified persons as possible;

(3) holds to no absolutes.

Science is a self-correcting system which has demonstrated considerable success in maximizing consensus. These are two of the major requirements for developing a viable ethic and value system which will "best fit man into the Universe."

211

MAXIMIZING RESOURCE ALLOCATION IN UNDERDEVELOPED AREAS--THE SOLUTION TO THE PROBLEM OF OVERPOPULATION

Morton Hirsch

Kingsborough Community College, CUNY

Much, possibly too much, has been written in regard to the population problem. If one were to ask one hundred people what they thought about the gravity of the world-wide population food-situation, ninety-five would stress that population is an overriding concern for mankind. The remaining five would shrug their shoulders, and remain indifferent.

My thesis is that the wrong part of the population-food equation has been stressed. In my view there is no population problem that cannot be solved by those affected. But there is most definitely a resource allocation problem. Too many countries, ostensibly suffering from overpopulation, are in reality victims of under-utilization of their scarce resources. This waste covers all the factors of production--land, labor, capital, and entrepreneurial ability--and transcends all ideologies--socialistic, democratic, and totalitarian regimes.

The re-emergence of the Malthusian theory of population is of recent origin. Thomas Malthus' theory was laid to rest during the early part of the 19th Century. The Industrial Revolution transformed Western societies not only in the industrial areas but also in the agricultural sector, which found itself caught up in the frenzied technological whirlpool of inventions and innovations.

The geometrical growth of population coupled with Malthusian arithmetic food growth was reversed in the advanced industrial countries. Food production grew so fast in the capitalistic Western societies that it enabled certain countries to embark on a no-growth population era.

The point to stress is that an intelligent allocation of resources over the last 150 years has resulted in a tremendous increase in the amount of food available as well as an increase in the standard of living of both rural dwellers and urban workers. A high standard of living usually limits the number of people in a family.

212

The birth rate of those countries that have high food production is nominal; at times, limited population growth may even be an indication of a future problem.

Western countries, specifically the U.S., have no population growth problem; in fact, history has proven that private initiative and enterprise can increase food production many-fold while limiting population expansion to a minimum. Underdeveloped countries must rid themselves of the "fiction" that their societies are efficient in their allocation of resources. The highest level of per capita inefficiencies are to be found in the over-populated countries.

The mix of skilled workers to non-skilled is practically non-existent (except for show place type of industries); in most countries acquisition of skills is extremely difficult and under the aegis of foreign managers who come and go and make no lasting contribution to the economy.

The problem is exacerbated by the lack of capital production in most over-populated areas. Domestic capital production is unheard of and must be imported from industrial countries, thus limiting a country's ability to develop a professional capital-producing class. The creation of a vicious circle, reminiscent of Hurkse's circle, becomes evident. A country must expand its industrial sector in order to raise the standard of living of its people. It cannot do so because it does not possess producers of capital; thus capital must come from outside the country and professionals must be imported to maintain the capital. The circle is complete and what one has is an increasing standard of poverty.

The mix of capital and entrepreneurial ability is also non-existent in most underdeveloped countries. Capital markets to capture savings (What's that?) and turn them into investments just don't exist in over-populated areas. No investment results in aborting any initiative fledgling entrepreneurs may have. In modern competitive societies a basic factor of production is the entrepreneur. It is this class that may invent or innovate and without them scarce resources cannot be utilized in a meaningful manner. It then falls upon government to perform the entrepreneur's function, but with disastrous results.

If one wants to pinpoint a major obstacle to increased food production it is government's intervention in the operation of the economy. The creation of a bureaucracy is not a substitute for efficiency. But unfortunately the greater the inefficiency in allocation of resources the greater the bureaucracy that is formed and perpetuated. Bureaucrats must maintain the status quo and what easier way to do this than by neglecting the resource allocation problem and stressing the over-population problem.

I suggest that energy should be expended in maintaining the right mix of labor to resources, capital to labor, capital to resources, human capital to resources, and entrepreneurial ability to land, labor and capital. The mixture and creation of proper production functions can only come about through hard work and dedication by leaders of underdeveloped and over-populated areas. I am afraid that this scarce resource--statesman-like leadership--so short in developed societies, is totally lacking in underdeveloped areas.

ACHIEVING POPULATION GOALS? THE TRIPLE LAG HYPOTHESIS

Carl L. Harter

Department of Sociology, Tulane University

Current population discussions basically deal with two key issues: (1) the goal--what is the proper population size/composition; and (2) the means--what are the appropriate methods to use in achieving whatever goal is selected. Even though most informed discussants concede that population growth cannot go on forever, there are substantial disagreements over whether "no growth" can or should be achieved, and by what date. Further, these sometimes sharp disagreements produce a wide variety of suggestions about the means of achieving no growth and/or about the viability of the population size/composition at the time the no growth becomes a reality. Notwithstanding these disagreements over the appropriate size of or the means to achieve a no growth population, implicit in the discussions is the notion that when an "appropriate" no growth state is eventually achieved, that population size will then be maintained ad infinitum because it is either the "proper" size or the smallest possible size. Hence the perhaps unconscious inference that someday we won't have the population problem to kick around any more.

Contrary to the implied notion that someday we will no longer be plagued with the proper population size/composition problem, the triple lag hypothesis presented below suggests that neither the social norms which regulate fertility nor governmental policies which influence fertility will be able to affect fertility behavior rapidly enough to achieve the population size/composition goal originally intended by those norms or policies. Further, every new population size/composition will bring about changes in the social norms or government policies which regulate fertility, and thereby initiate yet another "new" population size/composition goal.

The proposition developed here is based on the assumption that any population size/composition will not be maintained, either because it is not considered ideal, or because the current demographic processes are not appropriate to maintain it. If the goal is to maintain current size/composition, changes will have to be made in current fertility behavior. But there are three possible lags in this change process such that if and when the desired changes are made, the current

215

size/composition will have already changed and this will stimulate the selection of a new goal and new fertility changes to reach it, etc. Or, if the goal is to obtain some change in the current size/composition, fertility behavior will likewise have to be changed, but, again, there will be lags in the change process and whatever size/composition is eventually achieved will initiate another round of goal selection and fertility change attempts to reach that goal.

The normative change period, the governmental action period, and the demographic structure change period are the three time lags present in the process of adapting fertility behavior to obtain a selected population size/composition goal. The normative change lag is the time it takes to establish the new fertility pattern required by the population goal which is accepted as the "normal" fertility pattern. Indeed societies may have a number of significant sub-groups each with their own fertility norms, and making alterations in these family size norms is a process that takes years or even generations. The lag that thus occurs in making the fertility adjustments will result in missing the mark of the population size/composition goal selected.

With respect to governmental policy and action dealing with population goals and regulating fertility behavior, some people feel that such governmental action, at least in democratic societies, should not contradict the attitudes, beliefs, and practices (i.e., the norms) of the majority of the population; only when politicians are sufficiently sure of the fertility beliefs/behavior of their constituencies should they attempt governmental policies or programs that are consonant with those beliefs/behavior. According to this position, the people already want, and some may be illegally doing, what the government then decides to assist them with or give them permission to do. Another position is that government should not be so "passive;" rather, it should use its expertise, and then its power, to establish and achieve an appropriate population goal for the society. However, regardless of whether the government's role is passive or initiatory, from the time government "decides" on a population goal and begins to develop policies and programs to reach that goal, until the time at which the results or services of the new governmental action are in effect with the populace, there will be a time lag of years, if not decades. Such a lag in developing and effectuating fertility regulating policies and programs dictates that the population goal selected will not be met.

Even if a society is successful in establishing both normative desires for only replacement fertility and government policies and programs to facilitate its achievement, that society's population would not become stationary at that time. There would still be a demographic structure change time lag such that from the time replacement level fertility becomes a reality, the size of the population will still change before a no growth state is achieved. As a case in point, during the 1970s the average total fertility rate in the U.S. has been slightly below replacement level, yet even if that

216

rate is maintained our 1970 population of 204 million stands to increase until we reach the 270 million mark in the first third of the
next century. As stated by Ryder (Daedalus, 1973),

> The cause of this increase by more than one-third is
> . . . the considerable numbers of women below the high-
> est age of childbearing. . . . Each of those childbear-
> ing cohorts has an initial size of about 3.78 million,
> and each cohort member will live about seventy-two
> years. The size of the hypothesized stationary popula-
> tion produced by continual repetition of [replacement
> level total fertility] is simply the product of those
> two numbers, or 272 million.

Thus, even the achievement of replacement level fertility will not
maintain a population of desired size/composition. There will be a
demographic structure change lag of up to 70 years as the size/
composition adjusts to the effects of replacement fertility.

In summary, the triple lag hypothesis presented here suggests
that stationary population size/composition goals will not be obtained nor maintained. Impediments to the achievement of such population goals will be furnished by a lag in the development of the
appropriate family size norms, and/or by a lag in developing and implementing appropriate governmental action to regulate fertility,
and/or by the population size/composition changes that occur even after replacement level fertility has been established. As a consequence of these lags, any population size goal will be over- or
under-shot, and whatever new population size/composition is produced
will result in the establishment of yet another goal, which will in
turn also be affected by norm changes, governmental actions, and population structure changes. Population size/composition goal setting/
attainment is not and will not be a once and only activity--it will be
an ever re-occurring phenomenon.

BIBLIOGRAPHY

1. Blake, Judith. "Comment on Notestein's 'Zero Population Growth'," Population Index 36 (October-December, 1970).

2. Coale, Ansley J. "Should the United States Start a Campaign for Fewer Births?" Population Index 34 (October-December, 1968).

3. Daedalus 102 (Fall, 1973), The No-Growth Society.

4. Davis, Kingsley. "Population Policy: Will Current Programs Succeed?" Science 158 (November 10, 1967).

5. Frejka, Tomas. The Future of Population Growth: Alternative Paths to Equilibrium. New York: Wiley, 1973.

6. Hardin, Garrett. "Multiple Paths to Population Control." *Family Planning Perspectives* 2 (June, 1970).

7. Keyfitz, Nathan. "On the Momentum of Population Growth." *Demography* 8 (February, 1971).

8. Notestein, Frank W. "Zero Population Growth." *Population Index* 36 (October-December, 1970).

9. Pohlman, Edward, ed. *Population: A Clash of Prophets*. New York: The New American Library, 1973.

10. Westoff, Charles F., et al. *Toward the End of Growth: Population in America*. Englewood Cliffs, New Jersey: Prentice-Hall, 1973.

THE MALTHUSIAN GHOST AND ECONOMIC EXORCISM

Rohini P. Sinha

Department of Economics and Business, Muhlenberg College

The Malthusian theory of population is based on two structural relations: (1) the procreative drive propels population at a geometric rate, and (2) the niggardliness of nature makes it possible for man to augment his means of sustenance only at an arithmetic rate. These two disparate rates of growth of production and reproduction lead to an equilibrium population consistent only with a bare subsistence level of living. Any increase in the standard of living above subsistence, according to this theory, would induce larger numbers, which would bring the level of living back to subsistence, and a population size too big in relation to its supportive base would inevitably invoke "positive checks" by nature. Thus, man is seen as engaged in a losing battle when it comes to improving his economic lot.

While the past experience of the developed countries largely repudiates the Malthusian prognosis, the developing world is currently haunted by the Malthusian ghost of overpopulation. With the exhaustion of fossil fuels and raw materials, the world at large is now gripped by an almost universal sense of urgency, pessimism and helplessness with respect to the growth of population. This emanates largely from the assumption that population growth is an independent self-generating dynamic force which influences our socio-economic conditions without being influenced by them. In the model presented below, population is viewed as an endogenous factor which causes as well as is caused by economic forces.

An Economic Model of Family Size:
The Demand and Supply of Children

Like any other commodity, children are economic goods, the volume of which is determined by the interaction of demand and supply. For parents and relatives, children are desirable, simply because they are enjoyable. They promise to yield pleasure, pride, and, for some, economic protection. The production of children, very much like the production of other material goods, is also subject to the evolving technology and cost considerations. The parents--

the decision-makers--arrive at the optimal size only by rationally calculating, at the margin, the prospective benefits and costs of having additional children. In one respect, however, it differs from other market products, in that both the producer as well as the consumer originates from the same unit--the household. In analyzing the growth of population, therefore, the "household model" will be an appropriate model to use.

Demand for Children

A child may be viewed as a composite product: it has the properties of a consumer good which gives satisfaction to the buyer and of an investment good that has the promise of yielding income for the investor over time. The investment component of this joint product--the child--is, however, very strong and attractive only at an early stage of economic development, but as an economy develops, this component tends to wear out. The larger the family size, the greater is the labor pool from which the household can draw labor for the operation of its economic pursuits. Skills that are required to run primitive farms and businesses are less differentiated and demanding and hence require much less time and resources before children can be put to productive uses. Moreover, at the early stage of economic development, investment opportunities and financial intermediaries are few and far between. Hence, children are not only looked upon as a source of psychic income from cute "little darlings" but also as a monetary income.

But as the economy develops, alternative investment opportunities and institutions conducive to investment in material capital increase. This, then, makes children a less attractive source of future income. This, when coupled with higher risk associated with children, as they are all born with personalities and a will of their own, makes expected income from them still smaller. Thus, a child ceases to be a sound investment target. Consequently, in an economically developed society, a child is wanted because parents want to have them largely as consumer goods; we wish to have children simply because it is fun to have them. But this endearing aspect of children, paradoxically, militates against having larger numbers of children. One of the dominant characteristics of development is that it offers a bigger consumer basket of variegated goods. A child then has to compete for parental resources with all other material goods. This is possibly the reason that we almost invariably find lower rates of fertility in a developed country or developed regions of a country than in underdeveloped areas. Demand for children decreases as development increases. No wonder we come to recognize the fact that economic development is perhaps the most effective contraceptive available. The market demand for children may be represented graphically thus:

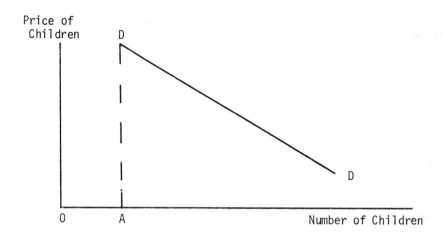

Price of Children

D

D

0   A   Number of Children

In the diagram above, OA number of children are demanded due to autonomous factors, such as religious beliefs, taboos, or just technological "goofs" (the infrequent failures of contraceptives). DD represents rationally determined demand for children. With an increase in income, DD tends to shift to the left. Shrinking family sizes essentially reflect this phenomenon.

Supply of Children

Inexpensive and effective means of contraception have enabled parents to control child production to a desirable level. The most significant role that the revolution in contraceptive technology has played is separating the recreational aspect of sex from its procreational aspect: children no longer have to be the unwanted by-products of sexual acts. It should be noted, however, that birth-control devices do not provide motivation to control births. The only function for them is to provide a means to control, if motivation for controlling births already exists.

The underlying determinant of supply is the cost of raising children. For parents, these costs are made up of two parts: (1) Direct costs--the expenses incurred from the prenatal stage to the point when the child enters the labor market and becomes self-supporting. These costs are highly and positively correlated with parental standard of living and the duration of child dependency. (2) Opportunity costs--these costs are in terms of earnings that parents, particularly mothers, forego in order to engage in child care at home. The higher the skill and education of mothers, the greater is the opportunity cost of rearing children. The sum of these two costs is the private parental cost of producing kids. It is reasonable to assume that the cost is higher for the first child than that associated with additional children. The supply curve would be the marginal cost curve (the cost schedule of

221

producing additional kids) and may be represented graphically by
the diagram below:

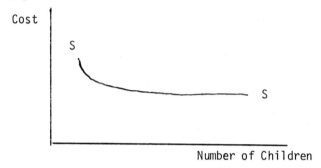

SS is the supply curve of children.

The equilibrium production of children would be where the demand
and supply curves intersect. In the diagram below, the optimum
size is ON; OA is the number of children born due to factors other
than economic, and AN represents the rationally determined number
of children.

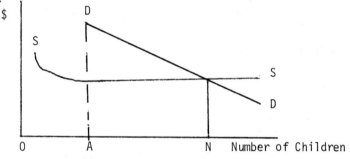

We also know that with economic development, the demand for
children decreases and the cost of raising them increases, especially the opportunity cost of mothers. This would result in smaller
sized families with expensive kids. Thus, we see that economic
forces work like a built-in mechanism to subdue the Malthusian
ghost in the long run, provided we succeed in raising the level
of living.

Social Costs and Overproduction

In determining optimum production level, the decision-maker
weighs the benefit he receives from producing another unit against
the cost he incurs in producing it. But there are costs which are
involved but not necessarily paid for by the producer. For example,
in the case of children, society pays for social and cultural infrastructure, such as schools, parks, playgrounds, roads, etc.

222

The total cost should include these social costs as well. If so included, optimum production would decline as a consequence of an increase in costs. If social costs are uncompensated, overpopulation is a logical outcome. Thus, we see that it will lead to a situation where what is privately optimal may socially be nonoptimal.

The policies contemplated or adopted to bring the size of population privately determined in conformance with social optimality fall in three main categories: (1) coercive methods, (2) fiscal disincentives, and (3) fiscal and/or community incentives to adopt birth-control measures. They all suffer from different degrees of inequities and/or ineffectiveness. For instance, the first approach to population control does not sit well with democratic principles. The second, if adopted, will result in a highly regressive burden on poor families and the third approach is essentially a bribe given to parents, who are, in this context, troublemakers for society. One possible way to exorcise the Malthusian ghost of overpopulation in the short run is to give consideration to the following approach. The approach is spelled out in steps:

1. Set up a socially desirable macro target or population for a given year, t_n. This will be the size of population for that year corresponding to the highest per capita income. This will project the number of persons needed in n years from now or in year t_n.

2. The number of girl babies in a year t_0 (or now) will be given equal number of "birth rights" certificates or coupons, based on the estimate in (1) above.

3. These coupons will be negotiable. Negotiability will make it possible for those who do not want kids to sell their "rights" to someone who does want more kids and has the means to effect those wants. Moreover, this will enable kids to be in the care of those who are both willing and able to raise them. It should be noted that this proposal does not involve trading kids. It only envisages trading of "rights" to bear kids.

This approach, I believe, will achieve the macro population target within the framework of decentralized micro decision-making.

223

DILEMMAS OF AN AVERAGE AMERICAN WONDERING
WHAT TO DO ABOUT GLOBAL POPULATION AND FOOD ISSUES

Eliot Glassheim

Population/Food Fund

The United States has not developed a very forceful policy in regard to world or national population growth, or world or national hunger. My assumption is that a number of mental or attitudinal conflicts keep us from having faith in any coherent policy direction.

Disagreement of Experts

The first paralyzing dilemma that faces the average American is that on every essential point expert opinion is contradictory. For example, there isn't any coherent public agreement among experts about how serious a problem the world's population is. Herman Kahn tells us that the world growth rate has peaked and will continue to decline, and that we have the technical capacity to provide a decent standard of living for 15 or even 30 billion people over the next 200 years.

On the other hand, Cargille and others say Kahn simply doesn't know what he's talking about. They cite ecologists who have general, though unsubstantiated, opinions that the maximum limit of people who can be adequately housed on this earth is 5 to 7 billion people. PaulEhrlich, Garrett Hardin and Georg Borgstrom all believe the world is already overpopulated and that ecological, environmental, food and resource disasters are well nigh inevitable.

There is equal disagreement among food experts. Lappe and Collins, who don't want us to believe that population growth is a significant factor in causing hunger, claim that there is no scarcity of food and that even during the food crisis of the early 1970s enough food was produced worldwide to feed every person in the world with ample protein and 3000 calories a day.

Using the same FAO figures as starting points, the Environmental Fund, which wants us to believe that population is the primary cause of the world's ills, claims that equal distribution of world food production would provide only an Afghanistan-level diet, and that we'd all be hungry together.

224

With such a serious division in the mind and knowledge of the country's food and population experts, action is bound to be minimal.

Attitudes Towards Children

Though most Americans are saying by their actual choices that two children are plenty, there is a lingering feeling that children ought to represent a reason for rejoicing because some new potential is released in the world, because the child represents a chance for improvement over the last generation. It's not easy to accept wholeheartedly the idea that children are simply a burden, that they keep families and societies from making social and economic progress.

Another aspect of attitudes toward having children is the feeling that carrying social responsibility into the bedroom is just too much of an invasion of private minds by the officers of the public good. There is hardly anything one can do any longer which does not have elements of public responsibility about it; can not even the number of one's children be exempt from the guardians of the public conscience? This whole discussion is tinged by weariness and exhaustion.

The Impotence of Large Things

Another dilemma which retards significant action on population or food issues is the immensity of the numbers usually involved. On the one hand, aggregate numbers--such as 4 billion people in the world, 15 million dying of starvation yearly, 1 billion suffering from malnutrition--have a certain power to shock and horrify. On the other hand, the numbers mean nothing, tell us nothing, hide whatever reality of suffering there is within that huge indigestible block. Billions, or even millions, of people is just too much for powerless individuals to do anything about. One might even hypothesize that people who pose problems in this way don't really want them to be solved.

Intervention

The last 20 years have taught us to be very careful about intervening in other countries' affairs, especially for their own good. After Vietnam, the United States should have less certainty that ours is the only way. Within the United States, Black, Indian, Chicano and women's movements have made a place for the idea that there is pride and power in being parochial rather than universal. Must all countries experience a decline in the rate of growth and in fertility rates, as Western countries have? Why are we out in front beating the drum to convince developing countries that they are overpopulated? You'd think they would come to that conclusion without our help. In The Politics of Ecology, James Ridgeway nastily raises the nasty suspicion that the heavy influence of Rockefeller money in the population movement signals more than disinterested philanthropy. Facts may refute such snide inferences, but the lessons of the past two decades do caution us against interfering in other countries' affairs without extremely good cause.

Solutions to These Dilemmas

The purpose of posing these dilemmas is so that others may clarify for me what I can't make sense out of. In the course of setting them down however, a number of potential solutions suggested themselves:

(1) Some very precise and extended research is needed to establish the degree of seriousness of overpopulation and/or food shortages.

(2) An extended series of private conferences among experts should be called for the express purpose of narrowing areas of public disagreement. Experts should put themselves under the discipline of labor-management type negotiations. After original circulation of a Population Memorandum of understanding, and then some exchanges and revisions, combatants might be locked in a room for three days until all parties agree on a position which is both true and workable. Such a document--signed by say 100 biologists, 50 nongovernmental organization heads and directors, 50 development specialists, 50 academic leaders in population--would be a strong statement to present to the American people and to Congress. It's time population people got their act together.

(3) The name of the game in the next decade may well be disaggregation of statistics. Thus we need to compile country by country--and, if Prosterman is correct, area by area within countries--studies of actual conditions, with estimates made of carrying capacity, food supplies, development needs, population pressures, etc. It seems to me unlikely that any world goal can be set for population or food unless it is composed of particular conclusions growing out of particular cases.

(4) These dilemmas might be resolved by pledging allegiance to the principle of quality over quantity. If the quality of the caring is good, then we may not need as many children to demonstrate that caring. If the quality of food is primary, monocropping and foreign exports may be less highly regarded. If we are interested in quality, devotion to mass production may be lessened, with a consequent reprieve for the environment and our resource base. Quality might well provide the rallying concept behind which population, food, resource and environmental problems could be unified.

(5) Finally, my wife has suggested that some of my dilemmas can be solved by setting up a mechanism whereby ordinary Americans with slight humanitarian leanings can be connected personally to overpopulation and world hunger. It's very simple. The churches--

226

being the only institution with a built-in ethical mission--make contact with churches abroad. They adopt a poor parish of the same or different religion; either each family adopts another family or each congregation adopts an overseas congregation. Letters and pictures relating to personal experience--working conditions, food, population, hopes, needs, efforts--are exchanged and the more well-off church than decides on some continuing commitment: money, time, things sent (socks, contraceptives, seeds, a local technical expert, whatever seems sensible).

This is no longer charity; it's a personal connection. It's no longer a huge and impersonal numerical problem. It's no longer merely the unreal invention of warring experts. Such a scheme could be organized on a huge scale, yet the actual doing would be in terms of individuals or small collective groups. The dilemmas of experts, of numbers, and of intervention would be eased by a broad church adoption plan.

To conclude, I may be naive, but I believe that the American people and the Congress will respond if they can be convinced that something is the case. Is the world overpopulated? How seriously? Is serious starvation inevitable if we continue as we are going? It is, I think, time for population and food groups to strongly demonstrate their case and then come out of isolation and join together in a common goal. If, as an average American, I am left with all these dilemmas, I guess I'll move to something smaller I can make sense out of.

OVERPOPULATION IN DYSTOPIAN LITERATURE

Richard D. Erlich

Department of English, Miami University (Ohio)

NASA's decision to name its new space shuttle The Enterprise is significant: it's NASA's rather elegant acknowledgment of the importance of Star Trek (and the sub-genre Star Trek ably represents) for governmental and popular support for the space program. All those space operas subtly, powerfully, and frequently repeat a basic lesson: space travel is possible; space travel is exciting.

We cannot hope for similar influence from cautionary fables about overpopulation. Such fables are often satires which question the mythic virtues of fertility and expansiveness. They cannot compete for a mass audience with the excitement of adventure stories and the celebration of fertility found in the symbolic weddings ending most comedies. Still, while science fiction is again attracting large audiences, it is important to encourage people to read and understand works that deal effectively with the themes of overpopulation and the ecological disasters that stem in large part from overpopulation.

In this paper I would like to comment on three works of fiction that analyze the causes of overpopulation and ecological disaster. Put into traditional terminology, the causes are familiar: the infernal trinity of stupidity, greed, and pride--with pride as the demonic father of greed and stupidity.

In Frederik Pohl and C. M. Kornbluth's The Space Merchants (1952), we see a good deal of folly, arrogance, and insensitivity. Indeed, the protagonist-narrator seems nearly uneducable and must go through two initiations and the entire pattern of Heroic development (Campbell, pp. 245-46) before he finally recognizes the evils in his world. Mostly, though, The Space Merchants shows us the horrible results of greed, of the worship of "the god of Sales." As a still-unreconstructed advertising executive, the hero reads Biometrika and notes that "Almost every issue had good news in it for us. . . . Increase of population was always good news . . . More people, more sales. Decrease of IQ was always good news to us. Less brains, more sales" (ch. 9, p. 111).

228

The greed of the corporations that rule the world of Space Merchants had brought about or encouraged overpopulation, pollution, protein shortages, and political oppression. By the standards of mid-20th Century America, no one in Space Merchants is really well off. But such a condition doesn't prevent greed, "For pride's criterion of prosperity is not what you've got yourself, but what other people haven't got" (More, p. 131). There is little hope for Earth in this novel, and its responsible people are forced to colonize Venus to give humanity a chance for survival.

Even less optimistic is the cause-effect analysis of ecological disaster by Ursula K. Le Guin in The Lathe of Heaven (1971) and The Word for World Is Forest (1972/1976). Le Guin's general philosophy is Taoist (Barbour), and she strongly disapproves of much of the outlook of "the Judaeo-Christian-Rationalist West" (ch. 6, p. 82); the target of her attack, however, can be described adequately as the sinful pride condemned, as well as condoned, by the Judaeo-Christian tradition.

In both of these works people have multiplied and filled the Earth, and have exercised dominion over it--and in both works we have very nearly taken a garden and turned it into a desert. The ultimate cause of such behavior is represented by the villains of the two works: the power-mad scientist Haber in Lathe and the macho Capt. Davidson in Word. Haber is one who cannot let the world be; he must exercise control. Davidson sees himself as a world-tamer, a modern incarnation of the old Conquistador: a man who will bring Terran guts and know-how to the subjugation of "New Tahiti," a logging colony of the deforested Earth (ch. 1).

Neither Lathe nor Word offers much hope for Earth and its people, but both strongly suggest the Way we must follow to avoid catastrophe: "[W]hen the mind becomes conscious . . . then you have to be careful. Careful of the world. You must learn the way. You must learn the skills, the art, the limits. A conscious mind must be part of the whole, intentionally and carefully--as the rock is part of the whole unconsciously" (Lathe, ch. 10, p. 161).

"The root of all evils," said the Church Fathers, "is pride." Of recent writers of dystopian fiction, Le Guin is clearest in teaching this lesson; but Pohl and Kornbluth know that the desire to be on top "and eat and drink and sleep a little better than anybody else" can be the source of much greed and "warped" thinking (ch. 13, p. 158). All three of these works give stern warnings to us to stop despoiling the Earth. They also tell us that, in order to save our world, at least some of us must radically change our attitudes and our lives.

REFERENCES

1. Barbour, D. Wholeness and balance in the Hainish novels of
   Ursula K. Le Guin. Science Fiction Studies. 1: 164-73 (1974).

2. Campbell, J. The Hero with a Thousand Faces. 2nd ed. Princeton University Press, Princeton (1968).

3. Le Guin, U. K. The Lathe of Heaven. Avon, New York (1971).

4. Le Guin, U. K. The word for world is forest. In Harlan Ellison,
   ed., Again, Dangerous Visions, Vol. 1. New American Library,
   New York (1972). Reprinted in 1976.

5. More, T. Utopia (1516). Trans. Paul Turner. Penguin, Middle-
   sex (1965).

6. Pohl, F. and C. M. Kornbluth. 1952. The Space Merchants. Ballantine, New York (1952).

A Brief, Selected, Annotated Bibliography of Works
Useful for the Study of the Vision of
Overpopulation and Ecological Disaster in Recent
Science Fiction and Dystopian Literature

I. Popularizations of Scientific Work

   Ardrey, Robert. African Genesis. 1961; rpt. New York, Dell,
   1963.

        A highly influential book that introduced to many people
        the idea of the biological limitations on human malle-
        ability. Deals with territoriality.

   _____. The Territorial Imperative. 1966; rpt. New York,
   Dell, 1968.

        An extended discussion of territoriality in humans and
        other animals.

   Calhoun, John B. "Population Density and Social Pathology."
   Scientific American (February 1962). Rpt. Science, Con-
   flict and Society: Readings from Scientific American.
   San Francisco: W. H. Freeman, 1969, pp. 111-18.

        Discusses the "behavioral sink" that can form when rats
        are overcrowded; suggests that further studies "may ad-
        vance our understanding to the point where they may

contribute to the making of value judgments about analogous problems confronting the human species."

II. Brief Review of SF Works on "The Population Explosion"

Berger, Harold L. "The Population Explosion" section of
Science Fiction and the New Dark Age. Bowling Green:
Bowling Green University Press, 1976, pp. 155-66.

Reviews James Blish and Norman L. Knight, A Torrent of
Faces; Harry Harrison, Make Room! Make Room!; Robert Bloch,
This Crowded Earth; Richard Wilson, "The Eight Billion";
J. G. Ballard, "Billenium"; Earl Conrad, The Da Vinci
Machine: Tales of the Population Explosion; Max Ehrlich,
The Edict; and Anthony Burgess, The Wanting Seed. Sug-
gests that all the authors he deals with present "a false
dilemma: Either man resigns himself to inevitable stran-
gulation through overbreeding or substitutes a different
disaster by some frightful circumvention."

III. Dystopian and SF Works

Blish, James, adaptor. "The Mark of Gideon" in Star Trek 6.
New York: Bantam, 1972, pp. 119-49. Based on the Star
Trek episode written by George F. Slavin and Stanley
Adams, 1967.

Kirk brings the gift of death to a planet that has become
overpopulated because of an inordinate love of life at
any cost.

Brunner, John. Stand on Zanzibar. 1968; rpt. New York: Ballantine, 1972.

I might have missed some subtle irony--but the ending of
this book at least seems inappropriately upbeat. Still,
this is the classic SF work on overpopulation and the
"behavioral sink" that may result from overcrowding and
the stringent "eugenic" measures justified by that overcrowding. Chad C. Mulligan, Brunner's mouthpiece, uses
the theory of territoriality to explain why severe overcrowding leads to social pathology (Context [5], "The
Grand Manor," pp. 73-79). A very long book.

_____. The Sheep Look Up. New York: Bantam, 1972/1973.

Often described as the sequal to Stand on Zanzibar. Deals
in great detail with the ecological disaster that probably
destroys the U.S. and makes life miserable for just about
everybody in this world of the near future. The "Prospec-
tus" of the book (on its first page of text) gives an

excerpt from "Christmas in New Rome" (1862), a poem that extravagantly praises the "noble goal" of subduing the Earth and making it fit for domesticated Victorian life. A very long book.

Clarke, Arthur C. Childhood's End. New York: Ballantine, 1953.

The utopian section of this novel presupposes that human beings reduce our population to human proportions. The utopian section quietly praises technology, but the novel goes on to find human likeness to the gods in the human spirit and not in gadgets and the power they give us.

_____. 2001: A Space Odyssey. New York: New American Library, 1968. Based on the screenplay for 2001, by Clarke and Stanley Kubrick.

Unlike the movie, the novel presents the problem facing humanity in 2001 as simple physical extinction. The basic cause for this threat of extinction is overpopulation, leading to hunger--in a world in which 38 countries possess nuclear weapons (with a strong likelihood that the number of nuclear powers will soon increase). This issue is handled quite briefly (ch. 7, pp. 43-44); then Clarke gets on to a mystic conclusion (both logically and esthetically) with the creation of Star-Child. As in Childhood's End, technology is OK, but mind or spirit is the ground of godhead.

Harrison, Harry. Make Room! Make Room! Garden City, N.Y.: Doubleday, 1966. Most readily available in the semi-legal British edn., London: Penguin, 1967. Based, according to Berger, on Harrison's short story, "Roommates"; the source for the overpopulation theme and some other elements of the MGM film, Soylent Green.

Harrison's book is generally inferior to Soylent Green (which isn't very good itself). Still, it is an attempt to deal seriously with the pathology of an overpopulated world, suffering from the "greenhouse effect" and the pressures of overpopulation. The book lacks the cannibalism gimmick of the film. In their images of overpopulation both book and film are effective propaganda: cautionary fables, warning us of what's in store if we don't begin to limit population growth.

Vonnegut, Kurt Jr. "Tomorrow and Tomorrow and Tomorrow." 1954; conveniently collected in Welcome to the Monkey House. New York: Dell, 1970, pp. 293-308.

A comic story of family life in a world overpopulated because of use of "anti-gerasone"--a drug that prevents death for an indeterminate, but very great, length of time.

_____. "Welcome to the Monkey House." 1968; conveniently collected in Welcome to the Monkey House, pp. 28-47.

A comic story set in a world where "the World Government was making a two-pronged attack on overpopulation. One pronging was the encouragement of ethical suicide . . . The other pronging was compulsory ethical birth control." Ethical birth control requires taking pills that "didn't interfere with a person's ability to reproduce, which would have been unnatural and immoral. All the pills did was take every bit of pleasure out of sex."

BACTERIAL GROWTH CURVES AND POPULATION MANAGEMENT

William M. Dowler

U.S. Department of Agriculture
Science and Education Administration

Perhaps the most important problem facing the world today is the struggle to achieve balance between world population growth and the food supply. This leads indirectly to other serious problems such as war, competition for territory, and threats of revolution. However, the ultimate concern is for adequate food, clothing, and shelter, all of which depends on achieving the critical balance between people and resources.

Two critical points merit serious consideration:

1. World population is expected to double in the next 35 years. This means we must at least double the food supply, learning how to produce as much again in 35 years as we have since the beginning of agriculture. Can we do it? Probably, but at great cost to our natural resources. And then what of the next 35 years?

2. Yields of major crops have not increased significantly since 1970. This is partially explained by weather and by the fact that we are bringing more marginal crop land into production. Scientists fear that it may take great efforts to obtain yield increases needed to provide the additional food required.

Let us consider a microcosm of the biological world for possible solutions to our dilemma. I have long been fascinated with bacterial growth curves. They begin with a long, slow adjustment phase; a rapid exponential phase; a stationary phase; and a death phase. The stages are predictable, and the end result in a closed system is always death. This occurs because of lack of space, lack of food, or accumulation of toxic compounds.

If one looks at the various depictions of our human population growth curve, one is struck by the similarity. We have moved from the adjustment phase to a point somewhere in the exponential phase, and we must surely wonder if the other stages will inevitably follow. Let us examine some options.

We have learned to manipulate bacterial cultures in such a way that the bacteria in the system do not die. Using this technique we continuously supply the bacteria with a certain proportion of new media or resources. With proper adjustment, the death rate becomes equal to the appearance of new individuals, and we achieve a steady state.

Can we do this with people? Let us hope so, for the alternative is to see our population climb to unmanageable proportions and decline traumatically through famine, pestilence, poisoning, or war. The sun is our extraterrestrial resource, but we lack the technology needed to utilize it properly. We must improve our management of photosynthesis and the use of the sun as a pollution-free energy source. Then, if we can learn how to manage our toxic byproducts, we will have a good chance of succeeding.

But time is short. The first requirement is to learn how to limit our population growth to zero without undue trauma. This must be followed by rapid development and application of other technologies needed to maintain the balance. We must be able to persuade governments that these activities take top priority and are more important than maintaining defense stockpiles or building bigger cities or machines. Although the task is enormous, I am optimistic enough to believe that we are smarter than bacteria and can learn to control our destiny. If we can, we will have satisfied the goal stated in the purpose of the Population/Food Fund: "To achieve a balance between population size and available resources for life support in a stable and healthful environment."

WHAT'S WRONG WITH POPULATION RESEARCH?--
AN ALTERNATIVE PROPOSAL

Emile Benoit

Senior Research Associate and Professor Emeritus
Columbia University

Most population research at present is narrowly demographic; it seeks improved estimates of present population size, and of future population trends under alternative assumptions. But improved estimates of this sort can have only a small bearing on whether or not mankind can avoid ecological catastrophe. Much potentially useful population research that is being done is specialized, disjointed, and unintegrated in any coherent social-science policy-oriented framework. In view of the gravity and urgency of the problems we face, we badly need a new approach, in which population research is so organized as to provide essential inputs into policy formation directed toward the supreme issue of human survival.

The three most basic questions which require research are:

1. What population size or trend would best contribute to human survival for as long as geological and astronomic conditions permit, with as high an average level of welfare as possible?

2. What economic, political and institutional measures would best facilitate the attainment of this optimal size or trend, with minimal cost for other values?

3. What interests, attitudes, and ideologies will oppose the measures required under (2) above, and how can such opposition be effectively overcome, reduced, or circumvented?

In category (1), one useful project would be a cross section analysis of a large number of LDCs to discover whether there is a statistically reliable inverse correlation between population growth rates and (a) growth in real per capita incomes; (b) reduced rates of unemployment and underemployment; (c) balance between rural and urban development; (d) literacy rates; (e) reduction in death rates. Research by the writer on (a) has given encouraging preliminary results for 140 countries during the decade of the 1960s, with a correlation of -.278, significant at better than a 1% level.

A second project in category (1) would explore the multiple determinants of dependency ratios. The first segment would project the increase in dependency ratios at various rates of decline in population growth, including negative population growth at various rates--assuming the continuation of present labor force participation rates. A second set of projections would be made on the assumption that recent changes in labor force participation rates comprise a trend, and the projections would be based on the assumption that this trend continues. A third set of projections would be based on estimates of how much this trend might be speeded up by changes in public policy, such as raising the required age of retirement for those willing and able to continue working; improving day-care facilities, thereby increasing female labor force participation; reducing school leaving age for those deriving no educational benefit from school; plus an effective full employment program (such as the one proposed by Dr. John H. G. Pierson). All of these policies would increase the ratio of employment to total population.

A third project in category (1) would be a retrospective econometric analysis of what per capita GNP, unemployment, fuel consumption, net oil and gas exports, pollution, reserves of nonrenewable resources, and soil erosion, might be today in the U.S. if the U.S. population had stopped growing in 1929, when world population was half, and U.S. population 52%, of what it is now. The analysis would trace the effects (based on latest findings) of reduced fertility rates in higher savings and investment ratios, and diversion of investment away from housing, elementary school building and transportation and into industrial building and machinery, and facilities for higher education, professional education, skill instruction and R&D, as well as reduced requirements for current expenditures on elementary education, police, firemen, etc. This project might make vivid the extent to which many of our key problems are attributable to the last doubling of our population, and the possible benefits of reducing our population by half--to the extent, of course, that these processes are reversible.

A project in category (2) would involve a detailed analysis and summation of encouragement to population expansion in the various countries of the world, arising from covert pronatalist policies, such as: welfare payments, family allowances, retirement benefits, food stamps, tax deductions directly related to family size, as well as tax subsidized housing and free education for large families. In some countries such a project would also need to examine direct obstruction of knowledge and procedures required for population control, as well as subsidization of religions preaching that such control is sinful.

A project in category (3) would involve motivational analysis to find out to what extent pronatalist policies derive support from the following attitudes and ideas: (a) ethnic imperialism (a minority student once asked me, in all seriousness, "if we stop population growth, how will we ever get to be a majority?"); (b) national security considerations; (c) the fear of politicians of losing part of their electorate; (d) the desire of national leaders, especially in LDCs, to gain international prestige and influence by representing large populations; (e) the wish of an affluent minority to keep unemployment high and wages low, so as to keep down costs and increase profits; (f) the wish of a middle class to have a large pool of indigent poor to supply personal services, and on whom they can look down, thus bolstering their own self esteem; (g) the machismo complex whereby men show their virility by having large families, and derive economic rewards thereby; and (h) sincere religious conviction that population control is sinful. A followup project might explore the extent to which these ideas and attitudes rest on assumptions which no longer correspond to reality, or were initially based on misperceptions, and the extent to which these ideas and attitudes are in fact changing over time.

The above proposals are, of course, intended solely to illustrate how population research might be modified so as to provide more relevant inputs into the determination of public policies affecting human survival.

INSTITUTIONALIZING POPULATION EDUCATION:
METHODS AND OUTCOMES OF A SUCCESSFUL
MODEL FOR TRAINING OF TEACHERS
AND ADMINISTRATORS

Elaine Murphy and Marge Dahlin

Zero Population Growth, Inc.

At present, Zero Population Growth, Inc. (ZPG) is midway through the third year of its national population education teacher-training project. To date, our national staff has led or cosponsored 34 workshops in 15 states, directly reaching a total of 2000 teachers, curriculum specialists, school administrators, and professors of education.

Supported mainly by grants from the U.S. Office of Environmental Education and private foundations, the project's purpose is to incorporate population education into the structures used by public school systems to introduce innovative topics or methods--for example, in-service courses or workshops, recommendation of new materials through department heads, curriculum writing and revision, and communication of new ideas through teachers' conventions and journals.

The ZPG project organizes workshops for those school personnel most likely to utilize these methods of institutionalization: highly motivated teachers, department heads, professors of education, curriculum writers, and supervisors of science, social studies, and other relevant disciplines. Participants are expected to leave the workshops with: (a) a basic understanding of population trends; (b) direct experience with existing pop ed lesson plans, games and activities, including a brief team curriculum-writing session; (c) knowledge of and access to the many written and audio-visual materials available for pop ed; and (d) a packet of pop ed materials directly usable in the classroom--the ZPG Population Education Resource Kit.

The Resource Kit, distributed to all participants, forms the basis of workshop activities. All the exercises and activities used in the workshop are provided in it. Materials and films used are listed, along with access information. The kit serves to reinforce the memory of what is experienced at the workshop and at the same time provides directly usable materials relevant even to persons who have not attended the workshop. Of course, participants are encouraged to adapt these resources to their own needs, the grade levels of their students, subject areas taught, and so on.

The workshops are a mixture of quizzes, films, discussions, small group problem-solving exercises, demonstrations, games, role-playing and lesson writing. The planning, content, and follow-up efforts of the ZPG project form a constantly-evolving workshop model, which we believe is a successful one. Some of the components of this model include:

1. The identification of cosponsors and participants whose school system positions or other networks enable them to multiply the effectiveness of the workshop. This may be accomplished through in-service courses, newsletters, and other ways.

2. An emphasis on "the local scene," to identify persons with expertise in population topics as well as materials and other resources available within the community--for example, locally-developed pop ed materials and films from nearby film libraries. Lists of local pop ed resources are distributed, and data on local or state population trends are included in the workshop activities. Cosponsorship of the workshops with local educational agencies and other community agencies is sought. The purpose of this local emphasis is to stress the idea that the project is a local commitment, not merely a one-time visit from an outside group, and to provide human and material resources at the local level after the workshop.

3. The selection of attractive written and audio-visual population teaching materials that come from a variety of sources and which are accurate, value-fair, appropriate to the needs and interests of the learner, easy to use or adapt and which utilize a large variety of teaching/learning methods.

4. The design of the workshop format around these teaching materials. Thus participants acquire population information, understanding of population dynamics, and values clarification by actually doing the quizzes, exercises, role-playing, games and discussions that they will use directly (or adapt) in their teaching programs. The written form of the workshop activities is then provided to each participant in the ZPG Pop Ed Resource Kit.

5. The provision of follow-up help with the implementation of participants' post-workshop plans for population education. This follow-up activity includes the mailing of new resource information to participants, data on participants' post-workshop activities, and notices about the availability of new materials. Help in planning "spinoff" teacher-training workshops and in obtaining free or low-cost materials is also given. The purpose of this continued

contact is to keep alive the enthusiasm for population education engendered by the workshop and to provide additional teaching tools to participants.

In 1976, the Office of Environmental Education funded a formal evaluation of ZPG's first year workshops in five states. Questionnaires were sent to all participants asking about their population education activities after--and, at least in part, as a result of--their attendance at the workshop. The validity of the results was established by an independent evaluation led by Andrew Leighton, now Assistant Population Education Director at the Population Reference Bureau.

In addition to the 67% of teachers who instituted a population unit in their classes, 58% of the administrators directed or encouraged the teachers under their supervision to teach about population, and 23% of the professors of education organized in-service pop ed workshops for teachers.[*]

---

[*]A full report of the evaluation findings, "The ZPG Population Education Program: Description and Evaluation," is available from ZPG, 1346 Connecticut Avenue NW, Washington, D.C. 20036, for $5.00. The Population Education Resource Kit is available for $2.00.

PLANNING POPULATION EDUCATION AS A COMPONENT
OF DEVELOPMENT POLICY

Muhiuddin Haider

School of Education, University of Michigan

Since the Bucharest Conference on World Population (1974), development policy has emphasized population planning in relation to man-land-resource ratios. It is widely accepted that education, as a major communications system, is one of the main strategies for reducing birth rates in developing countries. The magnitude of the problem of over-population calls for attention from beyond family planning programs, and the educational institutions of a country seem a logical place to communicate the message to youth.

Population education is a relatively new concept in the field of education, but it is increasingly being accepted as an essential component of fertility control population policy in developing societies. Elsewhere,[*] the author has discussed the conceptual relationship between development and population education in the context of socio-structural needs for a better quality of life. The central point to be made is that the nature of the population education message and its effects on reducing fertility depend largely on the level and structure of socio-economic development.

Because demographic growth in developing nations is exceeding peoples' capacities to satisfy their basic human requirements, development policies at national, regional and community levels must provide for population programs consistent with development goals. The ethical problem of how best to secure social intervention in family social systems is a final policy consideration. Client involvement in program development appears to be a logical approach to resolving it.

---

[*]Copies of the full research paper, printed in the Occasional Paper Series of the University of Michigan School of Education, are available from the Graduate Study Program on Education and Community Development, School of Education, the University of Michigan, Ann Arbor, Michigan 48104. The author acknowledges, with gratitude, the assistance of the School of Education Research Committee.

In view of the limited resources for educational investments in most developing countries, it seems logical to integrate population education into other educational programs and/or social services such as health, nutrition, and employment training, especially in rural areas.

PLANNING FOR HEALTH IN AN EXPANDING POPULATION

Robert Davis

American Health Planning Association

What I'm going to try to do is hit some highlights in the field of health planning as it relates to the expanding population in many parts of the country and of the world.

The first place you have to start when you look at health in an area of population growth, is to understand the nature of the population growth. The two questions that come to mind are: Is the growth a suburban, affluent, upper middle-class type of population explosion or is it really one of migrant workers, the indigent or the poor? Since good planning in the health business really refers to the provision of health care, the second key question is one of accessability. Cost factors are of secondary importance, and we'll come back to that in a minute.

What's been shown over and over again in research is that care should be close to the health consumer. People in all socio-economic categories will use facilities and services that are geographically in close proximity. Good planning attempts to respond to this truism and locate facilities and services as close to the population and needs as possible. This is especially true in the primary care delivery of health services.

You can't really discuss the topic of planning for health care without mentioning some recent developments. The first thing that comes to a lot of people's minds is the expansion of the HMO, the Health Maintenance Organization, type of effort in an area. HMOs are still in their infancy, but some of the studies which have been done suggest that the HMOs can cut down on the need for certain types of care and make it more efficient, especially hospital care or in-patient types of facilities, mainly because emphasis in the HMO development has been on the preventive aspects. However, there is really not a lot of evidence that HMOs will approach a broad range of the socio-economic population; although they're less costly than some types of primary care, they are still very costly. Only a very small percentage of the population has access to HMOs. But there is some hope in the future that this sort of thing will help an expanding population base to better primary care.

There has also been a lot of work done on the use of what is called physician extenders, often called paraprofessionals in the literature. I personally don't like the word paraprofessional since it implies less or different than professional, but there's no question that this has been helpful. But again, when we look at what has been done with the physician extenders and the nurse extenders and all this paraprofessional development in primary care, we find that it really doesn't address the increase in numbers. What it really involves is a qualitative increase. Extenders and paraprofessionals improve the quality of health care, but they make only a barely noticeable difference in terms of the numbers of people treated.

To look at it in a broad perspective, if you have a society that is chronically ill (however you'd want to determine that--you can use World Health Organization data on what is ill and what is healthy), you're talking about a situation that needs a top to bottom centralized control. What I'm really suggesting here is governmental control of the whole medical entity. Given the political realities of the situation, total centralization of medical care will be effective only in the future and probably only in Third World countries.

Again there's been some talk that one way to treat large numbers of people efficiently is by pre-diagnostic treatment, or what's sometimes called screening. The only problem with screening, we're finding out, is it does not appear to be cost-effective in terms of really finding the people that are ill and need treatment. There are many examples where several hundreds of thousands of dollars have been spent to do some screening in an area only to uncover three or four cases of the illness being sought after. One has to look closely at whether one would spend $50,000 to uncover three examples of something like skin cancer. I doubt if society would be able to provide that type of financial backing for this type of development.

Any discussion of health care and population now must mention the following: there is a very strong indication that improvement of the physical environment is directly related to improving the health of a community. This again cuts across all socio-economic levels; the poor as well as the less poor are affected equally by the environmental standards of an area. As a matter of fact we're beginning to think that it is quicker and, therefore, may be cost-effective, to improve the health status of a community by improving the environmental standards than it is to add, shall we say, inputs from the medical-technological standpoint. It may be in both the short and long term more effective to improve environmental quality, which seems to relate very closely to the health care quality of an area.

There's also been some talk about preventive care, self care and nutritional education, all of which fall under the general category of health education. There's no question that health education can improve the health of large segments of the population. Unfortunately, it's difficult to measure and therefore there is some reluctance to develop it a whole lot more. I think the special effects of health education programs are especially focused on prenatal care. They've been very effective in this regard and this is probably where the emphasis on prevention in health education will be focused in the next decade or two.

Any discussion of health has to talk about the problem of cost. Things cost money; especially to the poor, their disposable income being less than others, health costs become very important. This is something that the health planning field is taking a very close look at and this is something that's being federally mandated, slowly but surely, to look at costs of health in general.

Let me mention briefly the emergence of a new phenomenon in medical care, emergency medical services. Emergency Medical Services (EMS) has become in this country the main entry to the primary care health business for most of our people. I read an astonishing study about two weeks ago. They did a study of two EMS facilities in New York City and they found that 80% of the people who used the emergency medical services in two major hospitals were not emergencies, but merely needed entry into the primary care business. So if you're planning on looking at health care in an area that's growing quickly, especially a poor area, a lot of the focus might have to be on the quality of emergency medical service.

One thing for the future that's being worked on now is bringing private industry closer to the provision of health. The idea is that these non-health industries, like General Motors or DuPont, are beginning to see that the cost of health for all people in their community--not just their employees--is beginning to cause an increase in the price of their product. The indicator for this is the fact that in 1976 General Motors reached a point in its development where they were spending more on the health insurance package for the auto union workers than they were on the cost of steel and several other raw materials in the price of an automobile. If you want an important bit of trivia, approximately $1800 of every new American-make GM car is a health insurance premium that's paid for the workers by General Motors. So there are a lot of planners now who are trying to work hand in hand with large industries, because we feel that's an effective way to do it. For example, they may want to set up community outreach, or health education or HMO-types of development to better address the general population.

That, fortunately, or unfortunately, is the state of art. I can't cheer you up. There's no miracle cure for the growing population pains, especially as they relate to the health industry. As a planner, the best I can say is that we've got to keep trying to do a better job of planning for improved health care in an expanding population.

DISCUSSION

AUDIENCE: Is anybody doing studies on how an industry such as General Motors or the chemical industries are contributing to the ill health of their employees and consumers?

ROBERT DAVIS: It's usually not in the self-interest of industries to look at studies of how they contribute to the ill health of anything. But I think there is a growing awareness. It's very hard to show the correlations between some of these things to people, especially industrial executives, but it is slowly becoming more of a concern. I don't think it's happening fast enough, but at least they're becoming aware that they're part of the problem. And also the way we're addressing it is to show them that it's cheapter for them to be concerned.

CLIFFORD FIGALLO, The Farm, Summertown, Tennessee: I'm from an intentional community in Tennessee. We've set up our own primary health care system down there. We have one doctor, a couple of nurses, and others who are trained in the community. Our most effective practice is through the use of what you'd call physician extenders, although they're trained within the community. I was wondering what the main obstalces are to community outreach, especially in poor communities where you could go around and do a certain amount of screening for malnutrition, etc. and childhood diseases that the parents may not be aware of?

ROBERT DAVIS: That's a very tough question because there are about four components of it. First of all you have to remember the medical business is part of a free market economy, so you have to get providers to agree to that type of development. I suspect you have a closed community in some regards, so you have a little more control as to what the inputs are. For example, if you have a TV station, you know what's going on it so you can put health education messages on at a time when people are still awake. Your experiment is probably very successful and it's being duplicated elsewhere, but not on a massive scale. I think it's much too specific for a general population where the obstacles are just amazing.

THE NEED FOR RECONCILING NATIONAL ECONOMIC POLICY WITH CHANGING POPULATION STRUCTURE*

Chia-Lin Pan

United Nations Social Affairs Officer (retired)

Due to declining fertility since the early 1960s, the population age structure of the United States has been changing. It is now
shaped like a prehistoric flint-tipped spearhead. When a prevalent
low fertility is maintained indefinitely over time its eventual
shape will be rectangular like that of a brick. The current age
structure change has caused the U.S. population to be more and more
heavily weighted with adults. Widespread use of conventional phrases
such as "aging population" and "aging process" reflect general awareness of this changing age structure. Since practically every industrialized country in the world has undergone similar changes in
age structure, it is important to explore the phenomenon of "an aging
population."

In Figure 1, diagram A is drawn on the 1960 age structure of the
U.S. population with both sexes combined, expressed in percentage distribution. Since the year 1960 was prior to the onset of the recent
fertility decline, the structural shape should look like a folded
together age pyramid. And the diagram does resemble one. The
indentation at ages 30-34, 25-29 and 20-24 in 1960 was due to the
so-called birth "deficits" of the great depression years, corresponding to the birth cohorts of 1925-29, 1930-34 and 1939-39 respectively, as noted on the diagram. With nearly a decade of falling
fertility affecting annual births, the 1970 population age structure
(Diagram B) is, however, more heavily weighted with adults than that
of 1960 but bears a relatively closer resemblance to diagram A1 drawn
on the 1960 population by age in terms of adult-equivalent units (AEU).**
This comparison by visual inspection is, of course, very crude. For
a more precise comparison, diagram B1 is drawn on the 1970 population

---

*A version of this paper was presented at Capon Springs Public
Policy Conference #1 but was omitted from The Proceedings due to space
limitations.

**Conversion to adult-equivalent units (AEU) is based on the
following formula: for ages 0-1, 0.3 AEU; for ages 2-5, 0.4 AEU; for
ages 6-9, 0.5 AEU; for ages 10-11, 0.6 AEU; for age 12, 0.7 AEU; for
ages 13-14, 0.8 AEU; for ages 15-16, 0.9 AEU; and age 17+, 1 AEU.

by age in AEU. Furthermore, for the sake of simplicity, let persons aged 15 years and above be considered as adults. Then B1 (1970) is seen to be more heavily weighted with adults than A1 (1960) by some 1.5%. By comparing the two 1970 diagrams (which represent different categories) we find that B1 (in AEU)--which can be considered the type of adult-standardized age structure--is, of course, more heavily weighted with the segment aged 15 years and above than B (expressed

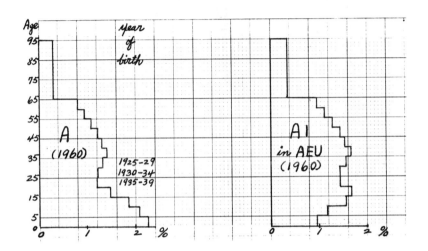

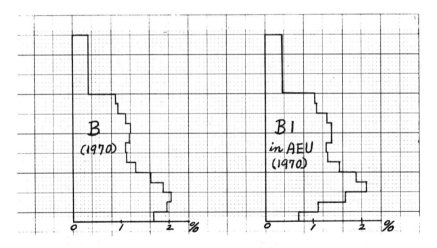

Figure 1. Percentage Distribution of U.S. Population Age Structure (both sexes combined): A for 1960 population, B for 1970 population, A1 for 1960 population in adult-equivalenc units (AEU), B1 for 1970 population in AEU.

TABLE 1

A TABULATION OF SOME SELECTED DATA OF THE UNITED STATES, 1960-75 with Projected Values to 1980

Year	Total Population (millions)	AEU (millions)	AEU as Percent of Total Population	Weighted Average Conversion Ratio of Population Aged 0-14 to AEU[1]	GNP in Billions of Constant 1972 Dollars	Per Capita GNP Dollars	Index	GNP Per Unit AEU Dollars	Index
(1)	(2)	(3)	(4)	(5)	(6)	(7)	(8)	(9)	(10)
1960	179.3	151.0	84.2	0.494	737	4,110	100	4,881	100
1970	203.2	174.8	86.0	0.509	1,075	5,289	129	6,149	126
1975	213.1	187.2	87.8	0.516	1,202	5,640	137	6,420	132
1980	219.2	198.3	90.4	0.575	...	...	...	...	...

[1]This weighted average conversion ratio of population aged 0-14 to AEU is taken to be 1 minus (difference between total population and AEU) divided by population aged 0-14.

in population) by some 15.5%. It is precisely the attribute of non-comparability that calls for a closer examination of what significance, if any, such noncomparability stands for. To facilitate the pursuit, Table 1 is given.

From column 4 of the table, AEU as percent of total population is seen to be rising consistently (with the negatively associated declining fertility) over time from 84.2% in 1960 to 87.8% in 1975; it is expected to reach a 90% level by 1980 (projected on condition of constant age-specific fertility and no international migration from midyear 1975 onward). Underlying this trend is the same experience expressed in terms of weighted conversion ratio of population aged 0-14 to AEU as shown in column 5. The noncomparability of data arising from a changing population age structure has indeed made significant differences in the time series data between, for example, per capita GNP and per unit AEU value of GNP as columns 7 through 10 indicate. Per capita GNP overstates the time trend of income and thereby unavoidably understates the serious state of the economy especially during, for example, the recent 1974-75 recession. This bias can not be dismissed as negligible during the present ongoing age structure change. Rather it calls for a reevaluation of major time series socio-economic data wherever the stated bias factor is involved.

Features of an age structure heavily weighted with adults

In the lower row of Figure 2, the 1970 U.S. total population by age and its rural-urban components, all expressed in AEU, are shown

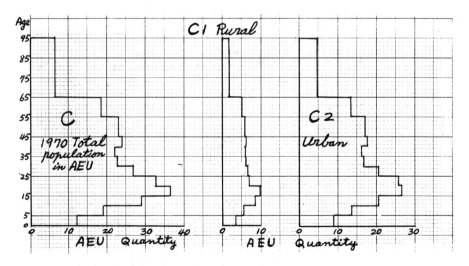

Figure 2. 1970 U.S. Population and its Rural-Urban Components in AEU (in 00,000 units).

251

in three diagrams. The features of the total population in AEU (Diagram C) are by and large reproduced in the overall urban population in AEU (Diagram C2), while rural population in AEU has been affected by emigration particularly at the young adult ages (Diagram C1). The conversion to AEU has rendered each aggregate for the rural and urban sector, for example, a quantified expression reflecting the population's general consumption function at the adult or its equivalent level. It is not surprising to see that at the designated level the weight of the young children's sector has shrunk drastically. Needless to say that children, like everybody else, have to consume in order to live and grow both physically and mentally. Yet the portions they have consumed are much smaller than an adult's on average whether it be the food eaten, the room-space occupied, the amount of materials that have gone into make the clothes, footwear and so on. We must not be confused with the price of consumer items for children in comparison with that for adults. In some market economies the pricing mechanism is highly influenced by "imperfect competition" which is altogether a different matter. Rendering a population in terms of AEU would readily yield a quantity reflecting aggregate consumption at the adult level.

Above the children's sector there is a bulge at the late teenagers and young adults segment. The proportion of those aged 15 to 29* can be read from the four diagrams in the upper row of Figure 1 and this is 19.5% according to the 1960 population diagram, 22.8% in the 1960 AEU diagram, 24.1% in the 1970 population diagram and 27.6% in the 1970 AEU diagram. As contained in diagrams B and A, this bulge will last until 1980, when the number involved will reach an alltime peak. Since the urban aggregate by and large reproduces the national features of the age structure, it is a foregone conclusion that there will be annual peak numbers of students attending schools at the senior high level and up through post graduate classes of the universities provided the enrollment ratio remains stable over time. Moreover, since this age segment coincides with that of candidate entries into the job markets there would have been a growing pressure on the urban job market. The appearance of two strange bedfellows in the form of a record number of employed persons and a record number of the unemployed occurring at the same time (as revealed in monthly tallies even during the 1974-75 recession period) was merely reflecting the effect generated by an ongoing age structure bulge.

At the higher ages the proportion of persons relevant to early retirement in the 55-64 age group has risen from 8.7% in 1960 to 9.2% in 1970, according to the population diagrams in Figure 1. According to the AEU diagrams this proportion has risen from 10.4 to 10.6% over that decade. As for those persons relevant to retirement in the 65 and above age group, the corresponding percentages are 9.2, 9.8 and 10.9 and 11.4, respectively. It should be noted that the growing proportion of the retirement age sector is a long term phenomena lasting

*This age grouping is useful for delineating migration effects.

252

through the next 50 years. Stated somewhat differently, the related
aspect of a declining average family size, too, is a long term phenomena.

The changing population age structure has brought about, among
other things, a shift in outlook away from family relationships towards a greater inclination to mobility, because there is a lowered
frequency of pending births and/or infants and young children to care
for to keep individuals and family members from moving about in migration. Moreover, urban communities with a steady stream of immigrants or a large migrant population turnover without causing local
net emigration are generally associated with spurred economic growth
while emigration communities are often stagnated. This is because
urban migrants are an effective catalyst on the economy.

Policy Responses to the Changing Age Structure

In the education field, the number of grade school and junior
high students has declined while those at senior high, college and
post-graduate levels continue to grow. With considerable inter-
regional migration from one urban area to another going on within the
country, it is conceivable that the receiving urban communities of
the South and West, for example, will be even more hard-pressed for
school expansions at these levels. And yet the current need is of a
relatively short duration; as mentioned previously, the present age
segment bulge will peak in 1980. What needs be done is to do the
obvious by rechanneling available educational funds into public institutions for higher learning. In addition, authorities should try cul-
tivating a system of resident student quarters in the form, for example, of adapted "YMCA" type dormitories on or near the campuses.
This will fully utilize the existing capacities of classrooms, laboratories and libraries of the educational institutions in the emigration regions such as the Northeast and North Central. In addition,
it would also contribute to reactivating the regional economy by moving in large numbers of resident students, some of whom will stay on
to become regular or career workers after graduation. Such a system
is nothing more than an institutional preference. It has been very
popular in Great Britain at the high school level and in many other
European countries as well. Table 2 shows school age population of
the United States by broad classifications (columns 2 through 5) for
1960 to 1975 at five year intervals and annually from 1976 through
1980, projected on the condition of no international migration since
the midyear of 1975.

The rising "boom" of job seekers at the labor force entry age
over the same time range, 1960-80, is shown in column 6. These persons
are consumers to begin with. Now that they have reached the age of
economic independence, they should become earners as well. It is the
government's obligation to see to it that they get settled in jobs;
for example, in various types of social work similar to that of the
Peace Corps. They can be trained to aid economically depressed areas
where there is a disproportionately large relative size of aged persons.

253

TABLE 2

TABLE SHOWING SELECTED FUNCTIONAL AGE GROUPS OF THE UNITED STATES POPULATION WITH
BOTH SEXES COMBINED, 1960-1980 (figure in thousands)

| Year | School Age | | | Post Graduate 22-24 Years | Labor Force Entry Age; 16-24 Years | Early Retirement & Retirement Age | | Small Children 0-4 Years |
	Grade School 5-13 Years	High School 14-17 Years	College 18-21 Years			55-64 Years	65 and Over	
1960	32,726	11,155	9,214	6,390	21,275	15,572	16,559	20,321
1965	35,899	14,482	11,916	7,897	26,863	16,966	18,156	20,434
1970	36,675	15,851	14,155	9,559	31,429	18,590	20,066	17,163
1975	33,456	16,941	16,330	11,028	35,776	19,780	22,400	15,896
1976	32,541	16,631	16,477	11,390	36,275	20,023	22,778	15,500
1977	31,705	16,459	16,481	11,689	36,526	20,304	23,084	15,386
1978	30,862	16,167	16,614	11,897	36,734	20,621	23,319	15,552
1979	30,132	15,855	16,679	12,260	36,962	20,873	23,482	15,842
1980	29,540	15,506	16,714	12,464	37,215	21,363	23,573	16,180

Source: U.S. Bureau of the Census, U.S. Census of Population: 1960 and 1970, vol. I; and Current Population Reports, series P-25. No. 614. The number of children under 5 years of age for 1976-1980 is estimated on the basis of assuming a constant annual age-specific fertility rate at a calculated "United Nations sex-age adjusted birth rate" of 14.8 per 1,000.

254

These persons are very much in need of rehabilitation in a healthy environment with semi-economic activities in a rural or small town setting. They can pay for themselves with their Social Security benefits. All it takes is appropriate business organization and management. However, they would need the assistance of a "domestic Peace Corps" to get them started on rehabilitation. The building of retirement settlements should include hospitals, nursing or convalescent homes and other related facilities. Retirement years can be made a period of continued productive and creative living. As retirement settlements get popularized, many workers would plan for early retirement, thus benefiting directly or indirectly job entrants at the young adult ages (see columns 7, 8 and 6 of the table).

In housing the changing age structure with the accompanying declining average size of the family calls for the building of efficiency apartments, condominiums and club houses. New housing starts, which has traditionally been the prime mover of the economy, ought to be guided at least in part to redeveloping the urban "blight" areas to (a) reverse the loss through non-compensated waste of once existing real estates (including abandoned tenement houses) and existing but underutilized community "overhead" of public services, and (b) recognize that private bank financed suburban residential housing is created to a certain extent artificially above the objective demand of the number of families having young children to raise. Continuation of this trend will only intensify the deterioration of the inner cities. A more informative figure than that on new housing starts should be the number of net incremental occupancy of dwelling units, to take account of the existing inventory of abandoned or otherwise vacated residential houses in the inner cities, appropriately valued according to the condition of the structure. Urban renewal is only next in importance to rebuilding disaster areas.

POLITICAL AND ADMINISTRATIVE REPERCUSSIONS OF POPULATION CHANGES DUE TO MIGRATORY OCCUPATIONS IN IMPACTED COMMUNITIES

Tim R. Miller

Northwest Community College, Powell, Wyoming

This paper is an excerpt from a larger inquiry into political and administrative ramifications of the dramatic population growth in energy impacted communities in the American west. The paper utilizes survey data obtained in three energy impacted Wyoming communities--Douglas, Gillette, and Sheridan--by the Center for Government Research at the University of Wyoming.

This paper considers one of four major topics covered in the full study. While the larger paper investigates problems and inadequacies of impacted community services and facilities, temporary and permanent population mutual assessments and perceptions and temporary and permanent population attitudes toward government leaders, this inquiry considers four political aspects of, and differences between, the temporary and permanent population groups.

Party Identification: Wyoming's political climate, much like that of other western states, is deeply ingrained by the conservative, ranching, individualistic ethic so prevalent in the region. The heterogeneous nature of the energy boom, some say, is changing the political landscape of the region. One question frequently raised is what the energy related population influx will do to both local and statewide political party balance. Accordingly, respondents were asked whether they think of themselves as a Republican, Democrat, or an Independent. Responses are shown in Table I. Clearly, the mobile resident population are not as Republican as the permanent population. However, they are not openly more Democratic. The disproportionately large "Independent" identification may mean any of several things. First, perhaps the mobile population is less likely to identify with a particular party, and is thereby "ahead" of the national trend toward party independence. Or, the figure may include sizable sample error, by not asking a follow-up question of which way, if any, the Independent identifiers lean. Another possibility, however, is that the figure represents political disinterest among the mobile population. After all, it is easier for survey respondents to answer "Independent" than "disinterested." This hypothesis is tested below.

TABLE I

TEMPORARY AND PERMANENT RESIDENTS BY
POLITICAL PARTY IDENTIFICATION

	Party Identification				
	Republican	Democrat	Independent	Other	
Temporary	25.0%	27.8%	43.0%	4.2%	100.0% (N=144)
Permanent	53.0%	26.8%	19.6%	.5%	99.9% (N=373)
		Gamma = -.50			

Political Participation: If over 40% of the new residents are indeed independent of the two major political parties, the political landscapes in impacted communities are increasingly apt to change. Increasingly, election outcomes will be determined by the voting patterns of the new residents, with their new and different values. Thus, the temporary residents may further compound the complexities of impact, by diminishing the permanent population's ability to solve their own difficulties. However, the first word of this section is the key: If they enter the political arena.

Respondents were asked questions dealing with both voting and political involvement. Table II shows responses to whether the residents voted in the 1972 Presidential and 1974 Congressional elections; the number of votes cast ranges from zero to two. As indicated by the .66 gamma coefficient, the temporary population was considerably less likely to vote in the 1972 and 1974 elections, than were the permanent residents. If this pattern is consistent, and it likely is, the political impact of the temporary residents is greatly diminished by their own absence from the polling place.

Likewise, respondents were asked whether during the 1972 or 1974 elections they had done any of the following: attended a political rally, donated any time or money, worn a campaign button, put a bumper sticker on their car, or put a sign in their window or yard. Of the temporary residents, 26.9% had done at least one of these things while 73.1% (N=145) had done none of them; 42.0% of the permanent population had, 57.9% had not (N=378, gamma = -.33). As shown, mobile residents were considerably less likely to vote, and somewhat less likely to participate in the ways listed above. Clearly, the mobile population's political impact does not match their social and economic impact.

257

TABLE II

TEMPORARY AND PERMANENT RESIDENTS BY NUMBER
OF VOTES CAST (1972 AND 1974)

	Number of Votes Cast			
	0	1	2	
Temporary	21.6%	29.7%	48.7%	100.0% (N=148)
Permanent	7.5%	7.0%	85.5%	100.0% (N=386)
		Gamma = .66		

Political Knowledge: As a test of political knowledge, survey respondents were asked to recall and identify the names of three government leaders--the Vice-President, Speaker of the House of Representatives, and Chief Justice of the U.S. Supreme Court. Correct answers ranged from zero to three. Two points were apparent. First, neither resident group was particularly more politically knowledgeable than the other (gamma = .11). Secondly, the number of respondents correctly knowing all three government officials (33.8% of the temporary population and 43.5% of the permanent residents) speaks rather poorly of the impacted community public. In fact, 12.8% of the temporary residents did not correctly identify any of the officials and 25.7% identified only one. Of the permanent population, 10.6% were incorrect all three times and 25.9% correctly identified only one government leader.

Political Efficacy: To assess respondent beliefs that they are able to have impact on, and affect the outcome of, government policy, the survey team asked, "Suppose a law were being considered by the state legislature which you considered unjust or harmful. If you made an effort to change such a law, how likely is it that you would succeed?" Answers are shown in Table III.

The correlation in Table III is weak (gamma = -.26). Still, a minor pattern exists: 25.0% of the permanent population believe they could prevent an unjust law, while only 17.6% of the temporary residents are as confident.

In addition, the two population groups were asked how likely it is that they would do something if the above situation actually arose. As might be expected from previous data, the permanent residents were slightly more likely to believe they would act (gamma = -.26). Thirty-eight percent of the permanent population said action would be very likely, compared with 18.3% of the mobile residents. Thus, efficacy differences between the groups were slight, but in the predicted direction.

TABLE III

TEMPORARY AND PERMANENT RESIDENTS BY POLITICAL EFFICACY

	Could Prevent Harmful Legislation?				
	Very Likely	Somewhat Likely	Not Too Likely	Not At All Likely	
Temporary	1.4%	16.2%	43.0%	39.4%	100.0% (N=142)
Permanent	4.6%	20.4%	50.4%	24.7%	100.0% (N=373)
		Gamma = -.26			

Summary: The data above have shown that while temporary residents living in energy impacted communities are as politically knowledgeable as their permanent population counterparts, they are significantly less likely to vote or participate in politics, and are somewhat less politically efficacious. Also, the new residents are less tied to the two major parties. These data confirm the hypothesis that occupational mobility decreases political concern and involvement. In impacted communities, this means that a disproportionately large segment of the residents who are visibly part of the problem, have no say in the problem solving process. Also, the temporary residents offer a potentially viable resource for whichever party is able to motivate them toward political action.

THE PLIGHT OF CHILDREN IN LATIN AMERICA

Mabel Lloyd

Yankton, South Dakota

I'm a retired teacher and a storekeeper.   If you're expecting
a scientific analysis, I'm afraid I'm going to disappoint you.

This past June I went on an International Goodwill Tour of
South America and Central America sponsored by the General Federation
of Women's Clubs. We visited all the capitals of South America, we
visited the American Embassies, and then we toured the countryside
to see how people lived and what they did. I was interested to see
that all South American countries seem to be composed of two kinds--
the rich and the poor. The rich seem to be doing all right for
themselves, so I won't say anything about them.

But the poor interested me, especially the children I saw and
what I heard about them. I came to this conference thinking that
I would listen to you folks and hear all the answers to the people
who are starving. It is said that 15 million people actually starve
to death every year and one-third of the world goes to bed hungry
every night. Every minute I'm speaking 28 people die of starvation;
21 of them are children! I'm horrified to think of the number of
children who die of starvation. As a mother and a grandmother I
feel strongly that children have a right to life.

In Guatemala we visited a remote resort town. There, sitting
on the step of a box-like house, was a little boy, perhaps seven or
eight, that I haven't forgotten yet. He had spindly arms and legs,
a fat stomach, and his eyes were watery and runny. I think he's a
symbol of many children who are malnourished because they're not
getting what they need. And why? I saw mothers who were doing
their best, but they had a lackluster look in their eye, and they
probably lacked some of the food they had to have. They tried to
sell us little trinkets and one lady tried to sell us a length of
cloth which she did up to make a platform on her head so that she
could carry a basket; she wanted to sell us that too. That was
their way of making a little extra money so they could add to their
annual income, which might be only $75--it could go up to $100. I
didn't see many fathers around in most of the places, but we were
told that most of them got their liquor first and paid for that
before the family got any food or clothes.

260

We went to see CARE workers in every place where we could contact them. The General Federation of Women's Clubs supports CARE and does what they can to help. Among other things our Federation gave the people of North Brazil a tractor like the Self-Help tractor on display at this conference, and the CARE people were to use it where it was best. Our Federation gave CARE workers projectors so that where people were illiterate and could only be taught by pictures, the CARE lady could use the projector to show pictures of how they were to prepare food and maybe get across the idea that protein was needed in food for these children.

I've thought of that boy I saw sitting on the steps many times. I'm sure he's dead now--he couldn't live. It is said that the children who have suffered from malnourishment between birth and the age of seven or eight never recover; their body is physically stunted and their brain is harmed. So they can't recover. That boy I saw is surely not here. But he might have had brothers and sisters, some of whom lived to go to school. There is school, usually. But if father makes $75 a year, maybe a little more than that, and if he isn't disposed, he won't buy a uniform for those children and there are many schools where you cannot go to school without a uniform. We were told that is why the children are not going to school--there's no money for that--so they run about the streets. I saw some in Rio de Janeiro, too, and they say they run about the streets, looking for purses to snatch.

Children are perhaps all that a family has, living in very poor circumstances. A father wants lots of children to show his manliness and he wants to be sure that one of them is going to grow up and take care of him when he gets old. The CARE worker told us that she taught birth control to the mothers who came to her classes but she had very little luck--she didn't think it was going to be successful-- because most mothers like children too and they haven't any patience with birth control habits which take some concentration and thought. From all we heard, birth control isn't going to help much.

The poor people in South America are always prepared for death. One day we saw a man going up a path, towards his little box-like home, carrying a coffin on his shoulder. We were told that when he got home he would take that coffin inside and fasten it to the ceiling so that it would be ready when a death occurred.

Political and economic conditions do not show much chance for improvement in South America. The Church does little to encourage population control. Dictators in every country are firmly against any change. Landowners will not agree to let a farmer take a couple of acres to scratch out a garden and have some rabbits and chickens. They're not ready for that, and so 15 million people starve every year because they don't know what to do nor how to do it. I had great interest in the children of Latin America; I hope some of you can suggest something so their life expectancy is longer.

261

NATURAL FOODS TO FEED THE WORLD

Paul Stitt

Natural Ovens, Manitowoc, Wisconsin

The conclusions I draw in this paper are the result of twenty years of work on international malnutrition. I've done research for Tenneco Chemicals and Quaker Oats. I've made single-cell protein from petroleum derivatives and from dairy plant wastes. I hold three patents on these processes, one of them a U.S. patent. So when I speak about nutrition and the food industry as it exists, I do so with some knowledge.

At present, unlike most people at this conference, I'm a private businessman. I employ about 35 people in a business which sells natural food to about 30 supermarkets in Wisconsin. I'm familiar with the difficulties of introducing new kinds of foods to people who are often not well informed about nutrition.

I've set up a number of standards to guide my selection of foods that I'll promote here in the United States or for Third World countries. The premises from which I start are that foods

1. must be highly nourishing;

2. must require low levels of energy to be produced, processed or transported;

3. must be appetizing and flavorful;

4. must not cause any religious problems.

My goal is to combat a problem that is common throughout the world--malnourishment. I believe that malnourishment is affecting the health of 75% of the people living today. Even in America we're generally overfed and undernourished. Americans, who could afford to eat better foods, eat poorly because food companies make and advertise nutritionally deficient foods. Why do the food companies do this? The reason why food companies choose to promote nutritionally deficient food is very simple and logical, though it may seem shocking to some. The reason is that the less nutritional a food is, the more people have to eat of it to be satisfied.

262

And the more people eat of it, the more the companies can sell.
The more they sell, the more profit they make. As long as companies control the manufacture of food, it is always in their best
interest to make the foods the least nutritional they possibly can.

I can give an example of the profitability of nutritionally
inadequate foods from my own experience. About a year and a half
ago I took over a bakery with the intention of turning it into a
natural food bakery. I had to keep making white bread to stay in
business, but I decided to make it nutritional. I went through
seven steps of gradually improving the white bread. I added oat
flour to it, then used raw sugar instead of plain sugar, then
used high-protein white flour instead of regular flour, etc. But
every time I improved it, people would buy less bread. They
couldn't eat as much, they didn't need as much to feel full. Except for some grumbling about a price increase of 10 cents--it
cost me 20 cents a loaf more to make good bread than to make cheap
bread--people got satisfaction from the better bread. One way to
eat better is to eat less, to desire less food of higher quality.

It's very easy to make nutritionally deficient foods. All you
have to do is to use white flour, white sugar, lard, artificial
flavoring and artificial coloring. About 90% of the foods in the
United States are made this way. Food manufacturers wouldn't
think of using the real thing because it would increase the cost
of the product and people would need to buy less if the product
were more nutritious. No honest businessman would ever risk putting himself out of business by doing this.

The foods we get in the supermarket don't satisfy because
they're not supposed to satisfy. Food processors aren't in the
business of satisfying people's appetites, they're in the business
of making a profit. Now there's nothing wrong with profit--I'm
making a profit--and I think all enterprises should be run on the
profit motive. But in the food industry it takes a watchdog to
see that the quality is not continually lowered while prices are
kept constant or raised.

There has lately been a great deal of concern about two problems which I believe are not directly connected--world food supply
and malnutrition. I did some calculations to show how much food
a person can grow on a small piece of land and meet all the recommended dietary allowances for protein, fiber, vitamins and minerals.

Suppose we take one acre of land and raise mixed species of
edible things on it, like sunflowers, rice, soybeans, wheat, corn
and a few fruits and vegetables. Add in a few nut trees on the
non-arable land. Suppose too that about a dozen farmers get together and keep a cow (feeding it with excess roughage from the
gardens) to produce animal-grade protein to supplement the diet.

263

Such an arrangement would produce 2500 pounds per acre. Assuming an average protein content of 20%, one acre would yield about 500 pounds of protein per year. According to the USRDA figures, the average person requires about 50 pounds of protein a year. In other words, 10 people could get enough protein off this one acre of land. If you make the same calculations for calories, you find that 6.25 people can live off this one acre of land. What this means is that one person can get all the protein and calories he or she needs from one-seventh of an acre. Most of these foods can easily be ground or mixed at home, thus cutting out large industrial complexes and concentrated energy needs as well.

At present, of course, most Americans foolishly desire to live on refined foods. According to the USDA, over 2 acres per person are needed to make this food, plus the tremendous amounts of energy which are imported to transport and make refined foods. In addition, the result of living on refined foods is a much higher incidence of heart disease, cancer, and diabetes.

The problem is, how does one go about inducing people who are used to refined foods to change to a natural foods diet? I think it can be done in the same way people were conned into eating junk foods, smoking cigarettes and drinking soda: make eating natural foods the "in" thing. Have movie stars tell why they love eating natural foods. Have people in power eat natural foods. Have popular songs espouse natural foods, etc.

Private enterprise and advertising have ruined cultural values. They can just as well rebuild cultural values and cultures. Natural food is no longer just a way of life for people who want an alternative lifestyle. It's the only way for Americans and for the rest of the world to be both well fed and healthy.

DISCUSSION

WILSON PRICHETT, The Environmental Fund: Mr. Stitt, would you run through those calculations again. I find it hard to believe that you can feed 10 people from one acre of land.

PAUL STITT: I'm saying that on one acre you can raise a total bulk of 2500 pounds of food a year. I don't think there should be any trouble getting that kind of yield from soybeans, sunflowers, corn and wheat. The average protein content of all these crops is about 20%. Sunflower seeds are about 26% protein, soybeans are about 40% of the whole bean, rice is 8%, corn is around 10% or more for some species, but the average is about 20% of the 2500 pounds, or 500 pounds of plant protein in a year. That's enough to feed

10 people 50 pounds of protein a year, or about a pound of protein a week.

WILSON PRICHETT: But that's all plant protein except for milk and cheese, and plant protein suffers considerable conversion loss in the human digestive system. You don't get the use of all that protein in the human body.

PAUL STITT: That's come out of studies which have been done with isolated soy protein, which is highly insoluble. But you can live on a lot less protein from natural food sources. People like the Hunzas live on just fruits and vegetables; they don't get near the Recommended Daily Allowance of protein and yet they live very well. The reason is that natural protein goes further. It's metabolized much more slowly by the body, but much more completely. I could be off by 30% or 50% on this figure, but that isn't the point. The point is that if people eat natural foods they can live on much less.

I'd also suggest that 2,000 calories a day is enough for a person living on a natural food diet because if you live on natural foods you need much fewer calories than you do if you're living on sugar.

AUDIENCE: It all depends on how much work you do.

PAUL STITT: No. Sugar goes into your blood stream very fast and is wasted. With natural foods it's metabolized slowly and not wasted.

WILSON PRICHETT: But you burn considerable energy in digesting that food too.

PAUL STITT: Okay, let's even say that I'm off by 100%. You wouldn't argue with that, would you?

WILSON PRICHETT: I'd argue that you're off by 200%. I'd say that at most you could feed 2 people on an acre of land.

PAUL STITT: I'd like to see your figures.

DONALD KEITH, Population/Food Fund: Let's turn the question around. How many acres does it take now to feed a person processed foods?

PAUL STITT: According to USDA, about 2-1/2 acres is required to feed one person. A lot of that goes to growing food to fatten animals. The only reason people in the U.S. need so much animal protein to supplement their diet is because they eat mostly refined (junk) foods that have had most of the protein removed.

265

DONALD KEITH: If I understood him correctly, Paul is saying
that a person can be well fed on anywhere from one-tenth to one-
seventh to one-third of an acre, instead of two acres. Even
if he's off by two or three times, there's still a substantial
benefit doing it his way.

GEORGE WEST, Delaware Valley College, Doylestown, Pennsylvania:
In referring to your bakery experience you said that people ate
less of your bread because it was more filling. Might not the cut
in sales be attributed to consumer preference in that as you changed
the product it became so different, so unfamiliar, that customers
no longer wanted it?

Secondly, you mentioned something about a watchdog. Who should
be the watchdog of good nutrition? How would we set that up?

PAUL STITT: Smart consumers is the way to watch things. Who
would watch the watchdogs? Who's watching the FBI, the CIA, the
ICC, the FTC and other agencies to see if they are doing their job?

GEORGE WEST: How do we make consumers smart? Government nutrition education programs?

PAUL STITT: I'm not sure government can do the job. But let
me respond to your comment about consumer preference. I'm not
talking about the people who stopped buying our more nutritious
bread. I'm talking about people who dearly love our 100% whole
wheat honey bread and won't buy any other kind but ours. But the
point is that our bread is so filling that people can eat only one
slice of it at a meal. One loaf of our bread is enough for a person to eat for a whole week. Now what businessman, except a nut
like me, would be interested in making nutritious food if it cuts
into his sales?

AUDIENCE: Do you feel there's a conscious policy decision by
food producing companies to make insubstantial or unhealthy food?

PAUL STITT: Sure. A lot of the information about that is in
the Congressional hearings on nutrition and on food production
held by Senator McGovern and Representative Richmond. If you knew
what manufacturers put in your food, you would literally say, "I
don't want to eat anything anymore."

AUDIENCE: I still think a lot of foods sell because people
want them. If there were no demand for these foods the companies
would stop making them.

PAUL STITT: I don't remember anyone banging on the doors of
General Mills asking for that junk bread they call Bunny Bread.
I don't know that people banged on the doors of these industries
and asked for more sugar and more garbage in our food and more DES

in our cattle. It's all a question of what they can market. If they can make a penny a serving on it, they'll do it.

BILL MARION, Iowa State University: I find some of your remarks totally opposed to a large body of prevailing thought. I can't believe the food industry is as misoriented as you say. And I just don't believe you when you imply that Quaker Oats, whom you worked for, was putting out Rolled Oats just as cheaply as it could with the intent of lowering the nutritive value of the oat product.

PAUL STITT: I'm not trying to malign any company, but let me give you one example of how things work in the food industry. I was digging through the literature when I was at Quaker Oats and I found that back in 1942 the company had published results of tests which showed that when test animals were fed Puffed Wheat they died within two weeks, whereas if they ate nothing but water and a few vitamins they lived for six weeks. I got all excited, went to my boss and told him about it. My boss went to the president of Quaker Oats Company, Robert D. Stewart III, and said, "Look what we've already published, in our own name. We said this, we said that Puffed Wheat has a nitrogen efficiency of -6." And the president said, "I know people should throw it on brides and grooms at weddings, but if they insist on sticking it in their mouths, can I help it?" That's a direct quote. That's what happens within the food companies.

Now, I should add that Puffed Wheat is not the worst food on the market. Puffed Wheat is even a so-called natural food because there's absolutely nothing added to Puffed Wheat. It's in the processing that it's ruined. Proteins are very closely related to toxic compounds and the processing may make them toxic.

AUDIENCE: Come on. How can puffing wheat make the wheat toxic? All they do is put it under pressure and then release it. That can't make it toxic.

PAUL STITT: The point is that the test animals died. I asked my boss, "I think we'd better do some research and find out what we can do about it," but he only said, "No, we're not interested. The product is selling, and that's all that matters."

So I never did get to do the research to find out what was happening. My theory is that the ring amino acids and the secondary amino acids are chemically very closely related to toxic compounds. When you put these amino acids under 1500 psi strange things can happen and, I suspect, they do. In any case, I didn't say it was toxic, the Quaker Oats research showed it was toxic.

267

A SOLUTION TO THE WORLD'S PROBLEMS--
COOPERATION INSTEAD OF COMPETITION

Clifford Figallo

The Farm, Summertown, Tennessee

We're all aware of the suffering created by rapid population growth, inadequate food for millions of people, and excessive consumption in the United States and other developing countries. In trying to solve these problems we often can think of changes other people can make rather than starting with ourselves. I'd like to describe changes in the way of life some of us have been developing at the Farm over the past seven years.

The Farm is a new-age intentional community of 1100 people centered on 1700 acres in Tennessee with sixteen branches in the United States and Canada. We're trying to settle on a lifestyle that is comfortable, graceful and healthy but one that anticipates and compensates for the growing problems of hunger and increasing population. Our goal is to live at a standard that is attainable by every person on the planet. We live closely together, and derive much of our strength from the fact that we are collective. We've found that when people cooperate towards a common goal, it takes less raw materials--and less money--to accomplish it. We consider ourselves voluntary peasants, and we relate to the greater culture somewhat like a lesser-developed country does. In the course of our growth as a community, we learned how to deliver our own babies, take care of our primary health care needs, and feed ourselves. We've developed a completely vegetarian soybean-centered diet which provides plenty of protein at a fraction of the cost of a cattle-based diet. We live on about a dollar a day per person for all of our needs.

Early in our community's development, we realized that we were strong enough to take care of some other people besides ourselves. Our policy has always been, not to take over the government, but to take over the government's <u>function</u>: to help the people take care of themselves.

So we've created an international development and relief organization called PLENTY, to try to help share what we've learned through our experience as a lesser-developed community with the advantages of a Western upbringing. Our first efforts were small, providing food for hurricane-struck Haiti and Honduras, cleaning up after tornadoes in Alabama and Omaha. But we started to make some connections, and we were able to act as agents for other relief organizations in locating and buying large quantities of food for their relief efforts.

More recently, we were able to help reconstruct a whole village in the highlands of Guatemala after the earthquake there in February, 1976. We set up a pre-fab house factory and taught the Indians how to run it. It was quite an adventure, because the usual level of technology available to them was thatching for huts. We were also able to build ten schools, with the help of the local Indians and materials provided by the Canadian government. PLENTY has also been active in Mexico, rebuilding after a hurricane in La Paz, and Bangladesh. We've learned a lot about overpopulation and food distribution from what we've seen.

What PLENTY has learned is that if you provide the people with the basics of knowledge about primary health care and nutrition, construction and sanitation standards, the people can take it from there without further intervention. We don't need more luxury-producing factories in the lesser-developed countries to make them more like the so-called "advanced" countries; we need more education about how to raise the quality of life--which doesn't cost a lot of money. Our experience in trying to support ourselves and in building our own community made it easier for us to transmit an accurate view of the physical world without disturbing other people's traditional ways. We've been teaching them about medical care and food while trying not to interfere in any of their economic, cultural or religious affairs.

We're only just starting to figure it out, but we have seen that a solution to the world's problems exists. It utilizes cooperation and education to abolish inequalities of opportunity and distribution. People can take good care of themselves if they have accurate information on how to go about it--and if they are allowed to. We've found this in our own experience on the Farm and in PLENTY's experiences overseas: anytime we approach people with a sincere desire to help--and with no profit to be made--they respond enthusiastically to the opportunity to help themselves.

But we have to stop educating people with misinformation that's profit-motivated. The conditioning that the culture has received through the media in the name of profit has made us so schizophrenic as a culture that we have performed the equivalent of a pre-frontal lobotomy on our people, causing many of us to ignore much of what is actually going on in the world: one-third of the people in the world are starving. Orange soda pop cannot replace fruit juice in the diet of malnourished children, and American corporations should not be permitted to make unrealistic claims in other countries any more than they are here.

Of the four basic foods we've all learned are essential to the daily diet, half of them are completely unnecessary. Our four basic foods on the Farm are beans, grains, fruits and vegetables. Relying on soybeans instead of meat or dairy products for our protein actually decreases the acreage required to grow our food to one-tenth of that which would be required to support us if we were meat-eating and milk-drinking. Soybeans are particularly relevant to countries such as Mexico, Ethiopia, India and Bangladesh--which are all among the top ten cattle-producing countries, and yet have large parts of their own populations living in chronic hunger. And in fact, PLENTY is working with the Mexican government to help set up soy "dairies" to make soybean ice cream available as a low-cost source of calories and protein. We are committed to raising the soybean's image from cattle feed to its rightful place as a valuable, tasty source of protein that can help feed the world.

We believe food should be removed from the profit system, so all the people can get fed. As it is now, we have the strange situation of one-third of the people in the world starving in the midst of abundant harvests while the farmers justifiably complain that the price structure of the economic system destroys their capability to earn a living. When people are hungry, as fellow citizens of the planet, we have a responsibility to do what we can, even if it calls for adjustments in our own lifestyles. In our community, we grow our own food. Anybody can, if they have access to land and water. People can take good care of themselves if the government will get out of the way.

Our community has also developed a safe, reliable method of natural birth control. We've been using it for several years on the Farm, and have had no unexplained pregnancies--and none of the side-effects associated with artificial methods of birth control. It seems ecologically sound for the human race to limit its population as best we can; but this should not be at the expense of any minorities, such as the American Indians, whose very ethnic existence is being threatened by government-sponsored programs of birth control; or at the expense of civil rights, which are seriously called into question when our government urges sterilization programs on countries as part of its foreign aid package.

We don't believe that abortion can be considered a responsible means of population control, either. We have to recognize that all life is equally precious. We believe that so strongly that the Farm's midwives make the following offer to anyone considering abortion: "Don't do it. Come to the Farm and we'll deliver your baby, naturally and for free, and we'll raise it for you and if you ever want it back, you can have it--with no hassle."

In our community, we've found that cooperation and agreement give us considerable strength--agreement to help each other out, and to put aside selfish ways that are a luxury we can no longer afford. It is time for us all to recognize that the technology and the resources already exist to enable everyone in the world to enjoy a comfortable, healthy lifestyle. What is lacking is the agreement. Imagine, for example, if the major powers agreed to a moratorium on the further development of nuclear weapons and decided instead to spend half their defense budget to feed hungry people and improve health and sanitation in the developing world. The best way to ensure peace is not through development and maintenance of elaborate weapons systems, but through a fair distribution of food, resources, services and education.

HEW Secretary Califano has said that the four horsemen of death for Americans are Smoking, Drinking, Obesity, and Accidents. These, in large part, are the symptoms of an overindulgent and fast society. The four horsemen of the world abroad are still Death, Pestilence, Famine and War. If we gave up our excesses-- the excesses that are actually killing us--to help conquer these ancient blights, we would all be the richer.

There are more and more people, all over the planet. It is our fundamental belief that all people really are created equal, and that every life is a sacred trust. We must each take as much responsiblity as we can to make sure our brother is well taken care of. In the words of Jesus, "Whatsoever you do to the least of My brothers--that you do unto Me."

DISCUSSION

QUESTION: I'm curious about your diet. Where do you get your Vitamin B-12? And what are you doing about meeting the riboflavin and calcium needs of your children and pregnant women?

CLIFF FIGALLO: We try not to be flower-childly about any of the aspects of our life style. We use supplements when our diet doesn't satisfy our nutritional needs. Pregnant women get calcium lactate and prenatal vitamins. Our children get vitamin supplements. For B-12 we use something called nutritional yeast, which is like brewer's yeast except that it tastes good.

QUESTION: Have you done any studies to determine what level of protein you are getting?

CLIFF FIGALLO: We complement all of our beans with grains. We have a cookbook and a meal planning guide where we've figured out a balance of amino acids and different things that go together to satisfy our needs. UNICEF has tested us to be sure we're healthy and to see what they can learn about Third World nutrition.

271

QUESTION: How do you make decisions at the Farm? Is there a council of elders or any organized way of making decisions?

CLIFF FIGALLO: We're not old enough to have many elders but we do have a council of straw bosses that we call a board of directors. One of the things they do is make sure that we have enough initial capital coming in from outside the Farm community. Since we don't concentrate on profit-making enterprises we sometimes run into trouble, like lesser-developed countries, of a "national debt." Within the Farm, though, we don't exchange money. It's all handled by a central bank.

QUESTION: Your way of life seems very demanding to me and I'd expect that a lot of people would leave. How do you keep people there, and what kind of turnover do you have?

CLIFF FIGALLO: Our population is surprisingly stable. We've been there for eight years and we've grown from around 250 people to 1100 people on the Farm in Tennessee and then the sixteen branches of the Farm bring us up to about 1700 people. There's also a group of about 40 of us down in Guatemala. Of course, people do leave. Like people who drop out of any society, their reasons for leaving vary from getting tired of living at what they consider lower than standard material levels to personal disagreements. It's one of the intangibles of living a lifestyle like ours that you have to learn how to get along with each other. We believe that your life is completely your free will and you do what you want to do, so it's very easy for people to leave the Farm if they want to, but we haven't really lost that many.

QUESTION: Do you use any modern machinery for work and transportation, or do you rely on, say, horses?

CLIFF FIGALLO: We do use horses, but we also believe in cars. It would have taken me a long time to get to Washington by horse. But we have very few cars because we share them all. At a farm with 1100 people we only have five or six tractors. I think it's a very efficient use of resources because most of the large things we use communally. We wear them out pretty good, but we still don't need very many of them.

QUESTION: Most relief organizations have a rather sophisticated fundraising apparatus. How do you manage to support the work of PLENTY?

CLIFF FIGALLO: We haven't really learned how to beat the drums and raise funds yet. We're a little timid that way, but we've managed to scrape it together. Sometimes we just support it on the money we make from the Farm, although that stretches us pretty thin because we have to support people all the way in Guatemala. We're still in the process of raising funds and looking for sponsors.

QUESTION: I'd like to ask you to explain how the birth control system works.

CLIFF FIGALLO: The birth control system is a combination of methods. We use a basal temperature method combined with a cervical mucus and also rhythm method. It's mostly based on the temperature. We don't rely too much on the mucus anymore, although we used to think of it as 50-50. But checking the cervical mucus is not as reliable, and if you start leaning on that one too heavily and stop taking your temperature every morning, you might get yourself pregnant. We call it a cooperative method because the husband and wife have to agree; it takes self-control since it uses abstinence during fertile periods. And that's the way it works most effectively-- through education and the use of counselors that you can talk to about questions you have about it.

QUESTION: Without the use of money to allocate jobs, how do you make sure all the community's necessary tasks are done? Is there any structure in your allocation of jobs?

CLIFF FIGALLO: Well, it's structured in that we know what we have to get covered and then we do what we can with the manpower available to cover it. Sometimes that means we'll take people who are doing one job and ask them if they could cover this other job because it needs doing. In most cases everybody's happy to do that. Once in a while you have somebody who's a little stubborn, but they don't have to do it if they don't want to. We don't have any forcing of things but everything seems to get covered pretty organically in that the manpower just sort of flows around and fills in where it's needed.

QUESTION: How is the work divided up between the men and women? Do the women always take care of the children?

CLIFF FIGALLO: No, there's no rigid division about that. It turns out that women mostly cook and women mostly take care of the kids, but it's not a rigid thing. We've had ladies go out and work on our framing crews, helping build houses at times, if they want to try that.

SOLVING THE POPULATION/FOOD CRISIS BY EATING FOR LIFE

Alex Hershaft

President, Vegetarian Information Service

The global tragedy of world hunger and malnutrition hardly
needs recounting. By various educated estimates, between 400 million and 1 billion people in the world today are not receiving sufficient nutrients to sustain normal bodily functions, and many of
these will die of this condition, in great pain and misery. With
population growth outstripping increases in food production, and in
the face of dwindling world supplies of fertilizers, water, energy,
and new land available for production, the future outlook is not
encouraging.

Some have proposed various ways to increase the food supply.
They range in complexity from food shipments and quick technological
fixes to fundamental shakeups of the social and economic structures
of the affected regions of the world. Others have argued with equal
fervor that these proposals would merely postpone the day of reckon-
ing and that world population must be stabilized first, as it is already running ahead of our ability to increase the food supply. I believe both sides would agree that, ultimately, the only long-term solution to the world population and food crisis lies in a stable balance
between demand and supply. And this requires stabilizing the demand
for food as well as increasing the supply.

I am in the fortunate position of not having to choose sides in
this raging controversy. My proposal does not require population
control or growing more food. It does not call for major social and
economic upheavals and has no other significant drawbacks. It has
been demonstrated to work on a world-wide scale. It can be implemented well within our lifetime. It is called eating for life.

Eating for life means abstinence from animal food products. It
means a drastic reduction in heart disease, stroke, cancer of the
colon and breast, and a host of other debilitating diseases. It
means saving some 700 million large mammals and uncounted billions
of small animals each year from living and dying in needless agony
to satisfy our wasteful obsession with meat. More pertinently, it
means reducing dramatically the demand for grains, the world's staple

274

food, and being able to feed adequately more than twice the present world population with current food supplies.

Of the world's total grain production of 1,100 million metric tons in 1974, 180 million tons, or 17%, went to feed cattle. Moreover, 28 million tons, or 40% of the world's 70 million ton fish catch is consumed by livestock. Noted nutritionist and demographer Georg Borgstrom estimates that present food supplies could adequately feed 8.7 billion people, or more than twice the world's present population, on a vegetarian diet.

The U.S. is setting a particularly dismal example for the rest of the world. Over half of our cropland and nearly 80% of our grain production are used to feed livestock. The average American consumes 2000 pounds of grain, or five times the amount consumed by the average inhabitant of the developing nations. Of that amount, only 150 pounds is consumed directly, while the rest is fed to livestock. The resulting national waste of 170 million tons of grain is estimated to amount to four times the world's current caloric deficiency.

This gross inequity is further compounded by the world's unbalance in purchasing power, as reflected in the international food market. The major importers of grain, meat, and fish meal are the world's richest and most developed nations: the Soviet Union, Japan, United Kingdom, France and Italy. They are literally taking this food away from the mouths of the starving masses in the developing countries.

But grain and fish meal are not the only precious resource wasted in the generation of animal products. Some $3\frac{1}{2}$ acres of cropland are required to meet one person's annual protein needs on a meat and dairy diet, but only 1/3 acre on a vegetable diet. According to current estimates, the world's arable land amounts to 3.5 billion acres, or less than one acre per person.

Production of meat requires up to 20 times as much water, energy, and fertilizer as production of vegetables containing an equivalent amount of protein. These are all limiting factors in any future expansion of the world's food supplies. Production of meat and dairy foods generates vast amounts of animal waste which is washed into nearby streams and results in their pollution and eventual eutrophication and death.

Compare this with the increase attainable by switching from a mixed to a plant diet. To be sure, claims of factors of ten have been made and documented in special instances. However, even on comparing such vast and populous areas as the United States, with an annual per capita meat consumption of 200 pounds, and South Asia, with a 7 pound consumption, the overall grain requirement drops by a factor of five, from 2,000 to 400 pounds.

Does this solution too require sweeping changes in social attitudes, land use patterns, and agricultural technology? Not at all. Meat consumption in the United States has fluctuated in the past in accordance with supermarket prices and level of consumer nutritional awareness. A public education program on the sanitary, economic, environmental, and ethical evils of meat consumption could accomplish wonders. The lands used to grow feed grains can be readily planted in human food grains just as soon as a suitable market has developed. Finally, the meat industry's investment in slaughterhouses and other non-convertible facilities is truly minimal for a $45 billion industry.

In summary, eating for life has been demonstrated conclusively to reduce demand for grains by a factor of five, over most areas of the globe. The improvements can be even more remarkable in more limited applications. These changes are accompanied by order-of-magnitude reductions in energy, water, and fertilizer requirements which are generally acknowledged as the limiting factors of future increases in agricultural production. Perhaps even more importantly, these dramatic changes can be achieved with a minimal impact on our social and economic structure, with a marked improvement in the consumer's health and life expectancy, and with a massive reduction in the needless suffering and destruction of billions of our fellow animals.

Indeed, eating for life reflects our noblest aspirations for our own health and welfare, as well as those of our other fellow beings on this planet earth.

DYNAMICS OF HUNGER AND FUTURE DIRECTIONS

Satish Kohli

School of Business Administration
Philadelphia College of Textiles and Science

Before offering a prescriptive strategy for the problem of global hunger, I would like to submit that my perspective stems from a synthesis of three disparate schools of thought: Tantric, Proutist and Social Marketing. For those of you who are unfamiliar with these stances, let me provide a brief background.

Tantra is an intuitional science that provides a holistic and spiritual world view and was propounded by Shiva about 7500 B.C. in India. It is the source of yoga, meditation and most of the Eastern-based religions and practices of physical, mental and spiritual development. Its primary tenet is that the whole universe is the metamorphosed form of Supreme Consciousness and to realize this is the very goal of human life.

Prout is a socio-economic theory propounded by Shrii P. R. Sarkar, a philosopher-seer of India. The cornerstones of this theory are the principles of cosmic inheritance (cooperative owner-ship), maximum utilization and rational-distribution of resources, moral and spiritual regeneration and decentralization of economic power.

Finally, Social Marketing, in an intervention sense, brings resources and human needs together in an economically viable way.

Roots of the Menace of Hunger

To locate the problem in a forest of symptoms is sometimes a most difficult task. Yet in order to be able to develop a coherent and clearly defined policy, an understanding of the nature of the problem and its causes is absolutely necessary.

My basic contention in this paper is that the roots of the multidimensional problem of hunger must be searched for not in the issues of overpopulation, economic stagnation, or energy crisis related symptoms, but in the misdirected longing of the human soul--the confused, narrowminded, materialist world view of the

277

majority of the human race. I have, therefore, taken a fundamentalist
approach to unravel the complexity of global hunger and offer a five
point strategy to deal with it.

The Way Out?

I. Sadvipras Leadership

The key to the way out of our societal problems (of which
world hunger is only one symptom) is the self-purification of individuals at all levels but especially at the level of political and
social leadership. Theories cannot solve problems. It is people
with high competence who bring about the fusion of hard realities
with ultimate meanings which only the visionary world can deliver.
To develop an able and informed leadership in all walks of life
(economic, religious, political, social, family, etc.) through moral
and spiritual education is, I believe, the need of our times. In
the words of P. R. Sarkar, "Only those people who are living by the
moral code of conduct (Yama-Niygama), have universal consciousness
and are prepared to fight against exploitation and injustice, are
worthy of being leaders (Sadvipras)." It is the will and motivations of these Sadvipras that will redirect physical, metaphysical
and spiritual resources of this universe for the good of all of
humanity. To create such Sadvipras will require discipline and
proper training in the early years. Meditation is one of the secrets
to foster the development of such leaders. Sadvipras are only those
who are perfect in morality and aspirants of Supreme Consciousness.

Abraham Maslow, in the same vein, has opted for such spiritual
leaders with the following reasoning:

> . . . Mystics and transcenders have throughout history
> seemed spontaneously to prefer simplicity and to avoid
> luxury, privilege, honors and possessions. My impres-
> sion is that the "common people" have therefore mostly
> tended to love and revere them rather than to fear and
> hate them. So perhaps this could be a help in design-
> ing a world in which the most capable, the most awaken-
> ed, the most idealistic would be chosen and loved as
> leader, as obviously benevolent authority. . . .

II. Progressive Utilization Approach

When the mundane world becomes the object of ideation, the
crudification of the human mind is a natural consequence. It is
the cosmic ideation alone that can break the fetters of the human
mind. The Tantric view, therefore, is a liberating mode which pro-
pounds that spirit and not the relative word must be the object
of ideation. To provide basic necessities to all of humanity so
that all can channel their human potentiality to spiritual

realization is therefore the second fundamental need of the hour.
To live simply with sentient diets is not only conducive to individual spiritual growth, it is also a way to unlock the creative
energy necessary to develop a harmonious egalitarian socio-economic
system. Shrii P. R. Sarkars' Prout socio-economic theory is based
on this spiritual view of economics and society. As Theodore Ros-
zak said, "We need a nobler economics that is not afraid to discuss
spirit and conscience, moral purpose and the meaning of life, an
economics that aims to educate and elevate people, not merely to
measure their low-grade behavior." E. F. Schumacher's discussion
of Buddhist Economics is a bold attempt in this direction. Shrii
Sarkar offers five fundamental principles of Progressive Utilization Theory.

Five Fundamental Principles of PROUT

1. No individual should be allowed to accumulate any physical
wealth without the clear permission or approval of the collective
body.

2. There should be maximum utilization and rational distribution of all mundane, supramundane and spiritual potentialities of
the universe.

3. There should be maximum utilization of physical, metaphysical, and spiritual potentialities of the units and the collective body of human society.

4. There should be a proper adjustment amongst these physical,
metaphysical, mundane, supramundane and spiritual utilizations.

5. The method of utilization should vary in accordance with
changes in time, place and person and these utilizations should be
of progressive nature.

III. Institutional Choices

Organizations and institutions have a tendency to create a
group flow that conditions individual human behavior. To create
egalitarian, cooperatively owned institutions is, therefore, the
third primary challenge facing us in the next few decades. There
is no dispute about the fact that we need more and better organization. The real question is who should control or own. My contention is that the decentralist approach of ownership of economic
resources offers the best potential for individual and collective
growth. As Huey Newton argues, "It is clear, that if you are in
control, politically and economically, of your existential entity,
there is no way in which you can exhibit or institutionalize your
culture, because you need political power, and to have political
power you need economic power, i.e., the economic freedom to express

279

yourself according to your image." Whenever possible, we should move towards cooperative ownership. This, of course, will demand lots of sacrifice, struggle and moral courage on the part of decision-makers.

IV. Shifting of Priorities

Accepting the principle of cosmic inheritance implies helping provide basic necessities to all people as the primary goal. In this regard, shifting priorities from funding development of nuclear weapons to the development of goods of basic necessities is our prime duty. China offers a few lessons for us in this regard, viz., recycling; cooperative spirit; self-reliance; balance between urban and rural development, small and large scale industries, capital and labor intensive industries; and minimum disparities in wealth. Furthermore, anti-exploitation sentiment and cosmic sentiment must go hand-in-hand as the watchwords of humanity at this juncture.

V. Nutrition Surveillance

To keep pace with the needs of consumers requires adequate information about their present nutritional status. In the spirit of successful social marketing, we must have constant nutrition surveillance lest anyone should lag behind.

If we can reach Mars, we can surely feed all of humanity. We may not have reached the limits of growth,but we surely seem to have reached the limits of humanity, cooperation, understanding and sense of human purpose on this earth. Let us resolve to purify our intentions and actions, and be unafraid to lock ourselves in a liberating mode--the path of Tantra.

SELECTED REFERENCES

Nature of Man

1. Markley, O. W., et al. Changing Images of Man, Stanford Research Institute, Menlo Park, 1974. Summary reported in Renaissance Universal Journal, 2239 E. Colfax Ave., Denver, Colo. 80206.

2. Anandamurtiiji. The Great Universe, Ananda Marga Publications (854 Pearl St., Denver, Colo. 80302), 1973.

3. Teilhard De Chardin, Pierre. The Phenomenon of Man, Harper & Row Publishers, Torchbook Edition, 1961.

4. Maslow, Abraham. The Farther Reaches of the Human Nature, Viking Press, N.Y., 1973.

5. Sarkar, P. R. Idea and Ideology and Ananda-Sutram, available from 854 Pearl St., Denver, Colo. 80302.

6. Proutist Forum of America. PROUT: A new idealogy for a New Era, Seattle Collective, Seattle, 1975.

7. Patanjali, Yoga Sutras.

8. Batra, Dr. R. A New Interpretation of History (Professor, Southern Methodist University, School of Humanities and Sciences, Dallas, Texas).

Will, Motivation and Leadership

1. Assagioli, Roberto. The Act of Will, Penguin Books, 1973.

2. Hyde, Douglas. Dedication and Leadership Techniques, Mission Secretariat, 1312 Mass. Ave. NW, Wash., D.C. Written by an ex-communist turned Catholic missionary.

3. Sarkar, P. R. A Guide to Human Conduct.

4. O. M. Collective, Organizer's Manual, Bantam, New York, 1971.

5. Nader, Ralph and Donald Ross. Action for a Change, Grossman, 1972.

FOOD UTILIZATION AND DISCARD AT THE HOUSEHOLD
LEVEL: A VIEW FROM THE GARBAGE CAN

William L. Rathje

Le Projet du Garbage, University of Arizona

Often problems of food availability are met with technical solutions which consume increased quantities of energy. Food loss is an important problem to examine at the household level because changes in consumer behavior may prove to be effective supplemental solutions without increased energy expenditures.

Recent pilot research at the University of Arizona in Tucson has found that there is significant food loss within sampled households. This waste represents between 7 and 20% of all purchased foods.

Based on these data, the GAO estimates that some 40% of all U.S. post-harvest food losses, possibly amounting to some $11.5 billion annually, occur within households. It is important to learn more about the nature of food loss at the household level, but it is not easy. Food waste is fraught with moral implications. In addition, interview and record-keeping studies require considerable time and effort on the part of informants. As a result, household food loss is difficult to study by traditional methods. The obvious lack of useful data is a barrier to effective planning.

At present Le Projet du Garbage, a cooperative University of Arizona and City of Tucson program, is the only long term effort to provide data on household food losses. The project has developed household residuals analysis as a quantitative measure of food management.

Since 1973 more than 3000 household refuse collections drawn from a stratified sample of census tracts have been recorded in Tucson, Arizona. Household anonymity is protected. Data are recorded to obtain quantitative information on food type, input volume, cost, packaging, and weight of any discarded edible food, not including bones, chunks of meat fat, tops, rinds, or other culturally inedible parts. Correction factors have been devised and tested to adjust for garbage disposals, food purchased without packaging and other biasing behaviors. The principal use for household residuals analysis is to monitor trends in food utilization and discard.

What types of food loss are patterned in ways which are amenable to technological or behavioral change? Answers to this question will require analyses in three areas.

Area One: How do specific food processing and delivery systems affect patterns in household food loss? Specifically, what consistent patterns of food discard are related to types of food purchased? For example, within Garbage Project sample houses, specialty breads, buns, rolls, muffins, were discarded at much higher rates than standard loaf breads. What patterns can be related to types of food processing? For example, frozen fruits and vegetables are discarded at a higher rate than canned fruits and vegetables. What patterns can be related to package configurations? For example, the waste of individually packaged servings follows different patterns from the waste of bulk packaged commodities. Data on these loss patterns could lead to industry programs to decrease food loss and increase consumer satisfaction.

Area Two: What are the patterned effects of socio-demographic characteristics and attitudes on household food loss? Can this loss be decreased by educational programs? Garbage Project analyses indicate that prospects are good for education programs because the primary correlates of efficiency in household food utilization are behavioral and attitudinal factors rather than factors such as household size. Direct garbage interview comparisons indicate that the most significant correlation with food waste is consumer knowledge of food safety. In neighborhoods where households knew when food was and was not safe to eat, there was little food discarded. This finding is tentative but points to the need for consumer education in the area of food safety, to promote both good health and food preservation. Education programs will require data on identifiable specific target populations.Available data indicate that middle income households discard up to 20% of purchased foods, twice as much as most low-income households, and would potentially benefit most from education programs. Also of value would be data on the total utilization strategies of efficient versus inefficient households. The households of low-income Mexican-Americans seem to be the most efficient in food utilization in Tucson, Arizona. Part of this is due to the fact that there is a relatively redundant diet using foods that can be readily saved and recombined as leftovers. Further study of Mexican-American households would be useful in planning consumer education programs.

Area Three: What patterns of food loss are related to changes in food prices and availability? Research along these lines has already produced results. One tentative pattern of discard behavior seems counter-intuitive. During the beef shortage in 1973, media interviews indicated that consumers were not only aware of scarcity and increased prices but that they were changing their behaviors to

283

correct for them. Surprisingly, residuals analysis found that consumer reactions were not conserving beef. Quite the opposite. During the shortage, beef was discarded at the high rate of 9% of input compared to 3% of input in the years following. It has been speculated that consumer experimentation, buying large quantities as a hedge against rapidly rising prices, buying new and unfamiliar cuts, trying out new recipes, led to new storage and utilization problems and increased inefficiency in consumption. Given this model, consumer reaction to the 1975 sugar shortage was predictable. As retail prices on sugar and sweets in Tucson nearly doubled, so did the percentage of high sugar and sugar substitute commodities discarded as waste. These data indicate that the short run response to rapid price rises or shortages is likely to be high rates of experimentation or crisis buying which result in increased food loss.

If food losses are to be exploited as significant future food resources, three tandem steps are necessary. The first is consumer education programs which focus on (1) food safety knowledge, (2) methods of meal planning, shopping, preparation and storage which conserve food, and (3) information on the value of conserving food both in terms of household food dollars and broader social costs.

The second element is education within the food industry. This program would focus on the magnitude of food losses related to specific processing and packaging systems and on the potential increase in consumer satisfaction that could result from modifying processing and packaging systems.

The third element is expanded collection of household residuals data to provide the foundation for consumer and industry education programs and to evaluate the effectiveness of resulting education programs in ultimately conserving food. All three steps should be taken together because the feedback between them can make an important contribution to their success. The goal of this outline for a process to decrease food losses in the U.S. is to turn food waste into a new food resource and increase the efficiency of utilization of a portion of our finite energy resources.

DISCUSSION

PAUL WOOLEY, Pennsylvania State University: I was interested in your comment about food safety as an explanation for discarding behavior. I was wondering to what extent you think food discard occurs because of dual career families and the time pressures that occur in terms of utilization of leftovers?

WILLIAM RATHJE: I'm sure that a lot of food loss occurs because of the fact that we're dealing with families where the people who prepare the food are also holding outside jobs. However, the largest quantities of food losses are not due to problems in consumption or even preparation and storage that would relate to that. There are other kinds of factors which our data found was more significant than the number of working individuals in a household, than income, than education and so forth. A lot of it does have to do with food knowledge. In the 170,000 items examined from our 3,000 households, we have found only one can that looks as though it was affected by botulism. But we found 300 to 400 cans that some poor stock boy had fallen on, or have gotten dented, which people threw out, perhaps believing that there was botulism. The same kind of thing with loaves of bread. One piece of the bread gets stale and the whole loaf goes. Likewise with cheese; when you get it in large blocks, a little mold on the outside and the whole thing goes. So we do feel that there are factors that go beyond the number of working people in the household.

CORNELIUS BODINE, Iowa Beef Processors, Dakota, Nebraska: I understand that the food for pets is about a $2 billion business in this country. I would imagine that the consumption of food by pets is substantial. Do any of your findings bear on that subject?

WILLIAM RATHJE: Several things bear on that subject. The pet population is incredibly substantial. Our data showed that if you add all of the solid food brought into the household in terms of solid ounces, 10 to 20% is pet food, depending on what income group you're dealing with. When you get up into the upper income group 20 to 25% of all the solid food brought into a house is pet food. But in lower income areas it's very much less. A lot of that, we think, has to do with the fact that people are feeding scraps of food which would otherwise be discarded as loss and end up in a landfill to their pets. I think it is significant that you have much less pet food bought in low income neighborhoods, although city records show just as many pets.

Another thing that's interesting in terms of consumption behavior is that status brand buying affects lower and middle income families much more than it does upper income families, with the exception of one area of food purchase and that's pet food. Nothing's too good for old Rex in the upper income neighborhoods.

COMMUNITY GARDENING AND WORLD HUNGER

B. H. Thompson and John Davis

Gardens for All, Shelburne, Vermont[*]

How can community gardening help the world hunger problem?

Let me start out to answer that question with a statement that you often hear from "shoot-from-the-hip" social thinkers: "Poor or hungry people would be a lot better off if they did more for themselves." Now, we know that that kind of solution to many of the social and economic problems facing people and nations today hardly ever comes close to answering the complex problems which we face. I haven't yet heard an easy solution to the problem of hunger and food shortages around the world, but if you permit me to devise one in the voice of, let's say, a hard-liner (which I don't happen to be), it might well be: "they should grow their own." I think here we might have something.

How does $14 billion worth of food sound as a starter? That happens to be the estimated value of the food that was grown in American backyards and community gardens in 1977 alone. Recent research shows that if everyone in this country who wanted a garden had the land for one, the amount of home grown fruits and vegetables could come close to $50 billion each year.

One example of how community gardening has been a factor in localized economies is the city of Chicago. The Chicago Housing Authority has a community garden project involving 6,000 residents. In the course of a summer they produce more than $300,000 worth of their own vegetables, which, when frozen or stored, is enough for many families for the entire year. If the urban poor, who have no land, were given the opportunity via community gardening--where people garden on land they don't own--those who most need food could make giant strides toward getting a lot more of it.

---

[*]Gardens For All is a non-profit organization which is concerned with organizing community garden programs in North America. Community gardening means putting people onto public or private land which they do not own but which they are allowed to use in order to raise some of their own food.

Community gardening in the United States is growing phenomenally. About 2 million people gardened last year in more than 25,000 organized community garden projects. This is about twice the figure that we found in 1974. The potential for community garden growth is excellent too. There are hundreds of thousands of acres of vacant land in our urban centers, as we found in a recent survey of municipal and county planners. And there are 6 million people who would get involved in community gardening if they and some of this vacant land could be brought together. The two of them are coming together, the land and the people, but much too slowly. The government, too, is pitching in in recent years with more down-to-earth people-oriented programs.

Let's think for a minute how individual food growing could benefit people around the world who are facing far more critical food shortages than we are. If we can grow $20 billion worth of food in backyard and community gardens here--and mostly for the pure pleasure of the activity--look at what hungry people around the world could do with a little assistance, guidance and technical advice. It's truly amazing, when you think about it, what one small garden, say 25 by 30 feet, can produce for a family. It costs about $25 to get it under way and can produce as much as 1,000 pounds worth of food, or just about enough vegetables for a small family to live on for all year long.

The United States has spent millions of dollars recently on Peace Corps and Vista programs, and much fine work has been accomplished in these areas. But how about weaving into these international self-help programs something like an international garden corps which would send trained people around the world helping impoverished people specifically to help themselves out foodwise. The trained manpower is obviously there. Recent studies have shown that only a very small fraction of the graduates of horticultural colleges around the country ever wind up after graduation in related fields. They go through four or five years of horticultural-related education and then take jobs in an office or in a stock brokerage firm. Many have a great interest in growing food, but there's nothing for them to do once they get out. This may sound idealistic, but I don't think it's impractical.

I don't think that individual food growing is the whole answer but it would at least be a step toward greater self-sufficiency for many poor people. In certain communities of the United States where a sizeable portion of the population are receiving food stamps, home gardening has done an awfully good job in reducing individual dependency on government, government food stamps, and other kinds of handout programs. I think the same thing could be accomplished, to a small degree, all around the world. If gardening assistance was concentrated on one major country that was experiencing extreme problems, it might well serve as a model for other countries around the world.

I think there's enough evidence that people are trying to pull themselves up from their problems, whether they be hunger problems or population problems or natural disasters; no matter who they are or what they are, they all want to help themselves.

I started with a typical "hard-line" statement to the effect that the world would be better off if people did more for themselves. With some modification, I think that statement could be more acceptable. I would put it this way: the world probably would be better off if we lent the expertise to _enable_ people to do more for themselves, particularly in the area of food shortages. Community gardening is one proven way to accomplish this.

FOOD RESOURCES FROM THE OCEANS: A PROMISING SOURCE
OF NUTRITIONAL ADEQUACY FOR LDCs' GROWING POPULATION

Raphael Shen, S. J.

Department of Economics and Management Science
University of Detroit

Kwashiorkor and marasmus, caused by protein and caloric defici-encies in infants and children, are prevalent in LDCs. UNESCO esti-mates that millions of children die of kwashiorkor before reaching the age of five.[1] One hundred million children in LDCs under the age of five are in danger of losing sight due to vitamin A defici-ency. An estimated 200 million people suffer from endemic goiter for lack of iodine supplement. And 30 million infants and children in LDCs are victims of rickets due to vitamin D deficiency.[2] These illnesses may be prevented or cured through a balanced diet. But a balanced diet is not available to more than 460 million world citi-zens. Population control and increased agricultural production have been the most preferred solutions. But a stabilized world popu-lation size and increased agricultural production do not result in a nutritionally balanced diet. New ways have to be found and some older ways re-studied to tackle the problem.

To secure vitamin intake adequacy, food products can be economic-ally fortified and vitamin pills inexpensively supplied.[3] But pro-tein must be "manufactured." The most productive yet most under-utilized protein source is harvests from the oceans and from bodies of fresh water. So far, what nature has "sowed" mankind has not fully reaped. The remainder of this paper limits itself to a dis-cussion of protein resources from the oceans by raising five ques-tions and answering four.

The potential types of ocean harvests include fish, krills, crustaceans, molluscs, phytoplankton and zooplankton. Phytoplankton are microscopic waterplants analogous to plants on land. They pro-vide food for zooplankton, which are small ocean creatures upon which larger ocean lives such as fish, krills and mammals feed in turn. Although protein and vitamin contents of phytoplankton and zooplankton have not yet been measured since they presently lack market value, results from scientific studies find a rich source of protein and vitamins in fish. Fish meals manufactured from various species of fish contain crude protein and minerals ranging

289

from 88.7 to 98.8% per unit weight.[4] Relative to better known food products, sardine proteolysate furnishes 25% more protein than meat flour and 300% more than powdered milk.[5] In addition, it provides a comparable amount of the indispensable amino acids and contains ten times more of vitamins A and B1 than either meat flour or powdered milk. As for vitamins B$_2$, B$_{12}$, PP and B$_6$, it also surpasses both meat flour and powdered milk per unit weight.[6] When compared with staples such as wheat and rice, fish flour yields seven to ten times more protein per unit weight. The nutritive value of fish can hardly be overemphasized.

Discussion may now be directed toward the questions. First, how much has been harvested from the oceans? By the turn of the century, world aquatic harvest was close to 4 million metric tons. Thirty years later it had approximately quintupled.[7] For the period 1930 to the early 1950s, aquatic harvest increased by less than 2% per year. But the decade of 1955 through 1965 witnessed a 100% increase, largely due to expansion of the Peruvian anchovy industry. Since then till the present, the annual growth rate has averaged no more than 3%, also primarily because of the decline in Peruvian anchovy catches.[8]

Secondly, what promises do the oceans hold for the future? FAO suggests that the potential annual harvest of living organisms from the oceans is close to 100 billion tons.[9] If close to reality, then the estimated potential of annual food source from the oceans is 700 times greater than the current annual harvest, though much of it might be in the form of phytoplankton and zooplankton for which there has been no market demand as yet. Current direct or indirect human consumption of aquatic harvest comprises only a few dozens out of an estimated twenty to twenty-five thousand species of marine animals. Many of these unused species are not only highly nutritive but also exist in what is thought to be very large quantities.[10] Hans Ackerfors estimates that the currently marketed fish harvest alone can be increased from the current 70 to the level of 106 million metric tons per year. Prickfish, living at great depth and not currently harvested for economic and technological reasons, could yield 100 million tons annually. Cuttlefish, whose present annual yield is in the range of 1 to 1.5 million tons, has a potential of 7.5 to 100 million tons each year. And krill, which are also not commercially marketed, could yield between 50 and 100 million tons per year.[11]

Earlier estimates of sustainable annual fishery harvest ranged from Graham and Edwards' 55 million metric tons to Chapman and Schmitt's 2 billion metric tons.[12] Graham and Edwards' second estimate, based on sea plant growth that could provide sustained fishery growth, was placed at 115 million metric tons per year. Although it is still the lowest of all estimates made during the fifties and sixties, it is 50% more than the current annual catches. And if Chapman and Schmitt's estimates, which were based separately on the

290

annual growth of phytoplankton, herbivores, and two stages of carni-
vores in the oceans, are to be accepted, than the current marine harvest is a mere 3.5% of the potential. For FAO, the estimated sustainable annual potential of fishery catches is 118 million metric tons.[13]
But as FAO noted, this 118 million metric tons per year is limited to
the conventionally marketed fish and crustaceans only. Mankind has
barely begun to scratch the surface of ocean potentials.

    Thirdly, how much can a fuller use of food resources from the
oceans benefit the world's malnourished? Great potential lies in
the utilization of marine species hitherto unfamiliar to commercial
markets. More specifically, if only krill in the Antarctic and
lantern fish in warmer waters were to be introduced into the market,
either for direct human consumption or processed into fishmeal and
protein concentrates, the food supply from the oceans could be increased manyfold. The annual Peruvian marine harvest is capable of
raising protein intake standards on the whole South American continent to a level equivalent to that of Southern Europe. Fish meal
manufactured from the sea harvest in Africa has the potential of
raising the protein intake level on the African continent by 50%.[14]
How many persons can benefit from a fuller utilization of ocean potentials? Assuming an average requirement of 60 grams of protein
per person per day, and assuming that marine catches can be effectively processed into fish protein concentrates,[15] between 1 and 16
billion persons' protein requirements could be adequately met by
marine harvest alone, not to mention the accompanying food calories,
vitamins and the essential amino acids contained therein.

    Fourthly, can LDCs benefit also from increased fresh water har-
vests? The answer is yes. For the world as a whole, an average
of 11% of annual aquatic catches are from freshwaters.[16] It can be
expanded. The largest quantity of freshwater fish comes not from
large lakes but from small rivers, lakes, ponds and reservoirs. This
means that the gear needed to harvest the annual catches need not be
as capital intensive as ocean-going vessels. Freshwater harvest
is closer to processing/packaging plants and market centers, thus
reducing the cost of transportation as well as that of freezing
equipment. And there is greater control over the presence of undesirable species of fishery in the freshwaters than in the oceans.
Besides, lower income people in LDCs would have access to freshwater
harvest in the form of aquaculture by using small bodies of water
at reasonably low investment outlays. In the Philippines, for instance, milkfish harvested on a fish farm in Bataan is able to meet
60% of protein needs in the area.[17] Shrimp farming has met success
in Puerto Penasco. Catfish farming is booming in Mississippi, Arkan-
sas and Louisiana.[18] A well fertilized acre of pond could yield
between 5 and 35 tons of trout. And to cite an extreme example, 500
tons of carp has been harvested from a one-acre pond in Japan.[19]
The prospects for freshwater aquaculture are encouraging.

    From this brief discussion, it is reasonable to conclude that

291

protein deficiency, vitamin deficiency and mineral deficiency that plague millions of the world's population could be made a matter of history if greater emphasis is placed on reaping more from what nature has provided in the waters.

The final question is whether we will succeed in doing so.

FOOTNOTES

1. Then there are more kwashiorkor victims who survive beyond the age of five. Their fate is: "growth retardation, impaired mental development, edema, enlarged liver, pigment changes in skin, low serum proteins, enzyme deficiency." Estimated protein deficiency victims in LDCs range between one-quarter and one-third of their entire population. Cf. Jonathan Power and Anne-Marie Helenstein, World of Hunger: A Strategy for Survival (London: Temple Smith, 1976), p. 48; United Nations Food Conference, The World Food Problem: Proposals for National and International Action, Item 9 of the Provisional Agenda, E/CONF 65/4 (Rome, August 1974), pp. 155-157; also, The White House, The World Food Problem: A Report of the President's Science Advisory Committee, Vol. II (Washington, D.C.: The White House, 1967), pp. 16 and 50.

2. United Nations Food Conference, op. cit.

3. Sufficient dosages of vitamin A pills may be supplied to every potential victim in the world for $3 million per year. This cost includes purchases, storage, transportation and distribution. The annual cost of iodinizing salt which, when taken, can effectively prevent endemic goiter is $1 million. And the cost of fortifying milk, milk powder and baby food with vitamin D to keep rickets away from 30 million infants and children is $2 million. Cf. United Nations Food Conference, ibid.

4. United Nations, Production of Fish-Protein Concentrate (Report and Proceedings of the Joint UNIDO/FAO Expert Group Meeting, Rabat, Morocco) (New York: United Nations, 1972), p. 32.

5. Ibid., p. 125.

6. Ibid.

7. Georg Borgstrom, Too Many (London: The MacMillan Co., 1969), p. 232. Cf. also FAO, The State of Food and Agriculture 1975 (Rome: FAO, 1976), p. 277, and FAO, Yearbook of Fishery Statistics 1974, Vol. 38 (Rome: FAO, 1975), p. 51.

8. FAO, Yearbook of Fishery Statistics, from 1950 to 1974.

9. FAO, Provisional Indicative World Plan for Agricultural Development, Vol. I (Rome: FAO, 1970), p. 274. Cf. also White House, The World Food Problem, Vol. II, op. cit., p. 345.

10. The White House, ibid.

11. Hans Ackerfors,"Trots dystra prognaserdet gar att oka fiske-fangsterna," Forsknig och Gramsteg, 1, 1977. ("Despite Pessimistic Forecasts, It is Possible to Increase Fish Catches," in Research and Progress, 1, 1977).

12. The White House, op. cit., p. 346.

13. FAO, Provisional Indicative World Plan for Agricultural Development, op. cit., p. 281.

14. Borgstrom, op. cit., p. 237.

15. Ibid. Daily protein requirement is less than 60 grams per person on the average. Cf. FAO, The State of Food and Agriculture 1964 (Rome: FAO, 1964), p. 103.

16. Borgstrom, op. cit., p. 215.

17. William Paddock and Paul Paddock, Time of Famines: America and the World Food Crisis (Toronto: Little Brown and Co., 1976), p. 184.

18. Science News, Vol. 113, No. 5, 65-80, Feb. 4, 1978, pp. 76-77. And Marylin Chou, David P. Harmon Jr., Herman Kahn and Sylvan H. Wittwer, World Food Prospects and Agricultural Potential (New York: Praeger Publishers, 1977), p. 110.

19. D. S. Halacy Jr., The Geometry of Hunger (New York: Harper and Row, 1972), p. 183.

AN ECOLOGICAL SOLUTION FOR FEEDING AN
OVERPOPULATED WORLD

Surendra Singh

Department of Biological Sciences, Kansas Newman College

The explosive growth of the human population we are presently experiencing on the global scale cannot continue indefinitely. No matter how far science and technology raise the carrying capacity of the earth for people, involuntary self-limiting forces will continue to determine man's population density. Overpopulation is linked with most of our global problems, starvation, disease, pollution and resource shortage. These surplus populations consume resources and contribute in general to various density dependent stresses, all of which make the environment less suitable, thus lowering its carrying capacity.

Most of the developing countries, when faced with several years of continued drought, experience starvation. Two options exist for eliminating the famine situation: mass shipment of food or long-range economic development assistance. However, if only emergency famine relief is provided, the root of the problem will remain. On the other hand, if we attempt to continue growth by increasing food output with fertilizers and higher yielding crops, we alleviate the situation only for a short period.

Whatever options we choose to solve the population and food problem, our goal must be to increase the benefits of the people alive today as well as all the people who are going to live on our planet in the future. Thus we are faced with one question in the impending global crisis: What are we going to do about the approaching collision between our growing population and the physical limits of the earth? We must design and implement a smooth transition to a non-growth situation--a global equilibrium, which is in accordance with our globe's physical limits. Global equilibrium is a necessity if mankind wants to have an equitable future on his small, fragile planet.

From the standpoint of both biocentricisms and population-related variables, the following suggestions may have relevance in solving population-related problems.

Carrying Capacity and Self-Limitation

The balance of nature is governed primarily by the suitability of the habitat and species-specific self-limitation, where members of each species involuntarily prevent any further increase in their kind. When other organisms follow a population growth curve similar to what man is currently experiencing, they can then become so destructive to their habitat that subsequent carrying capacity may be dramatically reduced, if not completely destroyed, thus causing not only mass individual suffering and high mortality but also a permanent destruction of the ecosystem.

Only self-limitation can stem the population tide, and the only voice man has in this matter is whether it will be done involuntarily by nature's undesirable stresses, or consciously by man not allowing his kind to exceed an optimum carrying capacity. Therefore it is extremely important that each country must determine its carrying capacity based on food habits of the people and natural resources of that country.

Food Habits and Nutrition

The challenge of feeding the millions is simultaneously a challenge to find new types of food and to engage in intensive research associated with human food habits. Getting adequate quantity of protein continues to be a problem for many of the world's people, especially for those who rarely eat meat or animal products and must therefore get most of their nourishment from grains and vegetables. This problem can be approached in three ways. One is that we should try to breed new strains of cereals and new maize strains with proteins of enhanced nutritional value. For example, the researchers at Purdue University found while screening some 10,000 varieties of sorghum from all over the world that two Ethiopian strains have triple the protein value of normal sorghum (Shapley, 1973).

The second way is to find alternate food crops, such as nutritious plants not now being exploited as food sources but having potential for development. For example, the Amaranthus are among the potential food plants that were once a stable of the Aztec diet; today most farmers think of amaranthus as weeds and nuisances, not as a source of food. According to Marx (1977), the principal merit of amaranthus is that both the grain and the leaves are sources of protein of unusually high quality.

Another area of great potential and increasing interest is single cell protein from various species of yeast, algae and bacteria as useful sources of protein and vitamins for human feeding. For example, dried brewers yeast, a residue from the brewing industry, and Torula yeast, resulting from the fermentation of wood residues, contain 45-55% of protein. Today only small amounts are processed for use in human foods.

295

Role of Affluent Nations in Feeding the Hungry

The developed nations can help developing and overpopulated countries in many ways, such as helping developing countries increase their production of food by implementing aggressive food production programs. This would allow time for effective population policies to be introduced and begin to take effect. Aid to developing countries may be based on the recipient country's effective population and food policies.

Affluent nations can also cooperate with the developing countries by sharing the information obtained from satellite information systems. Very few developing countries have accurate inventories of their resources. With the application of space technology, the information obtained on geology, soils, natural vegetation and water resources can be used in deciding where agricultural croplands, irrigation projects and improved rangelands can be developed and managed (Kingrey and Baumgardner, 1975).

Lastly, developed nations should seriously consider grazing livestock on rangeland of little agricultural value and save the cereal for humans. It appears rather unecological to continue feeding high-energy cereals to animals, and then derive our own energy from eating the animals. For example, about 78% of all the grain produced in the United States is fed to animals. The average ratio for protein conversion by livestock in North America is 10 to 1. Applying this ratio to about 20 million tons of protein annually fed to livestock in the United States, it appears that only 10% (or 2 million tons) is retrieved as protein for human consumption. Thus in a single year through this consumption pattern, 18 million tons of protein becomes inaccessible to man. This amount is equivalent to 90% of the yearly world protein deficit--enough protein to provide 12 grams a day for every person in the world (Lappe, 1972).

The present dilemma of uneven economic growth among nations, overtaxing our agricultural land, and the tremendous waste of energy by eating at the top of the food chain almost forces us to re-examine basic concepts of human nutrition and to probe for simple, inexpensive, and nutritious food. A move toward a more vegetable diet would have several economic and nutritional advantages: it would lower the cost of living, lessen our energy demands and reduce the ingestion of animal fat while increasing vegetable roughage. For ecological, ethical, financial and medical reasons, it appears important to rely more on plant protein and less on meat protein. The development of inexpensive, ecologically efficient, and nutritious food must be a matter of primary concern for us all.

REFERENCES

1. Kingrey, David and M. Baumgardner. _Now is Tomorrow_ (Friends United Press, 1975), p. 91.

2. Lappe, Frances Moore. _Diet for a Small Planet_ (Ballantine Books Inc., N.Y., 1972), p. 301.

3. Leeper, E. M. "Meat Without Feed Grain, Is It a Feasible Way to Go?" _Bio-Science_, 28, no. 1 (1978), pp. 65-66.

4. Marx, Jean L. "Amaranth: A Comeback for the Food of the Azetics?" _Science_: 198, no. 4312 (1977), p. 40.

5. Meadows, Donella, and Forgen Randers. "The Carrying Capacity of our Global Environment: A Look at the Ethical Alternatives," in _Western Man and Environmental Ethics_, edited by Sam G. Barbour (Addison-Wesley Publication Co. Inc., 1973), pp. 253-276.

6. Shapley, D. "Sorghum: Miracle Grain for the World Protein Shortage," _Science_: 182, no. 4108 (1973), pp. 147-148.

SOCIALLY RESPONSIBLE CORN FARMING

Donald Q. Innis

State University of New York at Geneseo

Corn and beans mixed together in the same field will give a
higher total yield than either crop grown alone. Chemical or organic fertilizers will provide a bigger total crop in a corn plus bean
field than the same fertilizers used in single crop fields. Experiments have shown that a 30% greater total yield due to intercropping
is quite common. In Tanzania it took 1½ acres, half corn grown
alone and half beans grown alone, to give the same total yield as 1
acre of intermixed corn and beans. The real reason why monocropping
(single cropping) is so common is that machines are only able to
harvest one crop at a time. Machines may provide higher wages for
the farm workers who still have jobs, and high profits to land
owners, but they lower crop yield per acre when the amount of nutrients used is considered.

In most fields with only one crop there is a lot of bare soil
in the field while the crop is young and after the crop has been
harvested. The sunlight and rain which fall on bare soil are largely
wasted and nutrients are washed out of some of the soil before the
crop's root system gets big enough to reach them. Intercropping of
corn and beans can be done by planting corn with regular spacing
and then putting bean plants in between the corn plants. A bean
plant is a more efficient way of using this empty space than an additional corn plant because the bean leaves are underneath the corn
leaves and bean roots get some water and nutrients from soil layers
below the level of corn roots. If chemical nitrogen is added to the
soil,bean plants are inhibited from their traditional work of fixing
atmospheric nitrogen to supply nitrogen to both the bean and the
corn. But as supplies of chemical nitrogen become scarcer and more
expensive there is an organic method of providing this soil nutrient
which farmers can resort to.

Small farmers can intercrop more efficiently than big farmers
because they can harvest crops by hand, one by one as each crop is
ready to eat. As long as gasoline is not too expensive small farmers can plow and plant with tractors but horses, oxen or hand labor
will most likely be the motive power of the future. Many small
farmers around the world have, in fact, never changed over from

intercropping and hand cultivation to "modern" methods. The small
farmer grows food for his family in the spaces between the crops
he is growing for sale. Sunlight, water and nutrients are used much
more efficiently this way and the land is better protected from erosion. Farm families on their own land do not need welfare payments
or charity hand-outs and tend not to have such large families as
landless workers. Many people have no land because plantation agriculture has been introduced in many countries. Since many plantation crops are weeded and harvested by hand, poor families near
plantations tend to have a lot of children because they can get
seasonal jobs on big farms. Small farms with several crops use labor more rationally throughout the year so there is not the same
economic incentive to overpopulate the country. If land reform cannot be carried out for political reasons, it would make sense to
allow landless laborers to grow food crops in between the plantation
crops.

Growing corn and beans together is better for the soil and for
the people and need not depend on the non-renewable resources of
phosphates, potash, natural gas (for nitrates) and petroleum which
are being exhausted so rapidly. There is still a serious problem,
however, in trying to design a type of agriculture based on renewable resources, which can provide the basis for a permanent civili-
zation. The nutrients which are taken from the soil in many developed countries are not being returned to the soil. Most of the
nutrients, whether derived from organic or non-organic chemicals, end
up in sewage which is dumped in the ocean, dried and burned, or applied to old strip-mined areas to grow trees. Treating sewage to
make it non-toxic and safe for farmers to use is not as simple as it
seems, because most modern sewer systems combine organic wastes with
industrial effluent which can be very poisonous. Even organic farmers cannot recycle the nutrients taken from their land by crops
they sell, because the nutrients have poison mixed with them in most
city sewage systems. In order to grow corn and beans or any other
crops in a permanent socially responsible manner, sewer systems will
have to be partially redesigned and rebuilt so that organic wastes
and industrial wastes are not mixed together.

REFERENCES

1. Aiyer, A, K. Yegna Narayan, "Mixed Cropping in India," Indian Journal of Agricultural Science, Vol. XIX, Part IV (entire issue), Cal-
   cutta, India, 1950, pp. 439-543.

2. Berry, Wendell. The Unsettling of America--Culture and Agriculture, Sierra Club Books, San Francisco, 1977.

3. King, W. H. Farmers of Forty Centuries, Rodale Press, Emmaus, PA,
   1972.

4. Lappe, Frances Moore and Joseph Collins. Food First--Beyond the
   Myth of Scarcity, Houghton-Mifflin Co., Boston, 1977.

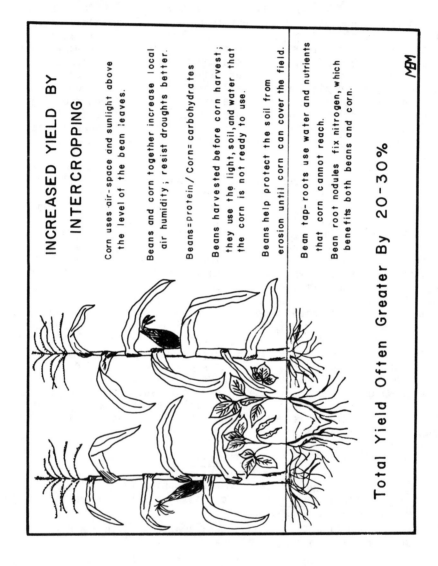

INCREASED YIELD BY INTERCROPPING

Corn uses air-space and sunlight above the level of the bean leaves.

Beans and corn together increase local air humidity; resist droughts better.

Beans = protein / Corn = carbohydrates

Beans harvested before corn harvest; they use the light, soil, and water that the corn is not ready to use.

Beans help protect the soil from erosion until corn can cover the field.

Bean tap-roots use water and nutrients that corn cannot reach.

Bean root nodules fix nitrogen, which benefits both beans and corn.

Total Yield Often Greater By 20-30%

A POSSIBLE NEW SOURCE OF PROTEIN TO MEET
THE WORLD FOOD CRISIS

Kenneth T. Vehrkens

Assistant Dean, Edward Williams College
Fairleigh Dickinson University

Perhaps the animal that has had the greatest impact on the history of the United States is the American buffalo. In the 17th Century, an estimated 60 million bison roamed North America. Never on any continent had there been such a population of an animal of this size. For the next two centuries, bison meat played a major role in the eventual settlement of the U.S. frontier.

Today, some 25,000 full-blooded buffalo graze in pastures scattered from coast to coast, a mere symbol of the buffalo's long history. But the species that has had such an influence on America's past may again become a key to the future of the United States and the rest of the world. The bison could very shortly make a dramatic recovery and provide a major source of sustenance.

About fifteen years ago in Wyoming, a rancher named D.C. "Bud" Basolo started an experiment in crossing a buffalo bull with a beef cow. After a great deal of time and more than a thousand attempts, a perfect mating was discovered. The experimenter found that half buffalo and half beef cow was not the ideal combination. The best hybrids, which are now called "beefalos," are 3/8 bison, 3/8 Charolais--a cattle breed developed in France and growing in U.S. popularity--and 1/4 Hereford beef cow.

Beefalos can be marketed to consumers at a price 40% cheaper than current prices for beef cattle. They do not have to be grain fed and can reach 1,000 pounds in less than a year on a diet of grass and roughage. After being corn and grain fed, the average cow takes twice as long to reach the same weight. The beefalo, like their ancestors, the bison, will eat tumbleweeds, sagebrush, straw, and even cactus.

Beefalo have more pounds of meat per carcass than regular cattle, with less bone and fat. Studies have indicated that beefalo products have 19-20% protein with about 7% fat. Regular cattle meat has approximately 10-12% protein with about 10% fat. Thus, beefalo meat is higher in protein and lower in cholesterol.

301

Another advantage to raising beefalo is that farmers do not have to supply heat to keep them warm. They have thick fur, instead of regular cow hides. Beefalo have 15,000 to 18,000 hairs per square inch. They are also more adaptable to hot weather than conventional breeds. The ability to withstand both heat and cold makes beefalo particularly suitable for export to any country.

Beefalo are very fertile and reproduce readily. The rate of conception through artificial insemination for this hybrid has run above that experienced with conventional cattle. Beefalo bulls seem to have longevity like bison, who are productive up to four times as long as beef cattle sires. They are also extremely free from diseases of all sorts and have demonstrated a resistance to pink eye and other common cattle maladies.

There are approximately 30,000 beefalo in the United States today, but this new type of meat will not be commercially available for another year or so. Consumer acceptance of beefalo meat will be a big factor. Beefalo meat has been sold in select test markets recently and the general reaction has been that the product was more tender, leaner, and tastier than comparable cuts of regular beef.

The potential of this new animal for both America and the world is immense. American consumers can readily recall the sky-rocketing beef prices during the spring of 1973 which led to a national boycott. As already mentioned, because of all of their unique advantages, beefalos can be marketed at a savings of 40% to American citizens. The raising of beefalo will not deplete the grain supplies of the United States and will also encourage the continued world leadership of American agriculture. In addition, the United States, through the exportation of beefalo bulls and semen, can lead the way in attempting to address the overwhelming problem of hunger on this planet.

Beefalo, with their adaptability, can be used as a supply of high protein food by many of the underdeveloped nations of the world. For example, Africa's hunger problems are largely due to the fact that cattle do not prosper there. Although there is an abundance of grass on the continent, there is a shortage of grain. Also, the presence of the tsetse fly, which spreads the fatal sleeping sickness, makes cattle raising very difficult. Preliminary experiments have indicated that beefalo are probably immune to the tsetse fly and could therefore prosper on African grasses without expensive grain. This new source of protein appears to have the capability of raising the sustenance level of the world.

Although there has been some negative publicity emanating from the sale of beefalo shares in the stock market and also breeding problems, some experts in the meat industry predict that by 1990 all domestic beef cattle in the United States will contain some bison blood. Once again, in a modified form, the buffalo will have a great influence on the destiny of America and, for that matter, on the future of life on earth.

PROVIDING FOOD SUFFICIENCY AND SOIL PROTECTION
TO A GROWING WORLD POPULATION

Walter W. Goeppinger

Farmer and Past Chairman, National Corn Growers Association

A newly increased awareness of the need to deal with and eliminate hunger and malnutrition in the world has surfaced in recent
months not only in the U.S. but around the world. With the knowledge, productive capabilities and resources now at hand, the goal
of ending world starvation in the next twenty years can be achieved.

Victor Hugo stated that all the forces in the world are not so
powerful as an idea whose time has come. The elimination of slavery
came despite the consensus among people that slavery was inevitable.
But when enough force was put into a context that it was time for
elimination of slavery, the idea's time had come. It took a cataclysm
to effectuate it, but it came.

When President John F. Kennedy decided in 1961 that we could
put a man on the moon within the next ten years and asked Congress
to fund the project, he decided that the idea's time had come,
despite many opinions to the contrary. He created the context for
the idea and the forces that believed it could be done went to work
and the seemingly impossible was accomplished.

There is no doubt that the end of hunger is an idea whose time
has now come. In mid-1977 the National Academy of Sciences published
a report based on a two-year study announcing that we have the ability to end hunger and starvation on our planet in two decades. The
report stressed that a key factor in ending hunger is the will to
reach that goal. That will exists and is being expressed throughout
the U.S. and in many other lands now.

Hunger is a condition that has already ended for more than half
the people on earth. Just since World War II, 32 countries with
more than 1.6 billion people--40% of our planet's population--have
eliminated hunger as a basic issue. When the population of the long-
time developed countries is added, the total comes to more than 2.1
billion people. These countries have brought about the end of starvation with a combination of measures that gave improved nutrition
and were complemented in each case with basic preventive health

303

measures such as immunization programs and clean water supplies.

Hundreds of thousands of minds with the full range of capabilities to end hunger are now at work and will, I am sure, be successful. But in the scope of that effort one paramount issue is being ignored. It is the world's soil. Most farmers are conscious of the present mistreatment of the soil but don't want to admit the serious problem facing them and their successors, let alone deal with it. Present day economics and governmental "cheap food" policies aggravate that attitude in many countries. As a result, more and more land grows intensive crops and less and less is devoted to crops that protect the soil from wind and water erosion, as well as loss of humus content from stimulated soil bacterial activity that converts humus into available plant food on a stepped-up timetable when in intensive crops such as corn, sorghum, wheat, rice, soybeans, and cotton.

As a consequence, when heavy rains or high winds strike these soils the protective absorptive sponge is no longer there to absorb the water and hold it in reserve for later dry spells. Instead, higher rates of run-off cause greater and greater rates of sheet erosion. This has left some parts of the world with little or no top soil remaining and crop failures and low yields are commonplace.

Half the top soil in the U.S. Corn Belt has been lost in just about 100 years of farming, mostly due to water erosion--and this was the best half as it contained the highest percentage of humus at the prairie's surface at the time man broke the land with the plow. So to speak, we are foolishly cutting the limbs off the apple tree to get the fruit.

Additionally, the profligate taking of our precious non-replaceable prime farmland for unnecessary road widening and new road construction, airport relocations and urban sprawl is eating it up at a rate few people realize. In the past 50 years we have paved over a land area equal in size to the State of Ohio. In the last eight years Iowa converted about 250 square miles, or half of an average county, to urban and transportation uses. At this rate Iowa will use up the land area of five or six of its 99 counties in the next 100 years. One hundred years is a fly speck of time in the history of man on this planet. If we continue at the present rate, what are we going to leave for future generations? Fortunately, states and the federal government are beginning to regulate land use to slow down unnecessary taking for non-agricultural purposes.

So the question is, can we end hunger, protect the soil, and provide food sufficiency? My answer is, "Yes, it can be done," but it requires a different kind of governmental leadership.

This leadership has been demonstrated by the U.S. Congress and President Carter in the past year through passage of the Food and

Agriculture Act of 1977 which protects domestic food supplies for consumers, provides for needed soil conservation and protection, aids developing nations in attaining food sufficiency, and establishes and maintains international grain and food reserves that are good for both world food producers and consumers. The act is a model for other major world grain producers to follow. It will no doubt take several years for it to be fully established, but the will and the format are there.

Interestingly enough, as a farmer I have been following through the years past approximately the same set-aside pattern in the operation of my home farm as provided for in the 1977 Farm Act. On the average I compute that the total gross production of our two major crops, corn and soybeans, is just as high with 80% of the land in these crops and 20% rotated to grass cover as if I were farming the entire 100% to corn and soybeans. This is because my higher humus levels produce greater yields with the larger amounts of stored moisture and more efficient use of fertilizers. At the same time, the land in grass is given maximum protection from erosion and the corn and soybean fields are much better able to absorb rainfall instead of being subjected to heavy runoff.

Conserving the soil for ourselves and future generations is the most important act we can perform in our food production cycles. However, there is one other conservation measure we can perform every day of every year if the proper steps are taken worldwide to prevent grain losses. It is estimated that we produce 1.2 billion tons of grain on this planet annually. Out of this an estimated 30%, or 360 million tons, are lost to rodents and insects, especially stored grain insects such as weevils. Translated to bushels at around 13-1/2 billion, it amounts to just about double the U.S. annual crops of corn and wheat combined.

A further 50 to 100 million tons eaten by people in the poor countries actually are consumed by the parasites that inhabit their digestive tracts. If we use the figure of 50 million tons as a reasonable possible saving, that translates into another 2 billion bushels. Combining the 13-1/2 billion bushels of insect and rodent losses and this 2 billion bushels makes a total of 15-1/2 billion bushels. If only half this amount were saved through application of currently known preventatives and determined efforts, it would support a population of 800 million people on an ample diet of 720 pounds per person per year using a diet of wheat, rice, corn, sorghum, barley or whatever other grain staple the societies of the particular areas involved were accustomed to.

Naturally, the diets would be bettered by the addition of soya flour and minerals or dried milk, but the main point is that our present basic food supplies are not being fully used. Of course, there is legitimate concern about continued population increase, but my belief is that science will continue to make breakthroughs in plant genetics that will give added production to the acres that we should be farming under a sound soil management system of agriculture in sufficient amount to meet our population increase needs in the foreseeable future.

The above takes no account of the transfer of excess agricultural production of the surplus grain producing nations to international grain reserves, just now in the initial process of accumulation under the terms of the agreement between world governments at the World Food Conference in Rome in 1974.

It is my firm belief that we can provide food sufficiency to a growing world population, for that idea's time has come. The soil can be provided for too if individuals and governments agree that its protection is a paramount issue whose time has also come.

USING ENVIRONMENTAL VARIABLES TO PREPARE
ACCURATE LONG RANGE CROP FORECASTS

Robert Phillips

Geography Department, California State University--Sacramento

Weather conditions have obvious impacts on crop production.
Many plants, if studied carefully, are found to respond in predictable ways.

Perhaps the major problem with using environmental variables
in crop forecasting has been the overbroad and careless application.
Sunspots have been blamed for vagaries in plant performance; some
crops are thought to have production cycles that are tied to three-
year, seven-year, or other cycles. The conventional wisdom of
growers or observers is often based on very casual or suspect data;
the vast majority of these predictions are erroneous but quickly
forgotten while the few accurate ones are remembered for a lifetime.

The second "problem," or perhaps warning, is that work must be
done carefully and in a thoughtful manner. Relevant variables must
be identified and their impacts estimated. It is critical that
irrelevant variables be identified and excluded; they burden any
equation and consume time and effort. The goal must be a stream-
lined methodology that can be worked fairly quickly but has enough
components to respond properly to changing conditions.

Many crops respond in predictable ways to aspects of precipitation, temperature, solar radiation, humidity, and soil temperature.
Among the grains there are maize, sorghum, wheat, rice and millet.
Tree crops are numerous, including almonds, prunes, cocoa, and at
least some aspects of coffee. Cotton and tomatoes respond well
to this system also. In recent years I have worked with maize, almonds, prunes, and tomatoes.

Maize in Africa

Maize: Zambia has adequate land for food production but often
the rains are light, causing a shortfall in maize production. Much
of the rural population lives near the subsistence level, growing
maize (Zea mays), sorghum (Sorghum bicolor), finger millet

(Pennisetum typhoidum), bulrush millet (Elusine coracana), and root
crops for their own use. The burgeoning urban populations of the
Copperbelt cities and Lusaka prefer maize as the staple food.
Nearly all the maize going into the commercial market was produced
in the southern portion of Zambia, and in the summer of 1968-69 the
rains there were not adequate for good maize production. Yields
were lower than those forecast, causing many local problems. Also,
Zaire had to look elsewhere for supplies for the Lubumbashi area
and it ultimately became necessary for Zambia to import grain.

The Zambian situation is similar to many areas in the tropics.
Temperature is important for maize but is not a factor in Zambia;
precipitation is the overriding environmental variable. There are
at least four considerations. The rains should begin on time; if
beginning much too early they may aggravate clearing, tillage, and
other practices. Once begun, the rains must continue, as droughty
periods cause stress and even death among the young plants.
Droughty periods of 8-10-15 days, not uncommon in the marginal
areas, may reduce yields significantly. Total rainfall is not as
important as distribution. Excessive rainfall can be harmful in
two ways; nutrients will be leached from the soil and lodging may
occur. Weeding is made more difficult also.

An accurate forecast of Zambian maize production and the amount
that would be moving into the commercial sector would not have made
more maize available. A good forecast would have helped in other
ways, however. By mid-December it was plain that the crop would
not materialize, but there was yet time to urge farmers to plant
sorghum and groundnuts; these shorter-season or more drought-tolerant
crops would have made more food available. In January a preliminary
search for imports could have begun, along with plans for transport
and shifts within the country. An early, accurate forecast could
have saved quite a bit of money, aggravation, and political erosion.

Forecasting American Crops

By way of establishing that it is possible to produce an accurate forecast through the use of environmental variables, I would
like to describe my work and how it has been carried out.

Almonds: In early 1973 I was doing research in an effort to
learn how the State-Federal[1] almond forecast could be done more
accurately; it had recently been in error by as much as 30%. It
developed that there were some broad environmental conditions that
have a profound influence on the almond crop. My 1973 forecast was
very good, although it was begun late and based on rather sketchy
data. Forecasts produced in 1974-77 have generally been good to

[1]The official forecasts are a State-Federal venture carried out
by the California Crop and Livestock Reporting Service in cooperation with USDA.

excellent. The early forecasts are delivered 10-15 days before those of the State and have always been more accurate than those of the Crop Reporting Service or any major handler. My late forecast in 1976 was a bit low and the Crop Reporting Service forecast was more accurate. Their forecasts are later, however, and cost 15 to 25 times as much money.

Precipitation is of great importance to almond production; timing and intensity are as critical as total rainfall. Temperatures are important in terms of chilling in winter for dormancy, adequate warmth for pollination, and the avoidance of frost after bloom. Humidity can be a factor at bloom and solar radiation is of obvious importance through the growing season.

Prunes: The prune (Prunus domestica) is a type of plum which can be dried without fermentation or other spoilage. Work on forecasting began in 1974. All of the early forecasts have been more accurate than those of the Crop Reporting Service or those of any of the handlers. Of twelve forecasts made, only once has the Crop Reporting Service been more accurate, and my forecasts are delivered 10-15 days before theirs. Over 50% of the forecasts have been within 1% of the actual crop.

Tomatoes: Work on an experimental tomato (Lycopersican esculentum) forecast for a large tomato canner began in late 1975.

The 1976 year was one of learning and was very promising. Heavy rain in our normally dry August reduced the harvest considerably. The final forecast was very close but had been lowered from the April-July estimates. Considering the very adverse and unusual circumstances it seemed that the forecasts were acceptable and promising.

The 1977 year was more nearly "normal," at least in summer. May was the coolest in many years and caused the early April forecast to be in error by 4%. Forecasts in early June, July, August, and September were reduced a bit and were in error by only .2 to 1.2%. The accuracy of these forecasts seemed to prove that environmental variables can be used to prepare forecasts of annual crops.

The 1977 Forecasts

Prunes			Almonds			Tomatoes		
June 1	157,000	tons	April 30	305,000,000	lb.	April 19	4%	error
June 25	157,000	tons	June 29	315,000,000	lb.	June 7	1.05%	error
Sept. 1	157,000	tons				July 12	1.20%	error
Final			Final			August 9	0.20%	error
crop:	158,000	dry tons	crop:	314,000,000	lb.	Sept. 13	1.05%	error

The Key

Carefully isolate the important variables; understand how they affect plant activity. Do not overload equations; keep them as simple as possible. Do not be distracted by trivia. Consider, but be wary of, the conventional wisdom. Develop a good data base, one that is lean and easily assessed. It is important to keep up with the plants on a day-to-day basis. And high technology cannot overcome faulty inputs, as our CIA relearned in 1977.

All countries are interested in knowing the magnitude of the coming harvest so they can begin to plan in terms of a food surplus or shortage. If a surplus is foreseen early enough it is often possible to divert some later plantings to other crops that can be exported. If it can be seen early that a long season crop will do poorly, it may be possible to plant the remaining acreage to shorter season or more drought tolerant crops. An early, accurate forecast can also allow a more timely search for import sources or export markets. Some countries, such as Ghana, which earn significant amounts from a single crop, could have an early indication of government revenue and employment-unemployment conditions.

Conclusion

An early, accurate forecast can be of great importance to many countries and peoples. Good forecasts can help in anticipating problems weeks or months before they become acute. It is feasible to use environmental variables to develop these forecasts.

APPROPRIATE TECHNOLOGY AND POPULATION--IMPLICATIONS FOR SELF-HELP AND TECHNICAL ASSISTANCE

Flemming Heegaard

International Development Staff, U.S. Department of Agriculture

My first caveat is that, although I'm with the international development staff of the Department of Agriculture, I am not here to make any official policy statement on the part of my agency. Secondly, I'm not an agriculturalist. I'm a behavioral scientist with a background in management science and public administration, and I've worked for three years at the grassroots level in Nepal. I've also worked for a number of years training people in population programs how to train other people.

I've recently become involved with a group of appropriate technology people in Washington who are planning a conference on appropriate technology for May 1979. This combined conference and fair is an attempt to bring to the attention of policymakers many recent low cost, low energy consumption level innovations in technology.

In the process of planning this, I've come across a great number of people here who are involved in the so-called appropriate technology movement. What has happened in the United States is that many people who used to be involved in the anti-war movement a few years ago have found their way into the appropriate technology movement. We also have some very high technology people from IBM and Univac and other places who want to get in on this movement, too. There's a very uneasy alliance between those people and the former anti-war people, since they come at it from very different points of view. In addition, a lot of wild-eyed inventors are coming onto the scene, and some very interesting dynamics are taking place between these diverse kinds of people.

The late Dr. Schumacher, the fountainhead of the appropriate technology movement, came to the United States not too long ago and was very well received both on the Hill and in the White House. Schumacher had a significant impact. The foreign aid bill had $20 million for appropriate technology, and Appropriate Technology International, a non-profit, semi-private arm of AID, was set up for the purpose of promoting the exchange of information on appropriate technology. The National Center for Appropriate Technology was set up by the Department of Energy, with headquarters in Butte, Montana, deliberately outside of Washington, to promote the development of appropriate technology at the local, particularly rural, level in the United States by providing small grants to support appropriate technology in farming, mining, transportation and many other areas. The Peace Corps has set up an office of appropriate technology. I could go on and on because, by my own rough count, about twenty offices that call themselves "appropriate technology" have been established in Washington within the last two years.

All this activity should indicate to our friends from other countries that there is, indeed, an interest in appropriate technology in the United States which is not simply aimed at exporting things to developing countries. In fact, many of us feel very strongly, and have data to back it up, that most of the valuable research on appropriate technology is being done outside the United States, and that we need to learn from what is going on in these places.

At this point, I'd like to take a brief look at the two terms which have been coupled together. First, what is "appropriate?" What do we mean by appropriateness? It's a very relative, very phenomenological concept, one which can only be defined in terms of the situation, the culture, the socio-economic system, and the needs of the people. From an economic point of view, an "appropriate" technology is one which gives the greatest return on investment, given the wage level of a particular country. In other words, that technology which is most economical and beneficial where the wages are $400 a month is certainly not economical where the wages are around $40 a month. In the past there has been a tendency for many foreign assistance agencies to recommend the same technology, regardless of tremendous differences in wage levels.

The concept of appropriate technology has its roots in a Gandhian philosophy and is compatible with Buddhist, Jain, Sikh, Moslem and Judeo-Christian social and ethical systems. But it is important to recognize that "appropriateness" is not a limiting but an opportunity factor. Between stone age technology and the latest space age technology there is a tremendous range of technological options waiting to be developed and used. I agree with Schumacher that four essential characteristics of "appropriate" technology are that

(1) it should be low cost;
(2) it should be easy to learn, operate and maintain;
(3) it should use renewable and locally available resources;
(4) it should be compatible with cultural values, particularly those regarding non-violence and respect for the relationship between man and nature.

It may be that the term "appropriate" is not the best one to describe what is needed, since it means so many different things to different people. It may be that a term used recently by

Congressman Long of Maryland--"light capital" technology--would be better. Certainly light capital technologies have become attractive in some developing countries where they feel they simply cannot wait for massive infusions of capital to develop energy needed for agricultural and industrial expansion.

In regard to the second half of the term, there's a tendency to think of appropriate "technology" as hardware, solar cookers, small machines, and so forth. I think we have to pay more attention to appropriate or light capital social technologies as well. Developing countries cannot expect to train sufficient numbers of doctors, nurses, health care and family planning people using models from advanced industrial Western nations. That is why the kind of models the Chinese have been using for delivery systems--paraprofessional training and the use of local midwives who can be upgraded to become helpful in family planning--are so important for developing countries.

Appropriate delivery systems, light capital social organization, which make the best use of the resources available, are perhaps as essential as appropriate hardware. For instance, in India only 12% of the rice-growing plots are covered by extension services. Why? Because the extension service model that India has adopted is so expensive that if they put enough people on the payroll to provide extension services to everybody, they would have to use the entire Indian budget to do this. There is a great need to adopt organizational models which are low cost and "appropriate." Outreach approaches, the Chinese idea for rapidly expanding literacy in their country--"each one teach one"--are the resource-saving, low cost, appropriate social technologies which can do some good.

Recent experiments in training indigenous people as health aids and community health workers, using "expert farmers" as local extension agents, training traditional midwives as family planning workers, and combining knowledge expansion with "learning by doing" in educational programs are all examples of appropriate technology approaches at the socio-technical level.

At the present time only 2% of the world's Research and Development money is being spent in developing countries where close to 50% of the world's people live. It is doubtful if much of that is being spent on innovations which will transform the lives of the 2 billion people who live in the rural countryside. There is an urgent need for stimulating development and introducing technological alternatives at the level and scale of the people themselves. The impact of such a movement could profoundly transform the world of scarce and poorly distributed resources as we know it today and would undoubtedly have an even profounder impact on the Western countries living on borrowed and bartered resources.

Innovations are needed in both hardware and social organization.

313

We need innovations that will provide communities with solar, wind
or biomass energy at a local, small scale level. We need the simple
machinery which will make tools and equipment to increase production
and free people from the drudgery of back-breaking labor. But we
also need health care kits which will provide the community with the
basic tools for dealing with community health care and population
problems in the absence of highly trained doctors and nurses.

Many countries, especially in the Sahel area, are facing very
desperate problems in regard to fuel and water. It has come to the
point where, within the next ten years, there will not be enough
cooking fuel or water in the Sahel area. Women in the Sahel already
spend as much as five or six hours a day gathering fuel and carrying
water from long distances. This is becoming true in Nepal and other
places as well. One of the problems in the past has been that
women's efforts in gathering wood and bringing water has not been
considered in calculating cost. But things are now reaching the
point where these communities are becoming aware of the true costs
and the need to look for alternative solutions. I think technological solutions which are truly appropriate at the local level
have a good chance of being adopted.

The choice of technology is a complex equation involving economic, social and political factors. Choosing a technology by the
exclusive consideration of only one of these ignores the substantial
costs that may be incurred in other areas. For example, a country
may choose a highly labor-intensive low-technology strategy for
the political and social benefit of distributing income among the
poor but may find that it cannot sustain the program for very long
since it generates little added value to the economy in the form
of additional taxes, spending power or export earnings.

At the village level, where it is generally considered most
attractive for introduction, the individual and the community face
a similar dilemma in evaluating the adoption of new innovations
and technologies. The question of using low-cost birth control
methods, for instance, assuming that they are available, raises
many questions about the perceptions of the costs and benefits
related to having children. As Mahmood Memdani points out in
his study The Myth of Population Control, having children who can
assist in the farm work, in the kitchen and as support in old age,
is often seen by peasants as a benefit which far outweigh the
costs of feeding additional mouths. The fact that this rationality
of "private wants," as Galbraith calls it, is in direct conflict
with the "public need" to control access to the total resources
available to the society, does not alter the difficulty of introducing contraceptive technology, and may in fact help to explain
it. Critical to the resolution of this gap is the spread of an
understanding of what Garrett Hardin calls "The Tragedy of the
Commons": When everyone acts to maximize his own advantage

against a pool of limited resources, the net effect will be the inevitable depletion of those resources. The great strength of the appropriate technology movement lies in its incorporation of both the ethic of conservation and the support of innovation required in order to deal with already existing demands for new life support systems.

Tubewells and water piped to the village only make sense as a project which can be owned, operated and maintained by the village once they have decided that their women should not have to spend many backbreaking hours a day carrying water from a distant well. If there is no sense of the value of benefits that might accrue from the change there will be no way to compare the cost of the investment required to make the change.

Let me end by sketching three policy proposals implicit in what I've been saying. First, the development of local energy sources should have priority over mechanization in developing countries. The Rural Electrification Program in the U.S. is an example of the positive impact on farming of low cost energy sources. Most countries cannot wait for huge dams, nuclear power plants, etc., but it's entirely feasible to make available--through solar energy, the use of streams, or even combustion engines--some low cost form of local energy which then can lead to many other things.

Secondly, while it is clear that alternatives for using this energy should be developed locally, I do not believe it can be done by the people themselves without outside help. The United States should attempt to provide technical assistance to countries which will reach local levels. The U.S. role should be a process assistance role, whereby we help train those who can design appropriate technology if those skills are not available, rather than one of directly providing equipment and machinery.

Thirdly, I would suggest that what we are all learning from appropriate technology should be applied to all phases of AID projects. There are many countries where the very way in which the AID people live is completely contrary to what we're saying those countries should be doing. AID housing, as well as that provided to World Bank and other overseas development officials, is totally opposite to the appropriate technology approach we are beginning to preach. It's energy wasteful, it's expensive, it lacks solar water heaters, etc. We need to take a very close look at the kind of model we provide, both in terms of specific projects and in terms of how foreigners actually live in developing countries.

If the term appropriate technology is to have any meaning then we must take our guidance from the term itself: a technology can only become appropriate after it has been rigorously evaluated and has had its costs and benefits tested against the context of the particular circumstances of a socio-economic system. If an

315

"appropriate technology" can send us back to take a look at all of the prjects and programs we are exporting to the Third World in the name of foreign aid, and analyze them in terms of their appropriateness, economic soundness and usefulness to the people we are supposed to help, then it will have done its job even if not a single windmill or solar panel is erected.

THE ROLE OF SOCIAL ORGANIZATION IN DEVELOPMENT

Rose Oldfield Hayes

Department of Sociology and Anthropology
State University of New York at Farmingdale

Physical evidence from Paleoanthropology and archaeology sites indicate that human groups have depended upon the social organization of technology for exploitation and control of the environment at least since the Homo Erectus stage of human evolution and the Paleolithic stage of cultural evolution. As hominid technology increased in complexity, there has been a consistent and concomitant increase in the complexity of social organization. Some scholars argue that the development of complex forms of social organization was a prerequisite to the development and effective utilization of the technology which accompanied the rise of civilizations and their urban centers. These scholars thus focus on social organization as the primary influence in cultural change and evolution, with technology playing a secondary role.

In modern developmental programs focusing on food production and/or population control, the emphasis has consistently been on technological modernization. Scant attention has been given to modernizing technology's prehistoric and historical accompanist, social organization. Indications are that low success rates in these programs are due to the lack of focus on requisite implemented changes in social organization.

It is fruitful to look to our past for guidelines into our future. Developmental problems were extant in the preindustrial pristine states that arose in the same geographical regions that are now the targets of modern developmental programs.

In ancient Egypt the state evolved around 3100 B.C. with evidence of dynamic changes and increasing complexity in social organization, but there is no indication that technolgical growth preceeded or even kept pace with changes in social organization. During the Second Intermediate Period there was widespread famine and even cannibalism, due to prolonged drought. Balance between the population and the environment was restored not by technological breakthroughs but by reorganization of existing technology and eventual restoration of the former social organization and order.

317

Chinese economic reform programs, such as those of the Han (207 B.C.-220 A.D.) and Sung (960-1280) dynasties were aimed at easing poverty and the burdens of the peasantry while simultaneously enriching the coffers of the state. These programs, like those of the Egyptians, consistently focused upon social reorganization rather than increased technological complexity. Each of these states has had a life span of several thousand years, which is a mark of outstanding success by any standards.

During my 1970 field work in Sudan I found that the almost universal custom of infibulating females (the excision of all external genitalia and almost complete closure of the vaginal opening) acted as a fertility depressant due to infections and deaths. The population growth rate there, however, is critically high (2.9 in 1970) and if the practice of infibulation is eventually curtailed, successful family planning programs must become its functional analog. This presents the scientific community with a serious challenge because I found that female infibulation was a vital and integrated part of the Sudanese sociocultural configuration, particularly functionally tied to Sudanese marriage practices, systems of ethics, family honor, women's roles and statuses, and the patrilineage which is fundamental to Sudanese society. Family planning programs could effectively curtail population expansion only if such programs were implemented as a component part of a system-wide program of change which sought to modernize both birth control technology and the social organization in which that technology was imbedded.

Developmental programs seeking to increase food production and curb population expansion should include a preliminary stage in which an anthropological structural and functional analysis of the target society and its culture is conducted in order to determine the manner and extent to which such technological innovations as Western birth control and agricultural practices require adjustments in social organization. Technological innovations can then be imbedded in a compatible sociocultural configuration, thus giving the programs a greater chance of survival at the least societal and monetary cost and disruption.

Technology has for too long been both the means and ends. This narrow focus and biased approach has resulted in a string of modern developmental disasters from the infamous ground nut scheme in Tanzania to the present Aswan Dam difficulties. With such empirical evidence before us to indicate the glaring deficiencies in the total technological approach, it is scientifically, monetarily, and humanistically untenable to continue ignoring the potentials for major adjustments in social organization as a means and ends by which we can help "underdeveloped" countries establish a more harmonious balance between their populations, the carrying capacity of their environments, and the manner in which these environments are exploited and controlled.

Further, I have serious reservations about applying Western solutions to non-Western problems. There are indications that emphasis might more profitably be placed, as the preindustrial Egyptian and Chinese governments did, upon the social reorganization of existing technology, rather than upon technological modernization.

FROM OXEN TO TRACTORS: FACTORS INVOLVED IN THE DEVELOPMENT, MARKETING, AND FINANCING OF APPROPRIATE TECHNOLOGY

Howard A. Dahl

Concord, Inc., Fargo, North Dakota

When one mentions the word "development," a great variety of connotations are evoked. For most of us in the Western, industrialized world, the simple definition offered by Webster would be satisfactory, viz. that development means to cause to grow gradually in some way; cause to become gradually fuller, larger, better, etc; to make stronger or more effective. The word has taken on a different meaning for many people throughout the Third World. For them it implies a strategy by the rich nations to pacify the poor nations, with the ultimate goal being that of continuation of the present economic order. The reasons for this skepticism are worth examining briefly.

The 1950s witnessed a period of great hope and optimism. It was to be a time when Third World countries experienced great "development" so that there might be more economic equality throughout the world. However, during this period of emphasis on "development" the gap between the rich and poor nations actually widened. As a result, the 1960s were years of disillusionment. Because many individuals in the Third World (especially philosophers and theologians) considered the economic and political path proposed by the rich countries no longer fit to be traveled on, a search for new models was undertaken. Many questions were asked. Assuming "development" is good, are there different ways to develop? Is economic development most important? Indeed, should affluence be the goal of development?

I bring up this brief historical sketch for two reasons. First of all, it helps one be cognizant of the complexity of any discussion of development. One can realize why so much of the rhetoric of Third World leaders is stridently ideological in nature, often being neo-Marxist. Secondly, I bring up the historical discussion of development as a reflection of the way in which I have been most actively involved in Third World activities to this point. For I believe that it is essential to understand the theoretical complexity of the whole issue of development, before one can most adequately contribute concretely.

320

In this paper I would like to examine a number of factors that relate to the increase of appropriate technology in the Third World. When I consider specific forms of technology, I will restrict myself specifically to farm tractors. The general comments on technology will be intended for broader application.

Before it is possible to speak of the development of technology which is appropriate, it is necessary to define the term appropriate. According to Robert Chambers, "There may at this moment exist a tragic gap between those who perceive the needs of rural societies and those who are creating the technologies that they will come to use and which will determine much of their form."[1] This can be seen most clearly in the ethnocentrism exhibited by those who think that Third World nations should seek to duplicate in toto the American agribusiness community. Fortunately, such proposals are quite rare today. However, there is still not enough utilization of local resource personnel in the selection of appropriate technology. This matter of selection is critical, for there are a number of serious criticisms leveled against mechanization. Stout and Downing[2] list a number of them:

1. land and capital are scarce in developing countries while labor is abundant and inexpensive;
2. jobs outside agriculture are not available for even a small fraction of the new workers entering the labor market;
3. mechanization ignores social problems;
4. the possibility of increased production by bringing new land under cultivation is limited;
5. mechanization encourages the large farm to grow larger, and only the large farm can obtain the capital;
6. agriculture should serve as a "sponge" to soak up excess labor or as a "storage" where workers can survive until something better comes along;
7. private cost does not reflect social cost--as a result it is more profitable to mechanize than to employ labor;
8. mechanization increases yield per unit of labor, but not necessarily yield per unit of land.

Nevertheless, in spite of these considerations, it is possible for mechanization to occur in such a way that it overcomes most, if not all, of these objections. A study by Giles demonstrated that machines used in a selective manner "in conjunction with multiple cropping will contribute markedly to: increased yields and production of food crops; increased utilization of labor (man hours per year, uniform output, reduction of peaks and productivity)."[3]

The proper utilization of labor has been one of the paramount concerns of those objecting to mechanization. There have been some statements indicating that a rapid mechanization policy could create 50% unemployment in some countries. The resulting social turmoil would be a worse situation than the present in most cases. But it is

321

the feeling of many that mechanization must occur for yields to increase. Better seed bed preparation and more uniform planting are more important to yields than fertilizer.[4] This can only be affected by mechanization.

Because of the need for machinery, and because of the many objections raised, scholars are calling for an integrated approach. Giles says in this regard that

> There are many centers throughout the world whose function is to develop and test agricultural equipment. As is well documented, many of these are concerned, as a top priority, with only one part of the system, as for example, a puddler. Although such objectives are important, the developing countries need a few exceptional centers that are geared, as a top priority, to the development of new systems designed to increase yields, production and labor utilization. It is suggested that a few be established at existing research and development centers where the required specialists are presently at work. To make such a center acceptable, three points seem important. First, there must be room to recognize the accomplishments of each specialist. Second, the name must carry the connotation of being as it really is, interdisciplinarian. "Operational Systems Institute" is suggested. Thirdly, we must recognize that it takes time to develop a machine as a part of a system. Basically the development of a machine is similar to the development of a new variety. Elements and characteristics are put together to achieve desired effects. Each promising result must be adequately field tested and evaluated.[5]

The development of a machine is indeed much like the development of a new variety. It is very costly and time consuming, but if the right machine emerges, it is of great value. In this regard, the United Nations Industrial Development Organization (UNIDO) in 1973 demonstrated the great need for a simple, yet durable, low-cost farm tractor for the developing nations.[6] It was while working at International Harvester's marketing research department in 1975-1976 that I became aware of this study. I.H. spent a great deal of time and money researching the market and, after considering carefully all the factors involved, decided not to go ahead with the development of any machinery. At about this same time Ford had a very bad financial loss in their efforts to market a two-wheel walking tractor. At the 1976 annual meeting of Deere and Co. some shareholders introduced a resolution asking Deere to commit themselves to develop machinery for Third World subsistence farmers. Management opposed this resolution and it was soundly defeated. Their reasoning--Ford tried to do something like this and couldn't make a profit.

322

I bring up these examples to illustrate a point. The major farm manufacturers have determined that there is little if any chance for profitability in the development of machinery such as was called for in the UNIDO study. This point was brought forcefully home to me in a letter I received recently from a former executive with International Institute of Tropical Agriculture in Nigeria. He stated, "There is a great interest in small agriculture throughout the Third World, but so far there has been little done that is helpful . . . several of the large American companies have given it a whirl, only to drop out of the picture. I don't think it was ever becoming of them, but there isn't much of a prospect of profitability at present, and the problems are many."[7]

It seems to be clear that other motives than financial incentives must be present in the development of appropriate machinery or, to use E.F. Schumacher's phrase, "intermediate technology." Schumacher's book Small Is Beautiful, which is subtitled "Economics as if people mattered," seeks to introduce many other factors to the economic discussion than simply GNP growth. This new way of looking at development was well demonstrated in a lecture given by Roger Darling at the Agency for International Development.

> Over the past decades Third World development has been largely discussed and described in terms of cold impersonal resources: aid flows, technology, credits, debt relief, commodities, feasibility studies, etc. This has tended to impersonalize development and obscure the critical role of human factors. It has also helped condition the public to view development as a matter of technology, complex international finance or mere resource transfers from rich to poor. The history of past decades has been one of relentless pursuit of resources for Third World development--all parties assuming that if you get the resources you get the development. As a consequence of these trends the public, and the international development community, have come to perceive development largely in terms of resources rather than human capacities![8]

It should be obvious by now that Third World development is so complex, involving so many disciplines, that it is not easy to render a simple formula to serve as a panacea. However, perhaps a modest proposal can be made that can serve as a foundation for further discussions.

First of all, it seems that it is going to take people who have motives other than a monolithic profit motive to be willing to take risks involved in developing appropriate technology. These people could be with foundations, government agencies, or with missionary organizations.

323

Secondly, the machinery that is developed must be done by individuals from various disciplines in both the developing as well as the industrial nations. Stated simply, it must be an integrated approach. In a recent article, four agricultural experts commented to this effect.

A rural strategy must be an integrated effort to promote economic growth and employment in all rural economic sectors. It is obviously far easier to plan than to implement such a strategy because implementation will require political commitment by elites as well as institutional restructuring and a large amount of trial-and-error projects, which must be tested at the farm, village and regional level.[9]

IITA is presently involved in a program in which they have 189 integrated agricultural test sites at which they are going to be experimenting with different approaches, hoping to find some adequate models that can be duplicated elsewhere.

Thirdly, mechanization is necessary for increased productivity, and it can be done in such a way that it will also increase the employment level. "The development of jobs of a tertiary character is undoubtedly one of the characteristics of advanced agricultural economics."[10]

Fourthly, because this intermediate technology is not deemed profitable by many companies, it will have to be marketed and financed through different channels than is normal in industrialized nations. As was mentioned already, this could come through foundations, government agencies, or mission organizations as well as normal economic channels.

Finally, in line with the purpose of this conference, it is necessary that a cogent policy of technological development is thought out. It must be one that takes into account social, economic, political and human factors. Giles comments that,

It is not surprising to find that government administrators and leaders in both developing and developed countries have vacillated somewhat in establishing firm continuing policies in mechanization for the non-industrialized nations. There is always an uneasiness among such leaders about promoting machines, largely because of the growing population and unemployment. As a consequence, a middle ground is hewed--some tractors, improved hand and animal powered tools, and local industries.[11]

FOOTNOTES

1. Robert Chambers, "Appropriate to What," Ceres 57:28, May-June 1977.

2. B. A. Stout and C. M. Downing, "Counterpull," Ceres 43:44, January-February 1975.

3. G. W. Giles, "The Reorientation of Agricultural Mechanization for the Developing Countries--Policies and Attitudes for Action Programmers," Effects of Farm Mechanization on Production and Employment, FAO, 7 February 1975.

4. Louis Malassis, "Toward a Technical Humanism," Ceres 55:73, January-February 1977.

5. Giles, p. 86.

6. "Report on Small Low-cost Tractors Suited to the Needs of the Developing Countries," UNIDO, July 25, 1973, p. 86.

7. Personal correspondence of February 6, 1978 with former IITA executive.

8. Roger Darling, Restoring Perspective on Third World Development (Vienna, VA: Lectures-Seminars, 1977), p. 6.

9. Derek Byerlee, Carl K. Eicher, Carl Liedholm and Dunstan S. C. Spencer, "Cut to Fit," Ceres 59:44, September-October 1977.

10. Jean Fauchon, "A 'Natural' Modernization," Ceres 58:21, July-August 1977.

11. Giles, p. 72.

THE SELF HELP TRACTOR--REPLACING DEPENDENCY WITH SELF-SUFFICIENCY THROUGH SMALL TRACTOR TECHNOLOGY

Fred Strohbehn

Self Help Inc., Waverly, Iowa

From its beginning, Self Help has believed in the old Chinese proverb which says: "If you give a man a fish he eats for a day. If you teach a man to fish he feeds himself for a lifetime."

Self Help believes and follows the advice of a Rhodesian minister who has stated, "Don't give us boatloads of your resources. They will only make us dependent--and dependent people are hostile. Help us develop our own skills and resources."

Farmers in developing countries want the information and guidance necessary for them to live with pride and dignity. Self Help Foundation is working to make that desire a reality.

Self Help, Inc. is a non-profit foundation attacking world hunger through rural industrialization in developing countries. Self Help was founded in Waverly, Iowa in 1952 by industrialist Vern Schield. Two goals were set forth. The immediate goal was to provide equipment to farmers, missionaries and others who wished to begin agricultural programs for rural improvement. Self Help's long term goal is to teach people to produce their own equipment in their own shops--in a way harmonious with existing cultures.

In 1963 Vern Schield designed a very simple, durable, 10 horsepower tractor which could replace an ox team or mule for soil tillage. Construction and maintenance costs were kept minimal to make the tractor affordable and reliable. Over 180 are now used in 48 different countries. In the past 15 years no change has been necessary in its basic design.

The "Self-Helper" tractor has many advantages designed specifically for farmers in developing countries. It is durable and performs more work than human or animal labor. The tractor is easy to maintain, is priced within an affordable range, and is suitable for local assembly or manufacturing.

Since 1977 about 80% of the tractors have been shipped with a long-life 7 H.P. Yanmar diesel engine, which is already sold and serviced in 130 different countries. In addition, Self Help offers more than 15 attaching implements for the Self Help tractor.

Self Help has established a two-phase program for assisting developing countries to acquire equipment and technology:

Phase one of the Self Help program is teaching the proper use of better tools. In this phase, emphasis is placed on making subsistence farmers aware of how farm machinery can increase food production. Before risking a change from centuries-old methods, a farmer must first be convinced there is a better approach.

Phase two of Self Help assistance is local assembly. In this phase Self Help determines if some items, such as wheels, tires or engines, can be obtained locally. For instance, Yanmar engines, produced in Brazil, are lower-priced in Honduras than the same model engine produced in Japan and sent to the United States. As familiarity with the product grows, the developing country can expand production and assembly with minimal capital and at a speed comfortable to them.

Ideally, complete local production will eventually be attained. If parts such as castings or gears are still not available locally, Self Help can supply them. The ultimate achievement of local manufacturing has many advantages, the most important being the employment of people, broadening their skills and in turn broadening their economic base.

For the first time in its 26-year history, Self Help is now achieving its second goal. Self Help is currently giving assistance to a school in Yoro, Honduras, which began building their own tractors in March, 1978. A department-head teacher from Honduras came to Waverly, Iowa in 1977 to work and study for two months in the Self Help factory. Several Nigerian students now studying at Malta, Illinois, are also considering a work-study arrangement next summer, hoping to gain experience to begin building their own small tractors in Nigeria. Several other groups in Africa are in the planning stages of building small tractors.

Several world-wide organizations have placed their support behind Self Help programs. A recent report by the United Nations Industrial Development Organization recognizes Self Help as a suitable supplier of assistance in Africa, Central and South America. The International Wheat and Maize Development Center in Mexico is another organization supporting and utilizing Self Help equipment. They have purchased a full line of Self Help equipment on the recommendation of Dr. Norman Borlaug. Several African governments are now using and studying the Self Help equipment in their own countries.

After using and observing the Self Help tractor over a two-year period, Jim Carpenter, Midwest agricultural recruiter for the Peace Corps, concluded: "That tractor is just what is needed in so many places where our volunteers are serving. It's so darn much better than the draft animals that eat three times the food that can be produced on their little plots of ground."

Since about 70% of the people in developing nations live on very small farms, and inadequate technology usually prevents them from best utilizing their land, there is a real need for this very simple, durable tractor and matching equipment. The tractor and the Self Help program have been proven effective over the past 15 years.

They have also proven the truth of the saying, "You can give a man a fish and he eats for a day. You can teach a man to fish and he eats for a lifetime."

INTERMEDIATE TECHNOLOGY IN FOOD PRODUCTION
IN THE THIRD WORLD

Godfrey Roberts

Livingston College, Rutgers University

There are a number of factors which make it important to apply village level technology in food production in Third World countries. First of all, most of these countries are poor. In many Third World countries more than 70% of family income is spent on food. Despite the fact that such a large percentage of family income in the Third World is spent on food, a large percentage of the population is undernourished. Secondly, the cost of commercial fertilizer is increasing faster than the ability of poor farmers to buy it and, in most Third World countries, there is very little cheap energy available to increase food production. Finally, in many isolated rural farm communities of the Third World there is little or no exchange of money. Since farming is the main activity, most transactions involve the exchange of food. For these reasons village level appropriate technology in food production is urgently needed throughout the Third World.

In this paper I wish to call attention to an intermediate technology model which is now working in Sri Lanka. It attempts to improve the nutritional levels in rural communities by combining appropriate social organization with village level technology. It is an attempt to take the rural development model and integrate it into the existing social structure.

The name of the rural development program is Sarvodaya. It's a program that was started in the early 1950s by a schoolteacher who believed that development in the rural sector could be achieved by communities organizing themselves to make maximum use of available local technology. The organization has a commitment to education, village-level development, and non-violent social change. Once a village has expressed an interest in the project, there is a voluntary work camp geared to food production or a comparable development project which creates some interest in development work.

When the project has been established in a village, the focus shifts to young people from the village who are invited to attend a

329

training program at the project headquarters in the capital city. There they are trained in various skills which would help them to introduce local technology in food production and village industries. At the training center, by participating in the Sarvodaya concept of learning through sharing, the young people become both opinion leaders and skilled in the introduction of development projects in their rural communities.

On a typical day in a Sarvodaya village, everyone would wake up very early in the morning and then participate in a community breakfast. After this the adults would go to work and the children would go to school. In the evening, the entire village meets for an extended family gathering where various issues and problems in the village are discussed. This is followed by an inter-religious worship and a community dinner. Two meals in the day are eaten in a community setting. This arrangement is called a community kitchen. The advantage of a community kitchen is that in rural agricultural communities, where there is little exchange of money, there can be an exchange of food products. Each person grows something and contributes it to the community kitchen, thereby increasing the nutritional standards of the population generally.

Leading nutritionists in Sri Lanka are involved in the development of this program so that some attempt can be made to balance the protein and vitamin intake of the community. A comparable community kitchen approach has been reported in some Chinese communities. The community kitchen is a unique idea in the application of village-level technology to improve nutritional standards at low cost to the individual farmer.

I believe that village-level food production is especially important in societies such as Sri Lanka where diet is dominated by food that is rich in carbohydrates and the little protein in the diet is obtained from rice and other local vegetables. Thus it is necessary that the utilization of vegetable products should be maximized in terms of nutritional efficiency.

An attitude survey of 200 farmers in one village involved in the Sarvodaya project gives some idea of the positive impact of the program. Responses to a few of the questions follow:

	Question	Response
1.	Has the rural development program had a positive influence on life in the village?	Yes--100%
2.	Is the community kitchen a success?	Yes--100%
3.	Do you now spend more time with your family?	Yes--75%

4. Would you like to move to a city if you   Yes--10%
    had the opportunity?

5. Are you happy with life in the village?   Yes--75%

6. What is the ideal family size?
        3 to 4 children   71%
        2 children or less   20%

The first two questions are self-explanatory. We asked the question about spending time as a family because there is some concern from an anthropological perspective about the effect of eating and preparing meals together on the traditional family structure. The fact that 75% of the respondents said they were spending more time with their families since the community kitchen project began is a good sign, but I think the impact on family structure should be carefully examined.

I should comment too about the responses to the question of ideal family size. Although almost three-quarters of the villagers said the desired family size was three to four children--a figure higher than most people in the population field would hope for--I think the figure is actually much lower than desired family size in most Third World rural farm communities.

Linked to my study, a health survey was also conducted by a medical team in Sri Lanka, and the health conditions in this village were very good.

The development program is not totally self-sufficient. It is being helped by AID-supported milk and a few other assistance programs. I should mention that I disagree with Congressman Scheuer and others who say that AID programs should have a measurable impact. This attitude is simplistic because in a program such as the one I am describing in Sri Lanka, American assistance is integrated into the village development program. It's very difficult to measure something like that.

Summing up the results of my study, it's very clear that the application of this intermediate technology model has had a positive impact on health and general quality of life in the village. If one has to measure results, perhaps the best standard for measuring the success of development projects was given by the Sarvodaya director, Mr. Ariyaratne. He said, "You are developed when you know what to do and you are able to do it." From my study of these villages in Sri Lanka, it seems that they understand what has to be done and they are doing it.

I would like to conclude this paper with several policy recommendations which grow out of my study of village development in Sri Lanka but are not a specific outcome of this study.

331

1. Research in intermediate technology should be emphasized in American universities and research organizations.

2. Courses and programs in alternate models of technology in food production should be encouraged.

3. Graduating U.S. college students should be encouraged to participate in intermediate technology programs in less developed countries.

4. Among funding agencies, there should be increasing support for food production programs that utilize intermediate models of technology.

5. As developed societies become increasingly concerned about the negative effects of big-time technology, we should reconsider the value of intermediate technology for the individual farmer in our own country. Models such as the one being developed in Sri Lanka are now being looked at in some European countries as approaches that could be used in developed societies. Perhaps some of the intermediate technology models that are emerging in developing countries should be looked at by developed countries as possible models for preserving small-time farms.

FOOD PRODUCTION IN THE ANDES: AN ALTERNATIVE STRATEGY FOR HIGHLAND AGRICULTURAL DEVELOPMENT

Sylvia Helen Forman

Department of Anthropology, University of Massachusetts, Amherst

As early as 1551, the Spanish viceroy in Peru registered complaints about the displacement of peasant populations from the rich agricultural valley bottom and their replacement by mostly cattle ranching. In the 400 years since Viceroy Mendoso registered this complaint, the pattern of disturbance of populations and agricultural production has continued to plague the Andean countries of Ecuador, Peru, and Bolivia.

The Andes, and other high altitude regions like the Himalayas and parts of Kenya and Ethiopia, have been seriously suffering in recent years from soil erosion, rapid population growth, population disturbances such as rural to urban migration, no increases in food production, and other less obvious things like loss of crop genetic diversity and rapid and often undesirable economic and cultural change.

Now, certainly most of these problems are common, at this point, to a good part of the world. However, they take a unique cast in the Andes. This is because mountain ecosystems require special considerations as food producing regions. They require special treatment because they're vertically, not horizontally, organized. Their topography and their climate make them particularly fragile environments, most importantly with regard to soil loss through erosion-- once it goes down the side of the Andes, you don't get it back up there again--and because of their slow cycles of soil production and vegetative growth, particularly at the higher elevations. So there are limitations of a rather severe nature on food production in highland areas.

Small farmers in the Andes--peasant farmers, primarily--are increasingly pressured by economic need (which is related to population growth), by poor advice, and by legal constraints to forsake the traditional forms of agricultural production.

The serious efforts at improving agriculture so far in the Andean countries have been almost entirely concentrated on large

scale commercial farming, primarily coastal lowland type plantations, and on cash crops--many of them not food crops--rather than
on subsistence farming. Yet, it seems obvious, first of all, that
a large proportion of the population of the Andean nations is
peasant agriculturalist, and that the topography, the labor pool,
the resource base, and the lack of capital in the rural areas makes
it imperative to move toward family size farms there (many of the
farms now are below family size) as the more desirable and more
productive kind of agriculture in the high elevation areas.

The traditional modes of peasant agriculture in the Andes
have been adapted to the vertical organization of the ecosystem and
to the tremendous local diversity in climate and soils that one gets
in a mountain environment.

Let me give a couple of examples of how that adaptation has
worked. There is a range of specific cultigens which have not been
grown elsewhere than in the Andes--pseudo grains and certain tubers
which were domesticated by the Incas and the Incas' predecessors--
which have the characteristics of being frost resistant or tolerant
of certain kinds of poor soils. That's one kind of adaptation. Crop
mixes, crop rotation systems and· fertilizing systems have all been
structured in a way which is different than they were in lower elevations to take advantage of climatic variation or to resist particular production problems that exist there.

Another set of specific adaptations include the elaborate terracing left by the Incas which tourists are so fond of looking at,
and the less well known, but fairly elaborate, irrigation systems
that work so well in terms of the particular kinds of drainage patterns and physical shape of the mountains.

Yet a third kind of adaptation that peasant communities in the
Andes have made for producing and distributing agricultural products
has to do with the control of land. Land use patterns elaborated
in the past, and to some extent still existent today, have taken
several forms. One pattern has been to control land in several of
the vertical ecozones at several elevations and thereby to provide
the communities with access to different kinds of crops, animals
and pasturage from different elevations.

When this direct control of more than one ecolevel hasn't been
possible, the other pattern has been one of establishing elaborate
networks of exchange among communities which are based at different
levels. A typical exchange pattern involves the trading of yama and
alpakison grown by a very high altitude pastoral community for
potatoes and corn from a lower elevation community. The corn, in
fact, has come from a still lower level to the intermediate elevation
community in exchange for potatoes.

However, many of these traditional adaptations are either

phasing out now or have completely disappeared. Terracing is one of the most striking examples of that. There are people still using Inca terraces, but new terracing is not done in the peasant communities in the Andes. The result is an increase in soil erosion.

The result of the disappearance or impending disappearance of these traditional adaptations is lower productivity for the peasant farm unit, a substitution of crops and farming methods which are less appropriate to the highlands ecosystem, and modes of economic exchange which operate purely through commercial markets. Two interesting effects of these changes are the direct undercutting of the peasant bias in a good part of the Andes and the diversion of a disproportionate share of potential peasant income to middlemen. I say disproportionate because there are some things about the way those markets operate that take advantage of the peasants.

Now, for me, the central point that comes out of this quick view of what is happening in the Andes is the question of how a highland peasant population can be enabled to continue farming, and not have to leave their land. How can they increase their subsistence production? How can they enhance the quality of their family's lives, at least to a level where they might consider some population control, without speeding up the degradation of this very fragile environment which will not take much more degradation?

One popular answer to these interrelated questions is the alternative technologies or intermediate technologies answer. And I agree with that but with some caveats. It seems to me that alternative technologies for mountain agricultural systems, much more strongly than alternative technologies for other kinds of productive systems, have to be based on the same kinds of special considerations that the traditional technologies were based on. The easiest way to do that, it seems to me, is to base them on the traditional technology, to modify, to elaborate, to enhance those without assuming that you can bring in "flatlander" ideas and biases and impose them on that very different environment. Flatlander experts have to be very aware of the particular kinds of biases that they bring to that environment. It would, for example, be more desirable to try to improve the strains of some of the traditional crops which I referred to than to introduce new cereals or new tubers from other parts of the world. Reintroduction of traditional terracing arrangements, and emphasis on manure which peasants already use for fertilizing their fields are other examples of how this might be done.

But even if the alternative technologies are handled in terms of the traditional adaptations, that is not sufficient in and of itself. In addition to these technological solutions, one would need intermediate or alternative economies also. The traditional adaptations made by the highland peasants were not simply a matter of how you plow your field or what crop you plant, but how you exchange products in this unusual stratified, selective and very diverse environment. When, for example, land reform actions forbid the exchange of labor directly for food stuffs, or when they consolidate the holdings of the community into a single ecozone, what they are in effect doing is undercutting the kinds of social and economic adaptations which are necessary for viable small farm units in this kind of environment. And the same goes for infrastructure decisions, roads, marketplaces, and so on.

Anthropological data are available to begin to use these traditional models. The goal has to be one of making the ultimate use of the diversity available in the mountains without degrading that environment further.

DISCUSSION

AUDIENCE: Could you say a little more about the economic relationships that you'd like to see?

SYLVIA HELEN FORMAN: I guess what I'm thinking of is kind of closing down the economic systems to a smaller local level. The national structures seem to be trying now to move them out and centralize them in region market towns and national capitals. I'm suggesting that, at least in some parts of the Andes, you can fall back on a much smaller regional basis which incorporates the ecozones that you need to have to operate in that particular locale. Your trade, then, is run primarily, though not exclusively, within that smaller system.

AUDIENCE: The political systems within the Andean countries are quite different, so I'm a little curious about your lumping them all together. Do you think the political answer lies in some kind of decentralist revolution?

SYLVIA HELEN FORMAN: Obviously there are major differences in the political systems. But I think that, with the possible exception of parts of Bolivia, they share a view of agricultural development which has created so many problems. Certainly the land reform efforts in Peru and Ecuador have caused as many problems as they've solved. The tendency to do agricultural development on non-subsistence crops and in the upper regions of the highlands is true for Ecuador and Peru and, to a large extent, for Bolivia also.

The politics of saying "decentralize" are obviously horrendous. It's kind of idealistic to even mention it. But it seems to me to be a very crucial issue if what the local political systems have in mind is anything approximating self-sufficiency. Last summer I was in Ecuador, which produces things like rice, sugar and beans. It seems outrageous to me that the people in the small town I was working in couldn't afford to buy any of those things.

336

POPULATION GROWTH AND SUBSISTENCE FOOD PRODUCTION IN THE WESTERN HIGHLANDS, PAPUA NEW GUINEA: IMPLICATIONS AND POLICY ALTERNATIVES

William H. Heaney

East-West Population Institute

The relationship between population dynamics, subsistence food production and ecological resources in Pacific Island societies has undergone substantial change as a result of sustained contact with Western societies. Following World War II, planned development projects have contributed to this change in two respects. The introduction of health services and a consequent reduction in mortality rates has led to a high rate of population growth. And the introduction of wage labor opportunities and cash crop agriculture in more remote areas has resulted in changes in diet and agricultural production.

The purpose of this paper is to outline briefly the interrelationship between rapid rates of population growth and food production and its implications for one area of the Western Highlands, Papua New Guinea.* Although the remarks will be confined to a particular area, the implications of population growth and the need for increased attention to the constraints and potential of subsistence agricultural production are relevant to other developing countries.

Pre-Contact Population and Ecological Dynamics

Before European contact, the central Highlands of Papua New Guinea had a stable, slowly growing population that was supported by

---

*The essays in Pacific Atoll Populations, edited by Carroll (1975), describe the changes in population dynamics that have occurred among island societies. The information for this paper was gathered during eighteen months of field work in the Western Highlands, Papua New Guinea, as part of a dissertation research project sponsored by the National Science Foundation and by the East-West Population Institute. The author gratefully acknowledges their generous support.

an efficient system of swidden agriculture (Brookfield, 1971: 83-85; van de Kaa, 1971: 72; Watson, 1965). The sweet potato was, as now, the staple food crop in the diet and was supplemented by endemic varieties of dry taro, bananas, yams, sugar cane and leafy greens. Pigs were one of the main forms of wealth, a medium of exchange between social groups and individuals, and a symbol of social status. Pork was, and continues to be, eaten infrequently, usually on ceremonial occasions. Other sources of animal protein--insects, birds, snakes and small marsupials--supplemented the diet. Their availability depended upon the terrain, population density (which affected the amount of available forest), and intensity of cultivation.

Consumption of animal protein was regulated by various cultural beliefs and dietary restrictions. These food sources provided a small, but significant amount of animal protein in the diet. The relative amount of protein and carbohydrates in the diet varies considerably between coastal and inland groups, and between groups practicing relatively extensive or intensive cultivation (Clarke, 1966; McArthur, 1974; Oomen, 1971). Swidden cultivation in Papua New Guinea takes a wide variety of forms, in which the practices of cultivation, varieties of crops and labor intensiveness reflect ecological constraints and settlement density. Recent studies of the nutritional status of these populations indicate that they have adapted to the particular environmental conditions very successfully, particularly with regard to their adjustment to low protein diets (Harrison and Walsh, 1974; McArthur, 1974; Oomen, 1971).

During the pre- and early post-contact period malaria, pneumonia and gastroenteritis contributed to relatively high mortality rates. Fertility levels were affected by social practices that included polygyny, post-partum sex taboos and abortion, which resulted in the spacing of children and a low rate of population increase (Bulmer, 1971). Warfare, homicide and infanticide also affected mortality levels, but their influence was not as important as the combined effect of disease and practices limiting fertility.

Post-contact Population Growth and Agricultural Change

Following the Second World War, the introduction of public health and development programs in the Highlands altered the quasi-stable relationship between population and resources. Mortality levels were substantially reduced; and, although the evidence is conjectural, increases in fertility due to changes in the observance of post-partum sex taboos may have contributed to high rates of population growth (van de Kaa, 1971: 72). At current rates of increase, it is estimated that the population will double within 25 years (van de Kaa, 1971: 215), thereby further increasing pressure upon subsistence cultivation. In some areas of the Highlands, in-migration also will increase population densities.

The introduction of cash crop agriculture during the late

1950s in the form of small holder coffee gardens and expatriate plantations has reduced the amount of land available for subsistence gardens and the raising of pigs. Within the constraints set by the
Highlands ecology for subsistence agriculture, garden production
can expand only so far before intensification is required to match
population growth. Papua New Guinea cultivation systems show evidence of evolution from relatively extensive to intensive systems
(Brookfield, 1971; Clarke, 1966), but this process has taken place
over a long historical period with low rates of population increase
(Watson, 1965). Under the ecological conditions present in the New
Guinea Highlands, intensification may also result in a reduction in
the quality and variety of foods in the diet; in addition, intensification may produce lasting changes in the forest ecology, as opposed to more extensive forms of shifting cultivation, in which the
tropical forest is allowed to regenerate between plantings (Clarke,
1973). It also remains a serious issue whether increased subsistence
production can keep abreast of population increase.

Income from cash crops enables cultivators to buy supplemental
food stuffs, but the desire for cash income and suitable land for
coffee gardens has stimulated migration to areas that already have
concentrated populations. Reliance upon coffee income raises the
issue of increasing dependence upon the stability of export prices.
While it is probable that nutritional levels have increased for
some groups with access to coffee income, it is unclear whether all
age groups benefit equally from purchased foods and how these food
patterns affect the consumption of other traditional nutrients.
Furthermore, it appears that little cash income is used to purchase
fertilizers to replenish soil nutrients involved in coffee growth.

Population growth and its long term implications for the future
of Papua New Guinea are recognized as serious problems (Papua New
Guinea, 1975; Tago, Lepani and ToRobert, 1976), and family planning
projects have been started in Highlands areas. It is most probable,
however, that the population will continue to increase because of
the growing number of young women in their child bearing years between 15 and 45. The problems of subsistence agriculture and the
effect of cash crops upon food production and consumption have received less attention. To date, the major emphasis in agricultural extension programs has been to encourage proper cultivation
of plantation crops for export, European-style vegetables (which
are usually produced to be sold for cash), and introduction of
livestock.

The subsistence sector has been neglected for the following
reasons: First, limited funds and the need to generate income for
development purposes and national self-sufficiency resulted in
administration programs to promote cash crop production; Secondly,
there was evidence that few incentives were available for increasing
subsistence production, as opposed to cash crops, and the increased
labor techniques would be resisted by Highlanders accustomed to

339

efficient, time-honored methods; Thirdly, the realization that extension work with native varieties of foods found in subsistence gardens would require specialized training in order to be effective, and that Papua New Guineans themselves took years to acquire the knowledge and skill for successful gardening.

These are important considerations, but they ignore two important problems. First, the production of cash crops and generation of income per se does not lead to a better standard or quality of living, and the reliance upon cash may have devastating, long-term effects upon the viability of the local subsistence system, especially if export prices fall (Shankman, 1977). Second, subsistence production may produce more food value per unit of land under current practices than can be purchased with the income derived from cash crops. This does not consider the actual distribution of cash crop income and how it is spent. Perhaps most important, the food requirements of the increasing population may exceed the rate at which the subsistence system can be intensified.*

The evidence from population projections suggests that increased pressure will be put upon the capacity of subsistence production to feed the population in densely settled Highland valleys. The development potential of the subsistence sector and the need for increased investment in rural production has been recognized by economists (Fisk, 1972; Conroy, 1973), but it has not received full attention from planners and extension officers. The continuation of present policies, which emphasize cash crop production, cannot meet the food requirements of a doubling population. Greater attention and support needs to be given to research and extension programs that deal with improving the productive capacity of subsistence agriculture. It has been emphasized also that without coordinated and effective population planning, agricultural intensification can only delay the negative effects of increasing rural population densities (Conroy, 1973: 82).

Although investment in rural extension efforts directed toward subsistence agriculture may appear to lack the direct return cash crops promise, increased efforts in agricultural extention can do much to develop means of meeting the future nutritional needs of an expanding population. Such efforts may also avoid the economic, agricultural and ecological risks that have been associated with cash crop expansion. Funding for these efforts can be obtained through subsidies levied upon coffee exports, which can be directed toward agricultural extension projects that encourage the planting of

---
*

This paper takes a neo-Malthusian approach by arguing that economic development projects have contributed to increased population growth, and that future population increase may seriously affect economic development and outweigh the productive capacity of shifting cultivation.

indigenous foods high in nutrients, as well as educational projects that urge the acceptance of new varieties of foods.

In many parts of the Pacific region, the delicate balance between populations and their resource systems has been altered. In some cases, subsistence agriculture can no longer support a percentage of the total population, and these people must migrate to other areas, towns and cities. In the case of Papua New Guinea, the low rate of employment expansion in urban areas, and the limited access to suitable environments in other areas, suggests that migration may not be able to alleviate the pressures of a growing population. This paper has suggested that increased attention be given to the development potential of subsistence agriculture. In order to be effective, however, a food and population policy requires coordinated efforts of national and regional governments, the department of health and the agricultural extension service. With simultaneous attention to population planning and the intensification of the subsistence sector, it may be possible to avoid future stress upon human and physical resources.

REFERENCES

1. Brookfield, H. C. and Doreen Hart. Melanesia: A Geographical Interpretation of an Island World. London: Methuen and Co. (1971).

2. Bulmer, R.N.H. "Traditional Forms of Family Limitation in New Guinea." In M.W. Ward (ed.), Population Growth and Socio-Economic Change. New Guinea Research Bulletin No. 42. Canberra: The Australian National University (1971).

3. Carroll, Vern (editor). Pacific Atoll Populations. Honolulu: The University Press of Hawaii (1975).

4. Clarke, W. C. "From Extensive to Intensive Shifting Cultivation: A Succession from New Guinea." Ethnology 5: 347-59 (1966).

5. _____. "The Dilemma of Development." In H. C. Brookfield (ed.), The Pacific in Transition, pp. 275-98. New York: St. Martins Press (1973).

6. Conroy, J. D. "Urbanization in Papua New Guinea: A Development Constraint." Economic Record 49: 76-88 (1973).

7. Fisk, E. K. "Development Goals in Rural Melanesia." In M. W. Ward (ed.), Change and Development in Rural Melanesia. Canberra: The Australian National University (1972).

8. Harrison, G. A. and R. J. Walsh. "A Discussion of Human Adaptability in a Tropical Ecosystem: An I.B.P. Human Biographical Investigation of Two New Guinea Communities." Phil. Trans. Royal Soc. Lond. B. 268:221-400 (1974).

9. McArthur, Margaret. "Pigs for the Ancestors: A Review Article." Oceania XLV (2): 87-123 (1974).

10. Oomen, H.A.P.C. "Ecology of Human Nutrition in New Guinea: Evaluation of Subsistence Patterns." Ecology of Food and Nutrition 1: 3-18 (1971).

11. Papua New Guinea. Nutrition for Papua New Guinea. Port Moresby: Department of Public Health, Nutrition Section (1975).

12. Shankman, Paul. Migration and Underdevelopment: The Case of Western Samoa. Boulder, Colorado: The Westview Press (1976).

13. Tago, S., Lepani, C., and H. ToRobert. "A Population Policy for Papua New Guinea." IASER Discussion Paper No. 4. Port Moresby: Institute of Applied Social and Economic Research (1976).

14. van de Kaa, D. J. The Demography of Papua New Guinea's Indigenous Population. Ph.D. Dissertation for the Australian National University. Port Moresby: Government Printing Office (1971).

15. Watson, J. B. "From Hunting to Horticulture in the New Guinea Highlands." Ethnology 4: 295-309 (1965).

DIETARY CHANGE DURING ACCULTURATION AND ITS NUTRITIONAL EFFECT: THE CASE OF THE HIGHLAND GUATEMALAN INDIAN

Nancy Erwin

Department of Geography, Jackson State University

While the basic food problem many countries face today is one of finding sufficient calories to ward off starvation, adequate total nutrition for all the world's people is far more difficult and complex. It is doubly saddening then to see dietary changes that move from more to less adequacy. It would seem meaningful to examine how and why such changes occur, their connection with population pressures and the possibility of slowing or even eliminating these changes.

This study was conducted in the highland and west coast areas of Guatemala. The highlands are an area of traditional Indian culture with a subsistence agriculture base. Sizeable population densities have existed from pre-Columbian times,[1] and crafts and local trade have long supplemented agriculture.[2] However, dropping infant mortality coupled with a very high birth rate has led to great population pressure, reduced farm land, erosion and, in general, a search for new sources to sustain one's family.[3]

Several alternatives are available to these Indians, including lowland colonization to the east, urban migration, and seasonal and increasingly permanent movement to the coffee plantations of the west coast.[4] Migrant Indian labor has long been used to supplement local labor, thereby making permanent change somewhat easier for the reluctant but hard pressed Indians. They have been even slower to accept the other alternatives.

Detailed studies were carried out in two Indian communities, one traditional--Santo Domingo Xenacoj, one transitional--Chocola.[5] Xenacoj, a municipio in the central highlands, covers 40 square kilometers and has a population of about 2500. Accessibility is very limited. There is no electricity. The birth rate is 50/1000, the death rate 27/1000, an increase of 2.3% per year. Twenty-five percent of the population is under seven. Other municipios feel more pressure because their greater accessibility has brought medicine, sanitation, and less infant death.

Farm land is limited to about 11 square kilometers, with tiny plots scattered on up to thirty degree slopes, so rough is the topography. Farming is done by traditional hoe cultivation of corn and beans, with low yields. Livestock is rare, even chickens. A single cow or pig is slaughtered every ten days for public sale.

The diet of Xenacoj consists mainly of corn atoles, tortillas, and boiled greens, many picked wild. Small quantities of lime in the water used to soak corn, chile pepper, squash, dark brown sugar and a local corn-based beer add significantly to the nutrient intake. While this diet may seem limited, nutritional analysis of average portions of a healthy adult indicate that minimal requirements were met or exceeded for eight of nine basic nutrients. Only riboflavin intake, whose major dietary sources are eggs and dairy products, doesn't meet the minimum (see figure 1). These results may appear to be at odds with other studies which focus on child malnutrition; however, children's situations vary widely from those of adults.[6] This paper contends that over centuries the people of this area, even with limited technology, have adopted cultural patterns that generally serve their nutritional needs.

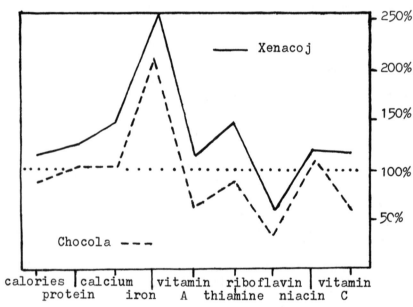

Figure 1. Diet Adequacy - Percent of Minimal Requirements

The second area, Chocola, is the major town on a government controlled coffee finca on the Pacific slopes. It covers 27 square kilometers and has three secondary towns. Fifty-eight percent of the
finca population of 4600 live in Chocola, and of these inhabitants,
80% identify themselves as Indians. Chocola is connected to a nearby
city by a bus that runs several times a day. Most houses have electricity. There are about a dozen stores that offer credit, and
meat is available daily. Liquor is illegal on the finca, but is sold
surreptitiously at high prices. Drunkenness is a problem. The birth
rate is 40/1000, the death rate 27/1000, an increase of 1.3% per year.
Perhaps this lower birth rate is explained by female hired labor and
unstable family structures. Twenty-two percent of the population is
under seven. Spanish is the language of store and street, Cakchiquel
of the home.

About 600 of the men are allowed to farm small plots, all in
corn, but none can sustain a family in spite of fertile soils. Most
of this corn, along with some chickens and pigs, is sold for cash.
The diet has more variety which is valued in itself. Foods available include white bread, white sugar, white rice, coffee, plantains,
meat, eggs, milk, some unripened cheese, and the highly prized canned
goods along with tortillas and beans. The cost of small amounts
of the former is paid by buying less of the latter. The use of
aguardiente, sugar liquor, eats up income and adds nothing but
calories. The adults of Chocola do not meet standards for five of
the nine nutrients: calories, Vitamin A, thiamine, riboflavin and
Vitamin C. Every single nutrient level is less than Xenacoj's.
Even total protein is less in spite of animal sources; Chocola--23%
of protein from animals, Xenacoj--7%. Figure 2 shows the contrasting
dietary sources for some selected nutrients.

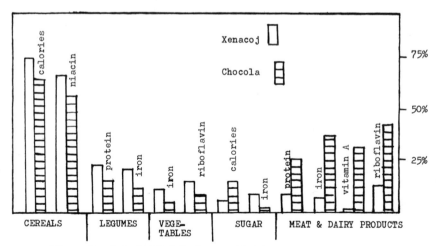

Figure 2. Selected Nutrients Provided by Five Food Groups
Xenacoj Compared to Chocola

345

The inhabitants of Chocola, while acknowledging their biological Indianness, show disdain for Indian ways and both envy and distrust their ladino neighbors. The obvious alteration in environment, work and language have broken up other traditional patterns including diet. When questioned about the purchase and use of specific foods, less than 20% referred to either nutritional value or personal preference. A healthy food usually meant a food purchased for a sick person.[7]

Most responses were social in nature. Two different attitudes affected food selection. The first concerns an attempt to not appear too rural, backward or Indian. For this reason, atoles, corn beer and wild greens are rejected. The women scorned picking "weeds." A second but related attitude is to show how modern, affluent and worldly one has become. This leads to the white bread, rice and sugar and especially the canned goods, a true status symbol. The people of Chocola understand that dietary change is a prestige item that is accessible, a financial possibility (though difficult) and demonstrated whenever shopping or eating. This is not the case with radios, bicycles, etc.

A people in transition become disoriented and many basic patterns alter (and suffer), particularly diet. This is probably even more true for those making an urban transition. Three basic points should be made in conclusion. First, population pressure is the major contributing cause of this transitional state. Second, as essential as diet and nutrition might seem to a scientifically educated American, status and personal worth, evidenced in whatever way possible, can assume great emptional importance. "Man does not live by bread alone." Third, to treat diet as an isolated element, separate from the entire culture in which it occurs, is futile. The outlook for the Guatemalan Indian is not good. Now is the time for the government here, and governments everywhere, to reassess priorities not only in the fields of birth control and food production but also in reinforcing or restructuring cultural patterns.

FOOTNOTES

1. T. T. Veblen, "Native Population Decline in Totonicapan, Guatemala," Annals of the Association of American Geography, vol. 67 (1977): 484-499.

2. N. Whetten, Guatemala: The Land and the People, New Haven, Conn., 1961.

3. O. H. Horst, "The Specter of Death in a Guatemalan Highland Community," Geographical Review, vol. 57 (1967): 151-167.

4. M. J. Frost, "La forma de poblamiento en Guatemala y los obstaculos culturales," La Geografia y Los Problemas de Desarrollo, vol. 2 (1966): 540-545. See also, J. R. Hildebrand, "Guatemalan Colonization Projects," Inter-American Affairs, vol. 19 (1966): 41-51; and R. N. Thomas, "The Migration System of Guatemala City: Spatial Inputs," Professional Geographer, vol. 24 (1972): 105-112.

5. The basic data for this paper is derived from the author's master's thesis which, in turn, largely used field studies and unpublished information from El Instituto de Nutricion de Centro America y Panama (INCAP). Nancy Erwin Rozman, Ecological Relationships of Diet and Nutrition in Three Areas of Guatemala, University of Florida, Gainesville, 1966.

6. P. R. Gould, and J. P. Sparks, "Geographical Context of Human Diets in Southern Guatemala," Geographical Review, vol. 59 (1969): 58-82.

7. R. N. Adams, "The Impact of Ladino-ization," in Social Change in Latin America Today, New York, 1960, 261-263.

THE ROLE AND RESPONSIBILITY OF AGRIBUSINESSES IN INTERNATIONAL FOOD PRODUCTION AND DISTRIBUTION[*]

David Balaam

Community and Organization Research Institute
University of California, Santa Barbara

Lately members of the international community have become sensitized to the effect that agribusiness firms, as part of increasing transnational business activity, have on the continued growth of the advanced nations and development of Less Developed Countries (LDCs).[1] This paper focuses on the influence agribusinesses have on global food distribution patterns. The structure of the international system does not include a well integrated global market or authoritative food regime that equitably distributes food.[2] Therefore, while the influence of agribusiness should not be overestimated as a viable solution to the world food problem, agribusinesses can be expected to play a more responsible and dominant role in future global food distribution processes, as part of investment and "diplomatic" objectives[3] of the advanced nations and development plans of LDCs.

Nearly 85% of the transnational agribusiness firms originate in the United States.[4] Before 1950, only a few of them had established foreign market positions, mainly in Canada, Argentina, Brazil, Uruguay, and parts of Central America. Since the mid-1960s they have grown in size domestically, and have horizontally integrated with and purchased facilities in Western Europe, Japan, all of Latin America, and are directing attention to the Middle East (see Table 1).[5] Their growth partially reflects four things: (1) an attempt to diversify overseas and thereby increase their competitiveness with domestic firms;[6] (2) an attempt to escape regulation at home; (3) changing political and economic conditions in host nations which are more receptive to them,[7] and (4) the attractiveness of increased per capita incomes in many LDCs and Western nations which have significantly altered dietary habits and generated a demand for more expensive and protein-rich foods.[8]

[*]This research is funded by the Rockefeller Foundation as part of a larger project entitled "The Political Economy of International Food Production and Distribution." Views expressed are those of the author. My thanks to my wife Debbie.

348

In order to lay a basis for policy recommendations, I have summarized below current research on the positive and negative effects
of agribusinesses on food production and distribution in the United
States and the LDCs.

The benefits of agribusiness to the United States are asserted
to be: (1) lower food costs to consumers between 1950-70, resulting
from the historical and economic process of organizing agriculture
into larger and more efficient economies of scale that (over) produce and more effectively market food; (2) as an integral part of
this continuing process, agribusinesses have been instrumental in
transforming American agriculture from labor to capital intensive
production and distribution and providing employment opportunities
in off-farm agribusiness industries; (3) since the mid-1960s, the
United States has benefited from increased agricultural production
which allows it to use grain company transactions and concessional
sales abroad to offset large balance of payments deficits.[9] Food
exports are needed by other nations as much as the United States
depends on them to fight inflation and maintain its political influence.[10]

The benefits of agribusinesses to LDCs are asserted to be:
(1) the stimulation of food transfers (much of the U.S. overproduction was used for P.L. 480 programs); (2) the transfer of technology,
managerial skills, marketing and production techniques;[11] (3) opportunities for employment, along with (4) additional national income
and foreign exchange accumulated from the sales of export crops.
The implied assumption is that agribusiness efficiency eventually
"spills over" and "trickles down" from the economic into other sectors, positively influencing political and social development.[12]
According to this view, agribusinesses have not been able to realize
their full potential for LDCs because host policy makers either dis-
criminate in favor of heavy industry or are suspicious of them for
political reasons.[13]

There is growing evidence to suggest that large economies of
scale are not the most efficient way to produce or distribute food,
nor are all the effects of agribusinesses on LDCs a positive influence on the total development of host nations.[14] Some agribusinesses
are more responsible than others.[15] The negative effects of agribusinesses in the U.S. and LDCs are asserted to be: (1) less efficient and more costly food production which does not realize the full
potential of labor-intensive agriculture, thereby displacing workers
and small farmers, and destroying the traditional institution of
farming in the U.S. and Latin America;[16] (2) this puts pressure on
urban centers for additional social services; (3) in the U.S.,
middlemen (food wholesalers, retailers, and advertisers) are accused
of causing high food prices and reaping excess profits in the face
of overproduction; (4) grain trading companies are accused of collu-
sion with the U.S. government to excessively profit from grain sales

349

(the Soviet wheat deals);[17] (5) agribusiness efficiency leads to overproduction and causes low farm prices and further displacement; (6) agribusiness externalities (e.g., air, water, land, and food pollution) are costs society cannot afford.

In LDCs: (7) many agribusinesses produce crops (e.g., strawberries, asparagus, tomatoes, bananas, sugar and coffee) that leave host countries dependent on export crops to earn foreign exchange, while many continue to import basic foodstuffs;[18] (8) agribusiness investment results in the consolidation of a transnational elite or commercial class around large-scale firms;[19] (9) this leaves the bottom two-thirds of the LDCs' poorest people still poorer as income is not being equitably distributed;[20] (10) agribusinesses do not substantially improve nutrition or alleviate hunger,[21] because (11) they focus their investment in high cost, low nutritional value, processed food items (e.g., Coca-Cola, hamburgers, fried chicken); (12) finally, they complicate ownership and land reform problems.[22]

Agribusinesses could effectively contribute to the total development of LDCs and still profit from LDC development if they considered in their investment strategies the economic, social, and political conditions of each nation.[23] I suggest that agribusinesses: (1) be more willing to invest on a Joint-Venture basis with LDC firms or governments;[24] (2) invest in areas where displacement is likely to be no greater than the number of people that can be employed elsewhere in that area; (3) encourage host governments to include in their development plans the agricultural sector as a primary force of development[25]--farmers are efficient producers when they have access to credit, technology, information,[26] etc.; (4) agribusinesses and host governments should promote and provide incentives for saving income, and cooperate in establishing supportive institutions that provide social services (e.g., health and education) to farm workers and the displaced; (5) agribusinesses should employ personnel to act as intermediaries who are familiar with both local conditions and the firm.

In one sense, food politics are not political enough, as the political and economic trade-offs to be decided upon by Congress and the American people are not fully understood.[27] In their formulation of regulatory standards, American policy makers are often forced by the question of agribusiness accountability to compromise a mix of economic and political influences and objectives. Congress can ensure agribusiness accountability both at home and abroad by: (1) taking a more positive stance toward liberalizing trade and commodity agreements that influence the amount of foreign exchange LDCs earn--the Lomé agreement is an encouraging example of a more desirable relationship of Rich to Poor nations; (2) confining food aid to short term crisis situations instead of using it as a dumping mechanism;[28] (3) encouraging food processing firms to produce more nutritional food at lower costs to local people. (4) Both

Congress and LDC governments can discourage displacement by indirect and direct measures of support to farmers. In the U.S., the Federal Trade Commission, aided by Congressional statutes and regulatory standards, can more aggressively ensure the competitiveness of agribusiness firms by emphasis on the breakup of "oligopoly" control over certain industries.[29] Consumers and economic efficiency benefit from competition. Likewise, (5) LDCs should encourage competitive investment in LDCs. Finally, (6) Congress should make all U.S. regulatory standards on inputs (e.g., pesticides, chemicals, fertilizers), food quality, packaging, pricing and labor applicable to U.S. agribusiness firms doing business overseas.

American agribusiness can expect to incur hostile reactions from LDCs for failing to be more responsible for the negative effects of their activity on host nations. LDC governments can expect the same reaction from within to national policies that do not do the same. Over the past fifteen years, there have been anti-government movements in Brazil, Guatemala, Ecuador, Costa Rica, El Salvador, Honduras, and Mexico. The cost of misunderstanding or indecision is continued malnutrition and even starvation in some areas of the world and a gradual erosion of American economic and social conditions which many have come to realize are dependent on a more equitable distribution of income, food, and goods and services to all.

FOOTNOTES

1. There is an abundance of material on the increasing role of transnational corporate investment. One of the more detailed is a history by Mira Wilkins, The Emergence of Multinational Enterprise: American Business Abroad from the Colonial Era to 1914 and also Ms. Wilkins' The Maturing Multinational Enterprise: American Business Abroad from 1914 to 1970, (Cambridge, Mass.: Harvard University Press, 1975). See also Richard Barnet and Ronald Muller, Global Reach, (New York: Simon and Schuster, 1974) and Abdul A. Said and Luiz R. Simmons, The New Sovereigns: Multinational Corporations as World Powers, (New Jersey: Prentice-Hall, 1975).

2. For a discussion of food markets and the global food regime, see Gary L. Seevers, "Food Markets and Their Regulation," and the rest of the articles in the upcoming issue of International Organization.

3. There are many current writings on the use of food to attain diplomatic objectives. One of the better ones is by Henry Nau, "The Diplomacy of World Food: Goals, Capabilities, Issues and Arena," in Ibid.

4. Thomas Horst, At Home Abroad: A Study of the Domestic and Foreign Operations of the American Food-Processing Industry, (Cambridge, Mass.: Ballinger Publishing, 1974).

5. See for example Japan's Fast-Food Industry: Export Potential for U.S. Products, USDA, FAS, (September, 1975) and M. H. Ghavamian, "New Approaches to Agricultural Development in Iran," in The Agribusiness Council, Agricultural Initiative in the Third World, (Lexington, Mass.: D. C. Heath and Co., 1975).

6. Horst, op. cit.

7. "Latin America Opens the Door to Foreign Investment Again," Business Week, (August 9, 1976).

8. This is discussed in Horst, op. cit. For an example of a speech focusing on what this means for agribusinesses see Robert H. Malott, "The World Food Equilibrium and Its Implications for American Agribusiness," in address before the Los Angeles Rotary Club, May 2, 1972.

9. For a brief summary of this trend, see Quentin M. West, "The U.S. Farmer in the International Food Situation," USDA, ERS, 651 (February, 1977).

10. Nau, "The Diplomacy of World Food . . ." op. cit., see also Charles Hanrahan and Richard Kennedy, "International Considerations in the Development of Domestic Agricultural and Food Policy," Agricultural-Food Policy Review, ERS, USDA, A-FPR-1, 1977.

11. J. David Morrisy, Agricultural Modernization Through Production Contracting: The Role of the Fruit and Vegetable Processor in Mexico and Central America, (New York: Praeger, 1974).

12. Ibid.

13. This view is not the view of all the authors, but represents a changing viewpoint of The Agribusiness Council, Agricultural Initiative in the Third World, op. cit.

14. Writings on this theme are popular and numerous. Some of the more radical are Michael Perelman, "Efficiency in Agriculture: The Economics of Energy," in Richard Merrill, Radical Agriculture, (New York: Harper and Row, 1977) and Cliff Connor, "Hunger: U.S. Agribusiness and World Famine," International Socialist Review, (September, 1974). More popular writings are Daniel Balz, "Exporting Food Monopolies," Progressive (January, 1975), Richard Barnet and Ronald Muller, "How Global Corporations Compound World Hunger," in Food for People, Not for Profit, (New York: Ballantine Books, 1975), Geoffrey

Barraclough, "Wealth and Power: The Politics of Food and Oil," New York Review of Books, (August 7, 1975), and Roger Burbach and Patricia Flynn, "Agribusiness Targets in Latin America," NACLA Report on the Americas, Vol. XII, No. 1, (Jan.-Feb., 1978). For more academic writings see Cheryl Christensen, "World Hunger: A Structural Approach," in International Organization, op. cit., and Frank Meissner, "Transfer of Marketing Technologies and the New International Economic Order," mimeo, paper for presentation Kansas State University Conference, (March, 1977).

15. There are signs that some agribusinesses are trying to reconcile corporate strategies with the conditional policies of host governments. Others aren't. See for example, "Dow banks on future growth," in Business Week, op. cit.

16. Sheldon Greene, "Corporate Accountability and the Family Farm," in Radical Agriculture, op. cit.

17. See for example, William Robbins, The American Food Scandal (New York: William Morrow & Co., 1974), James Trager, Amber Waves of Grain (New York: Arthur Fields Books, 1973), and for Congress's attempt to deal with the problem see Multinational Corporations and United States Foreign Policy, Hearings before the Subcommittee on Multinational Corporations, International Grain Companies (June, 1976).

18. NACLA Report on the Americas, op. cit.

19. Ibid.

20. Barnet and Muller, in Food for People, Not for Profit, op. cit.

21. NACLA Report on the Americas, op. cit.

22. Ibid.

23. James Grant, "A New Development Stragegy," in Food for People, Not for Profit, op. cit.

24. Many LDC governments are making this a condition for investment; see "Latin America Opens the Door . . ." Business Week, op. cit. For a discussion of this and other development problems see Denis Goulet, The Uncertain Promise: Value Conflicts in Technology Transfer, (New York: IDOC/North America, 1977).

25. Irma Adelman, Cynthia Morris, Sherman Robinson, "Policies for Equitable Growth," World Development, Vol. 4, No. 7 (1976).

26. James Grant, "A New Development Strategy," op. cit.

27. Leslie H. Gelb and Anthony Lake, Washington Dateline: "Less Food, More Politics," Foreign Policy, No. 17 (Winter 1974-75).

28. Controversy surrounding the negative effects of food aid on a long term basis in Bangladesh for example is discussed in McHenry and Bird, "Food Bungle in Bangladesh," Foreign Policy, No. 27 (Fall, 1977).

29. Compare discussion of the concentration of the food industry and government regulation in Dan Zwerdling, "The Food Monopolies," Progressive (January, 1975) with Kenneth R. Farrell, "Market Performance in the Food Sector," USDA, ERS, 653, 1977.

Table 1. Estimated Share of Foreign Assets in
Total Consolidated Assets of Various
Food-Processing Firms, 1971

Company Name	Share of Foreign Assets in Total (%)	Total 1971 Assets[c]
H. J. Heinz Company	49	753
The Coca-Cola Company	39	1107
William Wrigley, Jr. Company	25	163
Standard Brands, Inc.	23	697
Kellogg Company	23	378
General Foods Corporation	21[b]	1465
Libby, McNeill and Libby	21	268
National Biscuit Company	20	633
Pepsi-Cola Company	19	827
Carnation Company	19	594
National Dairy Products Corp.	18[b]	1163
California Packing Corp.	18	550
Beatrice Foods Company	16	934
Armour and Company	16	567
Hygrade Food Products Corporation	14	57
The Quaker Oats Company	13	423
The Borden Company	12	1257
Gerber Products Company	12	143
General Mills, Inc.	10	749
Campbell Soup Company	10[a]	667
Pet Milk Company	10[a]	391
Pillsbury Mills, Inc.	9	336
Swift and Company	7	869
Consolidated Foods Corporation	5[a]	781
Hershey Chocolate Corporation	5[a]	240
Oscar Mayer and Company, Inc.	5[a]	219
Stokely-Van Camp, Inc.	5[a]	167
Green Giant Company	5[a]	153
George A. Hormel and Company	5[a]	153
Campbell Taggart Associated Bakeries	1[a]	143
Iowa Beef Processors, Inc.	0	130
Fairmont Foods Company	0	118
American Bakeries Company	0	87
United Biscuit Company of America	0	63
The Rath Packing Company	0	40
Needham Packing Company	0	29

[a]Estimated

[b]Includes 5% imputed Canadian share

[c]Millions of dollars

Source: Horst, At Home Abroad, p. 102.

355

LAND REFORM, FOOD PRODUCTION, AND POPULATION GROWTH--IMPLICATIONS FOR U.S. POLICY

Jerald Ciekot

American Friends Service Committee

There are few absolutes in the realm of development, but some of the necessary conditions to increase food production and decrease birth rates are becoming clear. One of these is that the farmers have control over the land they work and derive the benefits of their labors.

If you consider the world's three major grain crops (rice, wheat, corn) for every country with five hundred thousand hectares or more planted, and compare this with the predominant system of agricultural production in each (i.e., whether it is owner-operated, tenant-operated under a landlord, or collectivized) you get some rather startling results:

1. In no nation of the world with a tenancy system have additional agricultural inputs significantly sustained increased food productivity.
2. Moreover, the most productive systems (in terms of output per hectare) are those organized on the basis of small owner-operators; and,
3. The most productive landlord system is less than 50% as productive as the most successful small-owner system.

Tenancy has proven to be an iron-bound constraint on increases in productivity. There are tens of millions of small farms in the less developed countries on which crucial productivity-increasing im - provements (such as irrigation works, ground leveling, water abatement projects, pond building, weed control, etc.) need to be made; but they have not been. The biggest part of the reason why is tenancy. Such essential improvements may mean at best an increase in rent, giving the landlord most of the benefits. Even worse, the landlord may decide to bestow this newly attractive piece of land on a favorite relative.

Moreover, without the fundamental motivation supplied through farmer control, the benefits of new technology, credit, extension services, and marketing support accomplish very little. In the

Philippines, for example, where the "green revolution" technology was widely disseminated, the results are particularly disheartening. After one small jump in productivity between 1968 and 1970 when the new technology and associated support were first introduced, production has yet to break through extremely modest levels.

But our concern is not simply with producing more food, but rather with a structure of food production that increases security, raises income, and significantly enhances general well-being, thus removing the necessity to seek security in a large family. Owner-operators (and those with owner-like tenure) are quick to make the improvements necessary to increase productivity. With more food to put in their children's bowls and more resources to spend on preventive health measures in the village (safe water, sanitation, vaccinations) they quickly find that fewer of their children are dying than in the low-productivity, high rent and physically unhealthy villages of the tenant-farmer. In addition, they have the old age insurance of assured tenure of their land. This combination of reasonably assured survival for their children and newly found old age security, assisted by health and education resources, provides the basis for the first time for a family decision to have fewer children. Family planning can now take hold and birth rates decline substantially.

In support of this common-sense argument, an examination of the infant mortality and crude birth rates for every nation with a population of one million or more reveals that: birth rates have never declined in the absence of a sharp decline in infant mortality rates (there is some evidence that this is true for regions within nations as well); and, this process is sequential with the drop in infant mortality preceding the drop in birth rates. The evidence suggests that having babies is by-and-large a deliberate, thought-through process even for the poor.

Although the U.S. cannot make decisions for other governments, we need not be passive or neutral on issues which signal life or death for so many. No government is homogeneous, and strong advocacy cannot be ignored.

But besides advocacy we can distinguish several other opportunities for directing our foreign assistance:

1. In countries where land reform has been largely accomplished, our assistance is needed for such inputs as: small farmer credit, training, extension services, health and education services.
2. In countries where there is already official commitment to land reform and labor intensive small-farmer development, U.S. aid geared to enhance such efforts can be decisive, especially if there is major opposition.

357

3. In countries where there is currently little or no commitment to basic reforms, the U.S. should be careful not to find itself funding projects that enable these governments to ignore or repress legitimate internal pressure for egalitarian development. To uncritically support such projects encourages government circumvention of needed reform and heightens the possibility of violence.

But the U.S. could do more. There is currently circulating in Washington a proposal for a Global Equity Fund. This fund would be designed to enable governments carrying out effective land reform programs to reimburse the current land owners for land they would lose under the reform effort. In so doing, one of the major impediments in many nations to successful reform efforts, landlord resistance, would be substantially weakened, if not overcome.

We should not forget that what the U.S. does, or fails to do, makes a difference. Championing this proven model of grass-roots development could be expected to affect both rich and poor. Immediate participants in such projects are obvious beneficiaries. Focused U.S. initiatives would also encourage other donor nations and multilateral agencies along this same route.

REFERENCES

1. Murdoch, William W. and Allan Oaten. "Population and Food: Metaphors and the Reality," Bio Science, Vol. 25, No. 9, Sept. 1975.

2. Paige, Jeffrey M. Agrarian Revolution--Social Movements and Export Agriculture in the Underdeveloped World, Free Press, NY, 1975.

3. Pohoryles, Samuel and Arieh Szesking, "Land Tenure and Economic Growth in Africa," Land Reform: Land Settlement and Cooperatives, FAO, 1975.

4. Prosterman, Roy L. and Charles A. Taylor, Hunger, Poverty, Desperation and Chaos, draft manuscript, Washington University School of Law, June 1976. See also Roy Prosterman, "Does More Food Mean More Babies (As Garrett Hardin Suggests) Or Fewer?" in Key Issues in Population Policy, ed. Eliot Glassheim, Charles Cargille and Charles Hoffman, University Press of America, Washington, D.C., 1978.

5. Stokes, Bruce. "Local Responses to Global Problems: A Key to Meeting Basic Human Needs," Worldwatch Paper 17, Worldwatch Institute, February 1978.

6. Thiesenhusen, William and Marion Brown. Survey of the Alliance for Progress: Problems of Agriculture, University of Wisconsin Land Tenure Center, December 1976.

THE POLITICS OF FOOD ASSISTANCE IN THE NINETEENTH CENTURY: VENEZUELA, 1812

Bernard J. Ulozas Jr.

Department of History, Carnegie-Mellon University

Contemporary studies of American diplomatic policy often include a chapter which focuses on the humane concerns of Americans and their government for the plight of distressed nations. During the 19th Century, disasters, accompanied by famines, occurred throughout the world, and some Americans felt a need to respond. In most cases, religious groups directed limited relief efforts for the starving victims. Private donations of provisions would be collected by various congregations, and the supplies would be shipped to the disaster area for distribution.

However, an expressed desire by groups of American citizens, encouraging the federal government to feed starving victims in foreign lands, reached the halls of Congress on more than one occasion in the 19th Century. This desire by private citizens to enlist the government as an agent of national humanitarian response represented a dramatic departure from the norm of totally private action.

The first recorded discussion of disaster-related food aid from the United States government for a foreign nation occurred in 1812. On March 26 of that year an earthquake leveled sections of Caracas, Venezuela and surrounding villages. The initial tremor killed "from 8,000 to 12,000," and "over 30,000 perished in the weeks that followed."[1] News of the tragedy traveled rapidly and "reached the United States with the arrival at Baltimore of the schooner Independence on April 23, 1812."[2]

Six days later, Representative Nathaniel Macon of North Carolina introduced a bill into the House of Representatives calling for the relief of the citizens of Caracas. Macon's resolution also included a provision for the relief of the citizens of Teneriffe, in the Canary Islands. Macon requested the Committee of Commerce and Manufactures to authorize President James Madison to purchase "barrels of flour and to have the same exported to some port in Caracas, for the use of the inhabitants who have suffered by the earthquake and to have the same exported to some port in Teneriffe for the use of the inhabitants who are likely to starve by the ravages of locusts."[3]

Congressional debates largely concerned the reliability of reports from the affected areas and the exact amount of money which
would be appropriated for the mission. Legislators generally expressed humanitarian concerns in suggesting approval for Macon's resolution. Representative John C. Calhoun of South Carolina envisaged
the bill as an opportunity "to aid the cause of humanity."[4] Representative John Randolph of Virginia sympathized with the "wretched
and unfortunate" people of Caracas, but inferred that a suspension
of the restrictive trade agreements between the two nations might
better relieve the long-term suffering in Venezuela. Randolph proposed an amendment to Macon's resolution, which later failed to
pass, "to authorize vessels laden with provisions to clear out for
any port of the aforesaid country."[5] In objecting to the proposed
amendment, Calhoun criticized Randolph's intransigent manner "as
not comporting with the sacred cause of distant and oppressed humanity."[6]

The first provision of Macon's resolution, relating to the
people of Caracas, passed unanimously. The remaining proposal, which
would grant aid to the people at Teneriffe, failed to pass. In the
latter case, Congressmen felt that unconfirmed reports of the impending famine did not constitute sufficient evidence, that privately
chartered vessels already had sailed to Teneriffe with provisions,
and that diplomatic relations with Venezuela superceded those with
the Canary Islands.

Randolph, however, offered a resolution which would delegate
the Committee of Commerce and Manufactures to "inquire whether any,
and what, relief ought to be extended to the inhabitants of the
Canary Islands, who are suffering by famine occasioned by locusts."[7]
The resolution passed, since it proposed only an inquiry, but on May
22, 1812, Representative Thomas Newton of Virginia, a member of the
Committee, reported that limited evidence from the Canary Islands
did not merit a full investigation.

Macon's resolution received Congressional approval on May 8,
1812. In final form the bill authorized the President to purchase
"such provisions as he shall deem advisable," and allocated $50,000
for the entire relief effort.[8]

American interest in Venezuelan affairs had been expressed at
least two years prior to the earthquake when rumblings of opposition
to Spanish rule in favor of a national government fomented civil
strife. In fact, royalist propaganda immediately following the
earthquake suggested that this calamity signified God's anger at the
opposition forces. Therefore, Congressional reaction indicated a
combination of humanitarian and political concerns. Some legislators undoubtedly were moved by a religious mandate to feed the
hungry. Apparently, this mission of mercy also "advanced the promotion of national interest in the Caribbean, toward which maritime
interests had been looking with anticipation of a brisk trade."[9]

The actual mechanics of distributing food to starving people seems to have escaped Congressional scrutiny. Of the "4,272 barrels of flour and 2,728 bushels of corn [that] were purchased and transported at the cost of $47,840.73,"[10] royalist forces stole "upwards of 3,000 barrels of flour" and resold them for over $100,000.[11] Furthermore, the six vessels which had been leased by the American government to transport the provisions to Venezuela were impounded by Spanish authorities. When the vessels returned to port, "the American authorities found that they had been so looted and damaged as to be of little value to their owners."[12] Still, Macon's resolution established a precedent for later use by those who would propose and oppose relief measures in the future for other starving human beings.

FOOTNOTES

1. Harold C. Bierck, Jr., "The First Instance of U.S. Foreign Aid: Venezuelan Relief in 1812," Inter-American Affairs, Vol. IX, No. 1, summer, 1955, p. 48.

2. Merle Curti, American Philanthropy Abroad: A History, (New Brunswick, New Jersey, Rutgers University Press, 1964), p. 10.

3. U.S. Congress, House, Annals of the Congress of the United States, 12th Cong., 1st sess., 1812, pp. 1348-1352.

4. Ibid., p. 1348.

5. Ibid., p. 1348.

6. Ibid., p. 1349.

7. Ibid., p. 1352.

8. Ibid., p. 2294.

9. Op. cit., Curti, p. 11.

10. E. Taylor Parks, "Foreign Aid--150 Years Ago," Foreign Service Journal, July, 1962, p. 39.

11. Op. cit., Bierck, p. 57.

12. Op. cit., Curti, p. 12.

REGIONAL FOOD PRODUCTION SYSTEMS:
A DECENTRALIST APPROACH

James R. Nolfi

Goddard College, Plainfield, Vermont

George C. Burrill

Center for Studies in Food Self-Sufficiency

Food production at the present time is largely related to a complex and increasingly fragile network of inter-relationships. This system is highly centralized in its control aspects, and is organized on an international basis. Consequently, the paradoxical situation may obtain wherein an agricultural region or nation faces the threat or actualization of food shortages in high production years, simply because the food production/consumption system has become unresponsive at the local level. A cash crop is produced on the largest portion of the arable land, perhaps linked through balance of payments to the national leadership's aspirations for industrialization. The crop is successful, and profitable to a small percentage of the population who act as absentee landlords, yet those who produce the crop cannot produce their own food, and are dependent on exogenous sources for their survival. The pattern has repeated itself through literally thousands of years of recorded history, and widely over the face of the globe.

Contemporary food production and distribution systems have become increasingly dependent on fossil fuels and other limited, or restricted resources. When this is combined with the increasing "disorganization" of the international control system, through rising nationalism in the Third World, and the resistance to "neo-colonialism" exemplified by OPEC's 1973 oil embargo, one begins to see a potentially frightening picture.

We propose that strong evidence can be mustered to question the continued viability of this centralized international monetary/market approach to food. The underlying but often unexamined tenets may no longer be valid. The notion of "comparative advantage" is being challenged by serious economists. A more regional, integrated food production/consumption system can be developed, wherein the range of foods eaten in a region represent principally what is produced in that

362

region. Parenthetically, except in the center of the few major empires that have existed in the millenia of recorded history, and within the last twenty years in the developed world, this has been the production/consumption system.

We began in 1974 to develop methodologies for development of regional production systems, and in 1976 published Land, Bread and History which summarized this work on the state of Vermont. The approach consists simply of a holistic analysis of the food production/consumption system. How many people are there in the region? What, and how much of each commodity do they eat in a given time period? What is the potential quantitatively and qualitatively for the land to produce food and forage crops? What resources would be required to produce the food on available land? What sort of marketing and distribution system is necessary to get the product to the consumer, and materials to the producer?

The techniques to approach answers to these questions are varied. An analysis of the history of change in agriculture in Vermont revealed that external market changes, often related to changes in transportation technology, were the most significant factor. Historical analysis also revealed an immense diversity of types and amounts of commodities produced. This stands in stark contradiction to the present monocrop picture of fluid milk in Vermont agriculture.

Analysis of a variety of sources, including detailed data on supermarket sales by commodity, allowed us to determine the per capita consumption by commodity. Comparison with potential crops and present food choices indicated that climate and topography would restrict diet only in a few cases.

A computer analysis of physical production potential for major crops indicated that all the food needed for the present population of Vermont (456,000) could be produced on 479,000 acres--53% of the Class I farmland or 21.5% of the combined Class I and II farmland in the state. The other farmland could be utilized for other crops, i.e., fiber, biomass for fuel, or "export" crops.

This exercise demonstrated the physical feasibility of linking production and consumption--in an area with "poor farmland," short growing season, and without asking consumers to radically change diet. The exercise utilized "conventional" agricultural techniques which conceivably could be modified to increase yields.

This approach need not result in "parochialism" or isolation, but in greater local self-reliance, increased vitality of rural areas, and increased national stability, as we may conclude from the experiences of the People's Republic of China. Modern communication technologies mitigate against isolation, and the relationship of the self-sufficient production/consumption unit to the greater whole can not be ignored. Clearly, systems theory, the paradigm of the emerging scientific revolution, demonstrates repeatedly that the "whole is greater than the sum of its parts." Such an approach might therefore bring greater good to greater numbers of persons, and would thereby have an unquestioned stabilizing effect at the international level. Quite frankly, the underlying values of the authors support this concern more strongly than concern for stability in the international monetary/marketplace, or profits and control for the privileged few.

THE COSTS AND BENEFITS OF FOOD SUPPLY STABILIZATION

Brian D. Wright

Department of Economics, Yale University

Every person who regularly pushes a cart through a supermarket checkout knows that food prices fluctuated wildly in the early 1970s. The worldwide economic havoc associated with recent food supply problems has made the question of food market stability an important policy issue.

Since the variance of the world supply of grains, the main staples, is small relative to production trends, and since the product is storable, it is natural to look to a buffer stock storage scheme as a means of market stabilization. However, economists have been rather critical of buffer stock proposals on several grounds.

Though there is now a consensus among economists that storage is an economically desirable activity, there is much less agreement that public intervention in storage activity is necessary or desirable. Further, simulation studies which take the response of private storage activity into account indicate that the costs of such schemes may well outweigh the benefits. The above objections become less daunting if the alternative to national or international storage schemes is not the free market, but the haphazard uncoordinated and often very costly market intervention of national governments, for thoroughly acceptable distributional reasons, which occurs in almost all countries when food prices reach extreme values.

In the brief space allowed here, I will concentrate on another difficulty with international grain storage scheme proposals, namely, the question of the distribution of costs and benefits of supply stabilization.

Both theoretical stabilization studies and storage scheme simulations have implied that serious difficulties may be experienced in obtaining international cooperation in a stabilization scheme. Since the seminal work of Massell (1969), the consensus of the theoretical studies of stabilization has been that in the standard linear demand and supply model, with additive supply disturbances, the net gain to society from supply stabilization is half

365

the gain to the producers, while consumers welfare losses equal the net gain. For demand disturbances, the reverse situation holds. Though different results have been demonstrated for nonlinear demand curves (Turnovsky, 1976), most storage scheme simulations (see Stein and Smith, 1977, for a review) reflect the gloomy conclusion that the interests of consumers and producers in stabilization are in direct conflict.

However, in a recent paper (Wright, 1978) I have shown that if producers are rational in their production decisions and in their formation of expectations, both producers and consumers may gain in a simple theoretical supply stabilization model, for a wide range of parameter values. In the linear case, stabilization is mutually beneficial if the long run supply elasticity exceeds the demand elasticity.

Given rationality, stabilization changes equilibrium output, even if the economic agents are risk-neutral, and this output change reduces the difference between the effects of stabilization on producers and consumers. The next step in this line of research is to incorporate this effect in a dynamic programming model, which can be used to analyze the costs and benefits of specific buffer stock storage schemes. Such an analysis should compare such schemes to the realistic alternative of haphazard uncoordinated and often very costly governmental market interventions, rather than to some rational free market situation.

Though I can see a real potential for conflict between the interests of producers in different regions in a more realistic, multi-country model, the results derived in this simple model lead me to take a more optimistic view of the chances of persuading the international community that we should act together to counter the wayward forces of nature.

On the other hand, no one familiar with previous commodity stabilization schemes should have any illusions as to the difficulty of designing and operating such schemes efficiently, free of the crippling influence of special interests. The alternative, however, is to leave the world community exposed to the possibility of larger shortages and greater economic disruption if the benevolent weather record of the past two decades reverts to the less stable historical norm, or if the margin of production is pressed to more risky areas as population increases. Now, in a possibly brief respite of relative abundance, we should undertake the research and design the institutions required to provide a safer barrier against the vagaries of nature.

REFERENCES

1. Massell, Benton F. "Price Stabilization and Welfare," *Quarterly Journal of Economics*, 73, No. 2, May 1969, 284-298.

2. Stein, John Picard and Rodney Topper Smith. A Report Prepared for the Council on International Economic Policy, Rand Corporation, Report R-1861-CIEP, Santa Monica, California, March 1977.

3. Turnovsky, Stephen J. "The Distribution of Welfare Gains from Price Stabilization: The Case of Multiplicative Disturbances," *International Economic Review*, 17, 1976, 133-148.

4. Wright, Brian D. "The Effects of Ideal Production Stabilization: A Welfare Analysis under Rational Behavior." Yale University, January 1978.

"EXCESSIVE" FOOD CONSUMPTION AND WORLD
FOOD SUFFICIENCY

Peter Svedberg

Institute for International Economic Studies
University of Stockholm

This note analyzes the link between what may be called "excessive" food consumption in the rich countries and food insufficiency in the poor countries in different time perspectives.

The Short Run. In this perspective--a year or so--there is
a significant causal relationship between food (meat) consumption
in the rich countries and the availability of food (grains) in the
poor countries, but only under rather special circumstances. This
is when (1) a global crop failure occurs in a year when (2) grain
reserves are insufficient, e.g., 1972/73 and 1974/75. In such a
situation, almost all countries try to secure a stable domestic
consumption level and price of food through trade interferences.
All countries, however, cannot succeed in securing a stable domestic consumption through trade simultaneously since short-run global
supply is given. The least affluent net-importing countries with
meager foreign exchange reserves are apt to be the losers when
world market grain prices go up. These countries (on the Indian
Subcontinent and in the Sahel area) are also the most vulnerable
to domestic food shortages. In order to relieve the food insufficiency in these countries effectively, it may be necessary to
reduce grain (meat) consumption in the rich countries, either
through rationing or through taxes on food (or reduced subsidies).

Food aid is not an efficient means of helping the poor countries out in the situation discussed. Since supply is assumed
given, food aid has to compete for the available quantities on the
world market, where prices will go up, forcing some countries to
reduce their imports; this is how the aid quantities are made
available. As before, the countries affected will probably be the
poorest ones which are also most vulnerable to reduced food imports.
Food aid may thus, to a large extent, only reshuffle food among
and within the poor countries, and it is not certain that the reshuffle will favor the most needy sections of the population in
the Third World.

The Long Run. In this perspective--a few decades--a reduction
in food (meat) consumption in the rich countries would not do much
to relieve food insufficiency in the poor countries. As hamburgers
cannot fly, the only way in which the poor, net-importing countries
can gain is through lower world market prices of grains. That is,
a drop in demand would make the marginal, high-cost grain production in the world unprofitable (cet par), output would fail, and so
would the average production cost and price. However, even a
drastic reduction of the rich countries' use of grains for feed,
say by one half (about 200 mmt today), would not lower prices by
more than 10% if the long-run aggregate supply elasticity is of the
order suggested in the literature (1.5-2.0). A 10% drop of the
world-market price of grains today would entail a terms-of-trade
improvement to the poor countries corresponding to at the most $1
billion annually, or about 0.1% of their GDP. Let alone its un-
likeliness, altered food habits in the rich countries thus seem to
be a very drastic and inefficient way of transferring $1 billion
to the LDCs. Even more important, there is no guarantee that the
governments in the net-importing poor countries would use the additional incomes to improve the situation for the poor and starving
population in their countries--the aim usually advanced by those
advocating simpler food consumption habits in rich countries.

The Very Long Run. Considering the world's capability to feed
its population in this perspective, the worst that can happen is
that the population in the LDCs continues to grow at precedented
rates. If this happens, and if no revolutionary technological breakthrough in agriculture occurs, the supply could become inelastic in
the very long run. The question is for how long supply could keep
pace with a rapidly growing population in the LDCs before this
happens. If this time span is short, a substantial reduction of
grain consumption in the DCs could be a means of improving or preserving food standards in the LDCs. If the time span is long, the
DCs' share of world grain consumption will probably be so small
that even a major cut in their share would only marginally improve
the situation in the LDCs.

The DCs' share of world grain consumption has decreased from
64 to 51% between 1934 and 1970. According to FAO projections,
the share will have declined to 44% by 1990 (Figure 1). As per
capita consumption of meat in all the rich countries by then will
have reached the for decades stagnant U.S. level, there is reason
to believe that the rich countries' share will fall even faster
in the years after 1990. Drastically reduced population growth
rates in DCs during the last decade also corroborates this notion.

If population in the LDCs continues to grow rapidly--the major threat to future world food sufficiency--the DCs' share of a
total world grain consumption, about three times as large as the
present one, will fall below 25% around 2030-2040. If, at that
time, the rich countries' consumption is cut in half and the grains

369

Figure 1: DCs' Share of World Grain Consumption;
Actual Data 1930 - 1970, Projections 1970 - 2030

Percent

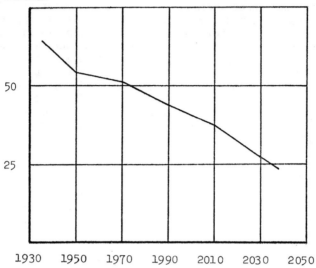

freed are transferred to the poor countries, in one way or the
other, these countries' consumption can only be increased by some
17%. It would then take only about seven years before the increase
is (literally) eaten up through further population increase. After that there is no way in which the poor countries' consumption
can increase (since supply is assumed inelastic) and their population will stagnate due to increased rates of mortality.

Finally, the important empirical question: can world cereal
production be increased three times before the production ceiling
is hit, i.e., when the supply turns very inelastic? A thorough
review of the literature suggests that the present effective production level can be increased many times over, even with present-
day technology, through productivity increases resulting from
institutional reform, by the use of additional physical inputs and
new varieties of seeds, etc., through bringing more land under
cultivation, and by reducing the spoilage and waste that occur in
all stages of production between harvesting and final consumption.

The above analysis leads us to conclude that if ever the food
situation of the world's poor hinges upon the availability of additional resources for the production of food, a major redistribution
of the quantities consumed in DCs will do very little to relieve

370

the food situation in LDCs. This is because, at that time, the DCs' share of world food consumption will probably be too small to free the quantities needed to really aid the poor. A reduction of food consumption in the rich countries can only in the very short run, and under rather special circumstances, be warranted as a means of relieving food insufficiency in the poor countries.

POLICIES FOR LESSENING WORLD FOOD DEFICITS

Doeke C. Faber, Earl O. Heady, and Steven C. Griffin

Center for Agricultural and Rural Development, Iowa State University

Organizations and leaders of the nation seemingly go through a frenzy cycle relative to the world food situation. We build ourselves to a high pitch of concern during periods of crop shortfalls in some world regions when grain supplies decline and hunger and malnutrition intensify. Then, when normal weather returns, grain supplies increase and prices in the United States soften, our concerns fade away as farmers favor programs which will reduce domestic food production and bolster farm incomes.

We were at the peak of the frenzy cycle in 1952 at the time of the "fifth plate scare," in 1966-67 with crop shortfalls on the India subcontinent and again in 1974-76 with the Russian and African droughts. But following each of these upswings in concern, we soon backed away and initiated programs to reduce food supplies. Currently, wheat farmers are invited to reduce plantings by 20% and feed grain producers by 10% for 1978. Nationally, it appears that we are again in the trough of the frenzy cycle. However, there is need for sustained attention to the world's food problems. We lack long-run solutions because the frenzy is so transitory.

There has been much speculation as to whether world agriculture can produce food at levels sufficient to maintain health in all countries at satisfactory levels. Because grain is the dominant component of world food consumption, a great deal of discussion has centered on the distribution of grains among uses and countries. There also has been great concern about the role of livestock in the world food system. The use of livestock to consume grain and produce food also has been subject to criticism. This paper emphasizes grain and the extent to which recommended nutrition levels can be attained worldwide under various alternatives affecting its production and distribution.

We estimated world food demands and requirements for the year 1980 under alternative conditions of consumption, production, and exports. Estimates include analysis of U.S. production and export capacity as a contribution to solving the world's food problems.

Alternative A: all-out exports

In Alternative A, U.S. exports increase 42% over the 1973-75 historically high levels. The amount of grain for export generated in this alternative is not enough to satisfy estimated world needs. A projected 58 million tons world grain deficit still exists. This deficit would leave about 375 million people, most of whom are located in less-developed countries with per capita incomes of less than $600, in a state of hunger or malnutrition.

Alternative B: consumption at recommended levels for all countries

In Alternative B, consumption for poor countries is increased to recommended levels, consumption for rich countries is reduced to it. The world food gap could be bridged under this condition. Relative to Alternative A, U.S. exports fall by 13% since a sizable reduction of consumption occurs in the other developed importing nations. These reductions more than outweigh the increase in imports to developing countries as their level of nutrition is raised.

Alternative C: consumption at recommended levels for the low-income countries

In Alternative C, perhaps a more feasible alternative, people in the developing countries (with incomes of less than $600 per capita) consume at daily recommended allowance levels while the other countries demand food as economic variables permit. Total world food requirements are greatest under these conditions. Alternative C shows a world food deficit of 113 million tons of grain and emphasizes the problems of poor nations faced with bidding for short grain supplies against rich importing countries.

Alternative D: 25% reduction in meat consumption

Alternative D includes a 25% reduction of meat consumption by the industrialized countries to free productive resources that can be used in the production of grains for human consumption. United States exports under this alternative increase by 18% relative to the base alternative. Relative to Alternative A, world grain deficits are reduced by 26 million tons. More than 200 million people would still have diets falling short of the recommended levels.

The results of this analysis contain a number of implications for a world food policy. The first implication is that U.S. agriculture (and large exporting countries in general) has a large capacity to produce grains. A second is that a reallocation of grain among consuming methods and countries could be effective in making more grain available for countries suffering malnutrition. A third implication is the fact that of the four alternatives studied, only one (Alternative B) would allow an adequate nutritional level in all countries.

The world food deficit is not a self-correcting problem, at least in the immediate future. Alleviation of hunger and malnutrition would require a strong world food policy. Extra-market policies would need to be implemented to distribute food to countries which need it but can't afford it. Also a successful food policy would need to provide countries with proper incentives to farmers of both exporting and importing nations.

Implementation of a food policy can be accomplished through either voluntary action, public market mechanisms, or government decree. A public market mechanism might be the most feasible alternative. If a strong market institution were created to purchase grain and, consequently, bid up grain prices, the purchased grain could be redistributed among the poor countries. At the same time, the higher grain prices would cause increased grain production, negating previous arguments that in the long run the grain supply would dry up due to low prices. A large world fund would, of course, be needed for these purposes. Also, it would be necessary for the world to have a long-run commitment to producing, storing and distributing food in a manner possible with current and prospective resources and technology. The concern must be more than cyclical and transitory.

DEMAND APPROACH TO WORLD FOOD RESERVES[*]

Jonathan J. Lu

University of Northern Iowa, Cedar Falls, Iowa

There is at present seemingly an irony in the world food situation. On the one hand, the shadow of the "world food crisis" a few years ago, which alarmed us into advocating "all out production," is still pretty much with us. On the other hand, we are now, in this country, facing a "farming crisis" as manifested in the recent farmer strike movement in which some even advocate "all production out." This irony seems to have been caused by the absence of a correct philosophy to guide food policies, especially in the area of reserves.

The fact that food reserve is an urgent matter may be seen in the actions by the FAO, in response to the recent "world food crisis," to propose a "minimum level of world food security" (1973), and by the U.S. Department of Agriculture to discuss short-run and long-run food security (1974, 40-47).

But food security is not a simple matter of putting food in storage, as it was recommended to the Pharaoh of Egypt, "that food shall be for store . . . against famine . . . that the land perish not . . ." (Genesis 41:36). Thus, the wisdom of Joseph which saved the world of old may not be wholly applicable to the 20th Century. Several questions must first be answered, such as: What quantities? how shall they be stored (and at what cost)? and for whom are they stored (cf Halcrow 1977, 1-19)? and who will be in charge?

Emphases in world food economy have traditionally been lopsided on the production side. The success in the late 1960s and early 1970s, with weather cooperating, has increased world food production ahead of population (USDA 1973, 44-50). This was especially true in the developed Western World and Japan which, ironically, were also burdened by huge carryovers and high costs of

---

[*]Financial support of the University of Northern Iowa toward the presentation of this paper is hereby acknowledged. I am indebted to Professors Basheer K. Nijim and Roy Chung for their helpful comments on an earlier draft of this paper.

storage. There arose, therefore, a desire among these countries to slow down the increase in food production. The slowdowns, coupled with vagaries of weather, contributed to the dwindling of world grain stocks in the mid-1970s, which then alarmed the world with a food "crisis," and the United States into advocating "all out production." Interestingly, it is also the result of this emphasis on production which is now plaguing the United States with sagging grain prices, and causing a "farming crisis" which drums up the farmer strike movement.

This paper, prescribing a "demand approach" to world food reserve, is based on the belief that consumption is the basic stimulant which generates demand and hence determines the level of production; that production, at its optimal level, should equal the level of consumption plus an appropriate amount of reserve; and that the optimum level of demand sets the ceiling for rational production. When production is rationalized, there should only be consumptive demand plus reserve demand without undue carryovers (Lu, 1971, 2-4).

A model, formulated by Lu and Morrill (1976) to deal with the spatial levels of world food reserve, is modified here to give emphasis on the demand approach to world food reserve. Let eR_t = estimated current optimum food reserve; eP_t = estimated current food production; oR_{t-1} = observed food reserve in the previous year; eS_t = estimated current food supply; eK_t = estimated current optimal minimum food consumption; oK_{t-1} = observed food consumption in the previous year; eN_t = estimated current per capita nutritional level; ePo_t = estimated current mid-year population; L_t = current land and other resources available for food production; T_t = current level of technology in food production; W_i = weather trend (i = t, t-1, . . . t-5); and

$$eK_t = f (eP_t, eN_t \cdot ePo_t, oR_{t-1}, oK_{t-1}) \dots \dots (1)$$

$$eP_t = f (oR_{t-1}, oK_{t-1}, L_t, T_t, W_i) \dots \dots (2)$$

whereas,

$$eS_t = eP_t + OR_{t-1} \dots \dots (3)$$

$$eK_t = eS_t - eR_t \dots \dots (4)$$

When emphasis is heavily placed on production, the attitude toward reserve is likely to be non-positive which, as a consequence is likely to lead toward either not enough reserve to ward off a food crisis or over production to depress grain prices. By taking the demand approach toward optimum reserve, the above problems could at least be alleviated, if not eliminated. For this reason, equation (4) should be rewritten as

$$eR_t = eS_t - eK_t \dots \dots (5)$$

Since eR_t takes into account all the variables defined above, it is treated as the optimum reserve. Expressed in concrete terms, the amount of eR_t, in my opinion, should be equal to one-fourth of eK_t. This is so because most crops are harvested in three to five months, and because grain harvests in different parts of the world span widely in a given year.

With eK_t and eR_t being estimated, the world then can plan for optimal production which allows no undue quantity of surplus to lower grain prices and to endanger farming. With the right amount of eR_t in storage, the world would always have enough food to tide itself over whether in rainy or droughty days.

However, equation (5) brings us to face three different degrees of effort. When,

$eS_t - eK_t > 0$, no difficulties to put eR_t in store;

$eS_t - eK_t = 0$, efforts are needed to put eR_t aside;

$eS_t - eK_t < 0$, reserves of previous year must be used to fend off a crisis, and it must be replenished as soon as possible.

BIBLIOGRAPHY

1. FAO. World Food Security: Proposal of the Director General. Rome, 1973.

2. Halcrow, Harold G. Food Policy for America. New York: McGraw-Hill Book Company 1977.

3. Lu, Jonathan J. The Demand for United States Rice: An Economic· Geographic Analysis. Dissertation. University of Washington, Seattle, 1971.

4. _____ and Morrill, Richard L. On the Spatial Levels of World Food Reserve. Paper presented at the 23rd International Geographical Congress. Moscow, 1976.

5. U.S. Department of Agriculture. World Agricultural Situation (WAS-4). Washington, D.C. 1973.

6. U.S. Department of Agriculture. The World Food Situation and Prospects to 1985. Foreign Agricultural Economic Report No. 98. Washington, D.C. 1974.

INSTITUTIONAL CHANGES IN THE LDCs AS AN ALTERNATIVE
TO ADEQUATELY FEEDING THE WORLD HUNGRY

Raphael Shen

Department of Economics and Management Science,
University of Detroit

The estimated population growth rate from 8,000 B.C. to 1 A.D. was .36 per year.[1] If close to reality, it must have taken nearly three thousand people to generate a net increase of one person per year during that period. At present, it takes only forty-eight persons to accomplish the same. In more recent times, world population doubled from the year 1650 to 1850. It doubled again from 1850 to 1925. Fifty years thereafter, it doubled again.[2] The next round of doubling will take only thirty-five years, if not less. There is cause for concern. And the concern is whether the world has not already reached its carrying capacity.

At the close of the Second World Food Conference in Rome in 1974 it was estimated that nearly 460 million people were suffering from malnutrition and hunger. Today, the figure 500 million has been reported.[3] Questions: First, has world population growth outstripped that of food production? The answer is no. For the period 1952 through 1969, the average worldwide population growth rate was 2.0% per year while that of food production was 2.9%. Even for LDCs as a whole, major staple production increases for the 1960 to 1975 period far exceeded their population growth rates.[4] Projected food production statistics into the next decade indicate a continued trend of food production increases over the rate of population growth.[5]

The second question: despite more rapid food production gains over that of population, is widespread hunger and malnutrition due to LDCs' inability to produce enough food calories on the average for their citizens? The answer is again no. The world average daily caloric intake in 1976 was 2,480 kilocalories. In Latin America, the actual per capita calorie consumption was 2,530. In the 1962 to 1964 period, the UN recommended 22 grams of daily animal protein consumption per person. An average Latin American consumed 23% more than the recommended quantity.[6]

Yet there is widespread malnutrition in Latin American countries. Fifteen to 17% of the population in 41% of Latin American countries

surveyed were malnourished. More than 40% of the children in over
one-half of Latin American nations suffer from nutritional deficiencies, and the mortality rate among children aged one to four in
one-third of these Latin American nations was 10 to 33 times higher
than in economically developed nations. Low life expectancy and
high incidence of malnutrition in LDCs is not due to low per capita
food consumption.

Question number three: have LDCs been able to increase their
food production in recent years? The answer is yes. Food production increases have indeed been taking place: "Bumper Crops in Tur-
key," "Bigger Grain Crops in India," "Record Rice Harvest in Sri
Lanka," "Rice Export Market Sought by Bangladesh," and "Emergence of
Brazil as an Agricultural Giant" are a few of the numerous recent
phenomena.[8] Yet there is hunger and malnutrition in these countries.
Production of most major crops is still below potential in many
LDCs, and a minimum of a 100% increase can be expected at least in
tropical areas.[9]

The fourth question: can agricultural technology be relied upon
to further increase world agricultural production in the future?
The answer is yes, both in quality and in quantity. Protein-rich
opaque-II corn has been developed. If adopted for production and
consumption, protein deficiencies in most LDCs can be eliminated.
Triacontanol, isolated from alfalfa and having the potential of re-
placing chemical fertilizer, has enabled an increase in yield between 3 and 63% for seven crops. Experiments to bring forth barley
and tomatoes from sand dunes irrigated with sea water have been
successful. The possibility of reclaiming vast savannah areas now
infested by tsetse flies in Africa is in sight. Not only production
area can be significantly expanded as a result, but supplementary
cattle population of about 120 million heads yielding 1.5 million
tons of meat for African consumers can be realized each year.[10]

In a short paper, these questions have had to be general in nature and the answers simplistic. But they do point to one fact,
namely the problem of world hunger-malnutrition is not caused by
human inability to produce a sufficient amount of food. Why, then,
is there such widespread and spreading hunger and malnutrition?
And how can this social malady be remedied? Increased food production which does not directly benefit the malnourished and the hungry,
is not an adequate answer. Only increased food production by the
hungry, with the resulting increase going to the hungry, can make
hunger a matter of the past.

Changes are required. Needed changes are not so much those in
terms of oversized tractors, shiploads of fertilizers, gigantic
water projects or technological adaptations of sweeping nature.
These yield-increasing, capital intensive inputs have their place,
but at a later stage of development. For the hungry millions, more
immediate and effective changes call for social and institutional
reform, reform that can provide investment and production incentives.

Space limitations do not permit a discussion of all required major social and institutional changes. Instead, the remainder of this paper limits itself to a brief exposition of the merits of certain infrastructural changes. These changes are: improvement in marketing channels, transport system, storage facilities and rural credit institutions.

Marketing channels. Profiteers in some LDCs quote fertilizer prices three to five times higher than that paid by farm producers of DCs and they buy farm produce from peasants at arbitrarily depressed prices. False weights and arbitrary deduction for produce impurities add to the problem.[11] Thus, it is no mystery that farm income and therefore consumer purchasing power for these peasants is low. And it is no myth that investment incentives are absent. Timely market information and farm level institutions such as purchasing and marketing cooperatives or government supervised agencies have a vital contribution to make.

Transport. The presence of transport facilities not only expedites the flow of produce from farm to non-farm areas but more importantly allows the flow of innovative ideas and newly acquired technical know-how between sectors. For instance, "visits to a village by extension agents, credit agents, health workers, and other government employees increased fourfold to tenfold after construction of a feeder road connecting it with a main highway."[12] Transport facilities serve as arteries through which flows life-giving blood of knowledge, capital, farm inputs and outputs.

Storage. Because of inadequate storage facilities, between 5 and 10% of grain products are lost annually throughout the world.[13] "A United Nations estimate gave losses as high as 35% in six Latin American countries from insects in stored cereals and pulses. An AID report from Brazil indicated losses of 15 to 20% in stored grains. Storage experts familiar with conditions in Africa indicate that one-third of the harvested cereals is lost to pests."[14] If only half of the grain loss were prevented, there would be an additional 55 million tons, sufficient to make the diet of 500 million malnourished and hungry more than adequate in calories.[15] Another important function of adequate storage facilities is the stabilization of food prices. Seasonal price fluctuations reach as high as 100%.[16] Farmers who sell produce cheap during harvest seasons must later on purchase back for consumption at a higher price what they cannot store themselves. If marketing facilities are adequate to absorb supplies during peak seasons and to distribute supplies during lull periods, then peasants' purchasing power can be effectively raised and their diet improved.

Credit Institutions. Many peasants in LDCs live from hand to mouth. Many more borrow from local money lenders to tide themselves over. Interest rates reaching 10% per month are not uncommon. There is only one direction the peasants can go--sink deeper into debt and reap all its consequences. Credit institutions could not only eliminate parasitic practices by usurers but could provide needed capital for timely investments by the peasant.

These are but a few of the numerous key infrastructural changes imperative to foster a healthier economic order in rural areas of many LDCs. Sketchy as these descriptions might appear, their policy consequences are unmistakable. If current emphasis is placed on changes relating to institutions and human factors rather than on physical increases in food production, then the world hungry and malnourished not only will have a chance, but an opportunity to lead a life befitting humans.

FOOTNOTES

1. Ansley J. Coale, "The History of the Human Population," The Human Population, A Scientific American Book (San Francisco: W. H. Freeman and Company, 1974), p. 17.

2. Ibid., Ronald Freedman and Bernard Berelson, "The Human Population," The Human Population, op. cit.

3. Cincinnati Enquirer, Dec. 8, 1977.

4. Food and Agriculture Organization of the United Nations, World Agriculture: The Last Quarter Century (Rome: FAO, 1970), p. 9. (PS/B0495/2. 71/E1/2900) International Food Policy Research Institute, Food Needs of Developing Countries: Projections of Consumption to 1990 (Washington, D.C.: IFPRI, December 1977), pp. 32-33.

5. International Food Policy Research Institute, ibid.

6. Shlomo Reutlinger and Marcelo Selowski, Malnutrition and Policy Options (Johns Hopkins University Press, 1976), p. 13. Cf. also Sylvan Kaplan and Evelyn Kirvy-Resenberg (eds.), Ecology and the Quality of Life (Springfield: Charles C. Thomas Publisher, 1973), p. 68.

7. World Report, July-August, 1976.

8. The Christian Science Monitor, Dec. 1, 1976; New York Times, Nov. 28, 1976; New York Times, April 14, 1977; Washington Post, April 22, 1977; and The Christian Science Monitor, May 6, 1977.

9. S. H. Wittwer, "Food Production: Technology and the Resource Base," Science, Vol. 188, May, 1975, p. 579.

10. *Detroit News*, Nov. 15, 1977; *News American*, Sept. 6, 1977; *Wall Street Journal*, Aug 18, 1977; and *The Washington Post*, Feb. 15, 1977.

11. Food and Agriculture Organization of the United Nations. *The State of Food and Agriculture* (Rome: FAO, 1967), p. 76.

12. President's Science Advisory Committee, *The World Food Problem*, Vol. II (Washington, D.C.: The White House, 1967), p. 522.

13. USDA, ERS, *Agriculture in 26 Developing Nations: 1948-1963* (Washington, D.C.: USDA, 1965), p. 107.

14. Morris D. Whitaker and Boyd E. Wennergren, "U.S. Universities and the World Food Problem," *Science*, Vol. 194, Oct. 29, 1976, pp. 554-555.

15. *Ibid.*

16. Lester R. Brown, *Seeds of Change* (New York: Praeger, 1972), p. 89.

INSTITUTIONAL APPROACHES ON PROMOTING RISK-TAKING AND DECISION-MAKING OF FOOD PRODUCTION TECHNOLOGY BY SUBSISTENCE FARMERS IN DEVELOPING COUNTRIES[*]

Allen Jedlicka

School of Business, University of Northern Iowa

In recent years the myth of the irrationality of the subsistence farmer has been largely discredited. Quite the opposite of the old conventional wisdom, subsistence farmers are exceedingly rational, and go through a very logical cost/benefit analysis to factor out the effect of an extensive list of environmental variables affecting their acceptance of technology. Too often the problem is that the change institution has not provided the framework which allows the farmer to effectively interact with the planning phase of a transfer program.

The perhaps simplistic answer is that it therefore becomes the change institution's responsibility to build this framework. That's no easy task. The first step, among several which I've intensively detailed in a book,[*] requires acceptance of the view that farmers must be involved in the decision-making aspects of technology transfer. That is, they must participate in this process, and the management of the change agency must promote that participation. That's difficult--particularly in an organization that adamantly does not accept that view--but it can be done. There are, for example, organizational development packages used to convert the thinking of top management along participative lines. Once that view has been accepted, there are organizational structural arrangements which describe how communication, feedback, and acceptance by all participants can be achieved.

To backtrack, I recognize that ideal conditions usually have to be compromised somewhat. Certainly the change institution has in mind a transfer of technology which will benefit both the client and nation. The client on the other hand may want something which wholly benefits him and not necessarily the nation. But providing a participative decision-making framework which allows both

---

[*]A. Jedlicka, Organization for Rural Development, Praeger Special Studies Series, 1977.

sides to fully understand the other's concerns can result in an accommodation for both. Fortunately, there are some examples of how participation works.

The first example comes from Mary Elmendorf[*] who has written on the introduction of water systems to villages in Mexico. In line with what was said earlier about farmers participating in decision-making, the Mexican extension agent spent a great deal of time talking with community elders and village forums to establish just what was needed for the development of a water system that would satisfy everybody. One village decided it would not build a system, other villages decided that it would be beneficial and modified the system so that it would be accepted by all the villagers. All these efforts were successful--even the rejected system--because that village established that it was not ready for a system, and did not accept a system which would not be utilized. The other villages implemented modified systems which satisfied their needs. In a non-participatory approach the end result could have been failure by all because an unacceptable system may have been pushed upon all the villages.

The second example deals with a quantitative technique--Hierarchical Structuring--which I have used in Mexico. This technique structures the variables affecting the adoption of technology in a hierarchical order from most important to least important.[**] In this approach change institutions can utilize a stratified random sampling procedure to select clients to establish environmental variables affecting transfer to all clients, and then add to the list institutional variables which they view as important to the transfer process. When one is through with the analysis, one is able to establish which are the truly important variables affecting transfer.

Of course, getting back to Elmendorf's simpler approach, the point is that the use of such quantitative analytical approaches can only come about when a change agency accepts the fact that clients need to be involved in the decision-making process in the field.

Obviously, the methodology and the specifics of these examples require a great deal more elaboration than is possible in a short paper. But to conclude, let me reiterate the major points of the presentation. The institutional barriers in technology transfer to subsistence farmers are perhaps even more insurmountable than the client barriers. Change institutions must recognize the role

---

[*]M. Elmendorf, "Public Participation and Acceptance in Development," paper for the Environmental Impact Analysis Research Council Convention, San Francisco, California, Oct. 17, 1977.

[**]A. Jedlicka, "Interpretive Structural Modeling and Transfer of Technology to Subsistence Farmers," National Meeting, American Institute for Decision Sciences, Chicago, October, 1977.

of participation by subsistence farmers in effecting transfer, and must make the organizational changes which will promote that participation. Once they make that commitment, there are a variety of behavioral and quantitative tools which can promote the participation of farmers.

While the tools to accomplish all this exist, the major, unsettled question is whether change institutions which do not share that participatory philosophy can adopt such a strategy in their work with subsistence farmers.

THE SCIENCE INFRASTRUCTURE OF NATIONAL
FOOD SUPPLY SYSTEMS*

John Blackmore

Department of Agricultural and Applied Economics
University of Minnesota

Two concepts are fundamental to this paper. These are the concept of a food supply system and the concept of an infrastructure.

Around the world there is a spectrum of food supply systems. Most all of these can be characterized as sets of interacting economic enterprises. They are economic enterprises in that they have maximizing and minimizing objectives, respond to incentives, and employ technologies. The enterprises that make up a nation's food supply system include farms and enterprises that manufacture production factors including fertilizers, machines, etc., plus all those enterprises that process, store and distribute food products to consumers.

One great difference between the well-fed countries and countries where hunger is a problem is the extent to which food is produced by technologies based on science. In the well-fed, developed nations, food production methods developed by producer experience and passed along by custom and tradition have largely been replaced by methods based on science. The varieties of crops grown, the methods of crop and livestock production, and the means of processing farm products into food are mostly derived from research in laboratories and experiment stations. On the other hand, most of the countries where hunger is a threat have not yet built a foundation or infrastructure of science for their food supply systems.

In societies where custom and tradition provided the essential technologies of food production, the productive enterprises were essentially self-contained and technological change was very slow. In contrast, food supply systems based on science are endlessly dynamic. Change is a central and constant factor. Productive enterprises in

*Miscellaneous journal article 1699 of the Minnesota Agricultural Experiment Station.

science-based systems need a continuing flow of technical information and support. Primarily because most enterprises in food supply systems are small, they and society have found it desirable to depend on external sources for technological support. For the most part the sources are external not only to the firms but also to the system. They take the form of an infrastructure, essential to the system, but not part of it.

The development of the science infrastructure of a national food supply system must proceed with or in advance of the development of the system itself. A review of the three principal elements of this specialized infrastructure will show why this is so.

The first element is a capacity for problem solving research. The results of some research is transferable from one country to another, but the world is enormously diverse as to soils and other factors that affect output. What works in the U.S. may have to be altered significantly to make it work in production systems in Bangladesh.

Research is important, but it is not enough. The second element of the infrastructure is a set of technical services. Some parts of this set are better recognized as essential than are others. There is now little disagreement that there is need for some kind of transmission system to get technical information to food producers from where it is developed in research laboratories and stations. But what is almost universally lacking is a two-way technical communications bridge between food producers and researchers. In addition to the information flow to farm and firm, there is a crucial need for a flow of information on problems to research centers.

This communication system is only one of the essential technical services. There are others which are essential for the development of effective food supply systems. There are almost universal needs for improved data collection. Agricultural statistics, hydrologic data and soil inventories are needed almost everywhere.

A third neglected part of the technical services group is the regulatory arm of the government. Undramatic as they may be, regulatory agencies play a crucial role in the workings of food supply systems. Some socially desirable attributes of a food supply cannot be assured by dependence only upon the unguided functioning of market mechanisms. The technical information required to assure that milk is safe to drink is available almost everywhere, but it isn't everywhere that one can drink the milk. Many developing countries have poor facilities for promulgating and enforcing necessary regulations relating to food products, or to such production factors as fertilizer and seeds.

The third element of the science infrastructure is a set of facilities for the training of professional and technical personnel

387

to operate the system and its infrastructure. The need for professional and technical personnel in the public service have tended to be better recognized than have the needs of the many enterprises in the food supply system itself.

Developing countries should look at the whole of food supply systems and their infrastructures. Too much of the effort thus far has been piecemeal.

The hunger-threatened countries should be encouraged and assisted in efforts to examine their food supply systems and to assess the needs for modifications in public policy and programs. These governments should be encouraged to assist the productive enterprises that make up these systems to perform better in the public interest. A central strategy should be the identification of bottlenecks and imperfections in the system that would lend themselves to treatment. Priority attention should be given to assessing the adequacy of the major elements of the science infrastructure. These are the facilities that provide a flow of problem-solving research results, those that provide needed technical services and those that provide trained people for the system.

FOOD SELF-SUFFICIENCY STRATEGY
FOR BANGLADESH FOR 2000 A.D.

M. Amirul Islam

Executive Vice-Chairman
Bangladesh Agricultural Research Council

Mofazzal H. Chowdhury

Research Associate
Agricultural Engineering Department
Iowa State University

Over four billion people now inhabit the earth and this number increases by millions every year. Under these conditions, there exists a grave doubt whether world food production can match the rate of population growth. Along with population growth, food imbalance is serious among different countries of the world. In most of the less developed countries there exists an acute food shortage and even starvation. Despite the fact that the economically advanced countries have food surpluses, two-thirds of the world's population are underfed or starved.

Most of the developing countries have less efficient primarily subsistence agriculture as the mainstay of the economy. They have very low per capita income, low literacy and a high rate of population growth. All these factors lead to the population-food imbalance in the developing countries. The poverty and hunger in these countries cannot be escaped unless population is controlled and agricultural productivity is increased. Bangladesh is a typical case in this group with the most unfavorable population-food imbalance.

The 1974 census found that over 71.3 million people live in Bangladesh, which has an area of about 55,000 square miles. This gives a population density of about 1400 per square mile as against a density of 978 per square mile in 1961. Bangladesh is one of the most densely populated areas in the world. Between 1961 and 1974 the population growth rate has been estimated to be 2.62 percent.

With the present rate of population increase it is estimated that Bangladesh will have twice as many people by the year 2000 A.D. This implies that during 1974-2000, the number of people will be increased from 71.3 million to 140 million and the corresponding total food grain requirements will also be elevated from 14 million tons to 27 million tons.

Bangladesh has been suffering from a chronic food deficit which has averaged about 2.5 million tons a year over the past five years. Every year, huge amounts of food grains are imported in an attempt to meet this deficit.

From a study of the production figures for rice in Bangladesh from 1960 to the present we find that rice production has increased at the rate of 1.2 percent. After the introduction of high yielding varieties of rice during the mid 1960s, we find that rice production increased at the rate of 2.1 percent. If rice production progresses at the rate of 2.1 percent, then by the year 2000 A.D., Bangladesh will produce 19 million tons with a deficit of 8 million tons. We are already seeing signs that the 2.1 percent growth rate is very hard to maintain. But, if we have to produce 27 million tons in order to reach self-sufficiency by the year 2000 A.D., then Bangladesh will have to maintain a steady growth rate of 3.5 percent (see Figure 1). With limited land resources and increasing population, one can hardly visualize what amount of effort will be necessary and what amount of technology will be involved in reaching that target.

In spite of the urgent importance of diversification in agriculture and change in food composition, rice will continue to be the principal component of the food mix. It is thus all the more important to improve the productivity of rice farms. Although improved rice production technology and the modern varieties have had some impact, the high yielding rice varieties have spread less rapidly in Bangladesh than in many other countries. Observers believe this is due to the fact that the high yield varieties and the necessary technology are not available enough to overcome local barriers in major rice-growing areas of the country.

If Bangladesh is to cope with the problems of projected food shortages, it needs both medium and long term policies. In the medium term, there must be an intensification of efforts to significantly reduce the population growth rate and improve the technological foundation to double production. The efforts should also include (a) improvement of the nutritional aspect of the diet; (b) an increase in the literacy percentage; (c) more productive utilization of women; (d) rapid diffusion of family planning and crop production technology; and (e) improvement of research.

For the long term, the necessity of research has been recognized as the basic need for sustained agricultural progress. This means that Bangladesh must develop the competence and skill of indigenous research personnel and improve the adequacy of research laboratories and other facilities.

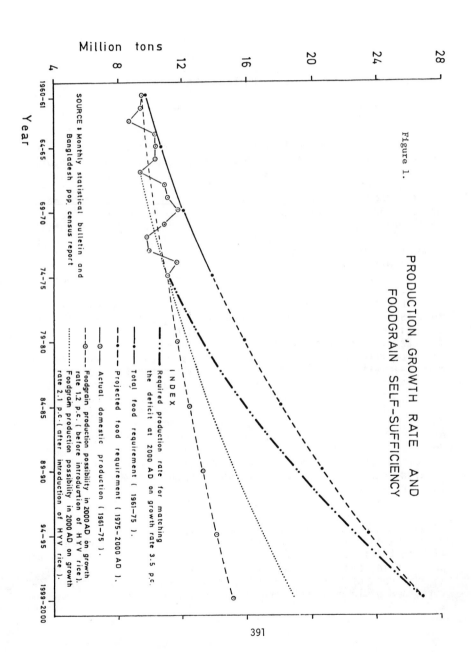

Figure 1.

PRODUCTION, GROWTH RATE AND FOODGRAIN SELF-SUFFICIENCY

Million tons

Year

SOURCE : Monthly statistical bulletin and
Bangladesh pop. census report

I N D E X

.... Required production rate for matching
the deficit at 2000 AD on growth rate 3.5 p.c.

——•——•—— Total food requirement (1961-75).

—•—•—•— Projected food requirement (1975-2000 AD).

————— Actual domestic production (1961-75).

——⊙——⊙—— Foodgrain production possibility in 2000 AD on growth
rate 1.2 p.c.(before introduction of HYV rice).

.... Foodgrain production possibility in 2000 AD on growth
rate 2.1 p.c.(after introduction of HYV rice).

THE TEACHING OF WORLD FOOD ISSUES AT THE
UNIVERSITY LEVEL

George W. Beran

College of Veterinary Medicine, Iowa State University

The teaching of world food issues to university students in the classroom and research laboratory is at once a unique opportunity and responsibility. The primary target student populations are U.S. students preparing for various forms of participation in feeding the people of the world, and foreign students from food needy nations who are in American universities preparing for careers in their own lands. The problems of feeding the world's population, along with the problems of controlling the increase in that population, rank among the top international issues. Students whose careers will involve any areas of feeding the people of food deficit nations can be helped by courses focusing on world food issues.

This report details preliminary findings in a survey of world food issues courses offered in the 47 land grant universities in the United States. At this time, information has been received from 22 of these universities. All 22 universities offer courses with specific international focus on food issues; the numbers vary from 1-44 with a median of 8 courses. All offer 1 or more such courses with a multidisciplinary perspective designed for students in a number of academic majors or in off-campus extension classes, and 91% of the universities also offer 1 or more courses in specific aspects of world food issues. These latter courses, offered by specific university departments primarily for their major students, comprise 71% of the world food issues courses. Only 18% of the universities offer undergraduate specialities in food related areas within an international studies co-major, and only 9% currently offer such a graduate major.

The courses offered by the responding universities center around three major broad objectives: (1) to expand the students' knowledge and capability in international aspects of their major fields; (2) to develop an understanding of international needs and problems in feeding the people of the world; and (3) to develop an awareness of the roles of other professionals in the total effort, and of levels of interaction needed.

Courses offered in land grant universities which deal with subject areas in world food issues as portions of courses or as entire courses are summarized in Table 1. Economics departments are most frequently involved in food issues courses, with 90% of the universities offering courses focusing on economics of international development, and 67% offering 1-10 entire courses in this area. Plant Science departments are the second most frequently involved, with 86% offering courses focusing on world crop production and 57% offering 1-6 entire courses in this area. This is in marked contrast to courses focusing on world animal production which are offered by only 62% of the universities and in world fisheries and seafoods which are offered by only 28% of the universities. Also ranking high in offerings are courses which include world population issues (86%), national and international food policies (76%), technology of food production (76%) and nutrition and health in developing countries (71%). Only a few universities offer courses which include material on world environmental issues (38%), on international education, extension and communications (33%), on world climatology (28%) and on international diseases and pests of plants and animals (19%).

Iowa State University, with an enrollment of 22,800 for the 1977-1978 school year, has drawn 6.4% of its students from abroad. Among these students, 91% are from developing countries and 26% are in food related curricula. Fourteen academic courses are currently offered with specific focuses on world food issues. Overall class enrollments have varied from 8-40 students. Foreign students have comprised 16.7% of undergraduate and 33.3% of graduate student enrollments in these courses, below a desired level. Table 2 shows offerings and enrollment data for 8 courses for students in a variety of major fields. The two broadest based courses, "Introduction to World Food Problems" and "World Food Issues" are newly organized for Spring, 1978. "Introduction to World Food Problems" and "Environment and Society" are offered both to off-campus extension and to on-campus students.

TABLE 1

COURSES IN WORLD FOOD ISSUES IN 22 LAND GRANT UNIVERSITIES

Subject Areas in World Food Issues	% of Universities Included	Teaching Subject Entire Course(s)
Economics of International Development	90	67
World Crop Production	86	57
World Population Issues	86	24
National and International Food Policies	76	33
Food Production Technology	76	10
Nutrition and Health in Developing Countries	71	38
Food Technology in Developing Countries	71	10
International Trade in Food	67	24
World Soils	62	29
World Animal Production	62	19
World Energy and Natural Resource Utilization	57	19
Sociology of International Development	52	24
World Environmental Issues	38	24
International Education, Extension, Communications	33	21
World Climatology	28	10
World Fisheries and Seafoods	28	5
International Diseases and Pests of Plants and Animals	19	5

TABLE 2

COURSES IN WORLD FOOD ISSUES--IOWA STATE UNIVERSITY

Course Title	Offering Department	Times Offered	Class Size Range		Student Level	
			All Students	Foreign	Undergrad	Grad
Climates of the Continents	Agronomy	> 3	25-30	1-2	20-25	5
Intermediate Technology	Agric. Mechanization	1	6	-	6	0
Introduction to World Food Problems	University Studies	New	-	-	-	Not Open
Seminar on World Food Problems	Food Technology	3	8-10	2	7-10	0-1
Population and Food	University Studies	4	30-35	3-4	30-35	Not Open
Environment and Society	University Studies	9	10-30	0	0	10-30
Adoption and Diffusion	Sociol. and Anthropol.	3	35-40	2-3	25-30	10
World Food Issues*	University Studies	New	-	-	-	-

*Principally for Graduate Students

395

APPLYING AN ECOLOGICAL SYSTEMS PERSPECTIVE
TO NUTRITION POLICY AND PROGRAMS

Laura S. Sims and Helen Smiciklas-Wright

College of Human Development, The Pennsylvania State University

There has been increasing attention to the use of an ecological systems approach in the analysis of health problems. It is an approach that is most appropriate for the study of nutritional problems because of the many complex interacting systems which influence man's use of food. The individual as an ecosystem is influenced by several exogenous or environmental factors which influence an individual's own personal food choices. These include values, attitudes, beliefs, and knowledge components. The individual uses these endogenous variables to choose his food from among those that are available as well as culturally acceptable. The interaction of factors is complex and resolution of nutritional problems must address these complexities. In being both an open as well as a dynamic model, the ecological systems approach can address this very complexity.

Nutrition Policy

There has been heightened interest among nutritionists in a well-articulated national nutrition policy. A number of attempts have been made to formulate such a policy. In general, these attest to the fact that nutrition and food policy do not lie within the purview of a single professional discipline. However, the inter-relatedness of systems is not always well addressed in the proposed policy statements. This is a significant issue because, in addition to being comprehensive and reflective of solid theoretical foundations, policy must also serve as the framework for specific programs and plans. Policy plays a pivotal role because it must translate the vague prescriptions of principles into a formalized plan of action in programs.

Nutrition Programs

Despite the lack of articulated nutrition policy, a large number of food and nutrition programs currently exist in the United States. These may be categorized into two major approaches: the environmental (external) approach and the personal approach (see

396

Fig. 1). In the first category are programs designed to increase food purchasing power (Food Stamps), those providing food or meals (Supplemental Commodity Foods, School Lunch) and those involving modification of the present food supply by enrichment or fortification processes so that foods currently available to the public may be made more nutritious.

Programs with a personal focus are usually termed "nutrition education" because in these strategies the individual is "taught" how to choose from among the foods available to him those which are more "nutritious" and thus more favorable to maintenance of good health. The Expanded Food and Nutrition Education Program, using indigenous paraprofessionals as nutrition educators, is the most obvious example of this approach. Nutrition Education components are also included in the Nutrition Program for Older Americans and the Women, Infants and Children's Supplemental Foods Program, and they are under consideration for School Lunch.

If programs are limited to one of the two domains, their potential for success may be restricted. Those programs which focus on changing the environment may be expedient. However, the question remains whether such temporary modifications--imposed from the outside--will result in long-lasting changes in the individual. But programs which provide information may also be inadequate for two reasons:

First, most educational programs are aimed solely at the cognitive level, while personal attributes such as attitudes, beliefs, and values which exert strong and powerful influences on behavior are not attended to. Attempts to address these endogenous characteristics of the population being served will also help to achieve greater effectiveness of the program. Second, the environment may not permit the individual to change or the program to succeed. The educational approach makes sense only as far as there are environmental resources available to implement the suggested changes.

It is our plea that a nutrition policy be formulated using the theoretical basis of the ecological systems approach. From this, nutrition programs can be implemented which address the total concerns of the population they serve. Not only should programs seek to change food supplies or purchasing power (environmental changes), but they should also incorporate strategies geared to the individual recipient so that he or she uses such resources to produce lasting behavioral changes in dietary practices.

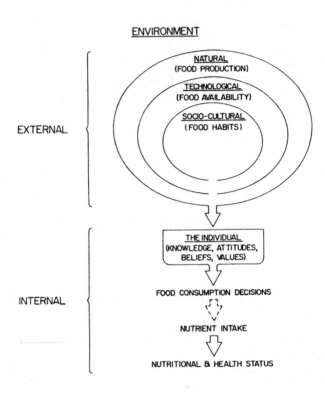

Fig. 1. AN ECOLOGICAL SYSTEMS MODEL

A MODEL FOR OVERCOMING NUTRITIONAL NEGLECT IN A COMPREHENSIVE HEALTH DELIVERY SYSTEM

Alice Tobias

Department of Family and Consumer Studies
Herbert H. Lehman College, C.U.N.Y., The Bronx, N.Y.

In the United States malnutrition has surfaced as a distinct problem. It is due to the same reasons it is found in the less industrialized countries: poverty, ignorance or misinformation, habit, uneven distribution and overprocessing of food.

Among the common disorders striking at middle-class Americans are heart disease and diabetes mellitus as well as an excessive intake of cholesterol, saturated fats. They are experiencing the same condition as the impoverished segment of society.

A survey conducted by the author focused on nutritional problems of patients admitted to two medical wards of two urban teaching hospitals for a six-week period. The subjects were 67 non-selected adult patients.

Medical records were surveyed and patients interviewed. Through observation of nutritional care personnel, 91% of these patients were found to have malnutrition problems--overt or potential. A large percentage confirmed that they had longstanding nutritional problems, such as obesity, alcoholism, gastro-intestinal disorders and nutritional anemias. Some had been neither identified nor treated.

Although they received diagnostic studies and complex drug therapy under hospital care, there was a basic neglect of nutritional diagnosis and treatment. There was failure to record or obtain diet history, body weight--on admission and at later intervals--nutrition counseling as well as referral services for such.

Another finding was the lack of communication between dietician and physician. Both physician and dietician failed to refer patients for follow-up to health and nutritional care services after their discharge. Many of these patients were the economically-deprived who could not afford this type of service. In this field there is a shortage of personnel, making rehabilitative and prevention care referrals after discharge unfeasible. There is neither federal health care legislation nor private segment coverage for such counseling.

Neglect of nutrition in health delivery is inappropriate, especially in the light of current technological advances in science. The American Dietetic Association has stressed that qualified nutrition personnel should be a component for all health related programs and that it should be designed to reach the entire population. It recognizes that nutrition is a critical factor in the promotion of health as well as disease prevention.

Demand for improvement in these areas by reduction of costs is necessary. There are underway efforts to restructure the health care delivery system to provide better quality care, greater utilization of health personnel, control costs and give consumer satisfaction. There is support for such a system (often termed Health Maintenance Organization,"HMO," or the Family Health Center, "FHC").

Such a program would provide "comprehensive care"--a full range of services offering completeness and continuity in dental, psychological and other health services from initial screening to followup. Such program would incorporate health promotion through prevention and periodic reassessment.

The implementation of a complete health care system would make possible a full range of essential nutritional services such as assessment of food practices and nutritional status, education to meet normal and therapeutic needs, provide resources for food service, special feeding equipment, and/or supplemental food assistance.

This framework calls for professionals from each discipline--medicine, dietetics and nutrition--and home economics to play important team roles. Since the efforts of all providers will be directed to maximizing independent functioning of individuals and their families, they also become integral parts of the system. Complete and continuous care will rely on how actively each participates in the program.

Medical associations, the federal government and educators must realize nutrition's importance at each level of health services. Congress should enact legislation to provide reforms so that nutrition diagnosis and counseling in health care delivery systems provide adequate coverage for patients.

I cannot emphasize too strongly that in the nutritional care of patients, there is no clear assignment of responsibility. The relative roles of physicians and dieticians vis-a-vis the nutritional needs of patients need to be more clearly defined.

BREAST FEEDING AND SOCIAL CLASS MOBILITY: THE CASE OF MEXICAN MIGRANT WOMEN

Carmen Acosta Johnson

University of Texas School of Medicine

Introduction

Differentials in the incidence of breast feeding by social class can be examined in nations with very different degrees of demographic advancement. Mexico, Figure 1a, with a relatively high birth, high death demographic regime, shows a pattern in which breast feeding is concentrated in the lower class. In Figure 1c it can be seen that in the British Isles, where both birth and death rates are low, breast feeding is virtually confined to the upper classes. In the United States, Figure 1b, with intermediate levels of birth and death, both patterns can readily be distinguished.

Figure 1. Patterns of Breast Feeding According to Demographic Advance and Social Class

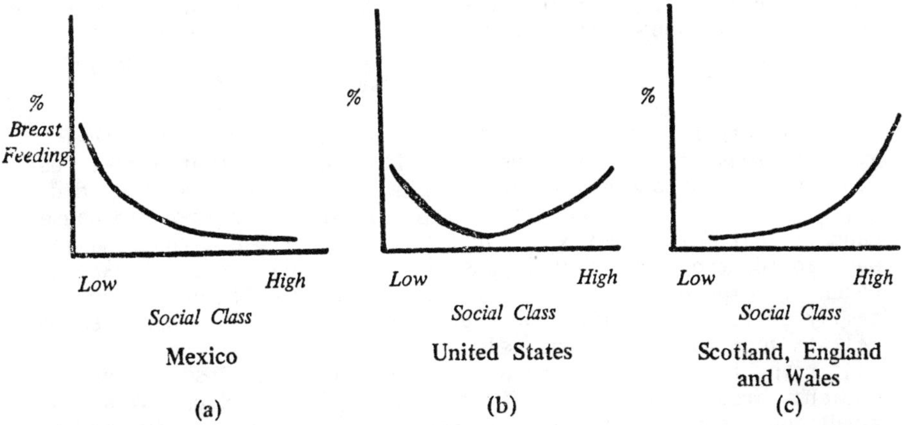

% Breast Feeding	%	%
Low High	Low High	Low High
Social Class	Social Class	Social Class
Mexico	United States	Scotland, England and Wales
(a)	(b)	(c)

We wish to know what elements in contemporary culture and society inhibit or enhance the choice of breast feeding by individual
mothers. Neither psychological, economic, nor biological analyses
have provided information which might explain such patterns.

This study presents interviews with 51 very low income Mexican
women who had been born in northern Mexican villages and had recently migrated into Houston, Texas. Small groups were assembled in
a charity clinic waiting room by inviting interested mothers to join
in discussion on infant feeding. Interviews were held in border
Spanish. Sessions were recorded by hand in full view of the participants and corrections and additions offered by the mothers as
the session progressed. Thus information was entirely public, not
at all privileged, and represents a consensus of the particular
small group which produced it.

Effect on Breast Feeding

Sixty percent of interviewed women delivering infants in Houston chose not to breast feed, but allowed their infants to be fed
commercial milks at first feed. Thus 40 percent chose to lactate
for varying lengths of time. While this proportion is high in comparison with American middle class norms, it is approximately the
same as the proportion expected among American lower class mothers
of rural, traditional backgrounds. It is a low proportion in comparison to Mexican lower class norms. The naturalness of lactating
when social supports were in order and the mother felt secure was
a distant memory, clearly separated from the situation of childbearing in Houston. With newly acquired modern viewpoints, women
reported feelings of pity at the memory of women in Mexico who were
so poor they had nothing to give the baby but their own breast,
even when it was not really milk in the breast. Women doubted that
the secretions of the lactating breast were really milk, or consti-
tuted infant food. They were pleased to report that salaries in
Houston, even though often below minimum wage, enabled mothers to
provide the highest status baby food, commercial formula for their
infants, an opportunity which was not available in Mexico.

All mothers reported that health personnel had advised them
against breast feeding for the following reasons: that breast feeding was considered a hippie behavior and all agreed that they did
not wish to be associated with hippie culture; that it would cause
cancer; that Mexican mothers had too much work to do; that the milk
was bad for the baby; that it was not really milk; that it was in-
decent to expose the lactating breast to other children in the
family or to the husband; and that mothers could not produce enough
milk to feed the baby adequately. Planning and decision-making
concerning the new baby were new and modern activities for the
mothers; breast feeding was never a matter for decision-making under
traditional conditions. Thus it was an unexpected question and

mothers were quite willing to take the advice of modern medical authority. Later when routine injection of Deladamone at delivery inhibited the milk supply, mothers felt that the advice had been accurate and that milk was impossible to produce under Houston conditions.

Substitutes. On payday all babies and young children received milk undiluted, but when the food budget was low at the end of a pay period, water had to be added to stretch the supply of either milk or substitute, and substitutes had to be used more frequently. Canned fruit punches and Kool Aid were popular for their sweet taste and red color. No babies rejected commercial nipples which allowed an easy flow of liquid into the baby's mouth. Nursing bottles containing substitutes were also used as pacifiers throughout the day, particularly in public.

Rice water is the water strained away from the refined cooked rice. It is white in color, thus seen as a satisfactory substitute for milk in the nursing bottle. Tea and rice cereal were frequently ordered by Houston doctors in the treatment of diarrhea, thus the prolonged use of rice water and tea was interpreted by mothers as prophylactic as well as traditional.

Summary

Small group sessions with women migrants from Northern Mexico into Houston, Texas revealed abrupt changes in the practice of lactation under urban, American conditions. A shift from high birth, high death regime to an intermediate birth and death regime occurred in mid-childbearing career. Psychological explanations appeared not to be relevant, as emotional trauma and satisfactions were reported in both traditional village settings and urban Houston.

Thus the proportion of breast feeders in the U.S. is elevated in the lower class due to recent in-migration from traditional settings such as Mexico, but declines quickly as purchasing power improves. Social supports for women in child bearing and child rearing will probably result in an increase in the practice of lactation. Such matters as nutrition education, good medical advice, improved lactation diets, and support for an at-home post partum period appear to be of vital importance.

COMPUTER MODELING AS AN ANALYTIC TOOL FOR
HEALTH PROBLEM DEFINITION:
PUBLIC POLICY IMPLICATIONS

Paul O. Woolley, Jr.

College of Human Development, The Pennsylvania State University

Barbara A. Underwood

Professor of Nutrition, Massachusetts Institute of Technology

Because data on the extent of malnutrition in developing countries is difficult and expensive to obtain by clinical surveys, the authors sought to develop a predictive model for determining vitamin A deficiency, one of the three remaining nutrient-specific deficiency diseases of world-wide public health significance.

The deficiency problem was defined in terms of T. J. Cartwright's typology of increasing levels of complexity:

1. As a simple problem, vitamin A deficiency means having an inadequate intake of vitamin A according to some specified criterion, e.g., some percentage of the recommended dietary allowance.

2. As a compound problem, vitamin A deficiency means having an inadequate intake of vitamin A because of low family income, ignorance, or inequity in intra-family distribution and/or excess demand resulting from infectious illness, parasitism, or rapid growth.

3. As a complex problem, vitamin A deficiency means having an inadequate intake of vitamin A because of the level of socio-economic development of the country, the availability of health services, agricultural productivity, or population growth.

To predict vitamin A deficiency, an extensive review of epidemiological and clinical literature was undertaken to identify possible causes, precipitating events, and indicators of vitamin A deficiency. The authors found that the available published data included too few variables to construct a suitable ecologic model. As a consequence, the primary focus of the study was shifted from vitamin A deficiency to protein-energy malnutrition (PEM) on the hypothesis that because vitamin A deficiency and PEM have been shown to correlate highly, it would be possible to estimate the prevalance of vitamin A deficiency from estimates of the extent and severity of PEM.

The authors attempted to determine indicators of first-, second-, and third-degree malnutrition in children under five years of age. Stepwise multiple regression for nutrition status on data from a study conducted in West Pakistan by one of the authors was employed to identify the strongest indicators. These were: per capita monthly income, average age totally weaned, immunizations, and number of days ill with diarrhea. The relatively high significance of the income variable as an indicator of nutrition status was seen as a surrogate for the operation of a cluster of variables not specified in the model. Similarly, other strong indicators were seen as clusters for related factors in the society.

To estimate the frequency of vitamin A deficiency in children with second- and third-degree malnutrition, findings from a variety of published studies were examined. On the basis of data analysis of these studies, it was estimated that approximately 10% of children with PEM would have vitamin A deficiency.

The model was tested using PEM rates reported in a study published by one of the authors and estimates derived from the authors' regression formula in order to determine an estimate of vitamin A deficiency for the child population of Haiti. The prevalence of second- and third-degree PEM was determined to be 27% of children under age five, and the estimate of vitamin A eye disease was consequently approximately 2.7%.

This estimate was compared with the results of a 1974 prevalence survey conducted in Haiti, which found a prevalence of xerophthalmia of .25%. Thus the predictive model overestimated the frequency of clinical eye signs by a factor of ten.

The overestimation was seen as due in part to a design factor, in that the model was designed to identify existing eye disease and members at risk in the child population, and thus sensitivity was one of the design parameters. The widely discrepant population bases of the data used to derive estimates of PEM may not have been fully appropriate to the setting in Haiti and thus also may have contributed to the overestimation.

While further testing is needed to validate the model, the authors conclude that it yields an estimate of the extent of vitamin A problems at a level sufficiently accurate to assist policy formulation. When applied to several settings, it could provide estimates of relative risk among several populations. It is clear that a more refined model would require data which address the interaction of causes.

The authors suggest that future research on the epidemiology of vitamin A deficiency and of protein energy malnutrition utilize an ecologic framework.

POPULATION GROWTH, POPULATION POLICIES AND FOOD PRODUCTION--POLICY PROPOSALS FOR SOLVING THESE INTERNATIONAL PROBLEMS

S. K. Kuthiala

Professor of Demography, University of North Florida

Some authors are of the opinion that the overpopulation crisis of the 20th Century will be a matter of history and that by the beginning of the 21st Century necessary political, economic, and social changes will have lowered fertility levels in all the rich and poor countries. However, even these optimists believe that there will be serious imbalances of population in the developing countries, which need desperate help for reformation of their social systems. Many of the poor countries are very much prejudiced against birth control, have enormous bureaucracies, and are politically unstable. So they remain unable to take action which would lower their fertility. Though you might find examples from India and Pakistan of 5 to 15% of couples practicing contraception, a vast majority of couples continue to ignore family planning and birth control measures.

Though population policies are espoused by many nations, there are as many definitions of population policy as there are nations. Sometimes family planning programs themselves are identified as population policy by a given nation. In fact, a population policy should be aimed at directly and indirectly influencing demographic variables. It is already accepted that the family planning programs alone cannot produce the results of a broad decline in births, a decrease in over-all population growth, and an increased standard of living. In my opinion, "modernization" of society must accompany family planning programs if there is to be an effective curb on fertility. It is not an either/or proposition, yet variables such as tax laws, rural development schemes, employment opportunities for the unemployed, self-help programs and public education programs by their own impetus can cut fertility. What is needed is a balanced and sophisticated view of population policy. Increasingly, we have to be concerned with environmental deterioration, which is related to increasing population.

In America we are prone to think of farm production in terms of bounty, of bumper crops which pile up beyond demand and depress farm prices. Much of the current economic difficulty U.S. farmers

407

face is, indeed, related to this vast production capability. Such
is not, however, the case all over the world. The Sahel countries--
below the Sahara in West Africa--are now experiencing the beginning
of another drought of as yet unknown severity. Similar weather
disasters in other areas, involving more millions of people, could
dramatically challenge the world's food supply. The intellectual
war over food production and human production continues merrily.
Poor nations need to increase their food production dramatically
and by no stretch of the imagination can poor nations do this job
alone. It has become a global task demanding a massive long range
effort. Further, if the promising changes occurring in agriculture
(such as the Green Revolution) are literally to bear fruit, they
must be accompanied by economic, technological, and social change.

POLICY PROPOSALS

Population Growth

Population growth cannot be curtailed by simply providing family planning information and contraceptives. Such programs simply
aim to achieve reduction in birth rates, yet at the same time they
continue to permit rapid population growth. India reached an
ironic state in population control and had to compulsory sterilize
couples with three or more children during Mrs. Gandhi's reign. A
rate of growth of 2.4% per year would allow India's already dense
population to double in 27 years. Population growth is real and
here. Thus,

(a) We should adopt policies of negative population growth,
sharply cutting fertility levels by provision of contraceptives,
abortion services, raised age of marriage, possibly yearly grants
to those who keep small families, and, worse, by compulsory coercion.

(b) There should be a vast expansion of literacy programs in
the poor countries, and research and development for a safe, cheap,
reliable contraceptive in the rich countries.

(c) There should be rapid modernization of science and technology in developing countries even if their surplus labor force
necessitates labor intensive growth and development in the industrial sector.

(d) In terms of reducing fertility, there should be strong
emphasis on over-all economic, political and social development.

Population Policies

A national population policy is designed to deal with changing demographic, economic, and social conditions in a country.
Such a policy on the part of a government seeks to change the number,

the growth, and distribution of a population. The United Nations and the Population Council have identified steps for establishing population policies. More important of these steps are:

(a) Establishing base-line demographic data from which annual or five year targets for family planning education, fertility reduction, and increases in literacy rates should be established.

(b) Establishing a commission to study the demographic situation and recommend policy.

(c) A non-bureaucratic and effective department where family planning services are part of an overall maternity plan. Integration of all population related programs.

(d) Allocation of increased budget for family planning, maternal and child health, and contraceptives.

Food Production

There are serious shortfalls in food production compared to food requirements in most of the developing nations. These shortfalls in food create continued undernourishment and probably are the source of more human misery than anything else in the world. This in turn has affected the health of a significant proportion of people and there is always the possibility of famine, starvation, and want erupting into violence. Thus,

(a) Tremendous resources should be invested in research and development to increase food supply. In the poor countries agricultural development should be the first priority.

(b) Food should be redistributed all over the world. Luxury consumption of food should be taxed and excessive food banked with a United Nations fund from which countries could borrow in case of critical need, to replenish it when there is a surplus.

(c) Farming should be made more productive and appealing. This would not only increase production but also slow down the mass migration of rural poor to the cities.

(d) Do something rapidly about protein-calorie-malnutrition (PCM) and Kwashiorkor among the world population--possibly by a technological breakthrough.

(e) Maintain an ecological balance and avoid any further degradation of arable land, deforestation, desert encroachment and threatened irrigation systems.

409

CAN THE WORLD FOOD PROBLEM BE SOLVED?

Elaine C. Charman and Maurice L. Albertson

Food Science and Nutrition, and Civil Engineering
Colorado State University

Demographers project that the population of the world will increase from 3.9 billion in 1975 to at least 5.8 billion in the year 2015. At this point, they feel there should be a balance or a 0% increase. There is no guarantee, however, when dealing with human nature.

In order to encourage family planning, particularly in the underdeveloped areas where there is the largest increase in births, education in the methods of contraception and the need for their use must be acceptable, both culturally and religiously. An incentive for family planning should be given consideration--e.g., rewards by way of old age insurance, money, praise, publicity and food supplements. Education and greater economic returns to the individual have been shown to decrease the fertility rate, and peer pressures in China seem to have been successful. Better nutrition, and consequently fewer deaths, in cultures where people depend upon children to care for them in their old age has influenced the birth rate. Perhaps a system of "barefoot doctors" in some of the populous LDC areas of the world could be a partial solution to educating and helping to structure the family planning system. Population increase <u>is</u> an area that can be controlled.

By 1985, world food demand is expected to grow annually at the rate of 2% due to increased population, and 0.4% due to increased income, while the production growth rate will average about 2.5% a year. However, for the LDCs, the figures are a 3.6% demand and only a 2.6% production increase. These figures do not consider political policies or the economic and environmental changes that will take place. This discrepancy increases the probability of: greater deficiencies in cereal grains, which is a major food supply in the LDC countries, and more than 500 million persons suffering from undernutrition or malnutrition.

There is not always a direct correlation between the amount of land per capita and the population that suffers from hunger. China and Taiwan are virtually self-sufficient in food, but Taiwan has one of the densest populations in the world, whereas Bangladesh has more land per capita and more hunger.

The more developed countries have, through genetics and good land and farming management, been able to increase their yield per acre. The LDCs, however, have increased their yields, but not to the extent that is possible. This is an area in which there should be a greater emphasis, along with improvement in storage facilities and better methods of distribution not only within countries but throughout the world. Inadequate storage and distribution account for tremendous losses in food materials. At the present time enough food is produced to give everyone in the world 2,000 to 3,000 calories per day. The primary problem is a matter of distribution. Small farmers should be given the knowledge and perhaps financial help to stay on farms and produce food crops. Cash crops are grown by larger combines and are needed for the economy of the country, but not at the expense of food crops that are within the budget of the poor majority.

Although animals, such as goats and sheep, can be and are grown for animal protein, cereal and legume crops along with green vegetables are necessary to prevent protein deficiencies and malnutrition in many areas. The balance of amino acids one gets by combining cereal grains and legumes is a less expensive yield of calorie input for calorie output than animal protein. Over 50% of man's food energy is derived from cereals. Therefore, research in improving the nutritional content and the yield of grains and legumes is needed, together with education in the planting, care, and use of these crops--which could help alleviate the many cases of marasmus and kwashiorkor in the world.

To do this one must consider the constraints of water quality and quantity. Sorghum and triticale are good drought resistant crops. Triticale used as meal has a higher protein content than wheat. Some strains yield 14-19% protein. In the U.S. there should be an increase in both the acreage and the yield of the soybean crop in order to provide protein alternatives. Attention should also be given to developing crops which are more resistant to saline water and desalinization techniques at an affordable price. Diverting rivers and manipulating rainfall patterns are other possibilities for helping to increase food production. In order to conserve water and soil, forests and reforestation should be included in the priorities.

Fertilizers yield better crops, but the United States uses a very great proportion and the price escalates. Alternate sources of fertilizer materials at more realistic prices must be found. Alternative energy resources must be found which do not deplete the nonrenewable sources of energy.

Another suggestion for feeding the world is exploration of less

411

conventional food sources. There is a need to continue to search for less expensive and more acceptable protein supplements--a case in point is the fish food concentrates. There needs to be greater emphasis on vegetable proteins in the more developed countries, and encouragement of fish culture in all countries for the basic production of protein.

The importance of manpower and other resources is shown in the Development Wheel (see Fig. 1). Manpower resources need steady improvement through continual educational programs. Nutritional education should begin in the elementary schools of all countries, and in the U.S. sound nutritional information should be reinforced by the school lunch program. The use of vegetable proteins should take a respectable place with animal proteins. The developed countries need to show the LDCs that animal protein does not need to be higher on the social scale than vegetable protein. Vegetable protein should become a status food.

One of the constraints that slows the process of enough nutritional food for all mankind is the instability of political systems. Frequently, this inhibits the distribution of land, food, and money, and the choice of how that money should be spent. A moral question is, "food or arms." The U.S. needs to take a long look at urban sprawl and the devouring of prime agricultural land. Cluster housing can be an alternative.

Even where there is affluence, and a choice of good nutritional food is available, without sound nutritional education and the desire to make use of it, people will continue to be undernourished, overnourished, and malnourished. The methodology and the technology exists to attack the issue. Do the people of the more developed countries of the world have the desire, the humanitarianism, and the willingness to change their life styles and food habits to meet the needs of the future?

Fig. 1

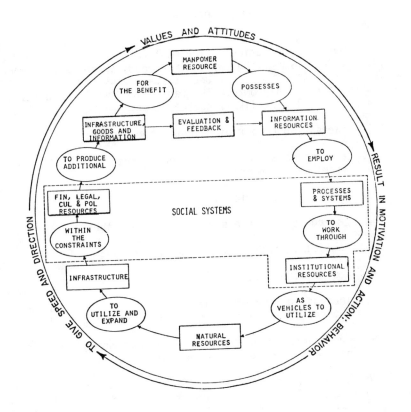

DEVELOPMENT WHEEL

413

IMPACTS OF RAPID POPULATION GROWTH--THE NEED FOR STATE FOOD AND POPULATION POLICIES

Beverly D. Grafel and Charles M. Cargille

Population/Food Fund

The world's population will almost certainly double in the next 38 years. Food production, which is already inadequate to feed an estimated 2 billion people at decent standards, may or may not keep pace with population growth. The rapidity of world population doubling has the following likely consequences:

1. Increasing number of malnourished people;

2. International maldistribution of food with resultant widespread hunger;

3. High consumer prices;

4. Low commodity prices to farmers, and thus

5. Lack of incentives for high production;

6. Loss of topsoil;

7. Increasing risk of nuclear war between rich and poor nations for dwindling resources, including food; and

8. Acceptance of the idea of "surplus people," that is, populations larger than carrying capacity.

Because of the disruptions in international trade brought about by excessive population growth worldwide, it is likely that food shortages will exist even in a country as well endowed as the United States. Although it seems blasphemous to speak of shortages at a time when surplus supplies have driven the price of wheat to $2.50/ bushel and farmers to the fear of bankruptcy, nevertheless, the long-term impact of rapid population growth will almost certainly undermine America's own food supply in 50 to 100 years. This is so because:

1. Birth rates in the U.S. have started to rise again after
    a long decline;

2. Legal and illegal immigration, especially via Mexico,
    may reach over 50 million illegal immigrants over the
    next 20 years;[1]

3. Hunger in Third World countries causes social disorganiza-
    tion; the U.S. is dependent upon Third World countries for
    industrial raw materials; American agriculture depends
    upon industrial raw materials; American agriculture depends
    upon industrial products for much of its productivity.
    With local disruptions, fueled by population growth, cur-
    tailing or cutting off the raw materials which go into
    tractors, fertilizers and pesticides, agricultural pro-
    ductivity in America would be severely cut.[2]

Historically, both food and population policy have been re-
linquished to the federal government. Yet the federal government
has not had a very impressive track record in either field. Their
food policies in the past have focused almost exclusively on short
term solutions to short term problems. Nor has the federal government embraced issues of population growth which require long term
planning.[3]

As Terry Sanford, former Governor of North Carolina, has written: "Little fault can be found with what was done through the
federal program. Much fault can be found with what was not done
. . . ." The criticism is that the vast national mechanism for
agriculture sealed itself off from new ideas and local innovations.[4]
Because of the lack of federal leadership on population and food
issues, and the serious dangers to America's future, we propose
that the states should take the initiative in developing integrated
food and population policies. The arguments in favor of such action are:

1. The consequences of inadequate federal leadership toward
solving population and food problems are suffered at the state
level. Thus, it is in the self-interest of each state to defend
itself against bad food policy:

2. Agricultural states possess great expertise in matters of
food production;

3. State legislation can control corporate farming, encourage
family farms, and reverse current dependence on food imports.
States can exert pressure toward decentralization of food processing and conservation of energy;

4. Food policy forged at the state level would better fit the
unique geographical conditions of each state;

5. States can best appraise the needs and preferences of their own citizens as consumers of agricultural products;

6. States can best decide upon the wisest tradeoffs between agricultural practices and protection of the environment, between alternative land use proposals, and between industrial and agricultural claims upon limited resources of land and water;

7. State policies can represent pilot projects for testing new approaches on a smaller scale prior to implementing them at a national level. This approach to national policy development is consistent with the political concept of Federalism. Thorough experimentation with a variety of policies at the state level can separate the successful from the unsuccessful without universal losses. The successful policies can then be incorporated into national policy by the federal government;

8. Finally, in a food short world resulting from national and international pressures of overpopulation, it would be well to have each state moving in the direction of food self-sufficiency, at least in supplies of basic foods. One spin-off advantage of state food self-sufficiency is a decrease in reliance upon costly transportation of food.

The idea that states should be involved in state food and population policy is not totally new. At present 31 states use some form of preferential taxation to help preserve agricultural land. Some states are now moving toward an integrated food policy. Minnesota is initiating plans for a Governor's Conference on Food and Nutrition. The National Conference of Lieutenant Governors in 1975 established a food policy committee. Its publication, Toward a National Food Policy, lays out a number of mechanisms for achieving policy objectives at the state level.[5]

Canada, which is roughly similar in population to California, has taken the lead in taking population and food policies seriously. In July, 1976, the Science Council of Canada made the following recommendation to the Minister of State for Science and Technology:[6]

1. That Canadian population growth should be slow;

2. That Canada's anticipated difficulties in meeting short-term energy requirements, especially in oil and gas, argue strongly for slowing population growth;

3. That careful land use planning is needed to prevent the population of major cities from spreading onto the limited amount of prime agricultural land;

4. That metropolitan centers can and should absorb further population without extending their boundaries, in order to minimize

416

transportation and other costs.

At first glance, the historical dominance of the federal government makes it seem impractical to conceive of individual states working toward solutions of world as well as local population and food problems. Yet the federal government has not shown itself capable of managing world or local population-food issues and the states will pay for what the federal government fails to do.

The time has come for the states to recognize that world food and population problems affect their well-being at home and that the federal government's response is not effective. To fill this vacuum, we believe that state governments must provide the leadership to:

1. Research ways of balancing population size and resources within each state;

2. Move toward food self-sufficiency at the state level;

3. Examine the seriousness of these problems at the world level and to increase public awareness;

4. Commit state resources and expertise toward developing global solutions;

5. Demand that the federal government give a high priority and sufficient funding to solve national and international food and population problems.

FOOTNOTES

1. Cargille, C. M. In Report of the House Select Committee on Population Hearings, February 23, 1978, Superintendent of Documents, Washington, D.C. 1978. Roughly one-fourth of the Mexican labor force may already have come to the United States. This suggests that the present population of Mexico may already exceed its social and economic "carrying capacity." If this is the case, then the entire national increase of population in Mexico over the next 20 years (66.7 million persons if present trends continue) may enter the United States in search of food or employment (statistics cited are derived from the 1976 World Population Data Sheet of the Population Reference Bureau, Washington, D.C.).

2. Mumford, Stephen. Population Growth Control: The Next Move Is America's. Philosophical Library, New York, 1977.

3. Barr, Terry, USDA. Statement to the N.D. Conference on Food and Famine, Bismarck, N.D. December 1, 1978.

4. Sanford, Terry. Storm Over the States. McGraw-Hill, New York, 1967, p. 72.

5. Toward a National Food Policy. Report of the National Food Policy Committee, Lieutenant Governor's Conference, July 30, 1976.

6. Science Council of Canada Report No. 25, Population, Technology and Resources (July 1976). Minister of Supply and Services, Canada, Ottawa.

A PLAN FOR STABILIZING WORLD POPULATION
BY INTERNATIONAL TREATY

Louise Chubb

Writer, Alexandria, Virginia

The recent famine in the Sahara desert is a very clear illustration of suffering and death caused by overpopulation. The farmers, as their numbers grew, kept farming poorer and poorer land, and it blew away, and they starved. Of course, the bad effects of overpopulation are only one of a number of factors in a multiple correlation type of causal chain. It does seem to be becoming more clear, however, that we are in serious danger of exceeding the carrying capacity of the earth. Though we do not yet have an accurate scientific measure of what that carrying capacity is, I believe that stabilizing population growth will allow us to bring some of our other serious problems under control. For the engine of population growth is the factor that presses against all our other problems, making them harder to solve.

This paper begins with the assumption that the present world-wide increase of population is a sufficiently serious problem so that a solution, i.e., stabilization of world population, is required.

The solution I am proposing involves developing a world consensus of agreement on this objective as a first step. Following educational efforts and the emergence of such a consensus, a treaty would be drawn up and submitted to each country for adoption. Because of the competitive nature of population growth, the treaty would provide that it not come into force until ratified by (a) 95% of the countries in the world and (b) countries comprising 95% of the population. Provisions of the treaty might be: (a) at a central point, such as Geneva, ampoules would be manufactured of two types, one with doses of contraceptive effective for one year, and the other containing only saline solution, but identical in appearance. Ampoules would then be mixed at this central point using proportions of contraceptive to placebo ampoules which would be required to reduce the number of births throughout the world to replacement levels; (b) public health teams would then travel around every country and administer an injection to every woman of childbearing age, once a year.

419

Neither the public health team which administered the injections, nor the women who received them, would know which kind of injection a woman was getting. This procedure has two important benefits: It reduces the likelihood of bribery or corruption, and it ensures that the possibility of pregnancy for specific individuals is left to chance. Each year women would get a new injection and would have a new chance of being in the non-contracepted group. Thus individuals could still plan to get pregnant from time to time as they wished.

Such a proposal clearly requires better vital statistics and rapid information retrieval than now exists. The exact percentage to be contracepted would be a fairly complicated calculation, but an idea of how the system would work can be gained from the following examples.

Take a random group of 10,000 people. Without specifying the age or sex composition, let us say that in a particular year these 10,000 people have 600 births and 400 deaths. They therefore have an increase of 200 people, or a 2% growth rate. In order to limit births in this group to replacement levels, we would have to contracept 33% of all the women of childbearing age. Thus, for this population, 33% of our ampoules would contain contraceptive solutions, while 67% would be placebos.

However, take another group of 10,000 people. It could easily occur that group 2 might have only 400 births and 200 deaths in a given year. They, too, would have a 2% rate of increase. Yet, to hold births in this group to a replacement level, we would have to contracept 50% of the women. It could even happen that a third group of 10,00 people might have 300 births and 100 deaths in a year. In such a case, contraception at the rate of 67% would be needed to hold births to a replacement level.

On a worldwide basis, it seems likely that the percentage of contraception to provide a replacement level of births would be close to 50%. But because of the uncertainty, we could provide that the treaty would be incrementally implemented over, say, a five-year period.

Because any such plan appears rather sweeping, it may be worthwhile to acknowledge some of the most recognizable problems with it.

1. We don't begin, today, to count births and deaths accurately enough to carry out such a plan. Even in the United States, we recognize a factor of error in our census, and I suppose that it is the most accurate in the world. So, before any such plan as I have outlined could be put into effect, we would have to have better vital statistics. Clearly, we would also have to have a sophisticated modern system for accurate and rapid data collection and retrieval.

2.   The particular countries and areas with problems from high birth rates would still, probably, have problems. although to a slightly lesser degree. I do not consider it appropriate for a world-wide plan to have differential impact in different places. It seems likely that countries would reject the plan if they were to be treated differentially.

I believe that stabilizing world population will have valuable effects on social attitudes (e.g., cooperation vs. competition) towards many other problems. For example, with a stable world population assured, the more affluent countries might be more willing to cooperate in measures to assure better nutrition, education, etc. of people born in less affluent countries than they are now with the prospect of an open-ended population explosion.

INDEX

abortion, 16, 19, 21, 22, 25, 26, 96, 161, 182, 188, 270;
    nontraumatic, 188; services, 96
adoption, 164
advertising, 264
Africa, 140, 302, 307, 308; women farmers in, 118
agribusiness, 348
agricultural attaches, 107
agricultural development, 144, 326, 383
agricultural experiment stations, 386
agricultural policy, 104
agricultural research, 105, 386
Agricultural Research Service, 105
agricultural statistics, 387
agricultural technology, 379
agriculture, improvement in U.S.
agriculture, subsistence, 337, 340
Agency for International Development (AID), 27, 60, 134, 135, 136,
    137, 144, 315, 331; budget, 135, 144; critique of, 136, 137;
    goals of, 139
aliens, illegal, 97
attitude surveys, 330
American Agriculture Movement, 108
American Dietetic Association, 400
Amin, Idi, 77
appropriate technology, 311, 320
Appropriate Technology International, 311
arable land, 33, 195, 275
Argentina, 348
Ariyaratne, Mr., 331
artificial coloring and flavoring, 236
Asia, 140
Aswan Dam, 55
Atlantic Union, 85
attitudes toward children, 225
Aztecs, 295

bacterial growth curves, 234
balance, 165, 235, 274, 417
Bali, 143
Bangladesh, 50, 67, 175, 270, 389, 411; rural leadership and
    population, 175
barefoot doctors, 410
basic human needs, 35, 292
Basolo, D. C., 301
beefalos, 301

422

beyond family planning, 242
birth attendants, 167
birth control, 172, 181, 270, 314; information, 181; programs, 172
"Birth Coupons," 223
birth planning, 165
birth rates, 142, 173, 415; and infant mortality, 357
Borgstrom, Georg, 224, 275
Borlaug, Norman, 327
Brazil, 8, 140, 348, 351, 380
breast feeding, 401
Brown, Lester, 207
Brzezenski, Dr., 71
Bucharest Conference, 44, 242
buffalo, 301
buffer stock storage, 365
Bunny Bread, 266
bureaucracy, 37

Califano, Secretary, 271
calories per capita, 264
Canada, 348, 416
capital markets, 213
Cargille, Charles, 138, 224
Carpenter, Jim, 328
carrying capacity, 1, 2, 9, 22, 42, 43, 47-52, 120, 138-141, 194,
    226, 236, 275, 294, 295, 414, 417, 419
Carter Administration, 39, 40
Carter, President Jimmy, 34, 62
cash crops, 338-340, 411
Census Bureau, 138
Central America, 348
Center for Population Research, 63
cereal production, 370
Chardon Plan, 148
"cheap food" policies, 304
children, as a consumer good, 220; demand for, 220; as an invest-
    ment good, 220
China, 7, 24, 39, 57, 142, 160, 280, 313, 318, 363, 410
Collins, Joseph, 224
commercial formula, 402
commodity prices, 414
community gardening, 286
community kitchens, 330
community living, 268
computer modeling, 404
condoms, 160
Congressional hearings on nutrition, 266
consumer education, 284
consumer prices, 414
consumption, 50, 52, 271; patterns, 52; levels, 50

contraception, 16, 19, 23, 63, 95, 96, 188; availability of, 95; practices, 188; research, 63, 96; for teenagers, 95; failure, rate, 63
cooperation, 268, 365
corporate farming, 415
costs of raising a child, U.S., 188, 221
Costa Rica, 351
crop forecasting, 307-310
crop yields, 234
cultural values, 264
cuttlefish, 290

de Castro, Josue, 207
decentralization of food processing, 415
Defense Department, 74
deforestation, 2
demographic structure lag, 216
Demographic Transition Theory, 11, 22, 23, 207
dependency ratios, 237
Depo Provera, 64, 182
desalinization, 411
desired family size, 66
development aid, 33, 269
development policy, 242
dieticians, 399
General Draper, 45, 75
dystopian literature, 228
Dyck, Arthur, 12, 20-23

eating for life, 276
ecological disasters, 228
ecological systems approach, 396
econometric analysis, 237
economic development, 131, 320, 323
economic growth, 172
economic model of family size, 219
economic theories of population, 200
Ecuador, 351
education, 97, 173, 242, 329
effective economic demand, 90
Egypt, 169, 317
Ehrlich, Paul, 206, 224
El Salvador, 351
Emergency Medical Services (EMS), 246
energy conservation, 415
energy costs, 8
energy impacted communities, 256
energy requirements, 416
entrepreneurs, 213
Environmental Fund, 138, 224
Environmental Protection Agency, 46

environmental standards, 245
environmental stress, 53
environmental variables, 307
erosion, 304
Essay On Population (Malthus), 200
Ethiopia, 169, 270
ethnic imperialism, 238
eutrophication, 275
export policy, 106; alternatives, 373

FDA regulations, 64
family farms, 415
family planning, 24, 95, 131, 160, 172, 178, 182, 190, 313, 410;
    and anxiety level, 190; evaluation, 182; Navajo,178, ser-
    vices, 95, 160; success, 57
Family Planning and Population Research Act of 1970, 88
family size, 186; ideal, 331
famine, 235
The Farm, 268
farm organizations, 108
farm parity, 120
farm prices, 112
farms, small, 299, 411
Federal Trade Commission, 351
female circumcision, 167
fertility, 131, 144, 186, 187, 212, 237, 242; control, 242; cumu-
    lative, 187; decline, 144; levels, 186, 338; rates, 131, 237
fertilizer, from sewage, 299; prices, 380, 411
fish catch, 1
fish consumption, 275
fish farming, 291
fish food concentrate, 289, 412
fish meat, 289
food: aid, 326, 350, 368; consumption, 362, 368; courses, university,
    392-395; distribution, 271, 348, 351, 362, 372, 411; imports, 146,
    368, 415; industry, 262; insufficiency, 368; maldistribution, 414;
    policy, 224, 372, 396, 415; purchasing power, 114; rationing, 368;
    redistribution, 370; research, 226; reserves, 305; self-
    sufficiency, 263, 389, 416; shortage, 390, 414; stabilization,
    365, 366; storage facilities, 411; subsidy, 104; sufficiency, 40,
    303; supply system, 386; taxes, 368; waste, 282
Food and Agricultural Act of 1977, 305
Food and Agricultural Organization (FAO), 104
food production, 113, 348, 362, 378, 389; constraints, 113; in-
    creases, 196, 379; proposals, 409; strategy, 388
food stamp program, 146, 317
Ford Foundation, 61
foreign aid, 33, 34, 36, 53, 56, 58; conditions, 296; "New
    Directions", 34
forest ecology, 339
Four Horsemen, 271

freedom of choice, 62
Frejka, Tomas, 203

Gabon, population policy, 100
Galbraith, John Kenneth, 314
Gandhi, Sanjay, 57
Gandhi, Indira, 68
gardening, 286, 339
General Mills, 266
Gilligan, John, 35, 60
government priorities, 235, 306, 388, 417
grain, 275, 295, 296, 305, 369, 370, 380, 410, 411; fed to ani-
    mals, 296; reserves, 305; storage, 305, 380; supply elasticity,
    369
Greep Report, 64
Guatemala, 269, 351
guinea worm, 38

Haiti, 269, 405
Hardin, Garrett, 224, 314
health, 244-247, 275-76; costs, 244, 246; education, 245; plan-
    ning, 244; programs in industry, 246, 247; services, 244
health care, 244, 245; accessibility, 244; screening, 245
Health Maintenance Organization (HMO), 244
hierarchical structuring, 384
Honduras, 269, 327, 351
House Select Committee on Population, 61, 68
human needs, 12, 25
human rights, 21, 36
Humanae Vitae, 16, 19
Humphrey, Hubert, 24, 34, 36
hunger, 14, 78, 378, 379
Hunzas, 265
hydrologic data, 387

immigration, 67, 96, 97, 415, 417; goals, 96; illegal, 67, 97,
    415, 417; legal, 97
income distribution, 350
India, 50, 270
Indonesia, 57, 143
industrialization, 165
industrial raw materials, 415
infant mortality, 38, 132
infanticide, 338
information retrieval, 420
intercropping, 298
intermediate technology, 329
international cooperation, 48, 365
International Confederation of Midwives, 668
International Federation of Agricultural Producers, 113
International Food Policy Research Institute, 117

426

International Institute of Tropical Agriculture (IITA), 323, 324
international trade, 414
International Wheat and Maize Development Center, 327
intervention in family social systems, 242
Iowa State University, 393
Iran, 149-152; census, 150; potential for stable fertility,
    151; population policy appraisal, 152
Israel, 54, 56
Ivory Coast, 169

Japan, 165, 348

Kenya, 169
Kool Aid, 403
Korea, 57
Kornbluth, C.M., 228
krill, 290
kwashiorkor, 289

labor force participation rates, 237
land reform, 35, 350
land use planning, 304, 416
Lappe, Frances Moore, 224, 296
land, 263
Land, Bread and History, 363
Latin America, 348, 378
leadership, 214, 278, 307, 415, 417
Le Projet du Garbage, 282
light capital technology, 313
literacy, 390
Lome agreement, 350
long term planning, 415
Loomis, Robert, 200

McGovern, Senator George, 266
McNamara, Robert, 5
machismo complex, 238
malnutrition, 103, 262, 289, 372, 378, 379, 399, 404, 414
Malthus, Thomas, 4, 200, 212, 219
manpower training, 388
marasmus, 289
Marshall, Alfred, 200
Marshall Plan, 54, 59
Marx, Karl, 67, 200
materialism, 8
maternal-child health, 132
meat consumption, 111, 269, 275, 373
mechanization, 321
medical care, centralization of, 245
Memdani, Mahmood, 314
Mexico, 58, 67, 132, 140, 270, 351, 401, 415, 417

Quaker Oats, 267

Ravenholt, Dr. R. T., 132, 135, 141, 163
recommended daily allowances, 265
regulatory standards, 351
reproduction: health conditions of women, 167; preventive
    care, 167; freedom of, 100
resource allocation, 212
resource scarcity, 201, 138
resource waste, 212
rhythm method, 16
rice production, 390
rice water, 403
Rich, William, 174
Richmond, Rep. Fred, 266
Ridgeway, James, 225
Right to Life, 69
Rockefeller Foundation, 61
rural development, 236, 329
rural people, disadvantage compared to urban, 120

Sahel, The, 314
Salas, Rafael, 131
Sarkar, Shrii P.R., 277
Sarvodaya, 329
satellite information system, 296
Saudi Arabia, 139
Scheuer, James, 61
school lunch programs, 397
Schumacher, E. F., 311, 312, 323
Science Council of Canada, 416
science fiction, 228
science infrastructure, 386
Seamans, Dr., 45
Self Help Foundation, 326; program, 327
"Self-Helper" tractor, 326
Senegal, 170
small tractor technology, 326
social change, 329
social class mobility, 401
social disorganization, 78, 415
social justice, 15, 24, 52, 84, 87; as policy motivation, 119
social organization, 72, 279, 317, 329
social technologies, 313
social reorganization vs. technology, 318
socio-economic development, 242
soil conservation, 303, 304
soil inventories, 387
solar energy, 235
sorghum, 295, 411
soybeans, 411
Space Merchants, The, 228

U.S. Puerto Rico Policy Commission, 145
unwanted births, U.S., 186, 187; pregnancies, costs to federal
    government, 188; child, 164
unwanted fertility, 186
Upjohn, 68
Upper Volta, 170
Uruguay, 348

vasectomies, 162
Vatican, 11, 13
vegetable diet, 296
vegetarianism, 274
Venezuela, food aid to, 1812, 359-361; political considerations in
    food aid, 360
Vermont agriculture, 363
village level technology, 329
vital statistics
vitamin A deficiency, 289, 404
voluntary peasants, 268

wealth, redistribution of, 35
West Pakistan, 405
white flour, 263
women, equaltiy of, 98
women-to-women self-help health care, 167
Word For World Is Forest, The, 229
World Bank, 315
World Fertility Survey, 141
World Food Conference (1974), 119, 306, 378
world food demand, 410
world food deficit, 374
world food policy, 104, 374
World Health Organization, 245, 68
world hunger, 274, 278
world population, size, 140, 410
world population growth, 72
World Population Conference (1974), 62, 242
World Population Society, 45
Wyoming, 256

Yanmar diesel engine, 327

Zambia, 308
zero population growth, 235; impact on schools, 102; population
    target, 93
Zero Population Growth, Inc., 239, Population Education Kit, 239